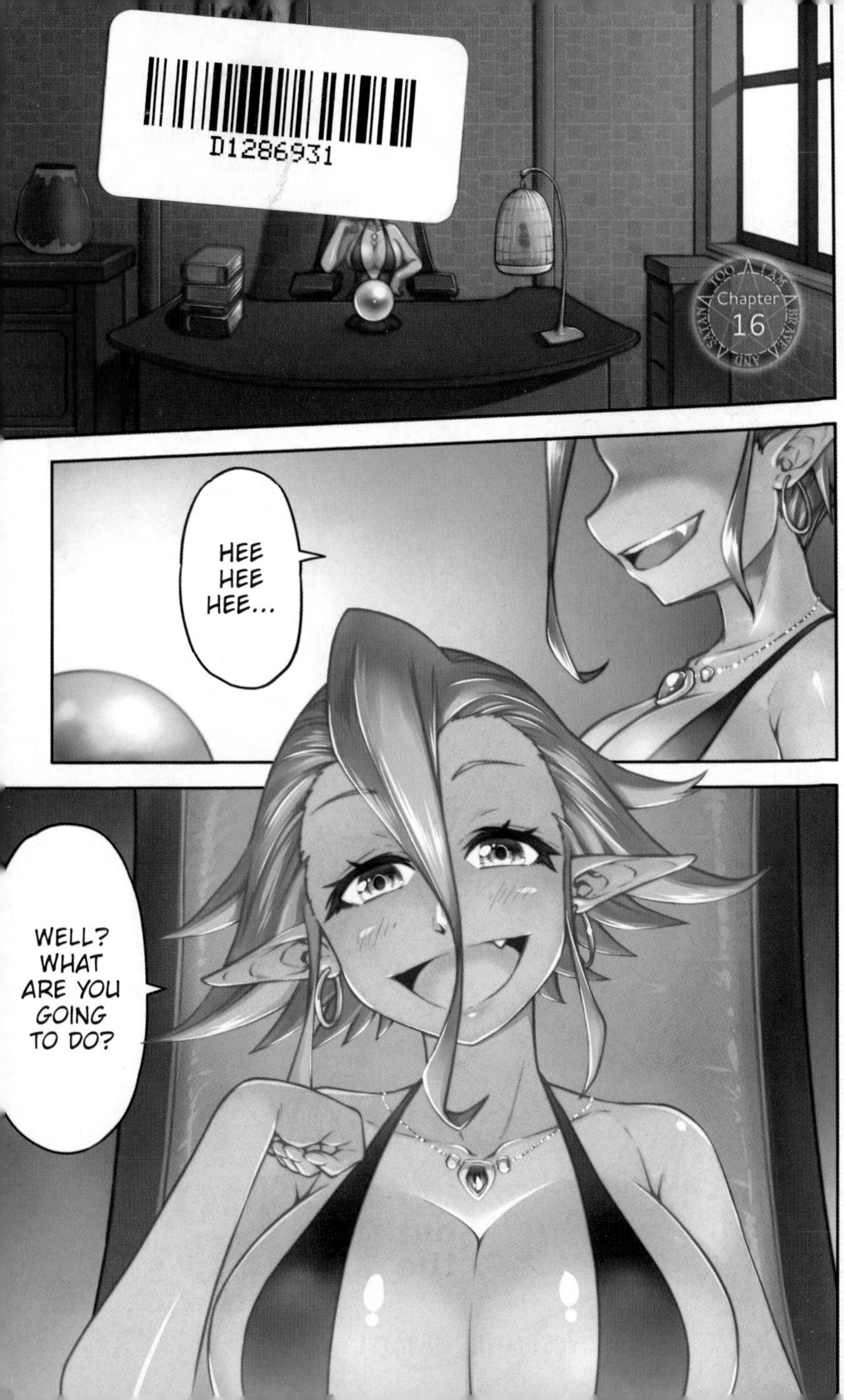
Chapter 16
HEE HEE HEE...
WELL? WHAT ARE YOU GOING TO DO?

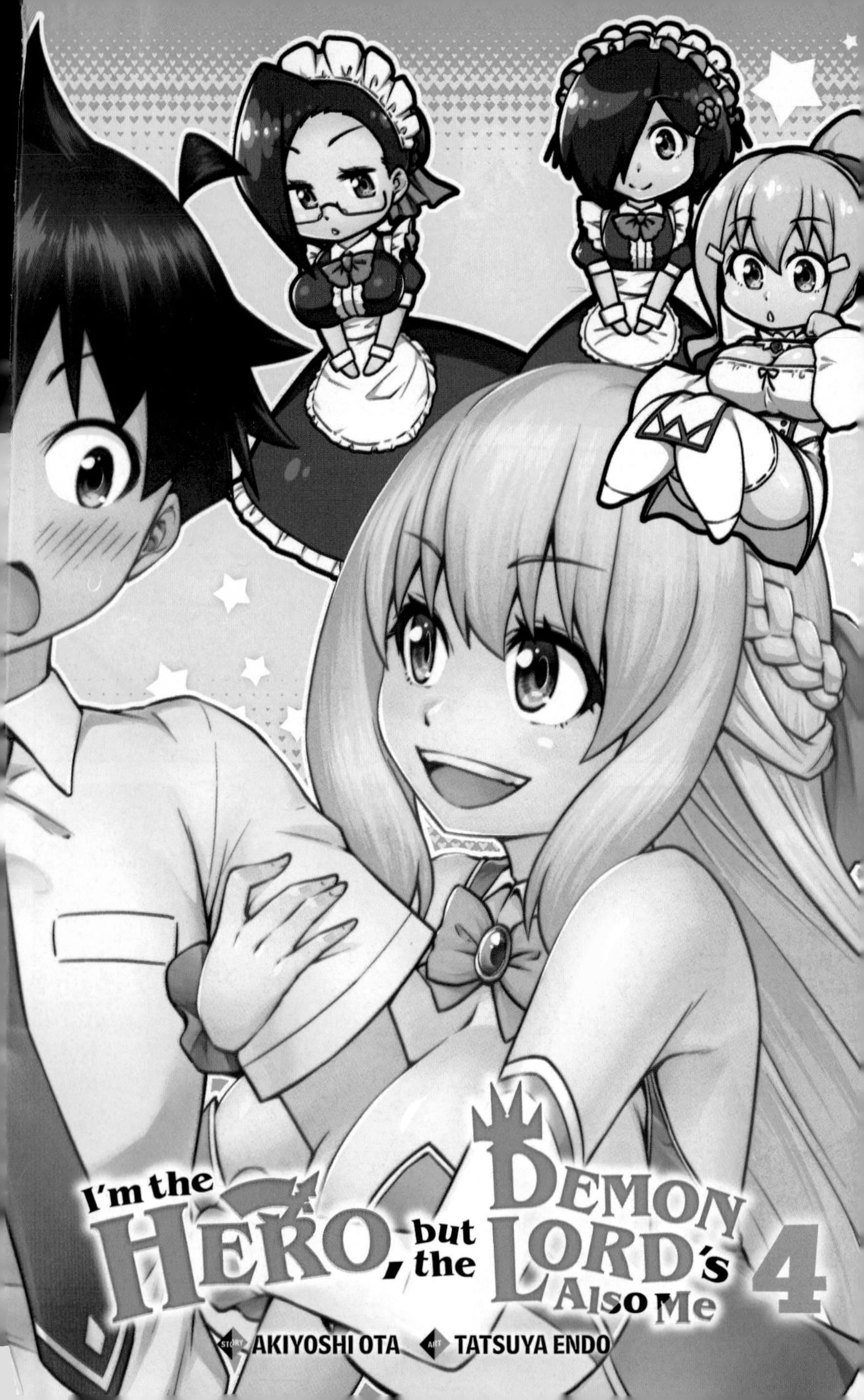
I'm the HERO, but the DEMON LORD's Also Me
4
STORY AKIYOSHI OTA
ART TATSUYA ENDO

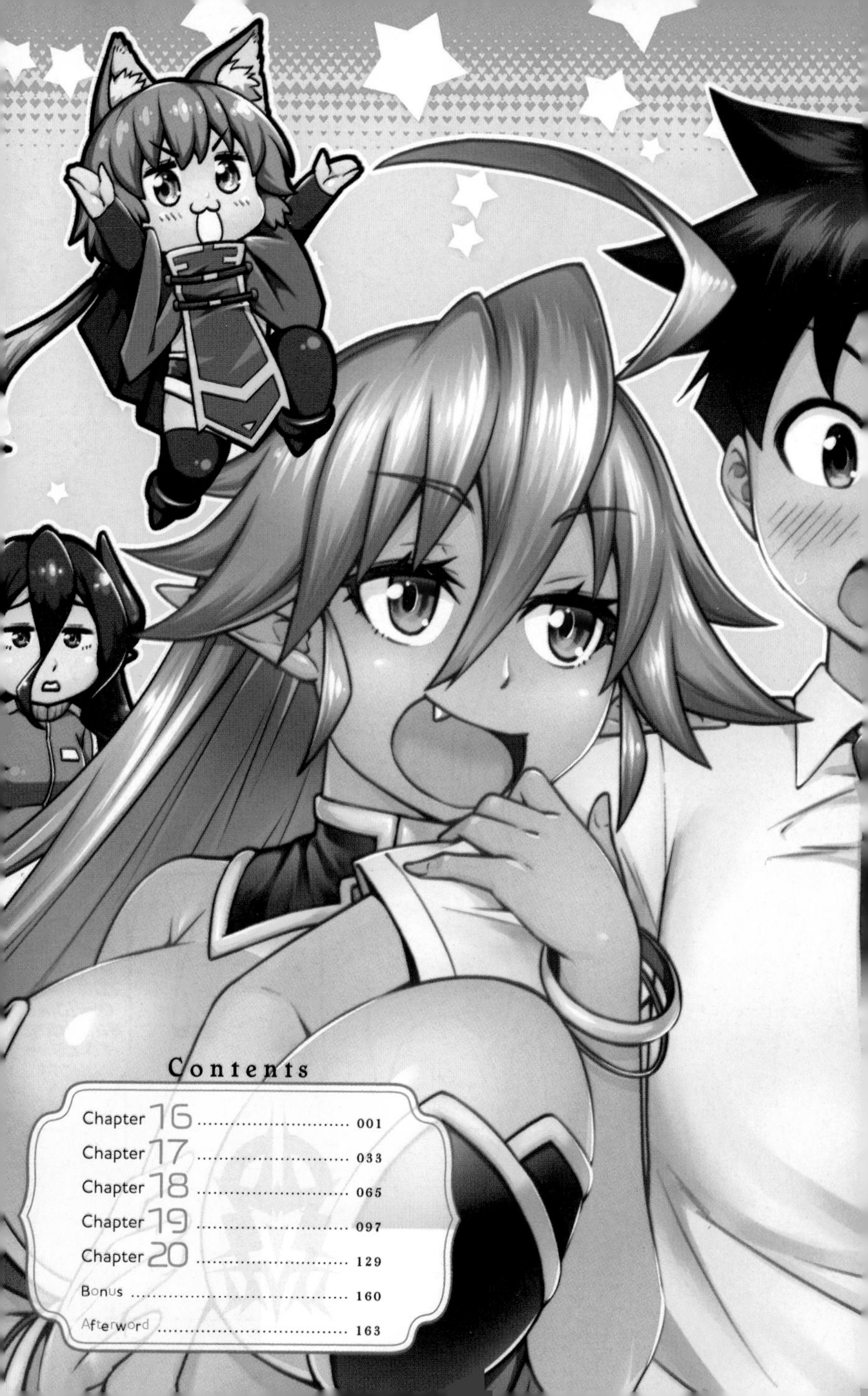

Contents

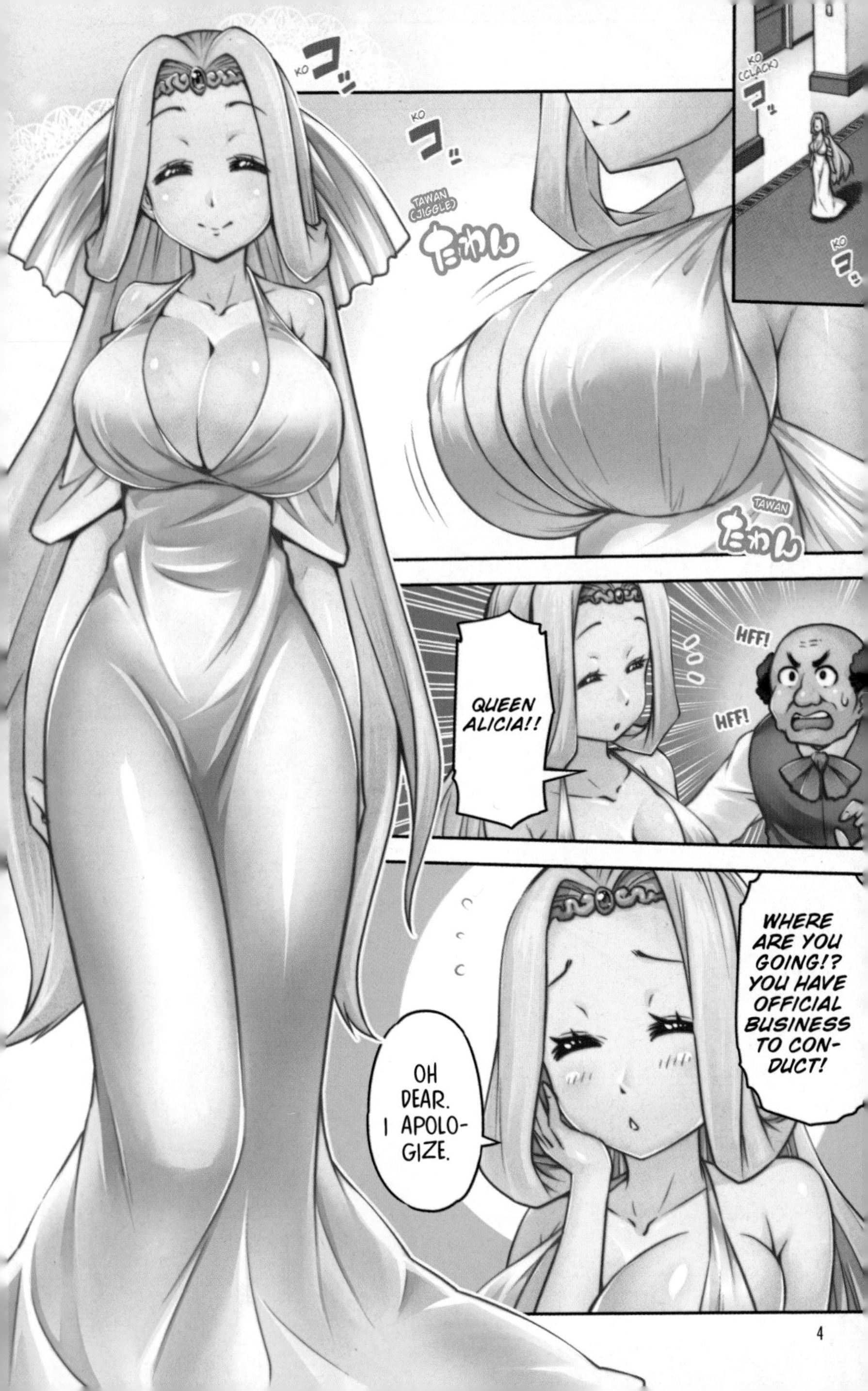
KO (CLACK)
コッ
KO
コッ
KO
コッ
KO
コッ
TAWAN (JIGGLE)
たわん
TAWAN
たわん
HFF!
HFF!
QUEEN ALICIA!!
WHERE ARE YOU GOING!? YOU HAVE OFFICIAL BUSINESS TO CON-DUCT!
OH DEAR. I APOLO-GIZE.

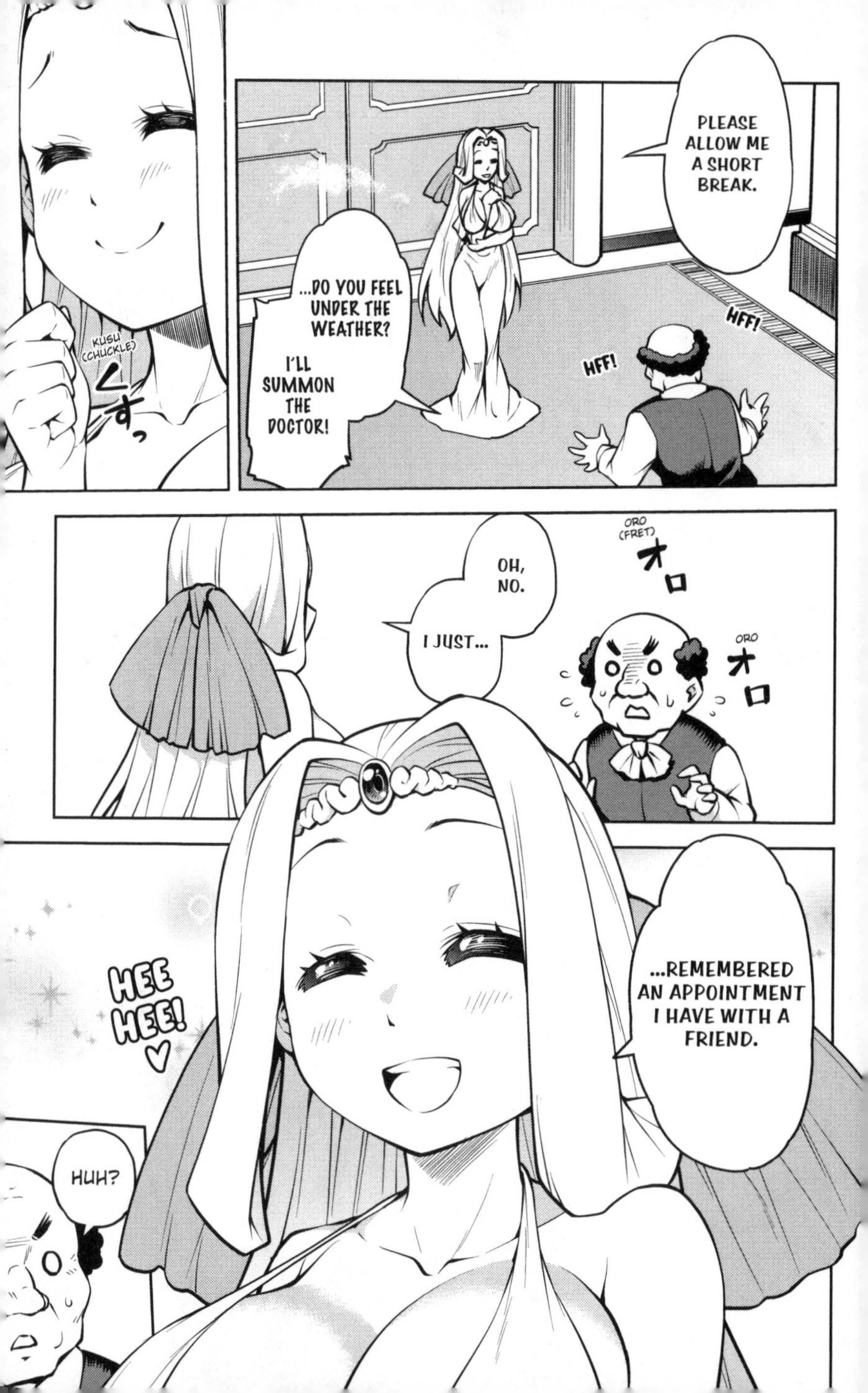
PLEASE ALLOW ME A SHORT BREAK.
HFF!
HFF!
...DO YOU FEEL UNDER THE WEATHER?
I'LL SUMMON THE DOCTOR!
KUSU (CHUCKLE)
くすっ
ORO (FRET)
オロ
ORO
オロ
OH, NO.
I JUST...
...REMEMBERED AN APPOINTMENT I HAVE WITH A FRIEND.
HEE HEE! ♥
HUH?

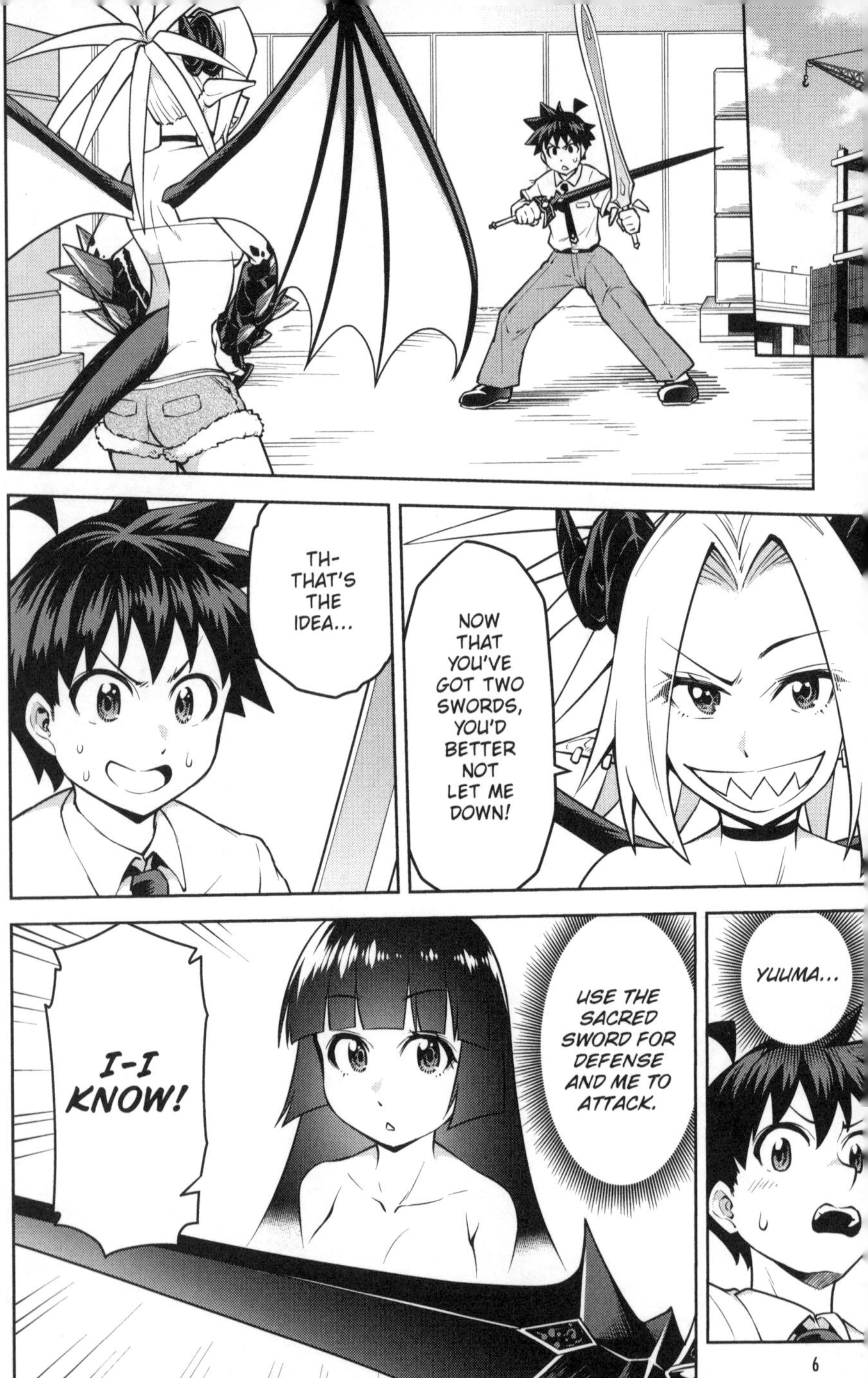
NOW THAT YOU'VE GOT TWO SWORDS, YOU'D BETTER NOT LET ME DOWN!
TH-THAT'S THE IDEA...
YUUMA...
USE THE SACRED SWORD FOR DEFENSE AND ME TO ATTACK.
I-I KNOW!

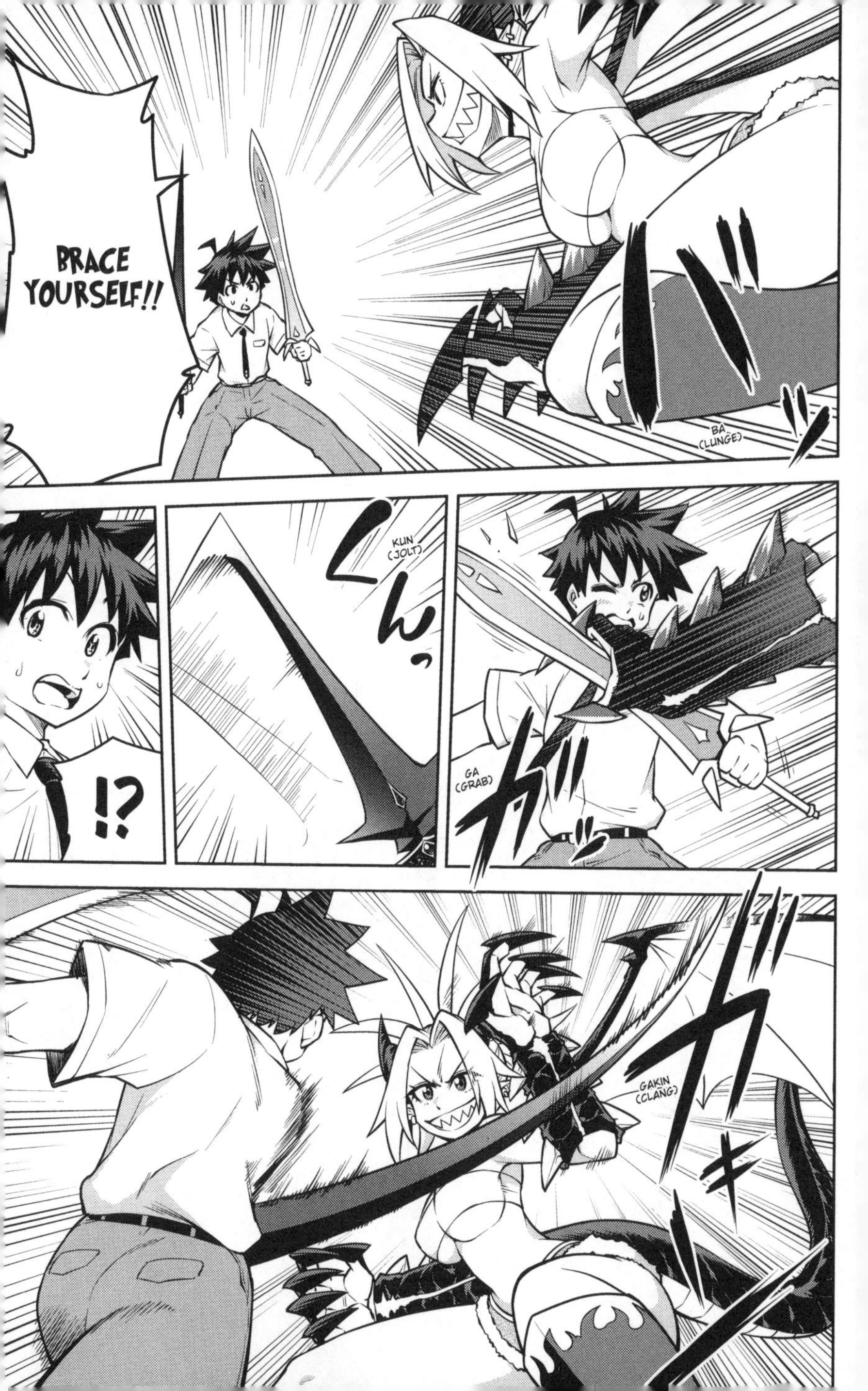
BA
(LUNGE)
BRACE YOURSELF!!
GA
(GRAB)
KUN
(JOLT)
!?
GAKIN
(CLANG)

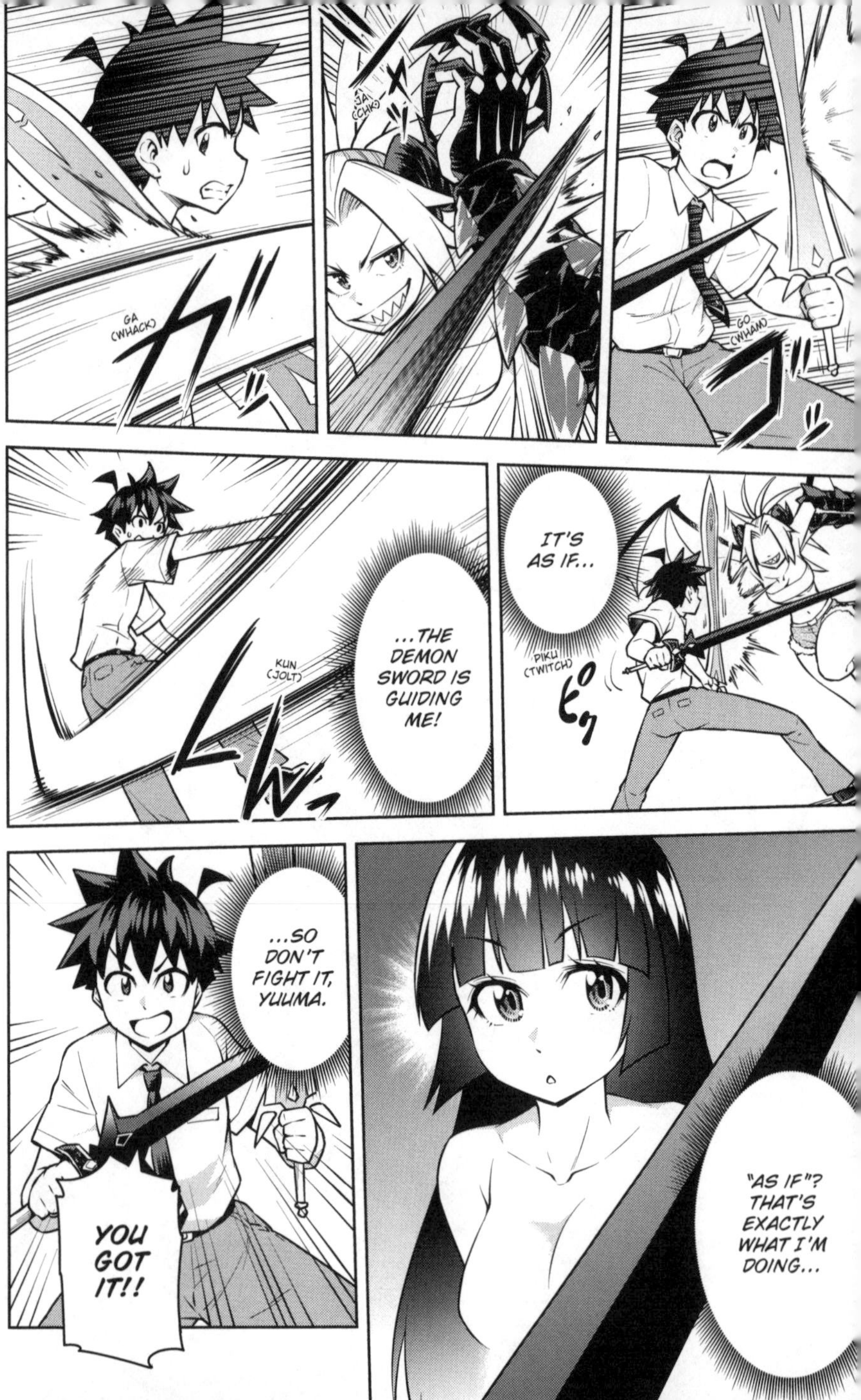
GO (WHAM)
JA (CHK)
GA (WHACK)
IT'S AS IF...
PIKU (TWITCH)
...THE DEMON SWORD IS GUIDING ME!
KUN (JOLT)
"AS IF"? THAT'S EXACTLY WHAT I'M DOING...
...SO DON'T FIGHT IT, YUUMA.
YOU GOT IT!!

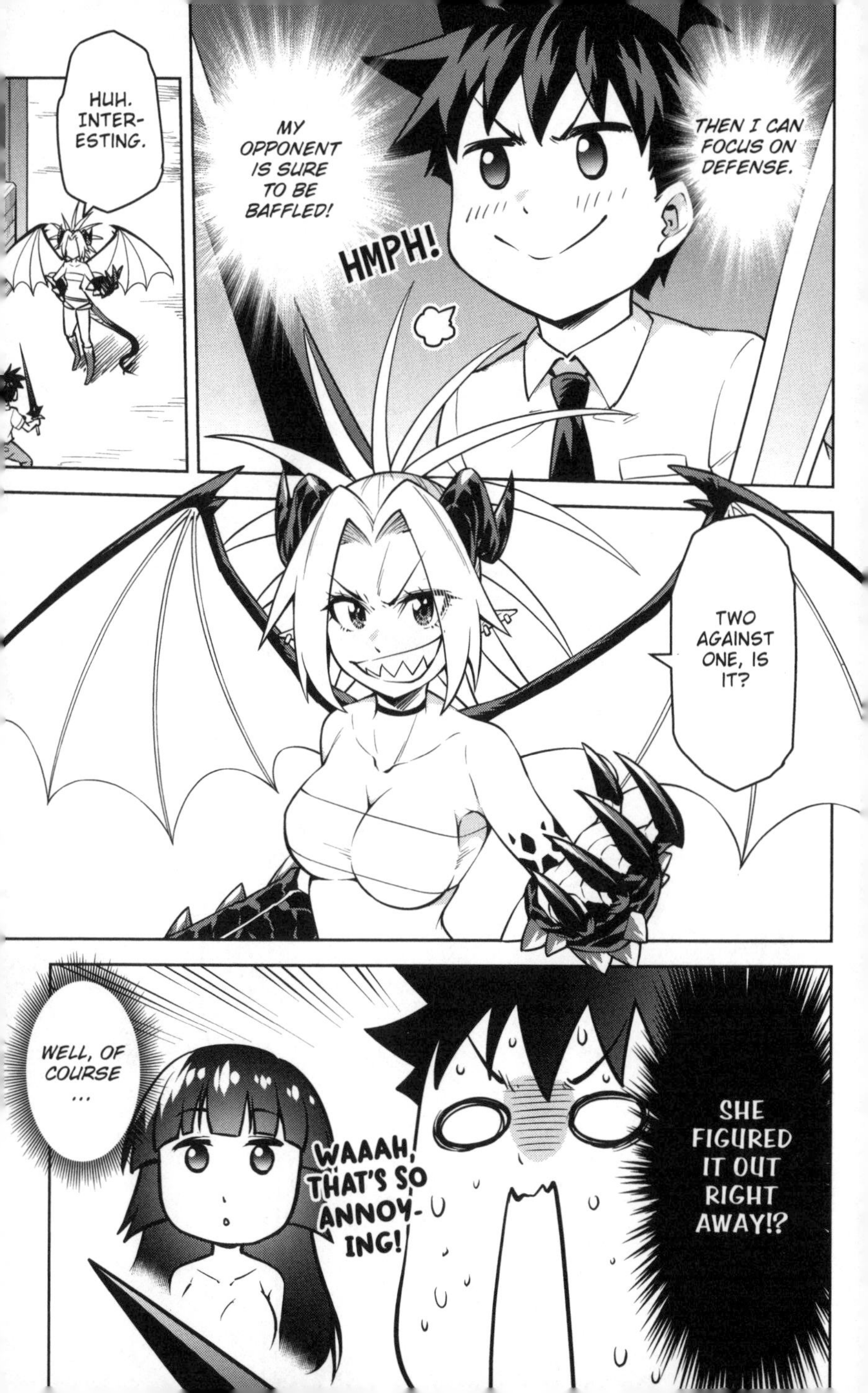
THEN I CAN FOCUS ON DEFENSE.
MY OPPONENT IS SURE TO BE BAFFLED!
HMPH!
HUH. INTER-ESTING.
TWO AGAINST ONE, IS IT?
SHE FIGURED IT OUT RIGHT AWAY!?
WAAAH, THAT'S SO ANNOY-ING!
WELL, OF COURSE...

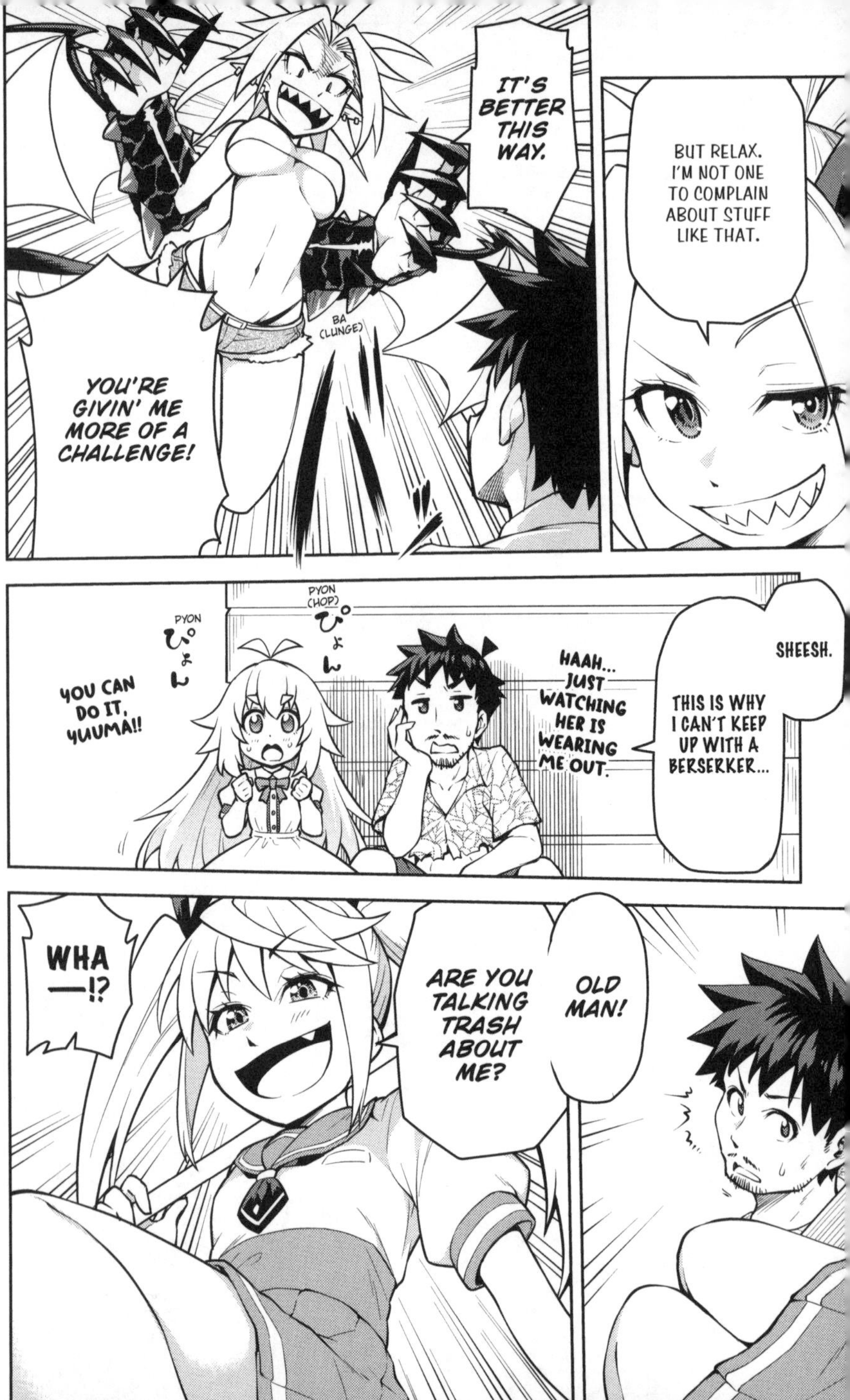

BUT RELAX. I'M NOT ONE TO COMPLAIN ABOUT STUFF LIKE THAT.
IT'S BETTER THIS WAY.
BA (LUNGE)
YOU'RE GIVIN' ME MORE OF A CHALLENGE!
SHEESH.
THIS IS WHY I CAN'T KEEP UP WITH A BERSERKER...
HAAH... JUST WATCHING HER IS WEARING ME OUT.
PYON (HOP)
ぴょん
PYON
ぴょん
YOU CAN DO IT, YUUMA!!
OLD MAN!
ARE YOU TALKING TRASH ABOUT ME?
WHA—!?

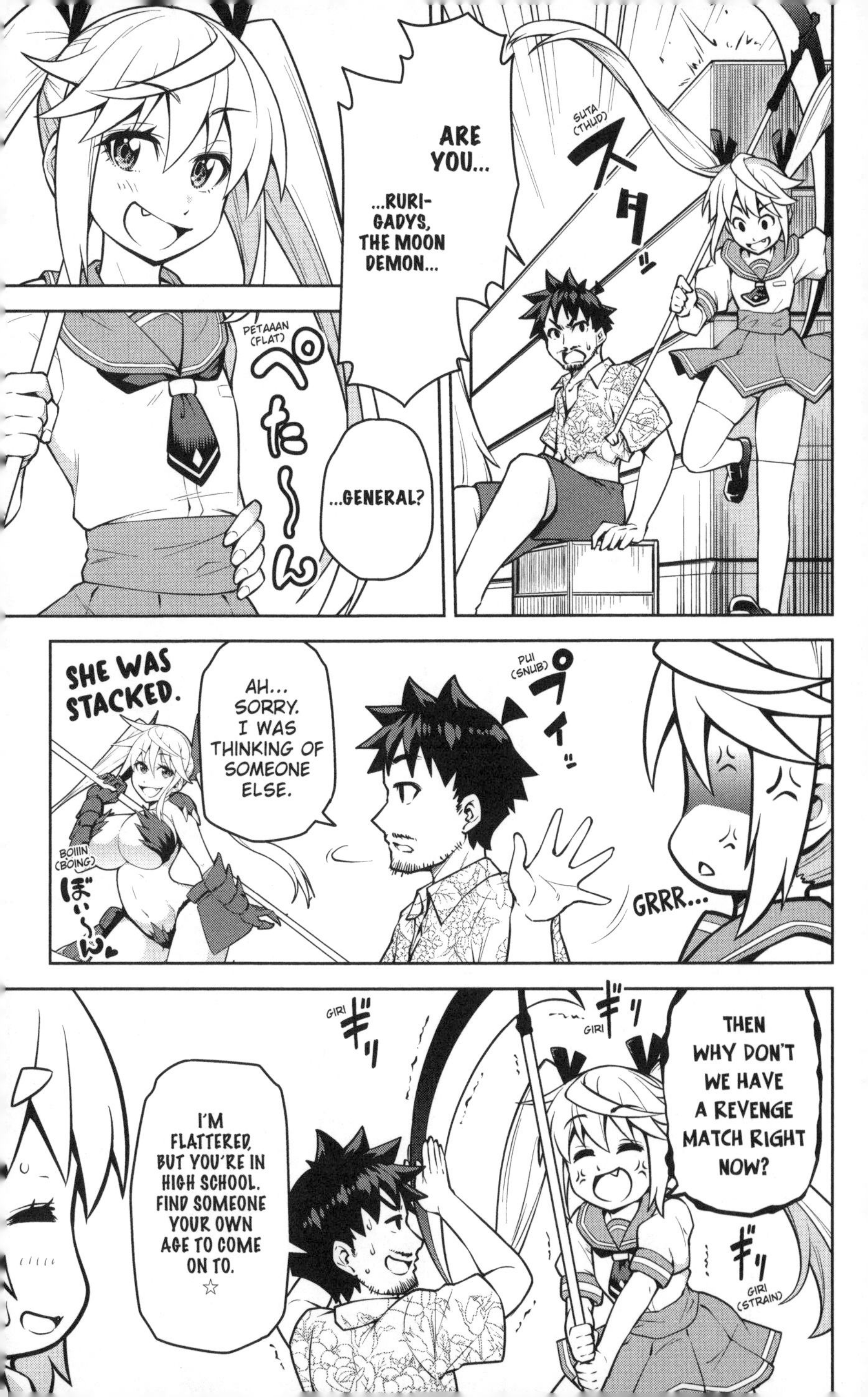
SUTA (THUD)
スタッ
ARE YOU...
...RURI-GADYS, THE MOON DEMON...
...GENERAL?
PETAAAN (FLAT)
ぺた～ん
GRRR...
PUI (SNUB)
プイッ
AH... SORRY. I WAS THINKING OF SOMEONE ELSE.
SHE WAS STACKED.
BOIIIN (BOING)
ぼい～ん♥
THEN WHY DON'T WE HAVE A REVENGE MATCH RIGHT NOW?
GIRI
ギリ
GIRI
ギリ
GIRI (STRAIN)
ギリ
I'M FLATTERED, BUT YOU'RE IN HIGH SCHOOL. FIND SOMEONE YOUR OWN AGE TO COME ON TO. ☆

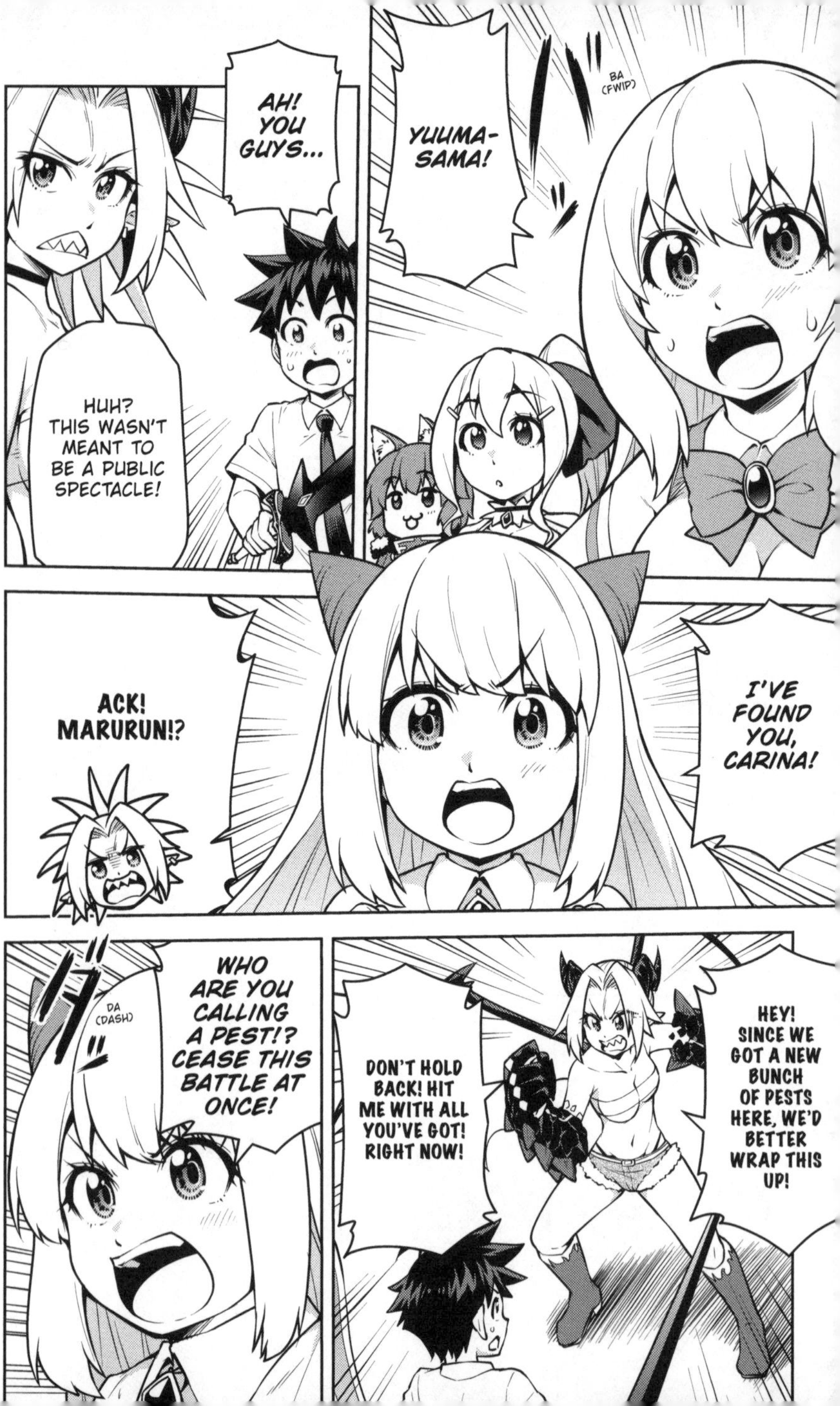
BA (FWIP)
YUUMA-SAMA!
AH! YOU GUYS...
HUH? THIS WASN'T MEANT TO BE A PUBLIC SPECTACLE!
I'VE FOUND YOU, CARINA!
ACK! MARURUN!?
HEY! SINCE WE GOT A NEW BUNCH OF PESTS HERE, WE'D BETTER WRAP THIS UP!
DON'T HOLD BACK! HIT ME WITH ALL YOU'VE GOT! RIGHT NOW!
WHO ARE YOU CALLING A PEST!? CEASE THIS BATTLE AT ONCE!
DA (DASH)

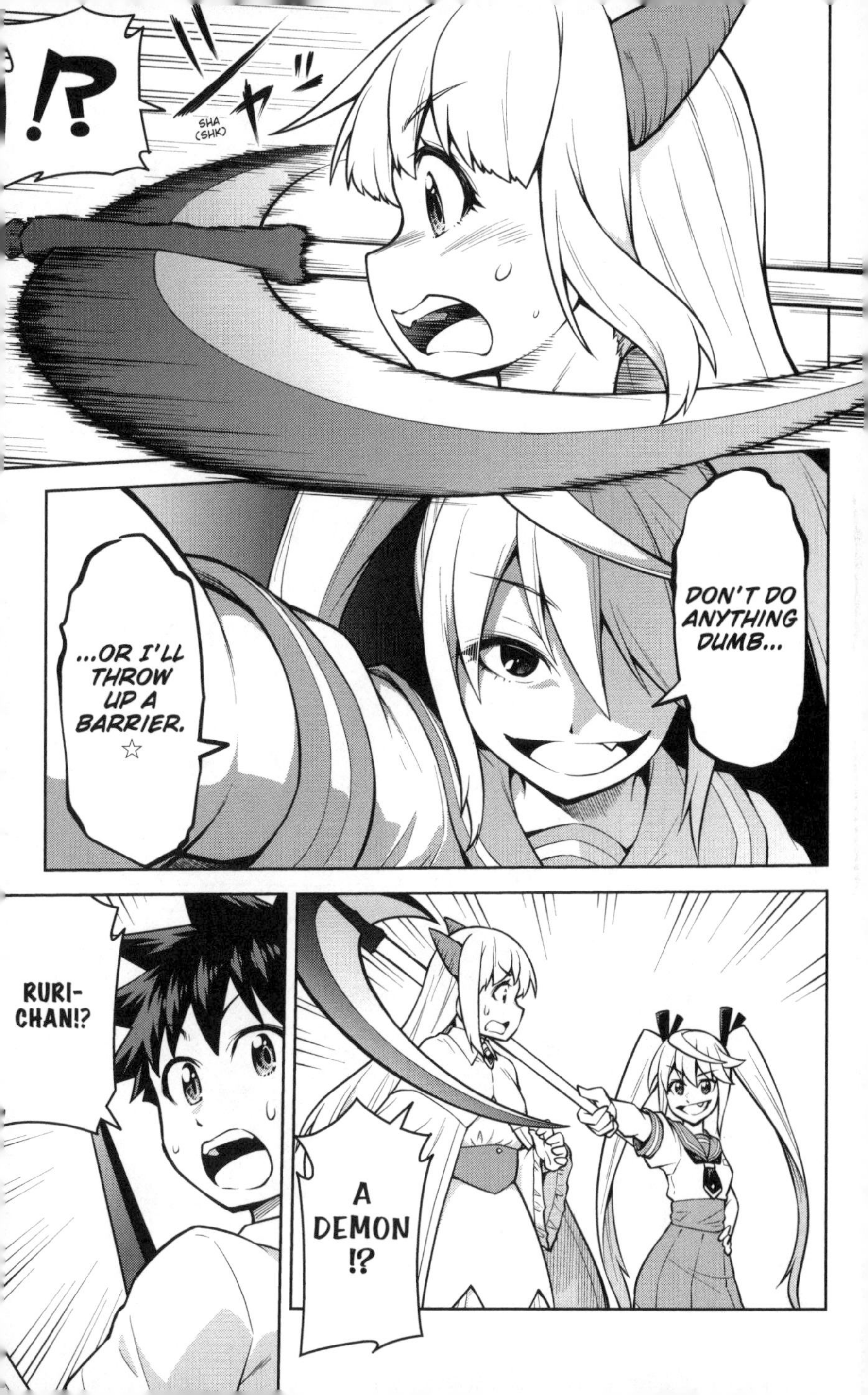
SHA (SHK)
!?
DON'T DO ANYTHING DUMB...
...OR I'LL THROW UP A BARRIER. ☆
A DEMON !?
RURI-CHAN!?

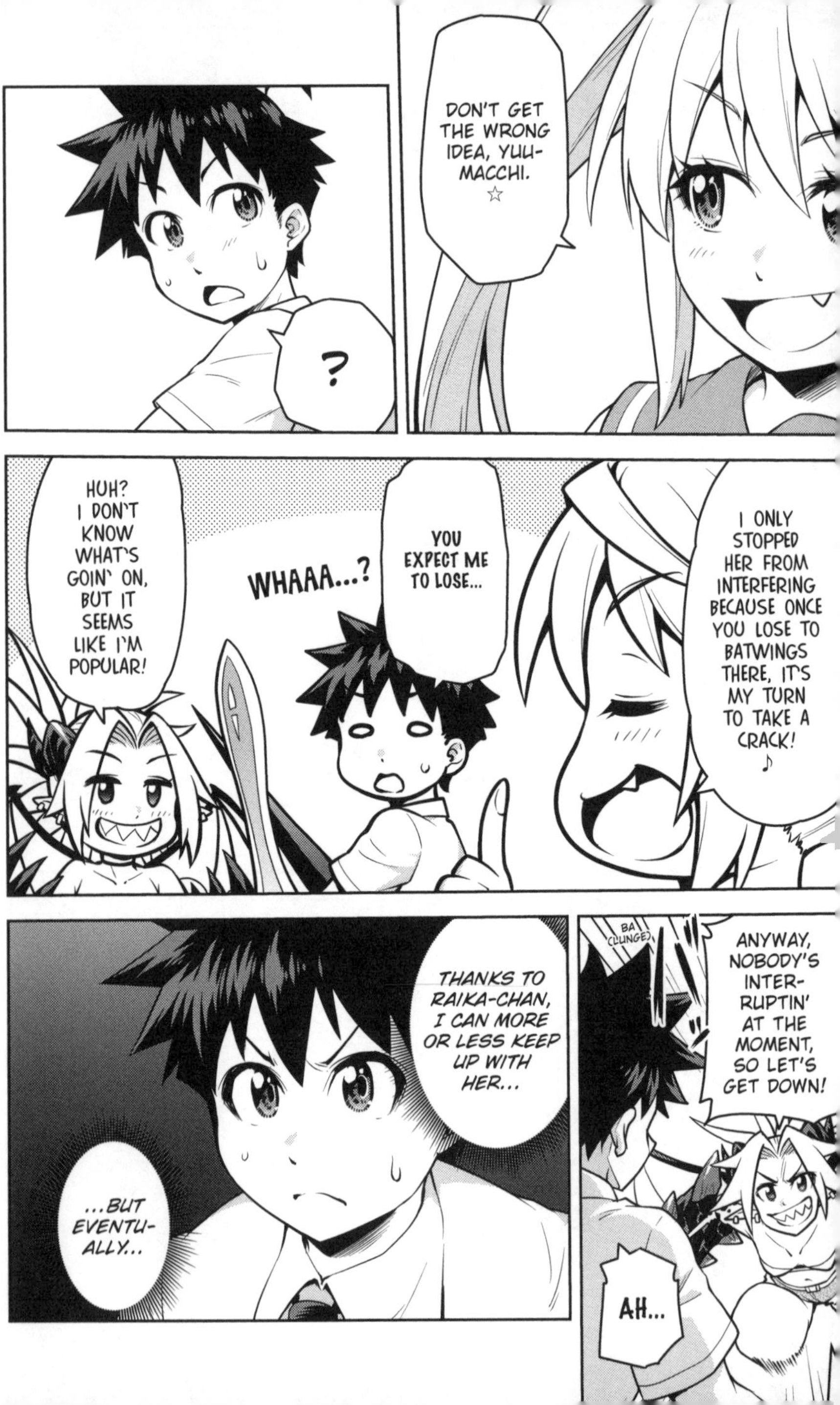
DON'T GET THE WRONG IDEA, YUU-MACCHI. ☆
?
I ONLY STOPPED HER FROM INTERFERING BECAUSE ONCE YOU LOSE TO BATWINGS THERE, IT'S MY TURN TO TAKE A CRACK! ♪
YOU EXPECT ME TO LOSE...
WHAAA...?
HUH? I DON'T KNOW WHAT'S GOIN' ON, BUT IT SEEMS LIKE I'M POPULAR!
ANYWAY, NOBODY'S INTER-RUPTIN' AT THE MOMENT, SO LET'S GET DOWN!
BA (LUNGE)
AH...
THANKS TO RAIKA-CHAN, I CAN MORE OR LESS KEEP UP WITH HER...
...BUT EVENTU-ALLY...

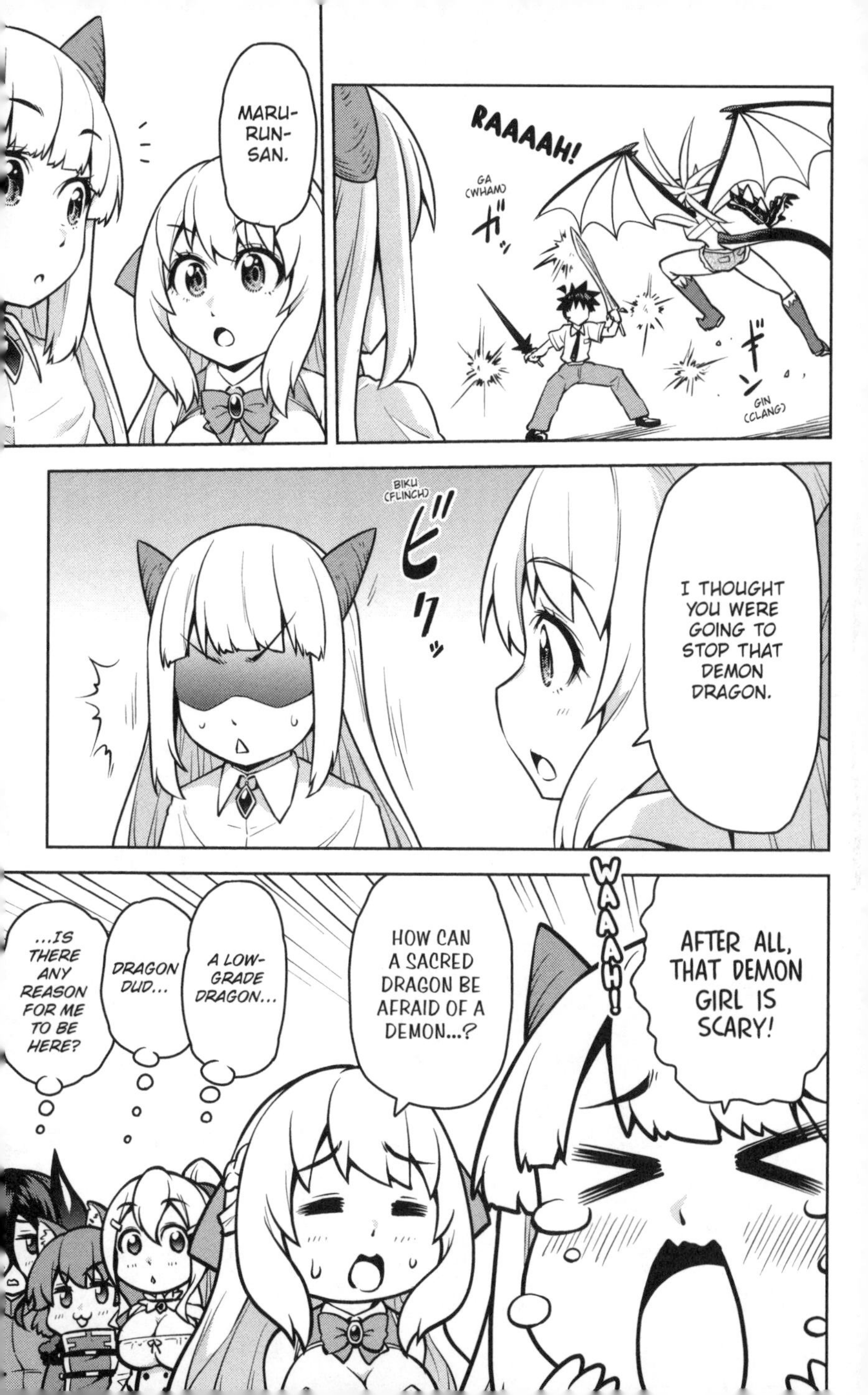
RAAAAH!
GA (WHAM)
GIN (CLANG)
MARU-RUN-SAN.
BIKU (FLINCH)
I THOUGHT YOU WERE GOING TO STOP THAT DEMON DRAGON.
WAAAH!
AFTER ALL, THAT DEMON GIRL IS SCARY!
HOW CAN A SACRED DRAGON BE AFRAID OF A DEMON...?
A LOW-GRADE DRAGON...
DRAGON DUD...
...IS THERE ANY REASON FOR ME TO BE HERE?

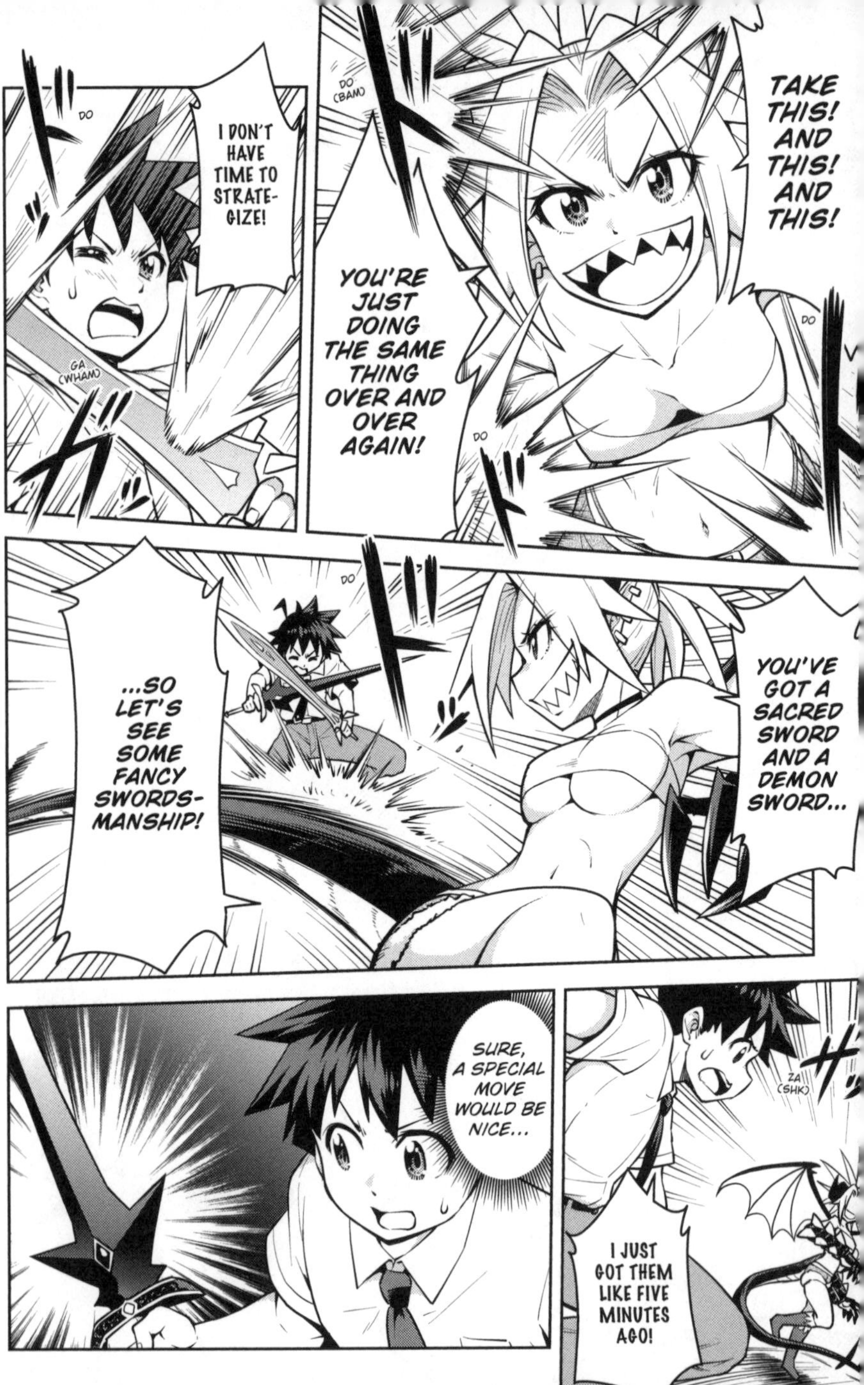
TAKE THIS! AND THIS! AND THIS!
DO (BAM)
YOU'RE JUST DOING THE SAME THING OVER AND OVER AGAIN!
DO
DO
DO
I DON'T HAVE TIME TO STRATE-GIZE!
GA (WHAM)
YOU'VE GOT A SACRED SWORD AND A DEMON SWORD...
DO
...SO LET'S SEE SOME FANCY SWORDS-MANSHIP!
ZA (SHK)
I JUST GOT THEM LIKE FIVE MINUTES AGO!
SURE, A SPECIAL MOVE WOULD BE NICE...

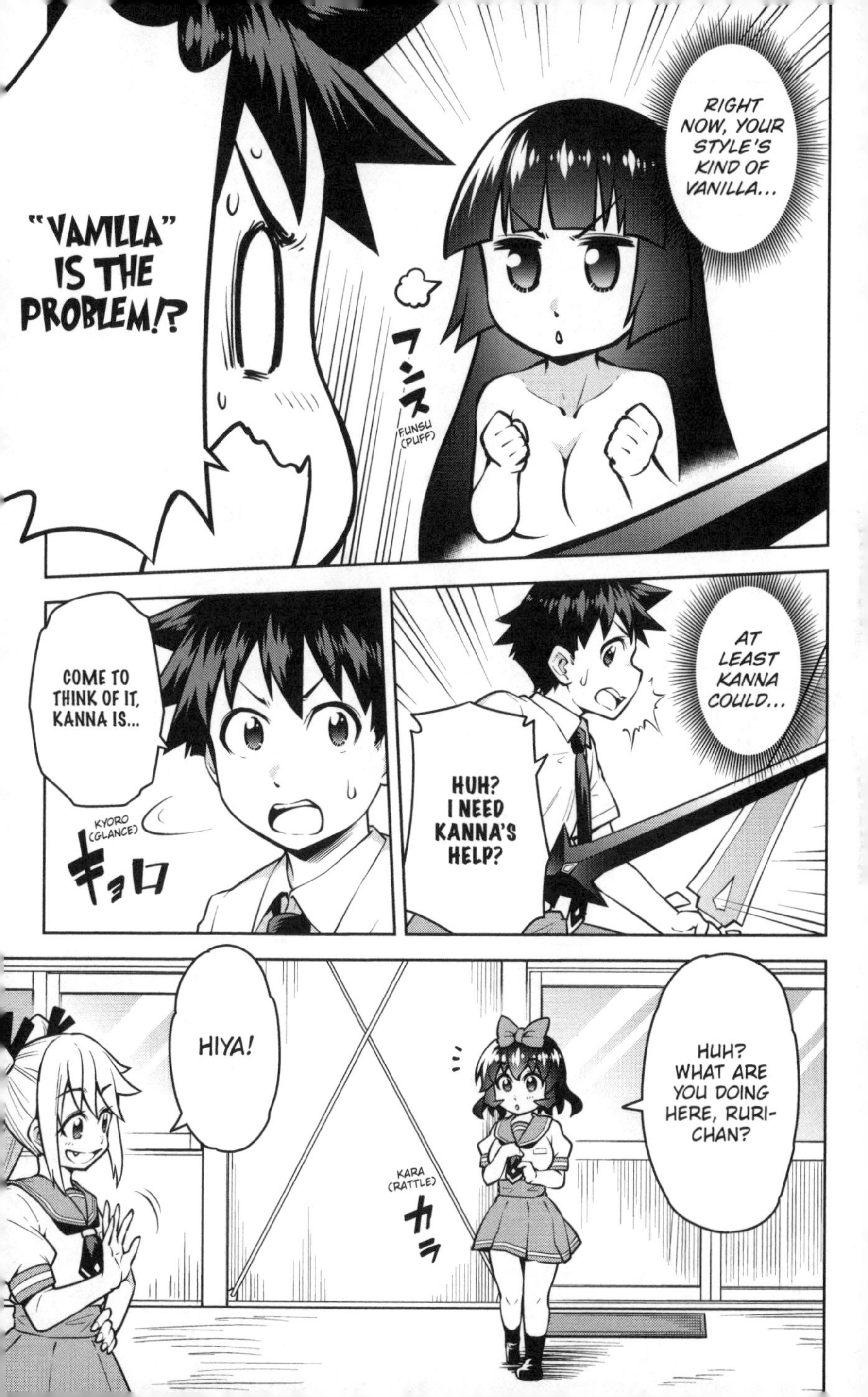
RIGHT NOW, YOUR STYLE'S KIND OF VANILLA...
フンス
FUNSU (PUFF)
"VANILLA" IS THE PROBLEM!?
AT LEAST KANNA COULD...
HUH? I NEED KANNA'S HELP?
COME TO THINK OF IT, KANNA IS...
KYORO (GLANCE)
キョロ
HUH? WHAT ARE YOU DOING HERE, RURI-CHAN?
KARA (RATTLE)
カラ
HIYA!

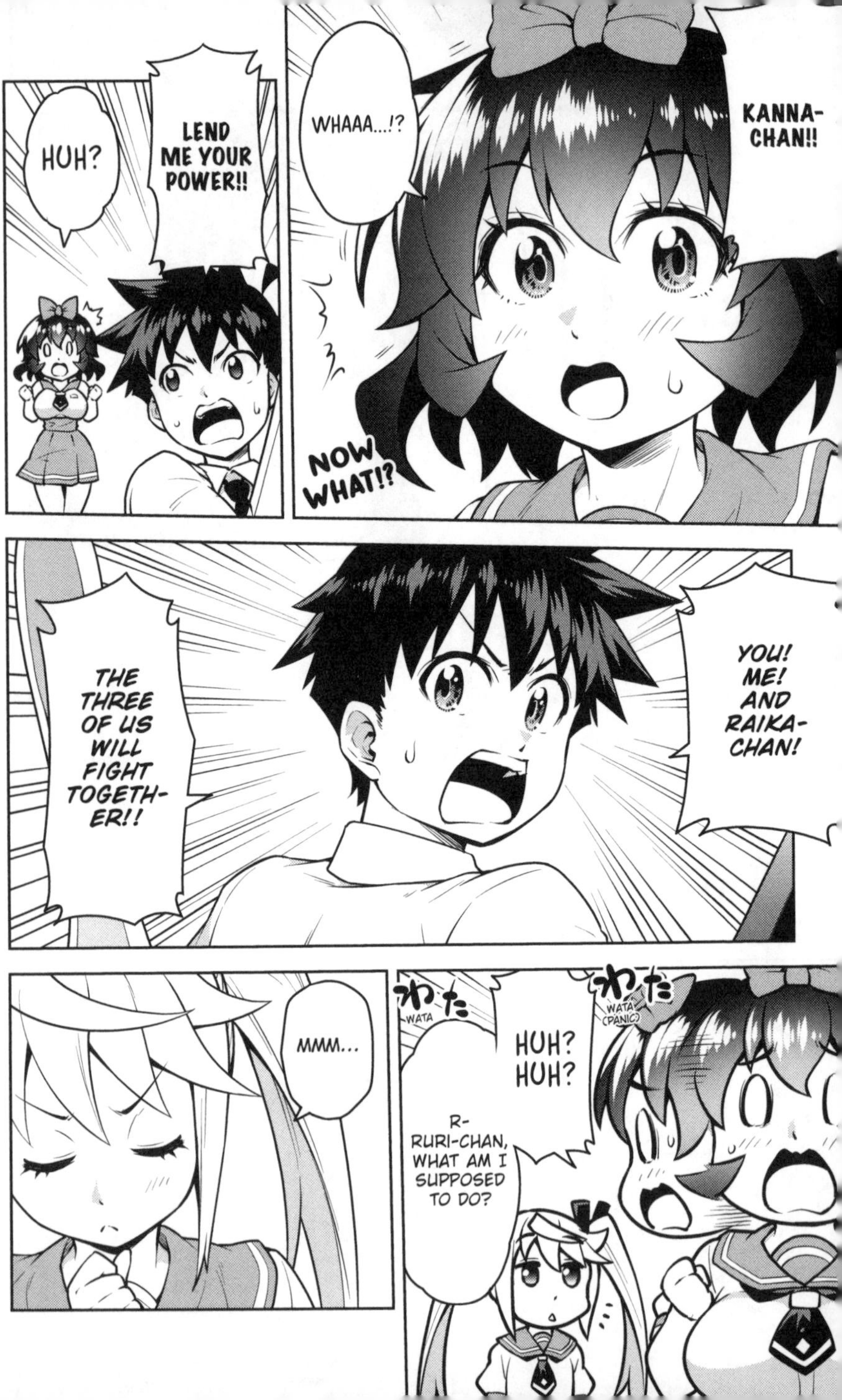
KANNA-CHAN!!
WHAAA...!?
NOW WHAT!?
LEND ME YOUR POWER!!
HUH?
YOU! ME! AND RAIKA-CHAN!
THE THREE OF US WILL FIGHT TOGETHER!!
わた WATA (PANIC)
わた WATA
HUH? HUH?
R-RURI-CHAN, WHAT AM I SUPPOSED TO DO?
MMM...

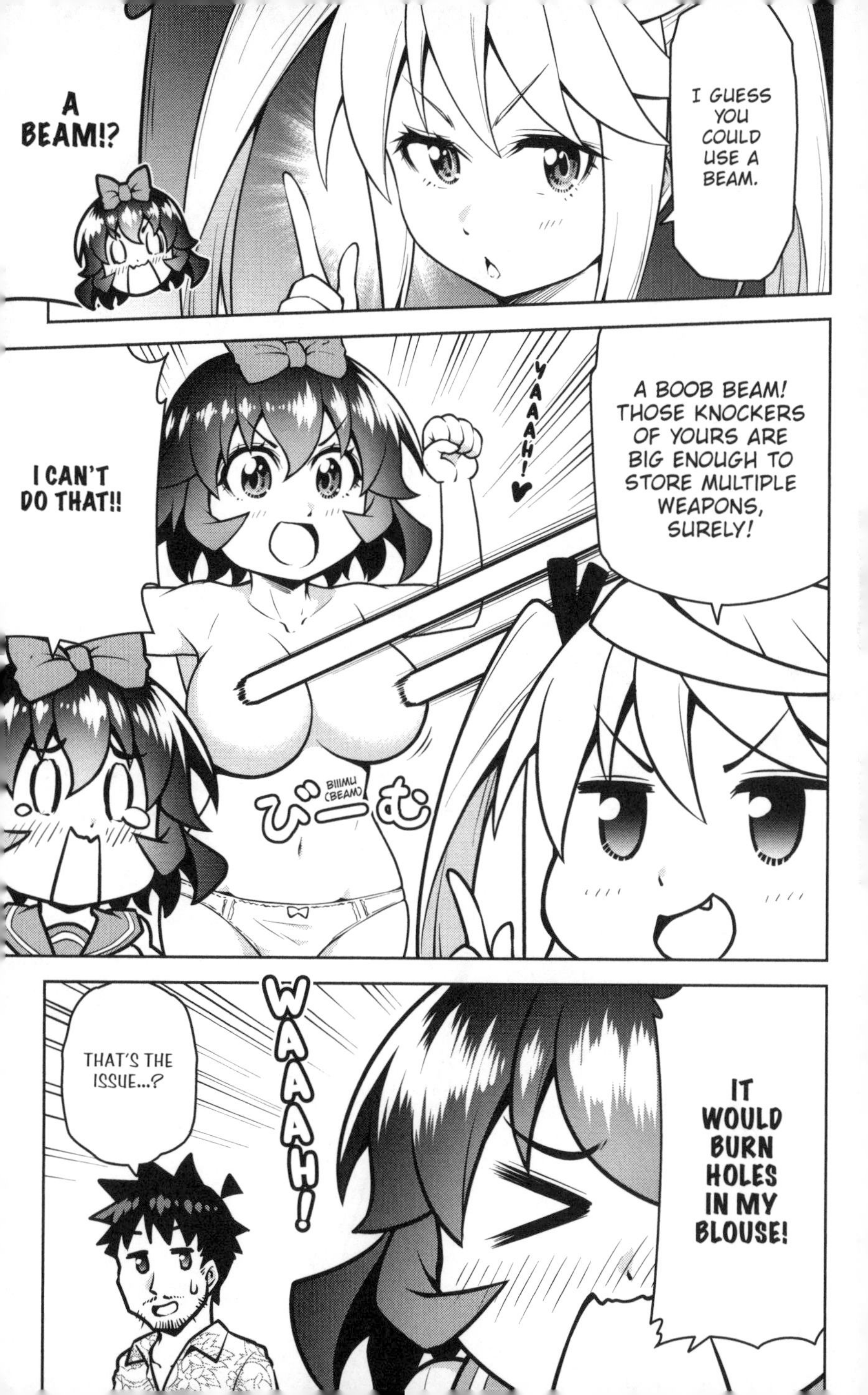
I GUESS YOU COULD USE A BEAM.
A BEAM!?
A BOOB BEAM! THOSE KNOCKERS OF YOURS ARE BIG ENOUGH TO STORE MULTIPLE WEAPONS, SURELY!
YAAAAH!♥
I CAN'T DO THAT!!
びーむ
BIIIMU (BEAM)
IT WOULD BURN HOLES IN MY BLOUSE!
WAAAAH!
THAT'S THE ISSUE...?

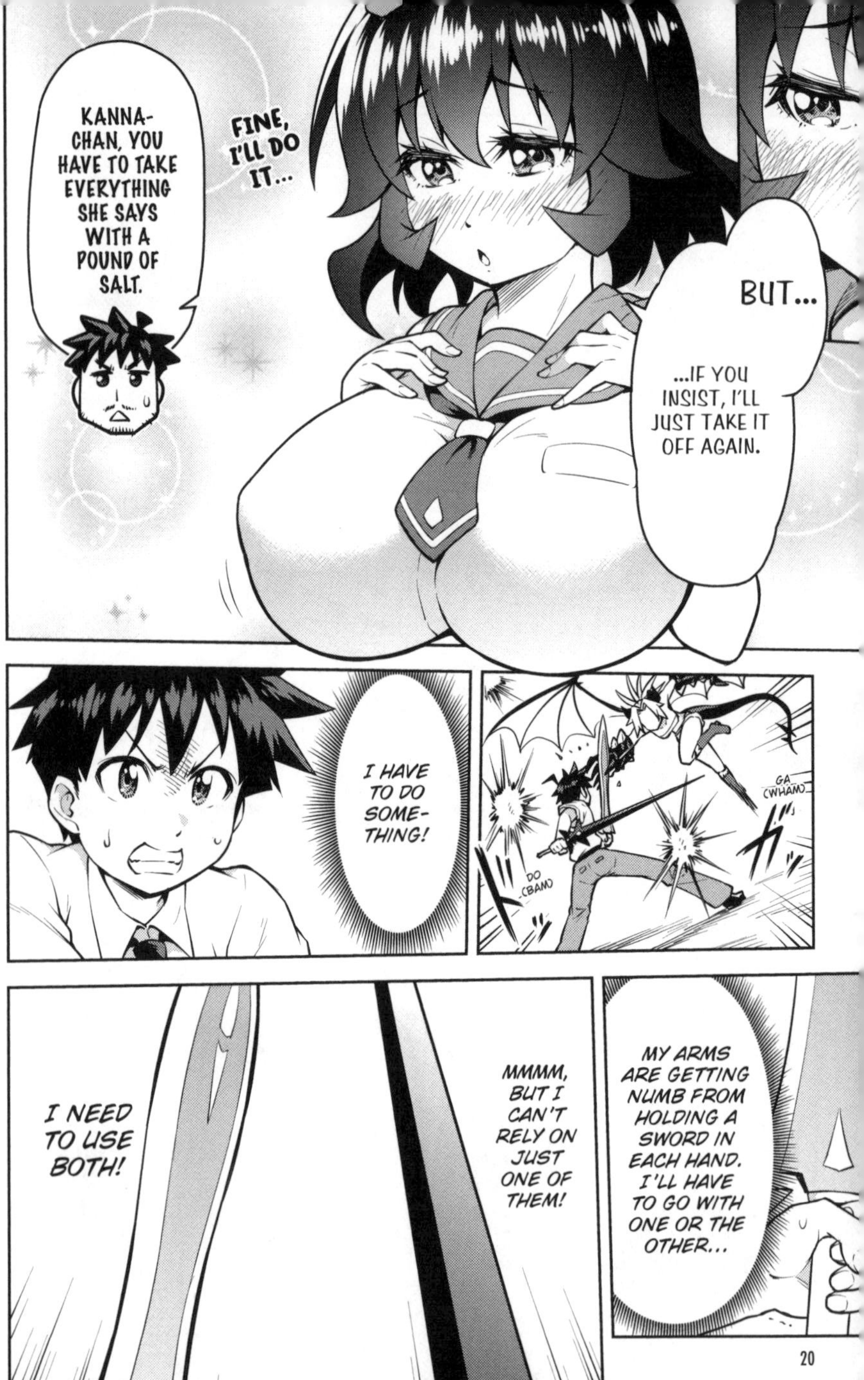
BUT...
...IF YOU INSIST, I'LL JUST TAKE IT OFF AGAIN.
FINE, I'LL DO IT...
KANNA-CHAN, YOU HAVE TO TAKE EVERYTHING SHE SAYS WITH A POUND OF SALT.
GA (WHAM)
DO (BAM)
I HAVE TO DO SOMETHING!
MY ARMS ARE GETTING NUMB FROM HOLDING A SWORD IN EACH HAND. I'LL HAVE TO GO WITH ONE OR THE OTHER...
MMMM, BUT I CAN'T RELY ON JUST ONE OF THEM!
I NEED TO USE BOTH!

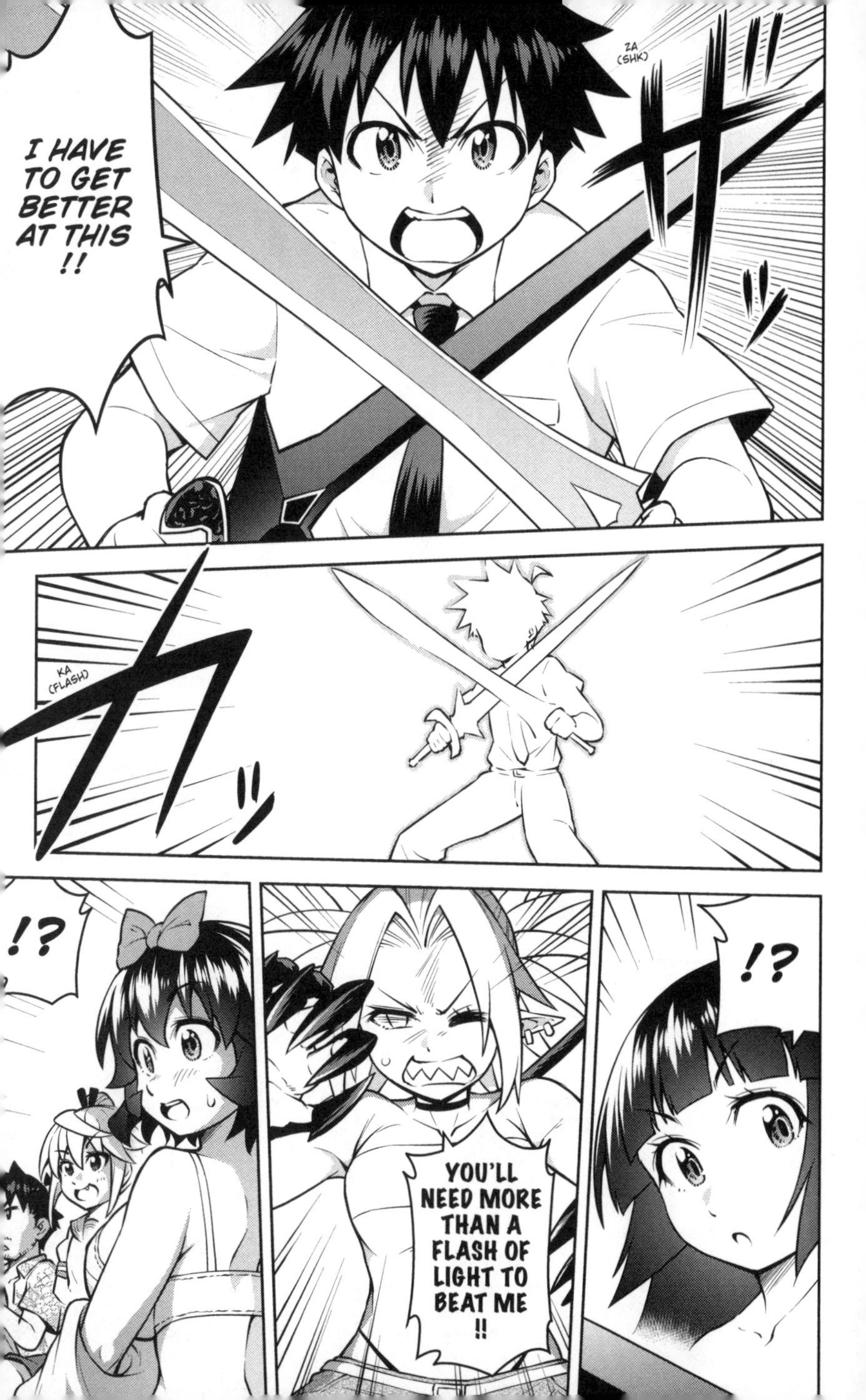
ZA (SHK)
I HAVE TO GET BETTER AT THIS !!
KA (FLASH)
!?
YOU'LL NEED MORE THAN A FLASH OF LIGHT TO BEAT ME !!
!?

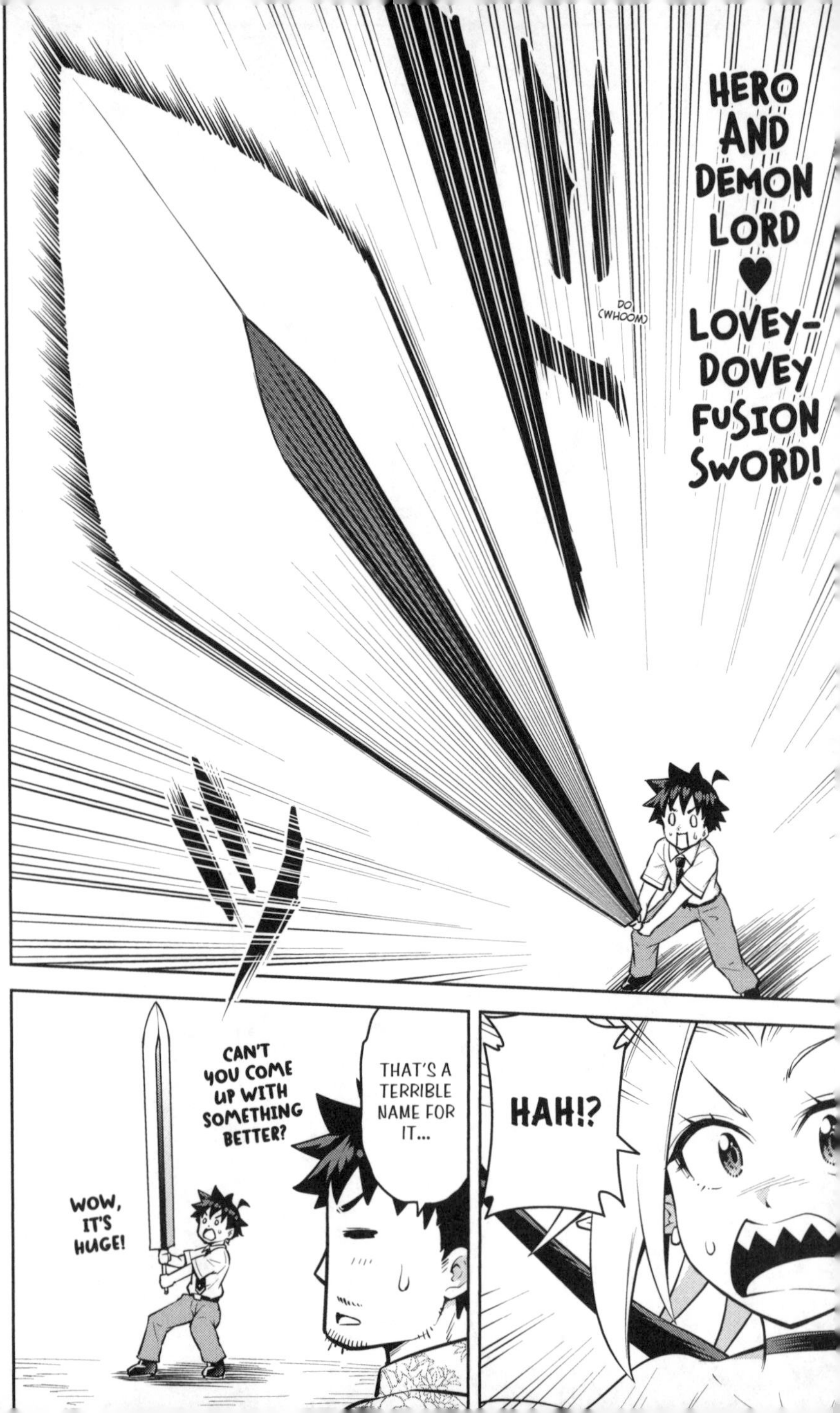
HERO AND DEMON LORD ♥ LOVEY-DOVEY FUSION SWORD!
DO (WHOOM)
HAH!?
THAT'S A TERRIBLE NAME FOR IT...
CAN'T YOU COME UP WITH SOMETHING BETTER?
WOW, IT'S HUGE!

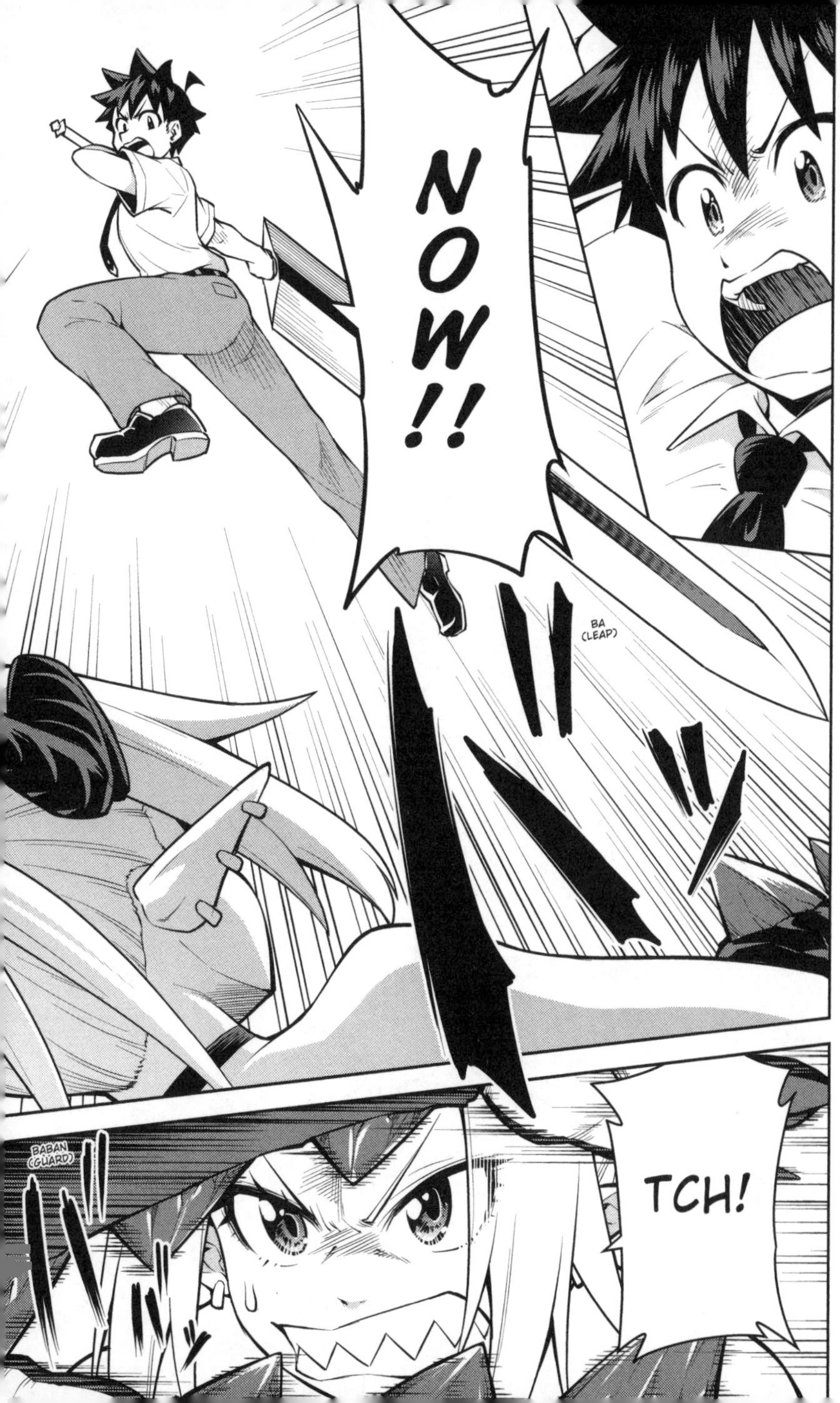
NOW!!
BA (LEAP)
TCH!
BABAN (GUARD)

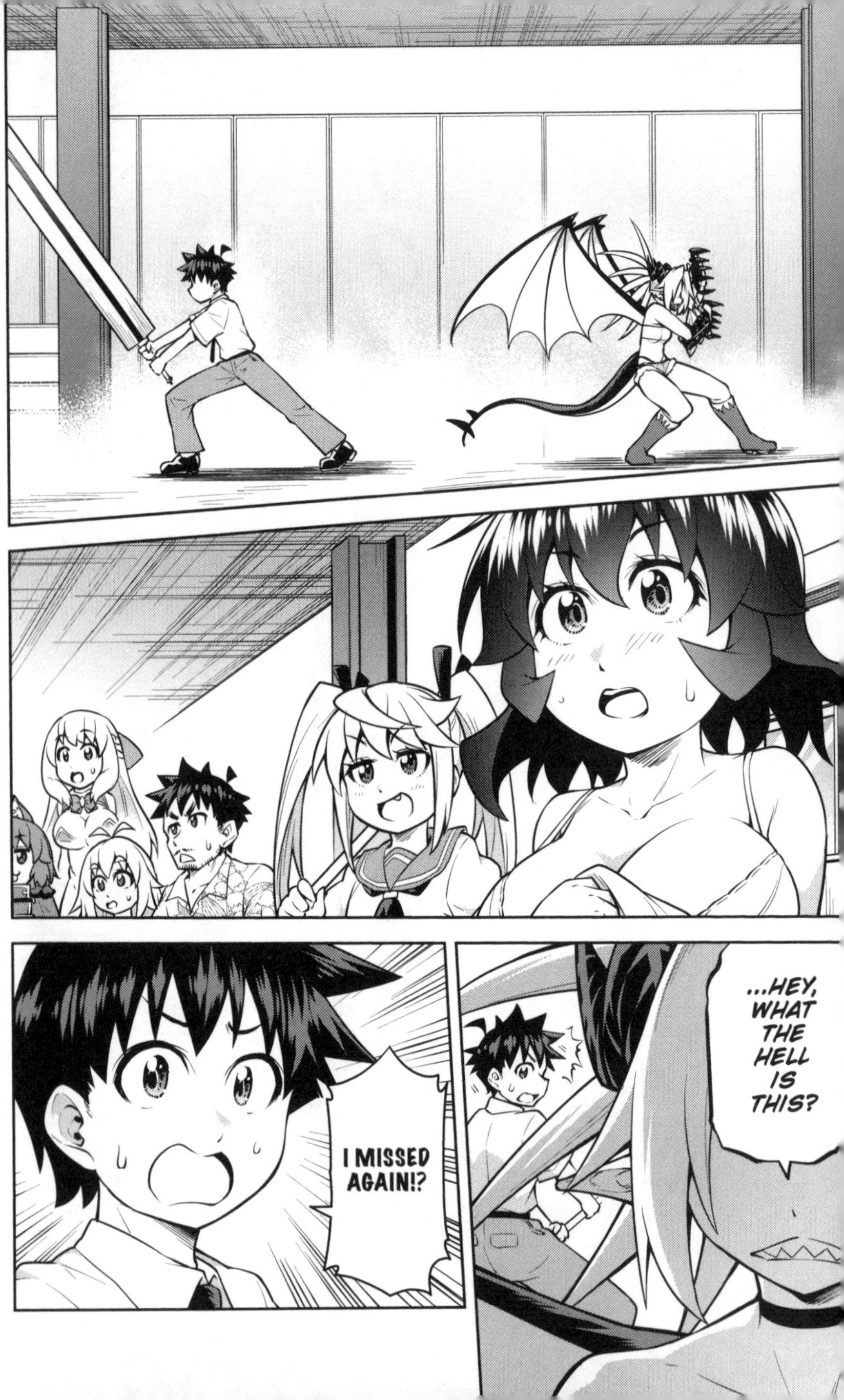
...HEY, WHAT THE HELL IS THIS?
I MISSED AGAIN!?

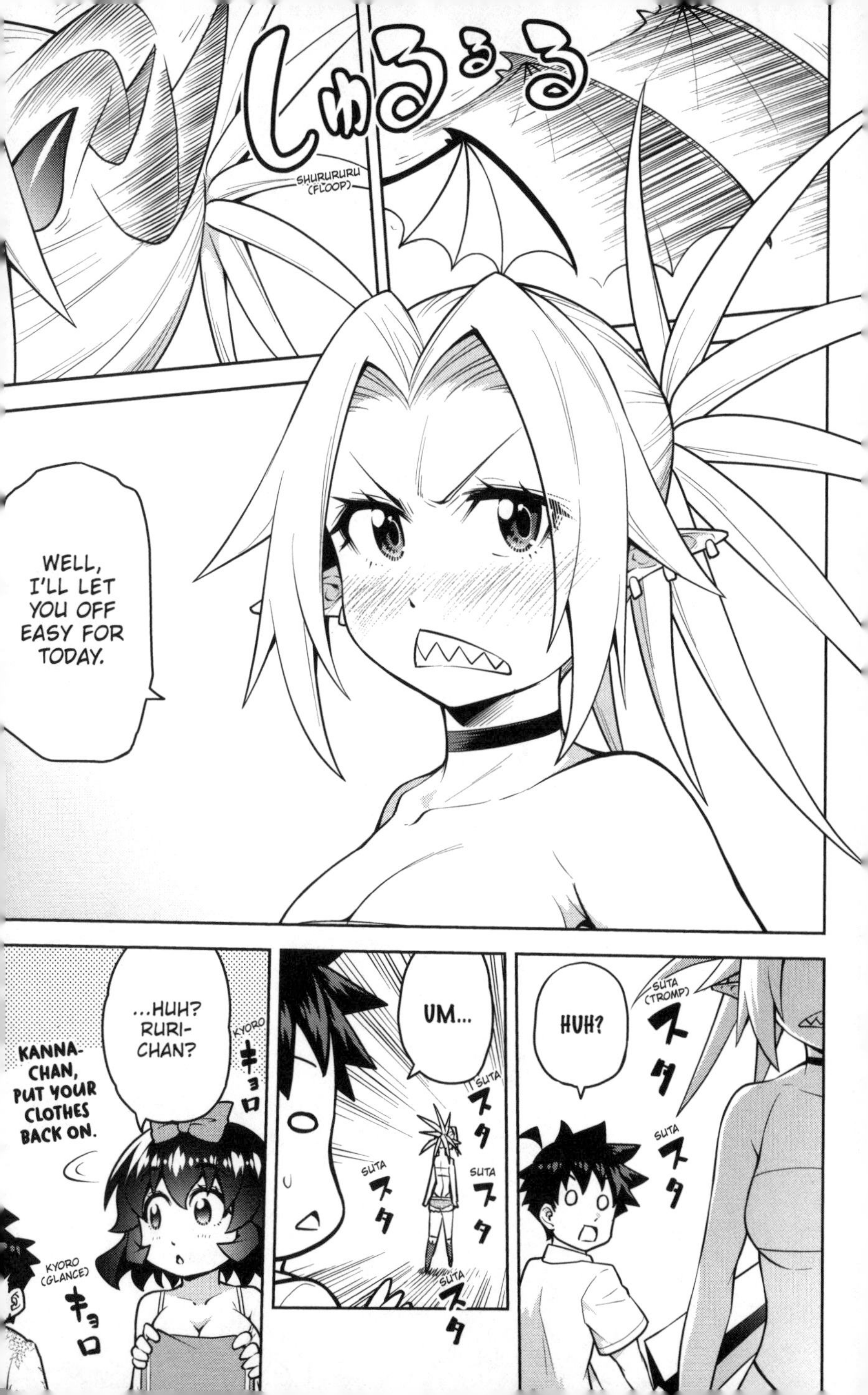
しゅるるる
SHURURURU (FLOOP)
WELL, I'LL LET YOU OFF EASY FOR TODAY.
HUH?
SUTA (TROMP)
スタ
SUTA
スタ
UM...
SUTA
スタ
SUTA
スタ
SUTA
スタ
SUTA
スタ
...HUH? RURI-CHAN?
KYORO
キョロ
KANNA-CHAN, PUT YOUR CLOTHES BACK ON.
KYORO (GLANCE)
キョロ

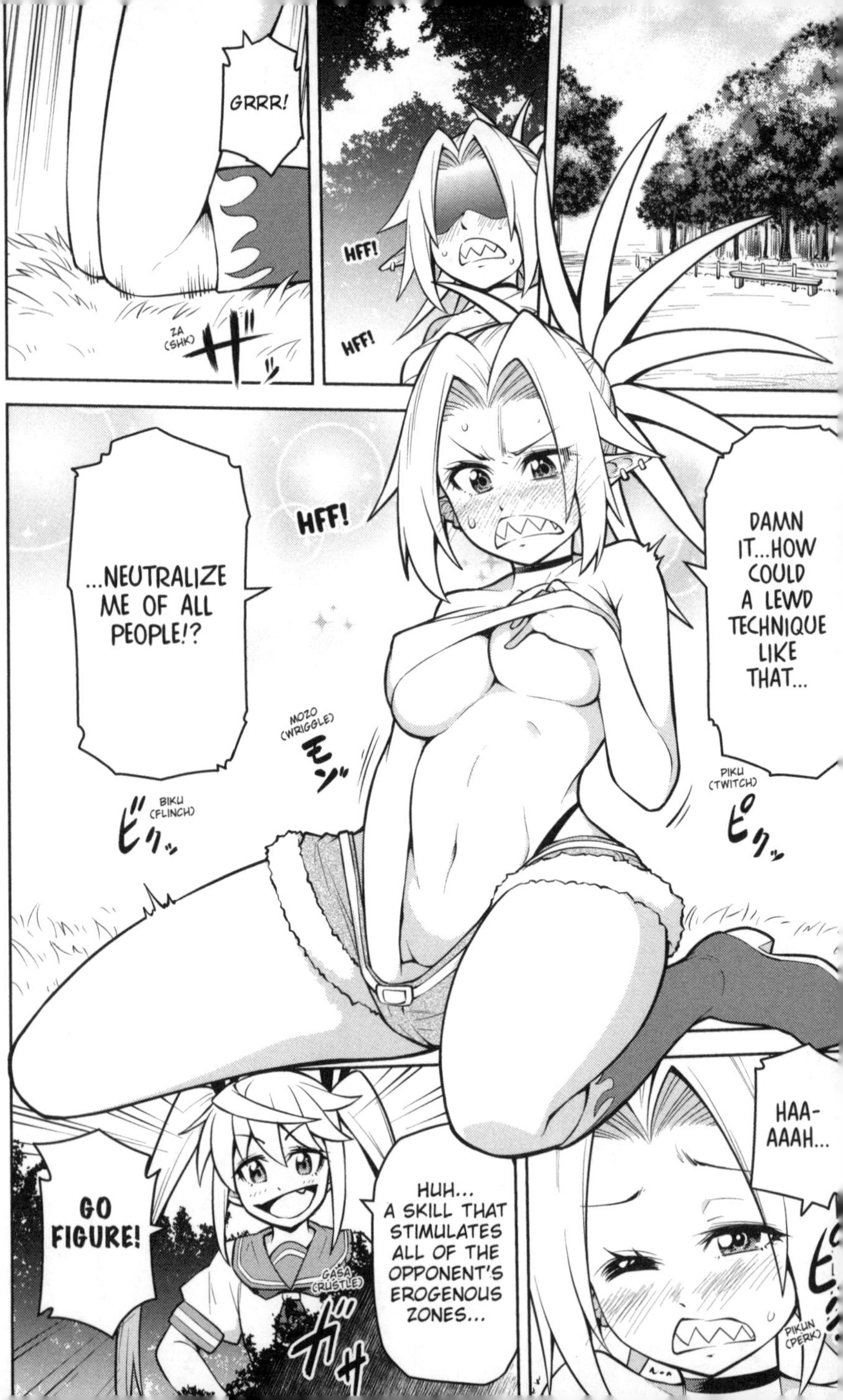
HFF!
HFF!
GRRR!
ZA (SHK)
DAMN IT...HOW COULD A LEWD TECHNIQUE LIKE THAT...
HFF!
...NEUTRALIZE ME OF ALL PEOPLE!?
PIKU (TWITCH)
MOZO (WRIGGLE)
BIKU (FLINCH)
HAA-AAAH...
PIKUN (PERK)
HUH... A SKILL THAT STIMULATES ALL OF THE OPPONENT'S EROGENOUS ZONES...
GO FIGURE!
GASA (RUSTLE)

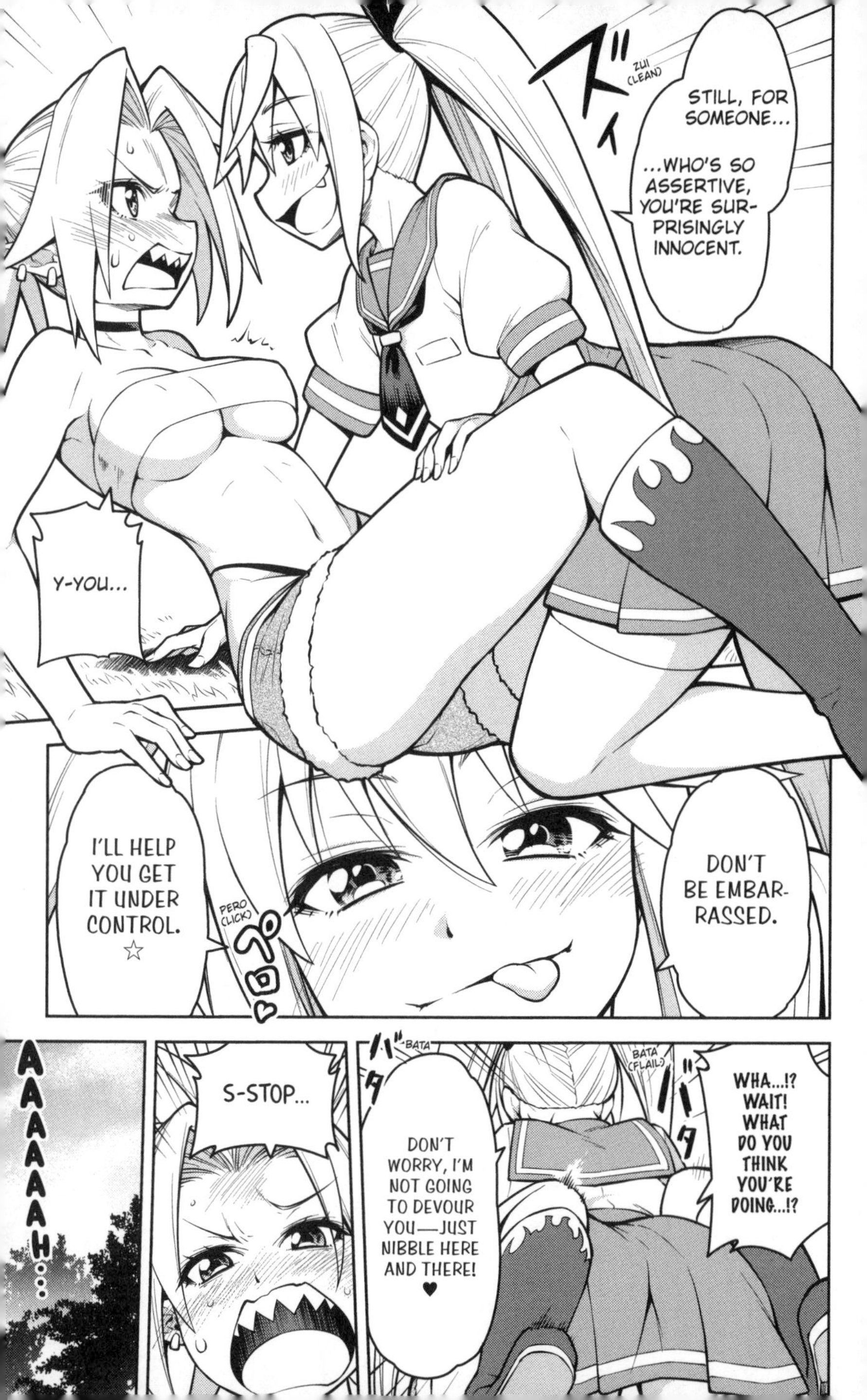
ZUI (LEAN)
STILL, FOR SOMEONE...
...WHO'S SO ASSERTIVE, YOU'RE SURPRISINGLY INNOCENT.
Y-YOU...
DON'T BE EMBARRASSED.
PERO (LICK)
I'LL HELP YOU GET IT UNDER CONTROL. ☆
BATA (FLAIL)
WHA...!? WAIT! WHAT DO YOU THINK YOU'RE DOING...!?
BATA
DON'T WORRY, I'M NOT GOING TO DEVOUR YOU—JUST NIBBLE HERE AND THERE! ♥
S-STOP...
AAAAAAH...

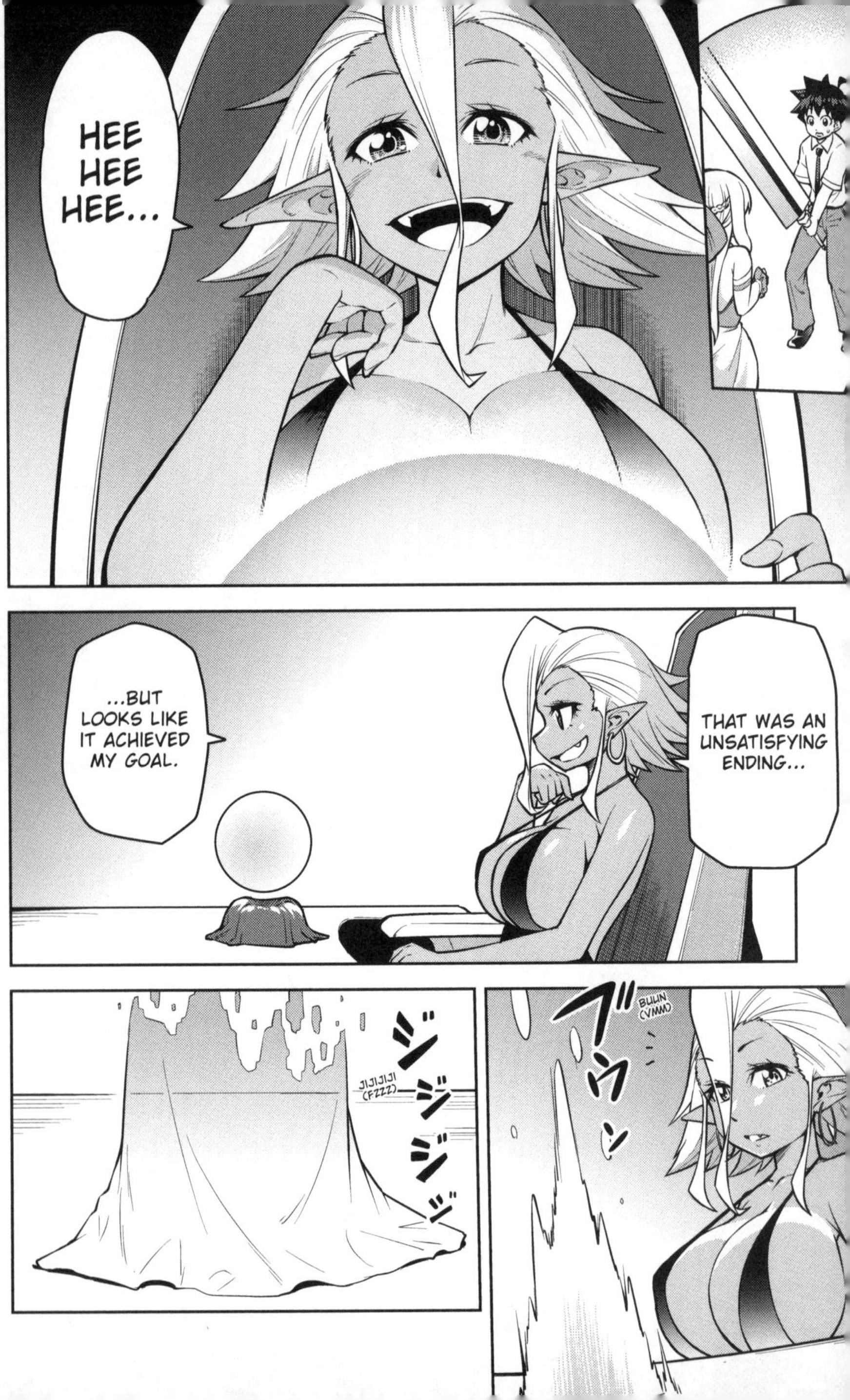
HEE HEE HEE...
THAT WAS AN UNSATISFYING ENDING...
...BUT LOOKS LIKE IT ACHIEVED MY GOAL.
ブゥン
BULUN (VMM)
ジジジジ
JIJIJIJI (FZZZ)

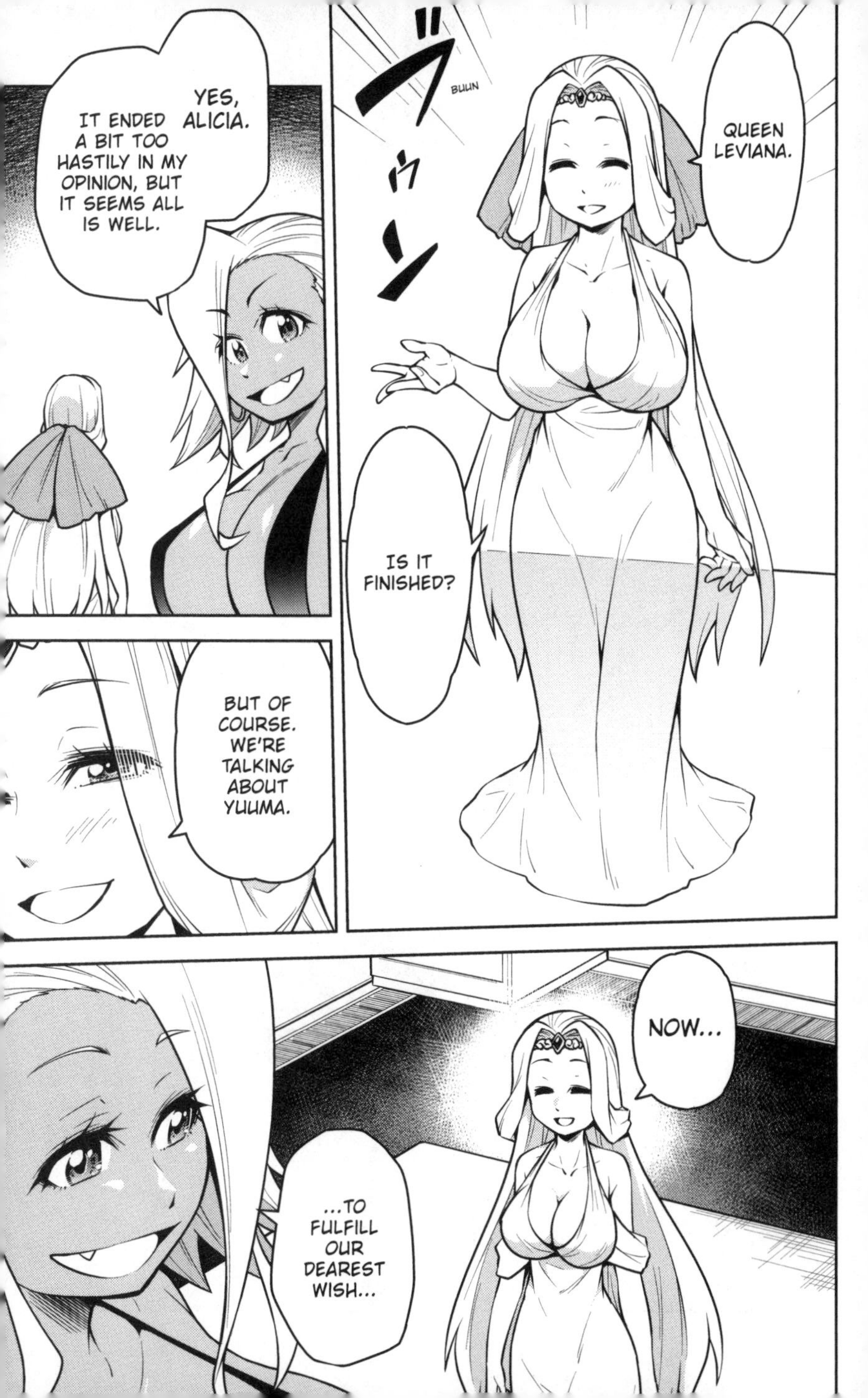
QUEEN LEVIANA.
ヴゥン
BUUN
IS IT FINISHED?
YES, ALICIA. IT ENDED A BIT TOO HASTILY IN MY OPINION, BUT IT SEEMS ALL IS WELL.
BUT OF COURSE. WE'RE TALKING ABOUT YUUMA.
NOW...
...TO FULFILL OUR DEAREST WISH...

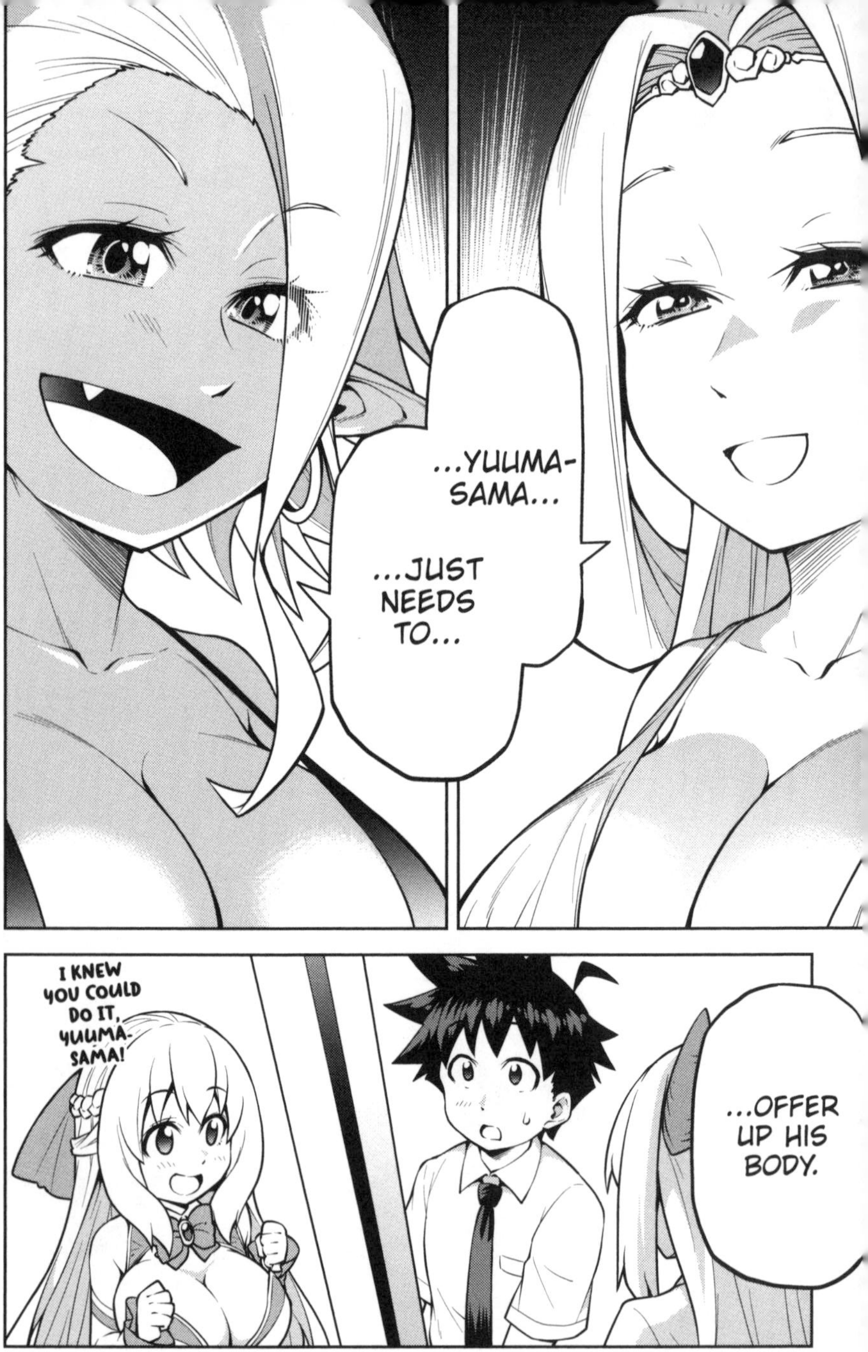
...YUUMA-SAMA...
...JUST NEEDS TO...
...OFFER UP HIS BODY.
I KNEW YOU COULD DO IT, YUUMA-SAMA!

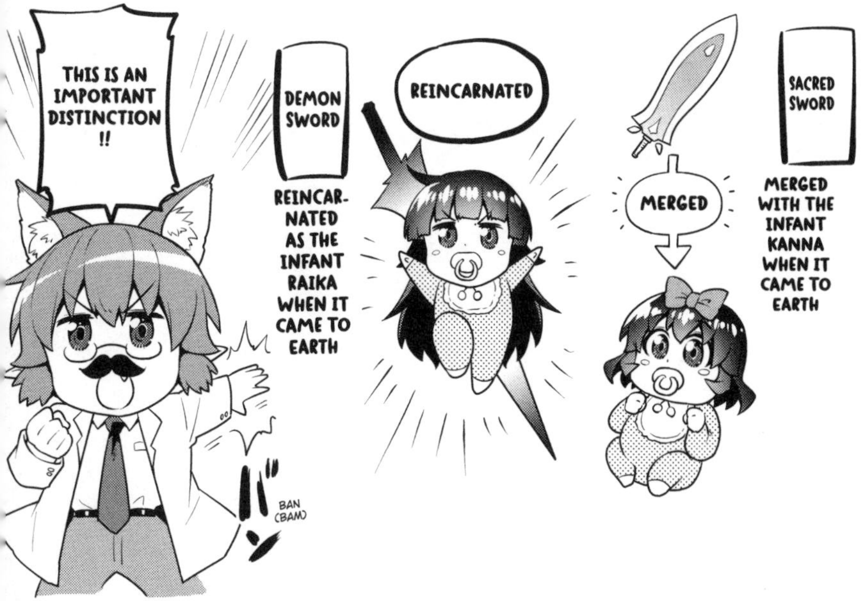
SACRED SWORD
MERGED WITH THE INFANT KANNA WHEN IT CAME TO EARTH
MERGED
REINCARNATED
DEMON SWORD
REINCAR-NATED AS THE INFANT RAIKA WHEN IT CAME TO EARTH
THIS IS AN IMPORTANT DISTINCTION !!
BAN (BAM)

I'm the
HERO, but the DEMON
LORD's
Also Me

SIGN: OKONOMIYAKI

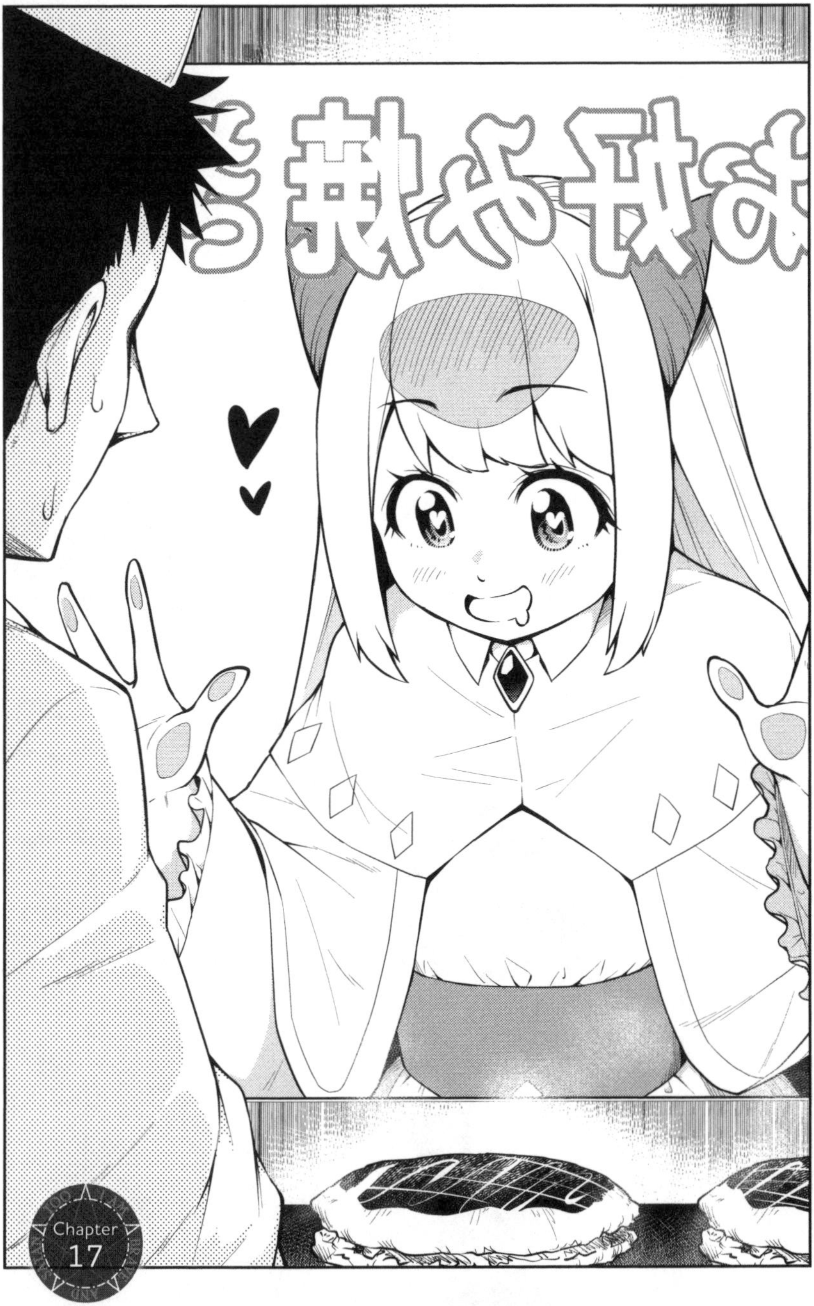
Chapter
17

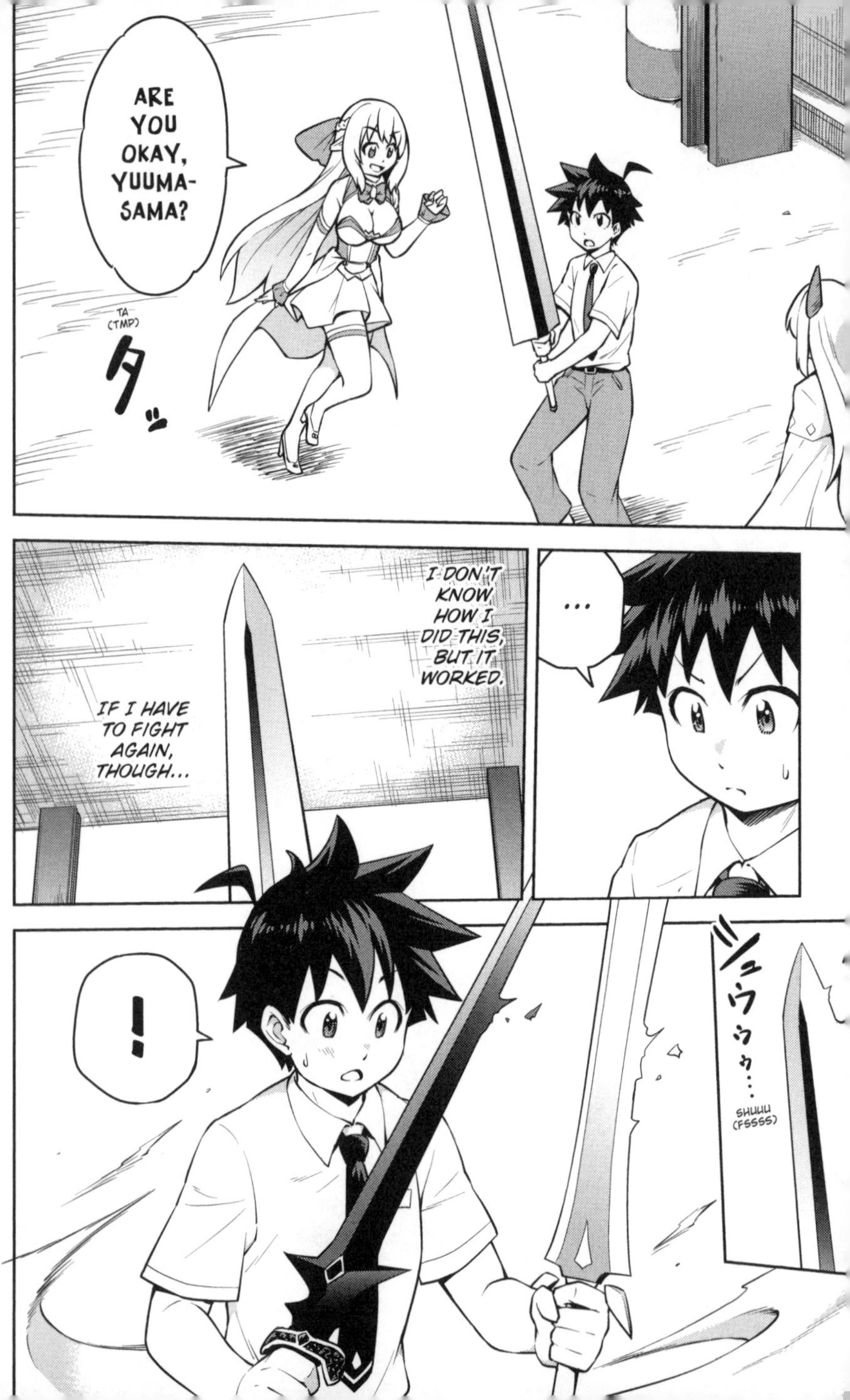
ARE YOU OKAY, YUUMA-SAMA?
タッ
TA (TMP)
...
I DON'T KNOW HOW I DID THIS, BUT IT WORKED.
IF I HAVE TO FIGHT AGAIN, THOUGH...
シュウゥゥ...
SHUUU (FSSSS)
!

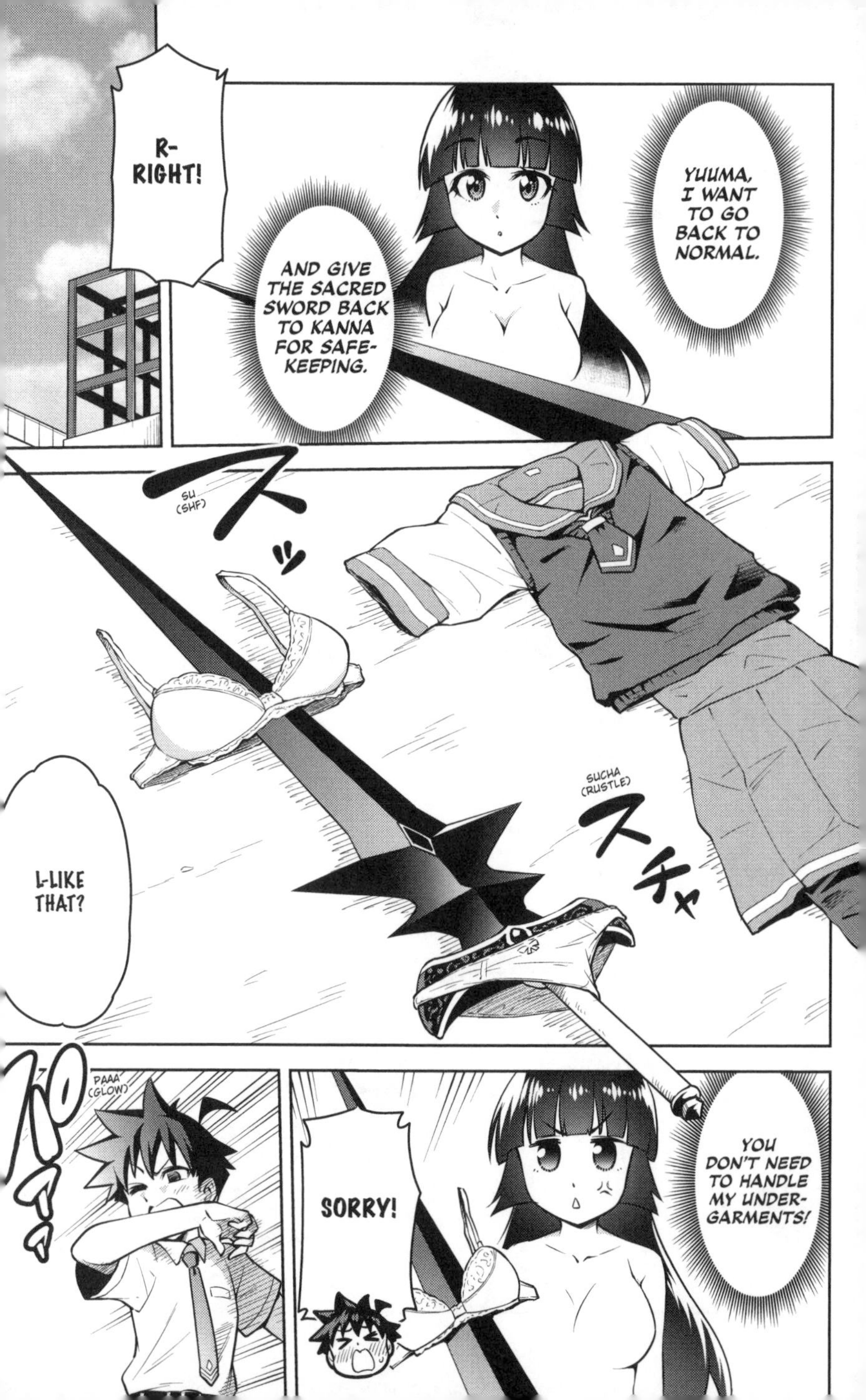
YUUMA, I WANT TO GO BACK TO NORMAL.
AND GIVE THE SACRED SWORD BACK TO KANNA FOR SAFE-KEEPING.
R-RIGHT!
SU (SHF)
SUCHA (RUSTLE)
L-LIKE THAT?
YOU DON'T NEED TO HANDLE MY UNDER-GARMENTS!
SORRY!
PAAA (GLOW)

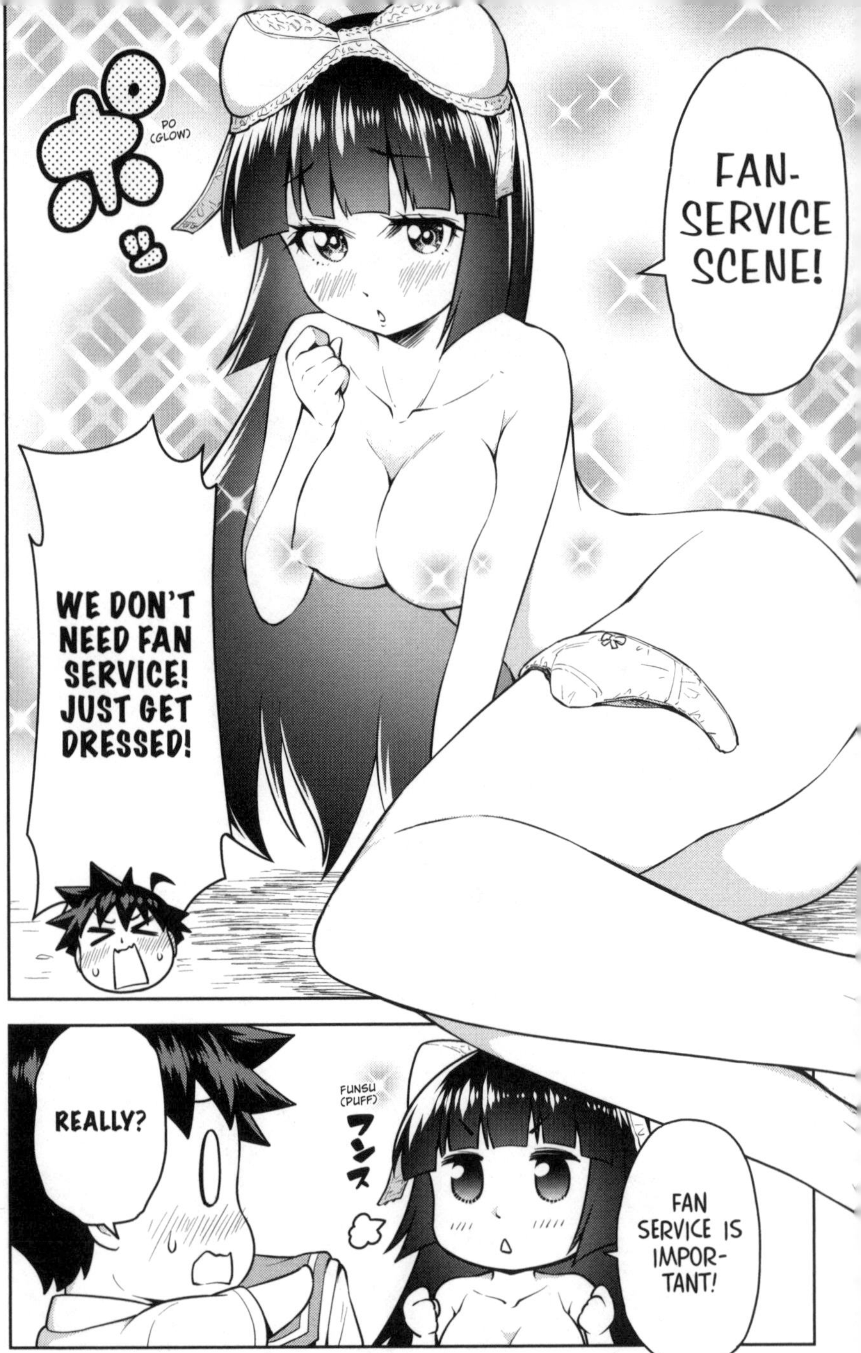
PO (GLOW)
FAN-SERVICE SCENE!
WE DON'T NEED FAN SERVICE! JUST GET DRESSED!
FAN SERVICE IS IMPORTANT!
FUNSU (PUFF)
フンス
REALLY?

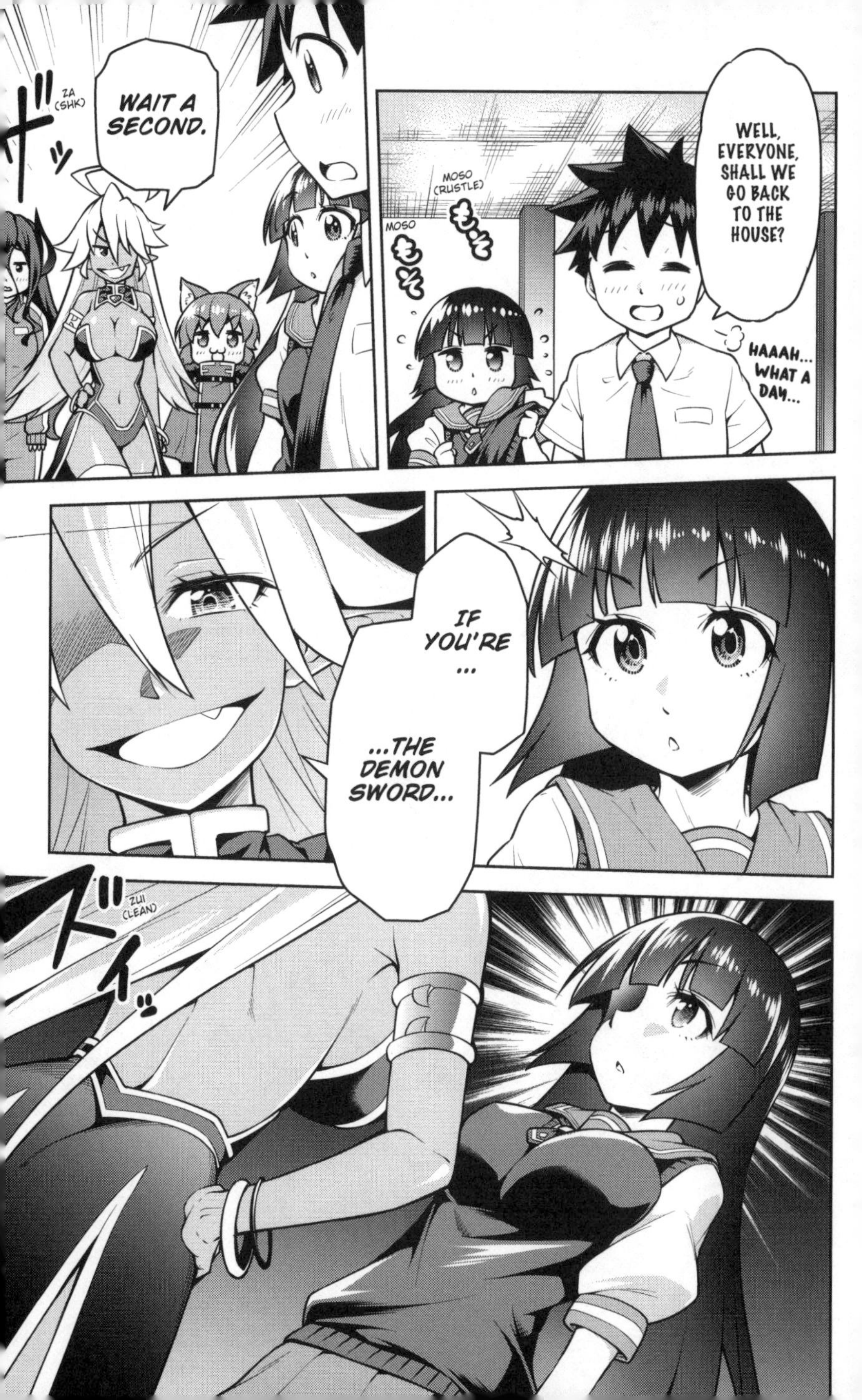
WELL, EVERYONE, SHALL WE GO BACK TO THE HOUSE?
MOSO (RUSTLE)
MOSO
HAAAH... WHAT A DAY...
WAIT A SECOND.
ZA (SHK)
IF YOU'RE ...
...THE DEMON SWORD...
ZUI (CLEAN)

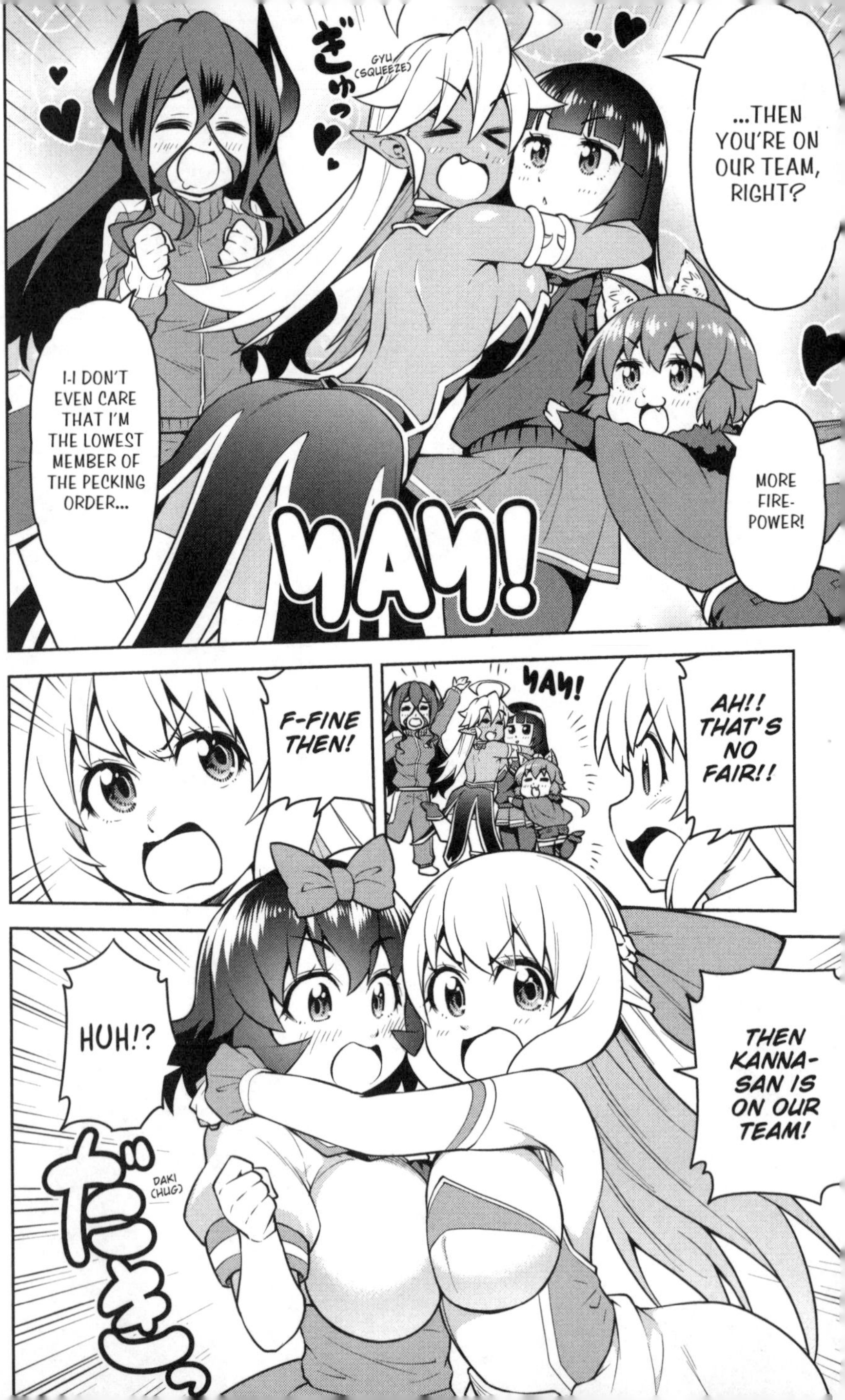

...THEN YOU'RE ON OUR TEAM, RIGHT?
ぎゅっ
GYU (SQUEEZE)
MORE FIRE-POWER!
I-I DON'T EVEN CARE THAT I'M THE LOWEST MEMBER OF THE PECKING ORDER...
YAY!
AH!! THAT'S NO FAIR!!
YAY!
F-FINE THEN!
THEN KANNA-SAN IS ON OUR TEAM!
HUH!?
だきっ
DAKI (HUG)

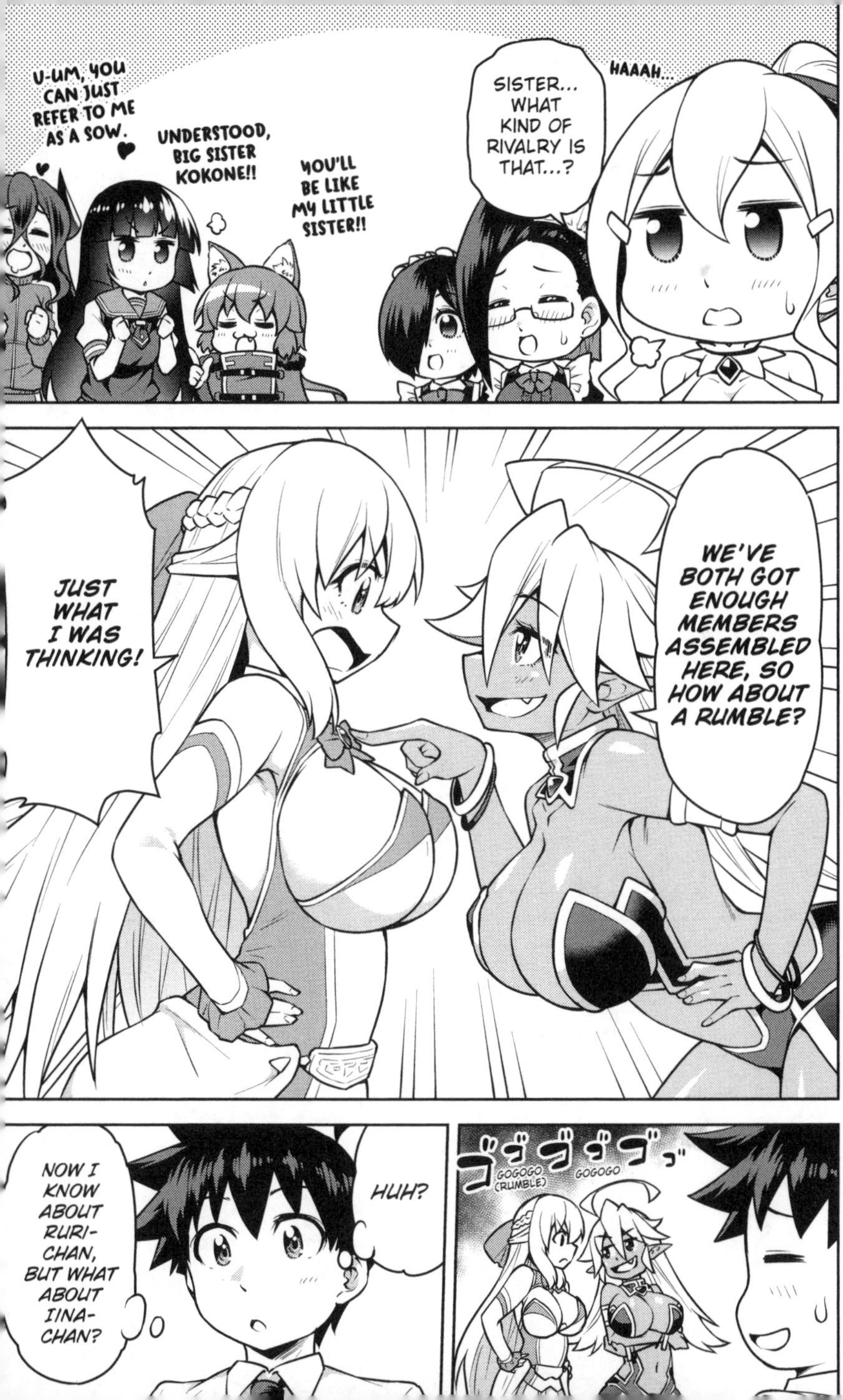
HAAAH...
SISTER... WHAT KIND OF RIVALRY IS THAT...?
YOU'LL BE LIKE MY LITTLE SISTER!!
UNDERSTOOD, BIG SISTER KOKONE!!
U-UM, YOU CAN JUST REFER TO ME AS A SOW.
WE'VE BOTH GOT ENOUGH MEMBERS ASSEMBLED HERE, SO HOW ABOUT A RUMBLE?
JUST WHAT I WAS THINKING!
ゴゴゴゴゴッ
GOGOGO (RUMBLE)
GOGOGO
HUH?
NOW I KNOW ABOUT RURI-CHAN, BUT WHAT ABOUT INA-CHAN?

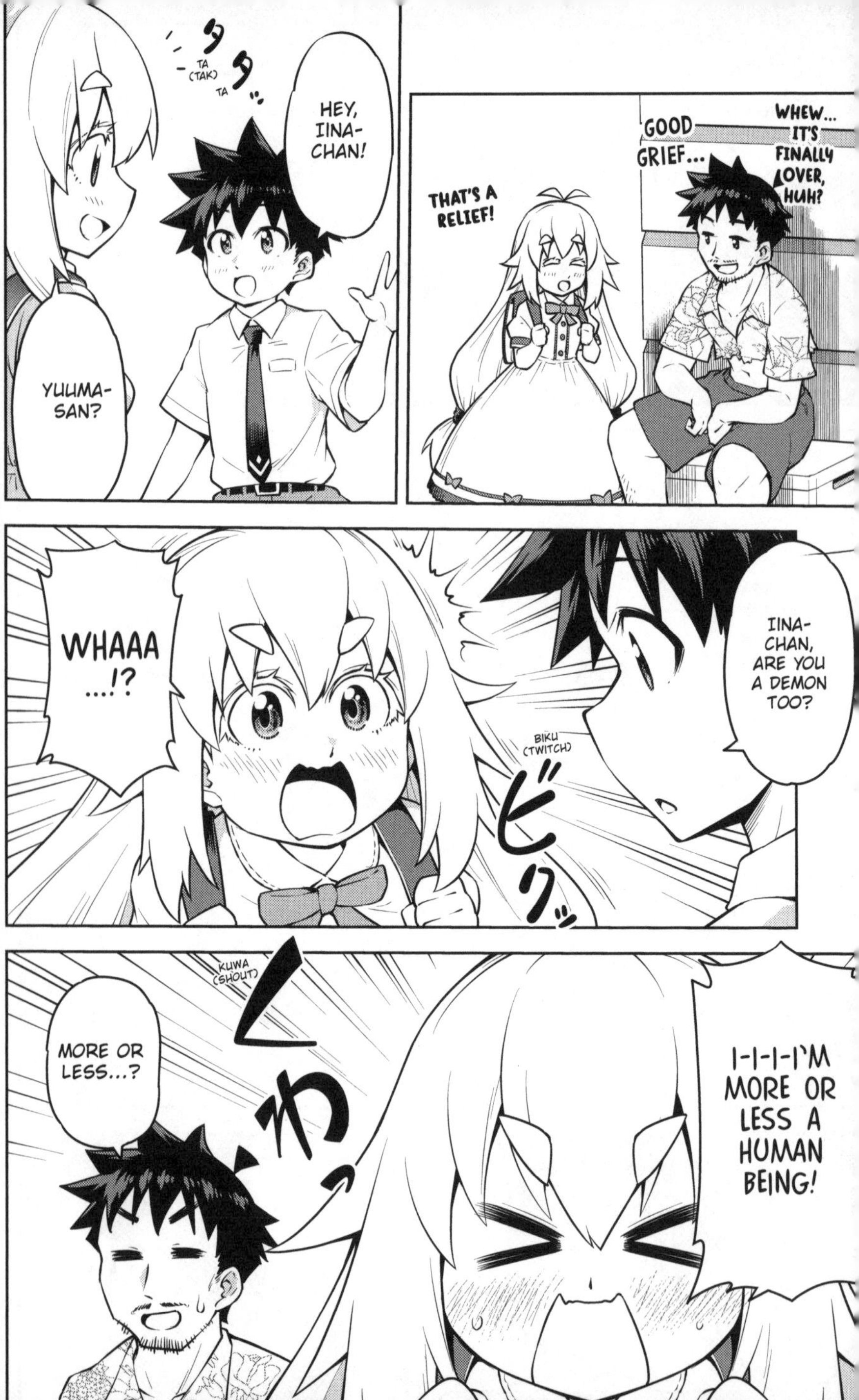

WHEW... IT'S FINALLY OVER, HUH?
GOOD GRIEF...
THAT'S A RELIEF!
TA (TAK) TA
HEY, IINA-CHAN!
YUUMA-SAN?
IINA-CHAN, ARE YOU A DEMON TOO?
BIKU (TWITCH)
WHAAA ...!?
I-I-I-I'M MORE OR LESS A HUMAN BEING!
KUWA (SHOUT)
MORE OR LESS...?

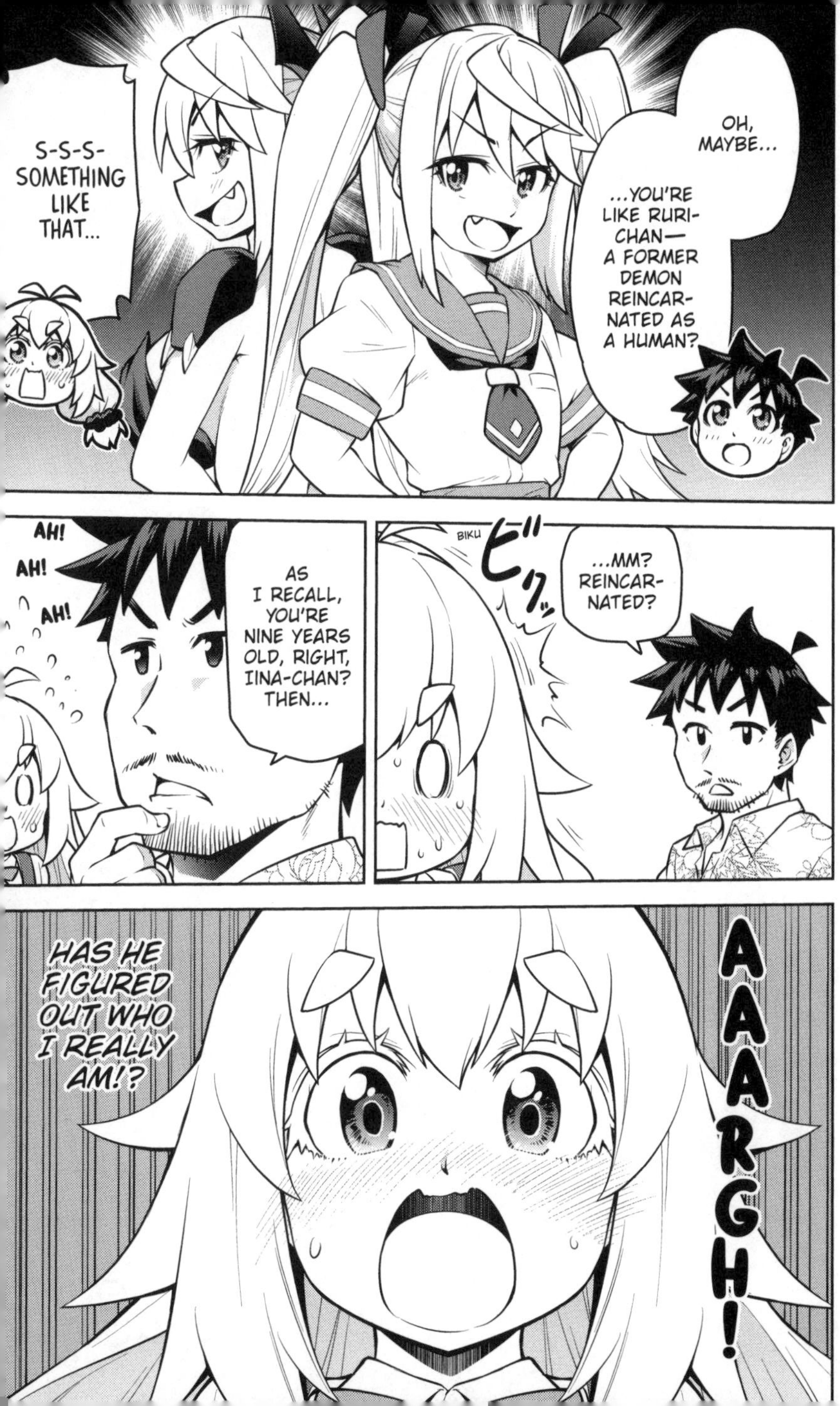
OH, MAYBE...
...YOU'RE LIKE RURI-CHAN—A FORMER DEMON REINCARNATED AS A HUMAN?
S-S-S-SOMETHING LIKE THAT...
BIKU
...MM? REINCARNATED?
AS I RECALL, YOU'RE NINE YEARS OLD, RIGHT, IINA-CHAN? THEN...
AH!
AH!
AH!
AAAARGH!
HAS HE FIGURED OUT WHO I REALLY AM!?

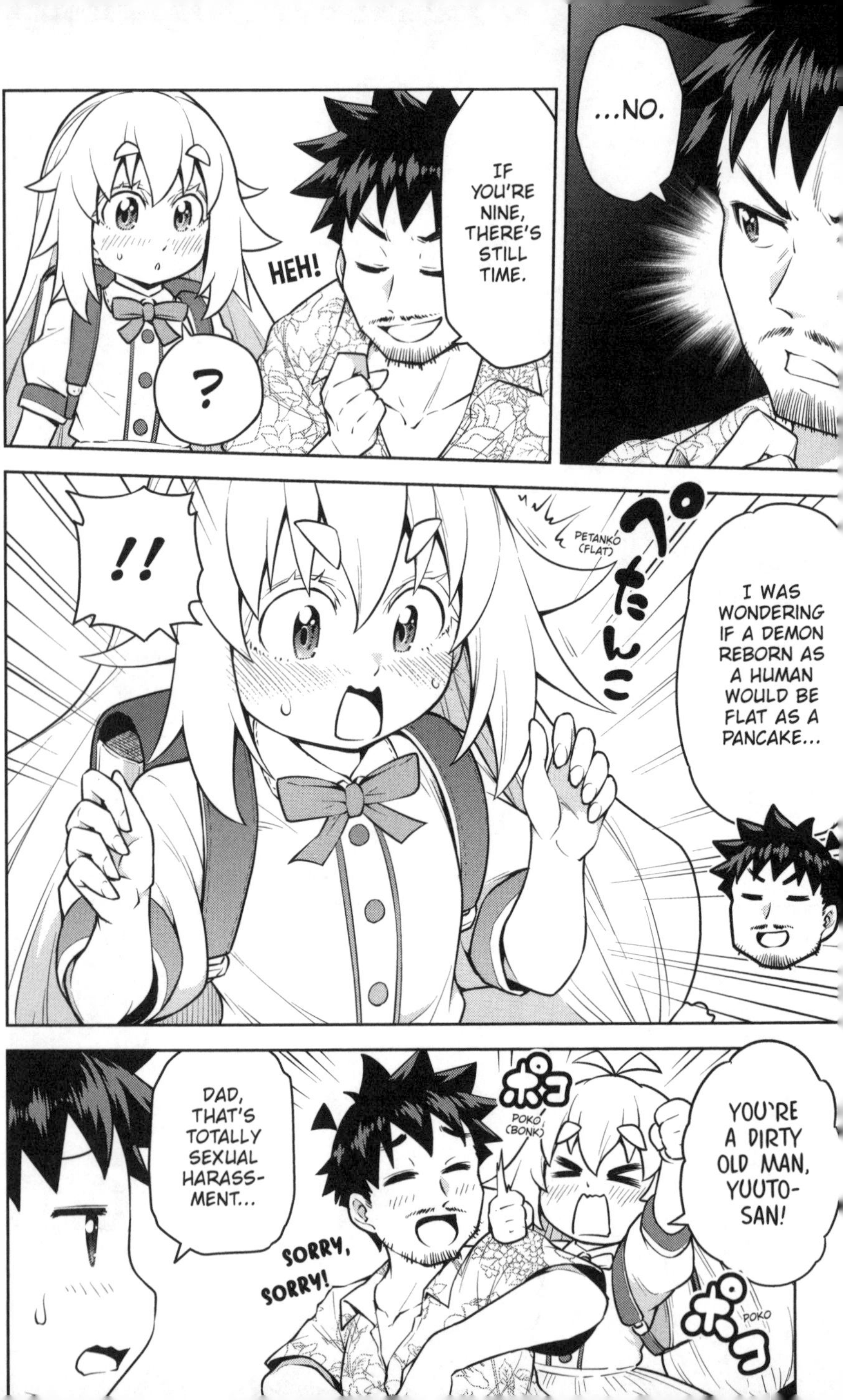
...NO.
IF YOU'RE NINE, THERE'S STILL TIME.
HEH!
?
I WAS WONDERING IF A DEMON REBORN AS A HUMAN WOULD BE FLAT AS A PANCAKE...
ぺたんこ
PETANKO (FLAT)
!!
YOU'RE A DIRTY OLD MAN, YUUTO-SAN!
ポコ
POKO (BONK)
DAD, THAT'S TOTALLY SEXUAL HARASS-MENT...
SORRY, SORRY!
ポコ
POKO

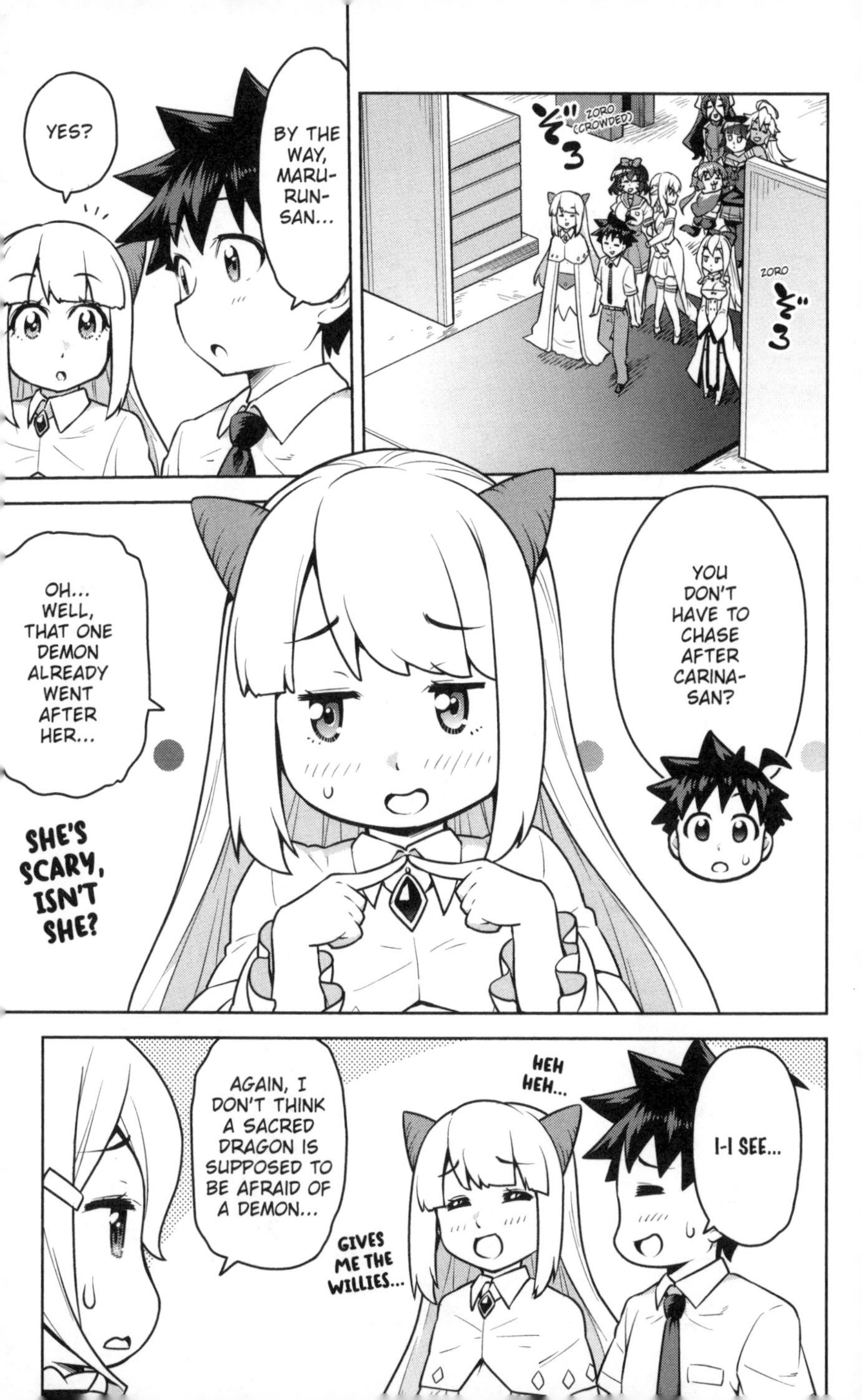
ZORO (CROWDED)
ZORO
BY THE WAY, MARURUN-SAN...
YES?
YOU DON'T HAVE TO CHASE AFTER CARINA-SAN?
OH... WELL, THAT ONE DEMON ALREADY WENT AFTER HER...
SHE'S SCARY, ISN'T SHE?
I-I SEE...
HEH HEH...
GIVES ME THE WILLIES...
AGAIN, I DON'T THINK A SACRED DRAGON IS SUPPOSED TO BE AFRAID OF A DEMON...

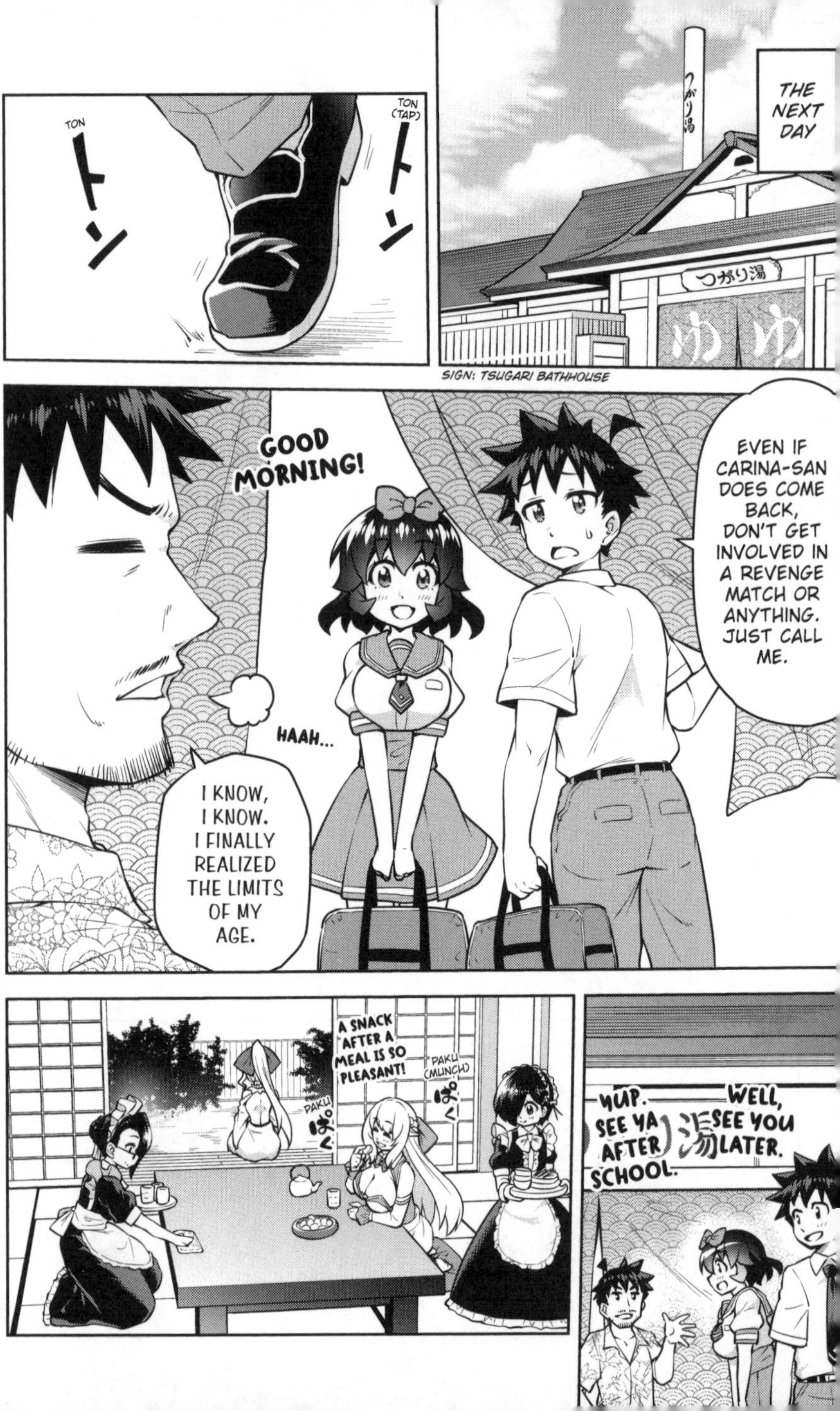
THE NEXT DAY
つがり湯
SIGN: TSUGARI BATHHOUSE
TON (TAP)
トン
TON
トン
EVEN IF CARINA-SAN DOES COME BACK, DON'T GET INVOLVED IN A REVENGE MATCH OR ANYTHING. JUST CALL ME.
GOOD MORNING!
HAAH...
I KNOW, I KNOW. I FINALLY REALIZED THE LIMITS OF MY AGE.
WELL, SEE YOU LATER.
YUP. SEE YA AFTER SCHOOL.
A SNACK AFTER A MEAL IS SO PLEASANT!
PAKU (MUNCH)
ぱく
PAKU
ぱく

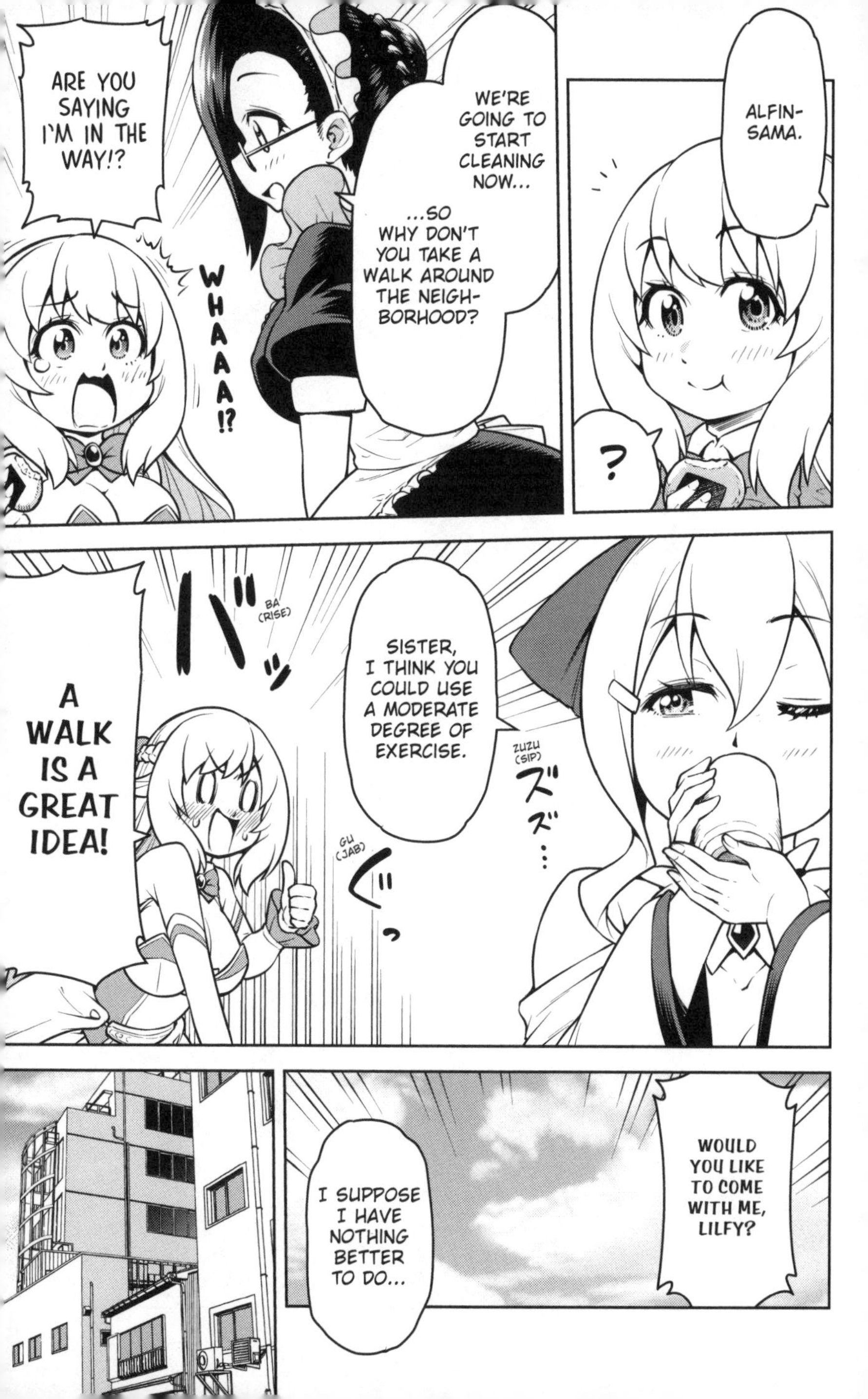
ALFIN-SAMA.
?
WE'RE GOING TO START CLEANING NOW...
...SO WHY DON'T YOU TAKE A WALK AROUND THE NEIGH-BORHOOD?
WHAAAA!?
ARE YOU SAYING I'M IN THE WAY!?
SISTER, I THINK YOU COULD USE A MODERATE DEGREE OF EXERCISE.
ズズ…
ZUZU (SIP)
バッ
BA (RISE)
A WALK IS A GREAT IDEA!
ぐっ
GU (JAB)
WOULD YOU LIKE TO COME WITH ME, LILFY?
I SUPPOSE I HAVE NOTHING BETTER TO DO...

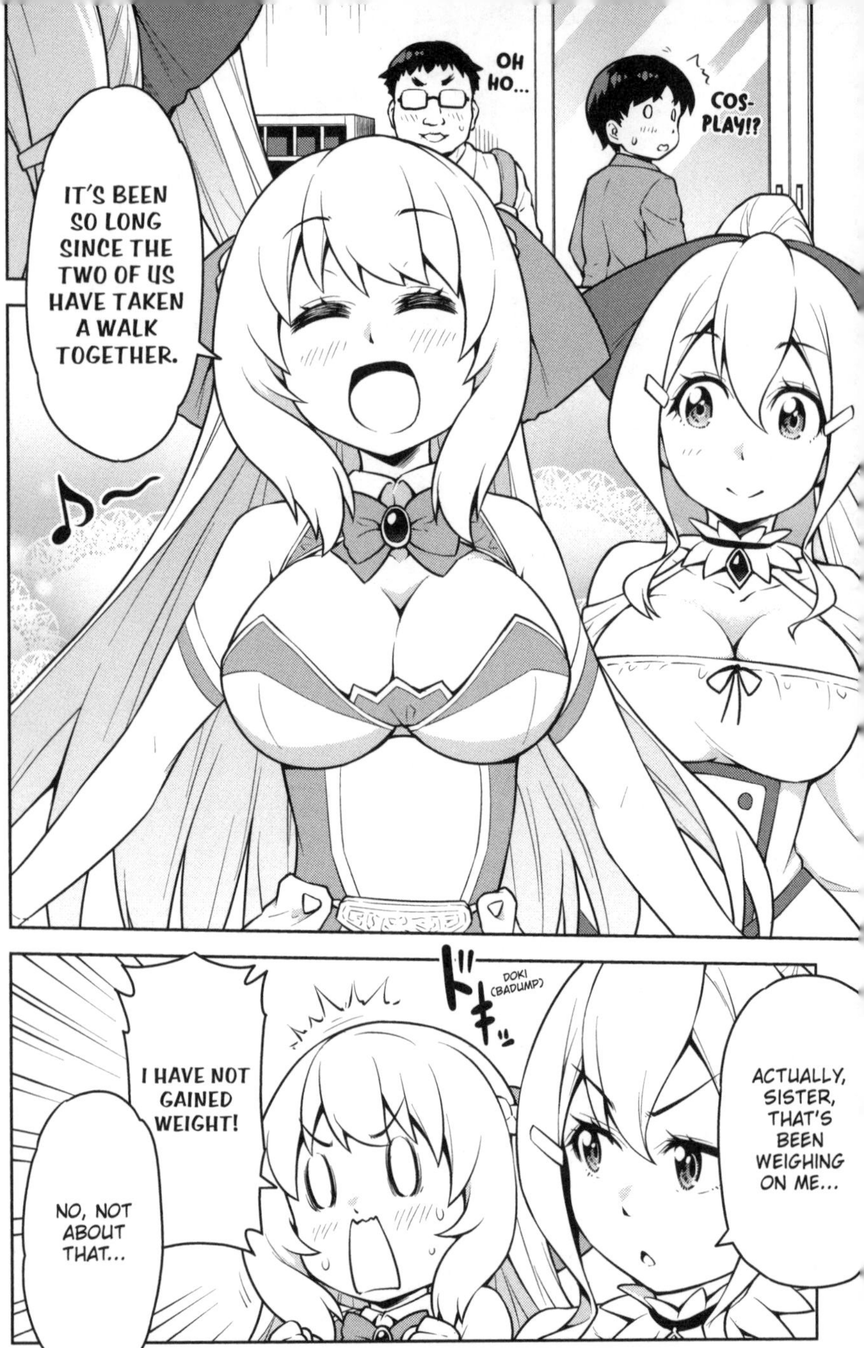
COS-PLAY!?
OH HO...
IT'S BEEN SO LONG SINCE THE TWO OF US HAVE TAKEN A WALK TOGETHER.
♪~
ACTUALLY, SISTER, THAT'S BEEN WEIGHING ON ME...
ドキッ
DOKI (BADUMP)
I HAVE NOT GAINED WEIGHT!
NO, NOT ABOUT THAT...

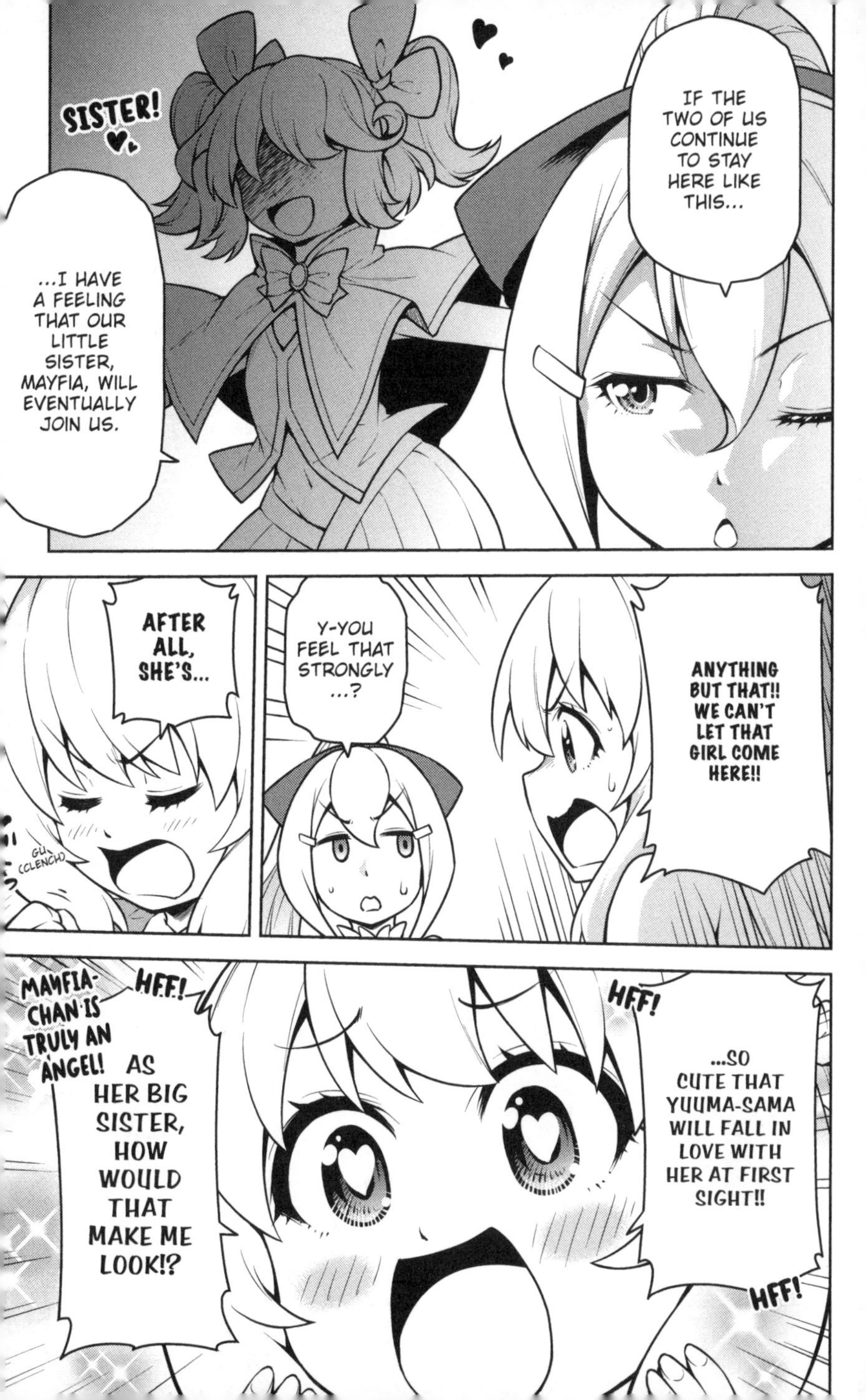
IF THE TWO OF US CONTINUE TO STAY HERE LIKE THIS...
SISTER! ♥
...I HAVE A FEELING THAT OUR LITTLE SISTER, MAYFIA, WILL EVENTUALLY JOIN US.
ANYTHING BUT THAT!! WE CAN'T LET THAT GIRL COME HERE!!
Y-YOU FEEL THAT STRONGLY ...?
AFTER ALL, SHE'S...
(CLENCH)
HFF!
...SO CUTE THAT YUUMA-SAMA WILL FALL IN LOVE WITH HER AT FIRST SIGHT!!
HFF!
HFF!
MAYFIA-CHAN IS TRULY AN ANGEL!
AS HER BIG SISTER, HOW WOULD THAT MAKE ME LOOK!?

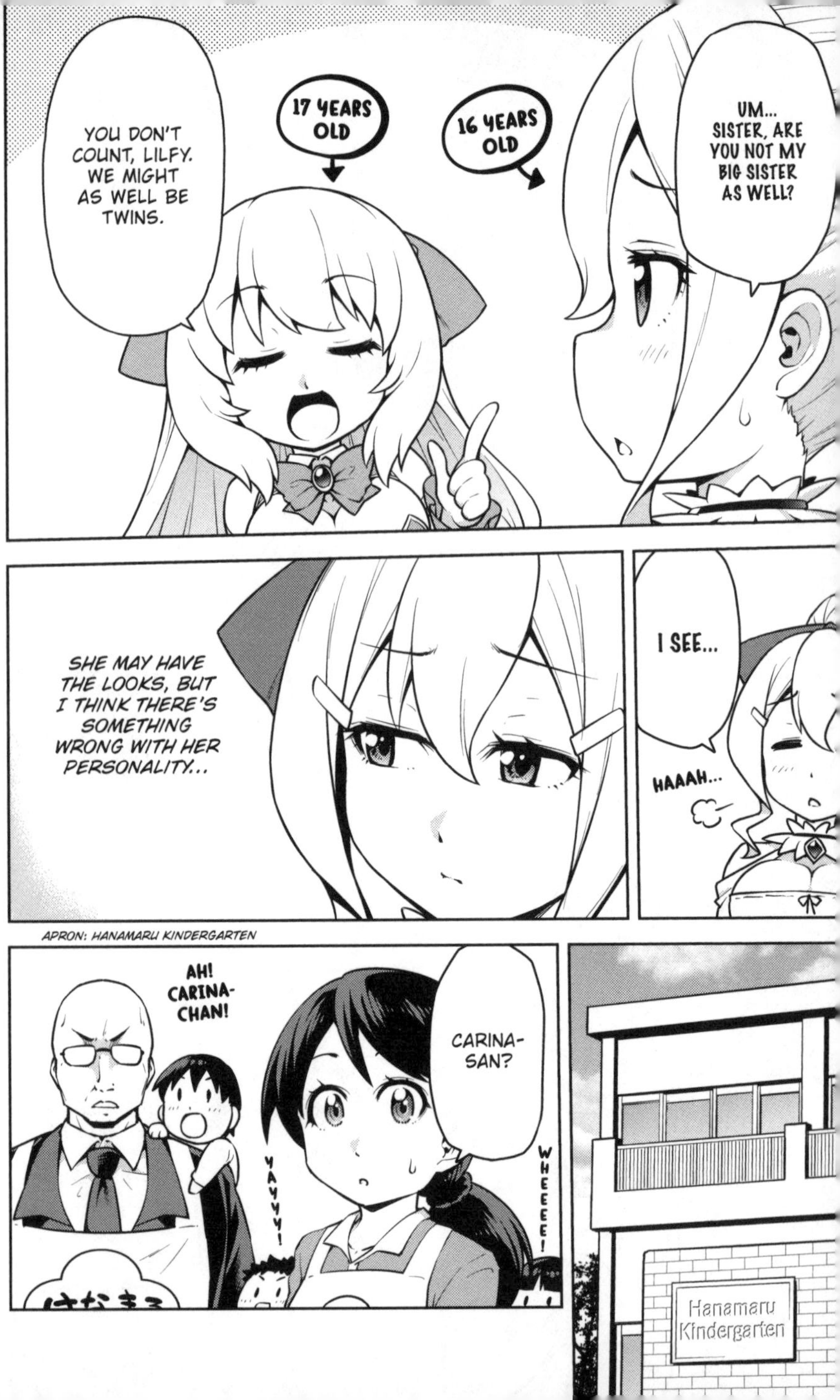
UM... SISTER, ARE YOU NOT MY BIG SISTER AS WELL?
16 YEARS OLD
17 YEARS OLD
YOU DON'T COUNT, LILFY. WE MIGHT AS WELL BE TWINS.
I SEE...
HAAAH...
SHE MAY HAVE THE LOOKS, BUT I THINK THERE'S SOMETHING WRONG WITH HER PERSONALITY...
APRON: HANAMARU KINDERGARTEN
Hanamaru Kindergarten
CARINA-SAN?
WHEEEEE!
AH! CARINA-CHAN!
YAYYY!

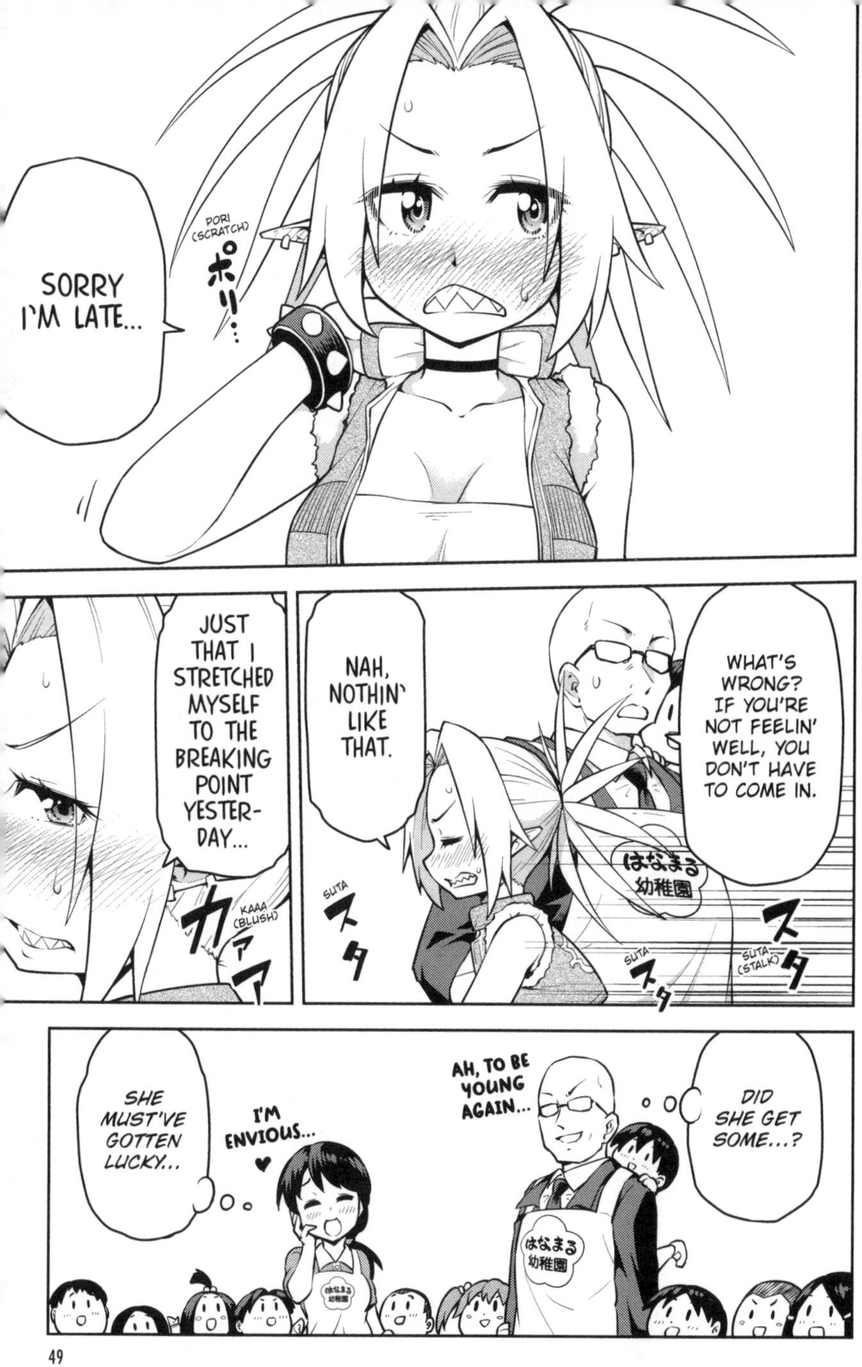

POR I (SCRATCH)
ポリ…
SORRY I'M LATE...
WHAT'S WRONG? IF YOU'RE NOT FEELIN' WELL, YOU DON'T HAVE TO COME IN.
SUTA (STALK)
スタ
SUTA
スタ
はなまる幼稚園
NAH, NOTHIN' LIKE THAT.
SUTA
スタ
JUST THAT I STRETCHED MYSELF TO THE BREAKING POINT YESTER-DAY...
KAAA (BLUSH)
カァア
DID SHE GET SOME...?
AH, TO BE YOUNG AGAIN...
はなまる幼稚園
I'M ENVIOUS...
SHE MUST'VE GOTTEN LUCKY...
はなまる幼稚園

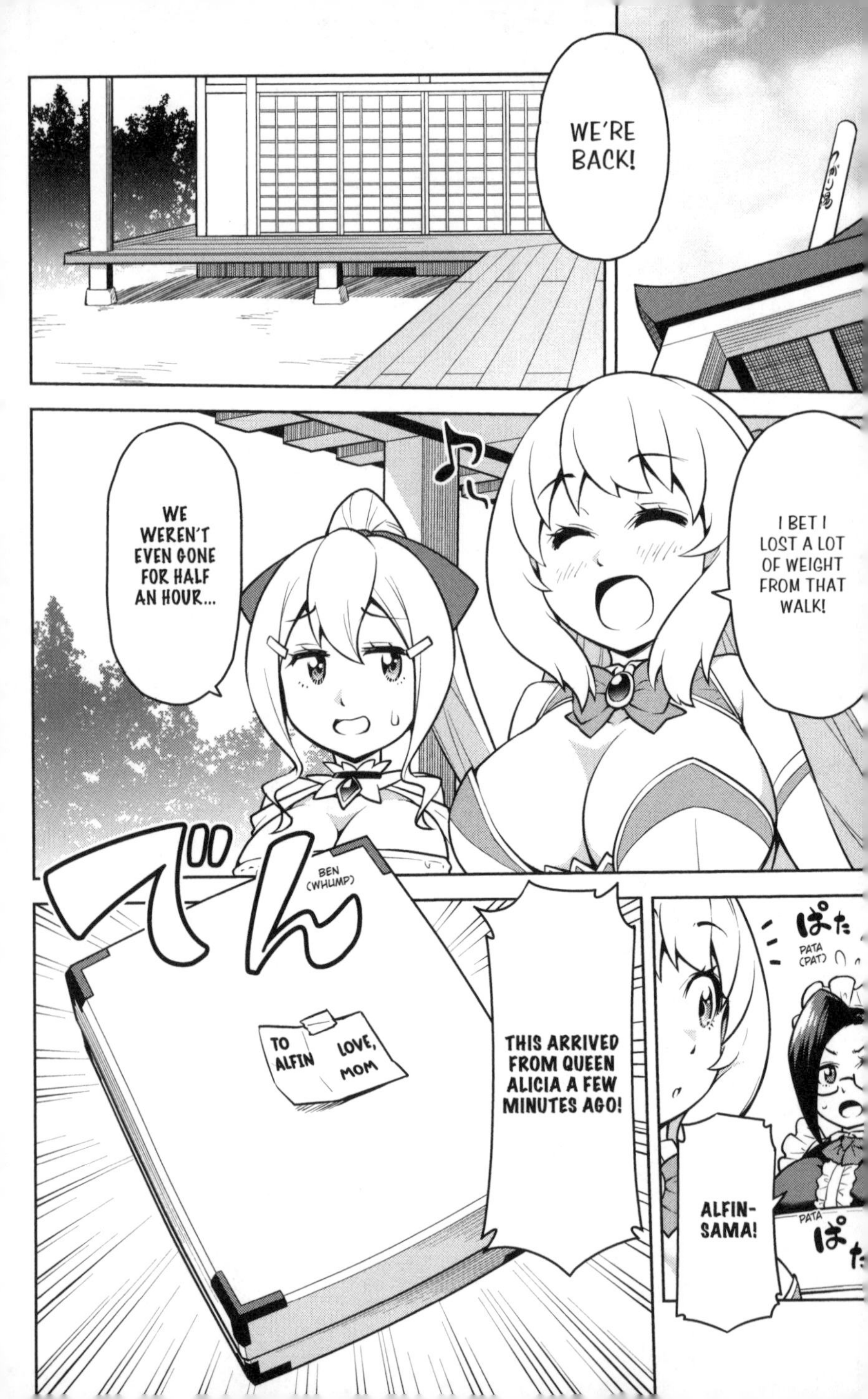
WE'RE BACK!
I BET I LOST A LOT OF WEIGHT FROM THAT WALK!
WE WEREN'T EVEN GONE FOR HALF AN HOUR...
ぱた
PATA (PAT)
PATA
ぱた
ALFIN-SAMA!
でん
BEN (WHUMP)
TO ALFIN
LOVE, MOM
THIS ARRIVED FROM QUEEN ALICIA A FEW MINUTES AGO!

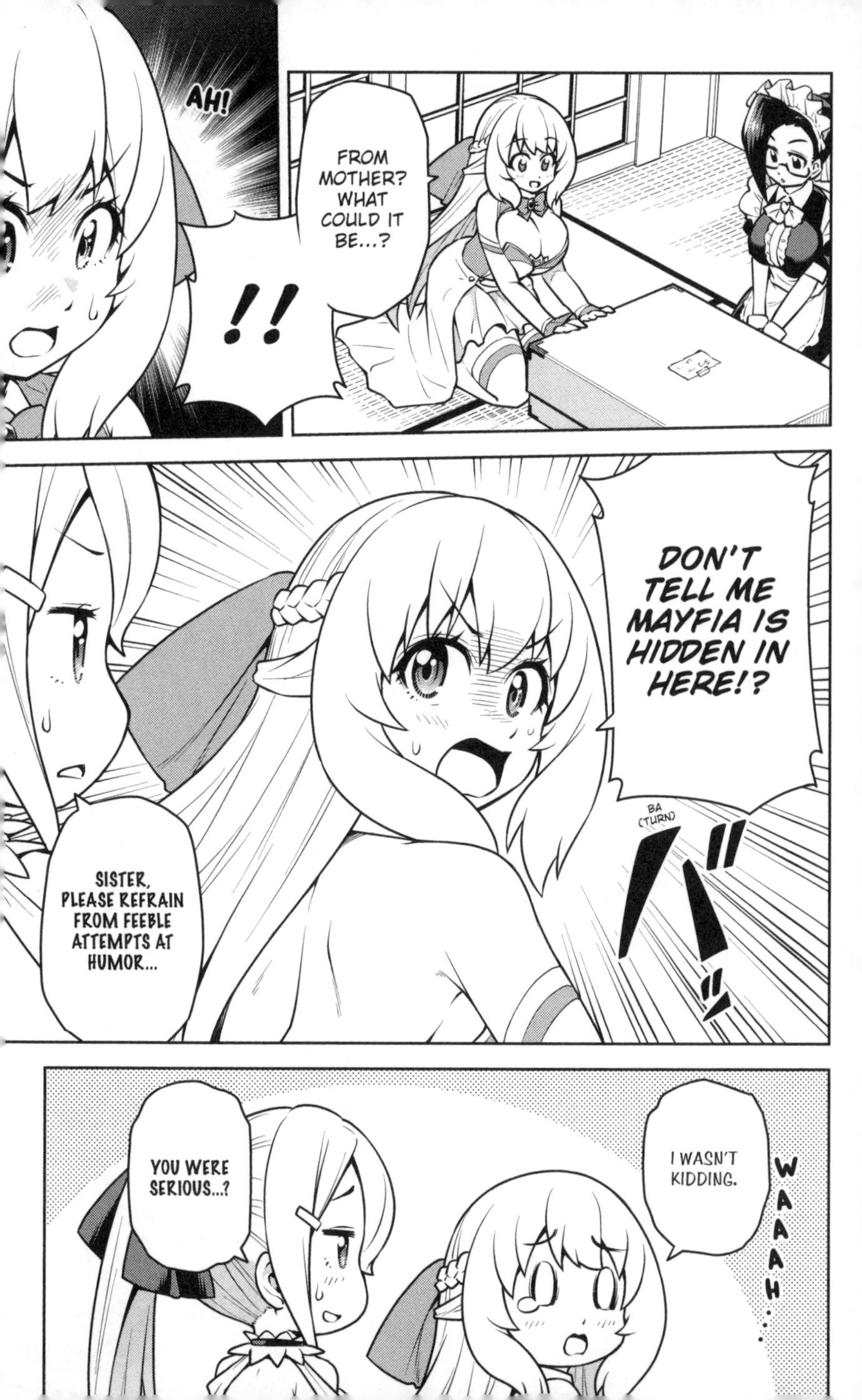
FROM MOTHER? WHAT COULD IT BE...?
AH!
!!
DON'T TELL ME MAYFIA IS HIDDEN IN HERE!?
BA (TURN)
SISTER, PLEASE REFRAIN FROM FEEBLE ATTEMPTS AT HUMOR...
I WASN'T KIDDING.
WAAAH...
YOU WERE SERIOUS...?

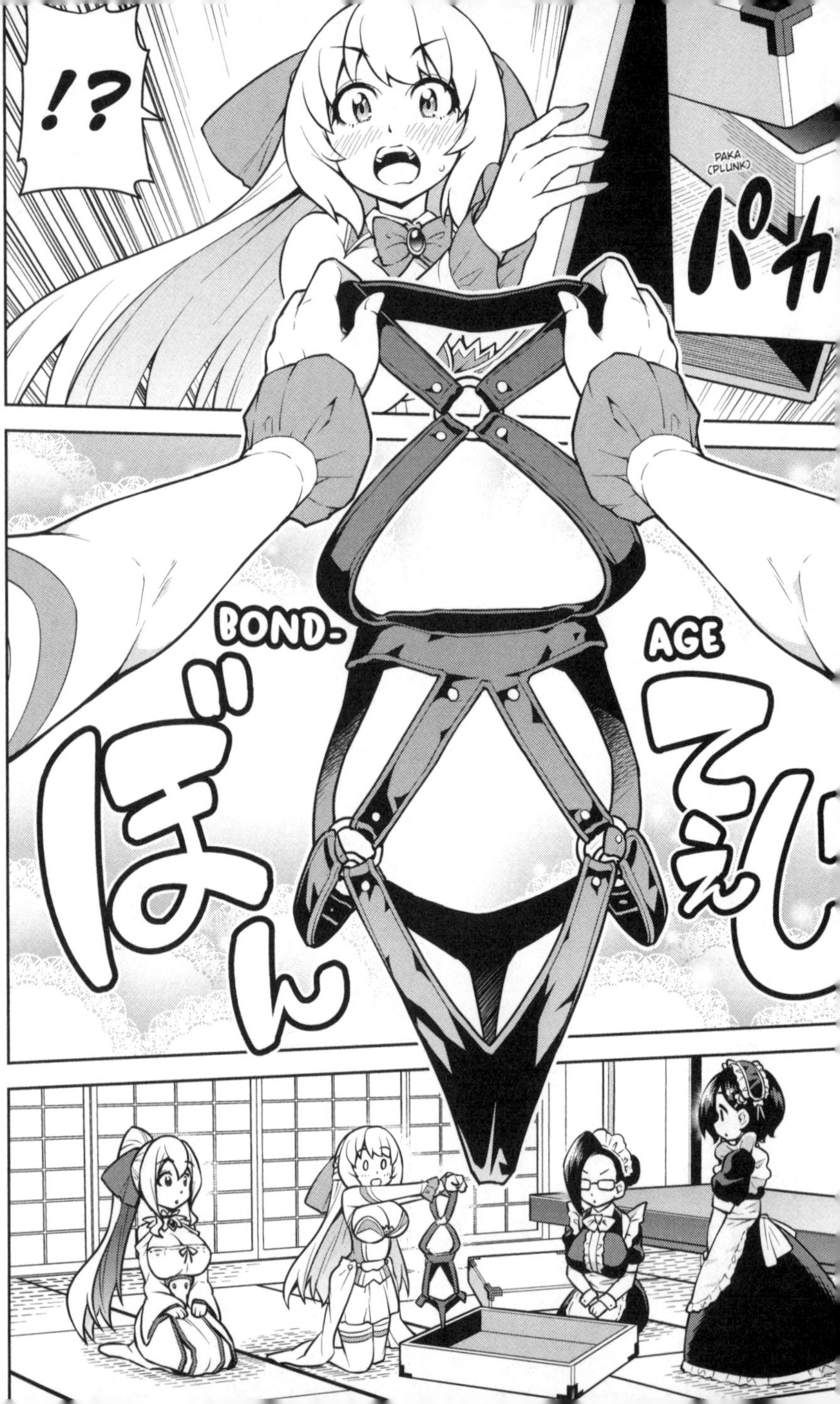
PAKA
(PLUNK)
パッカ
!?
BOND-
AGE
ぼん
てえ

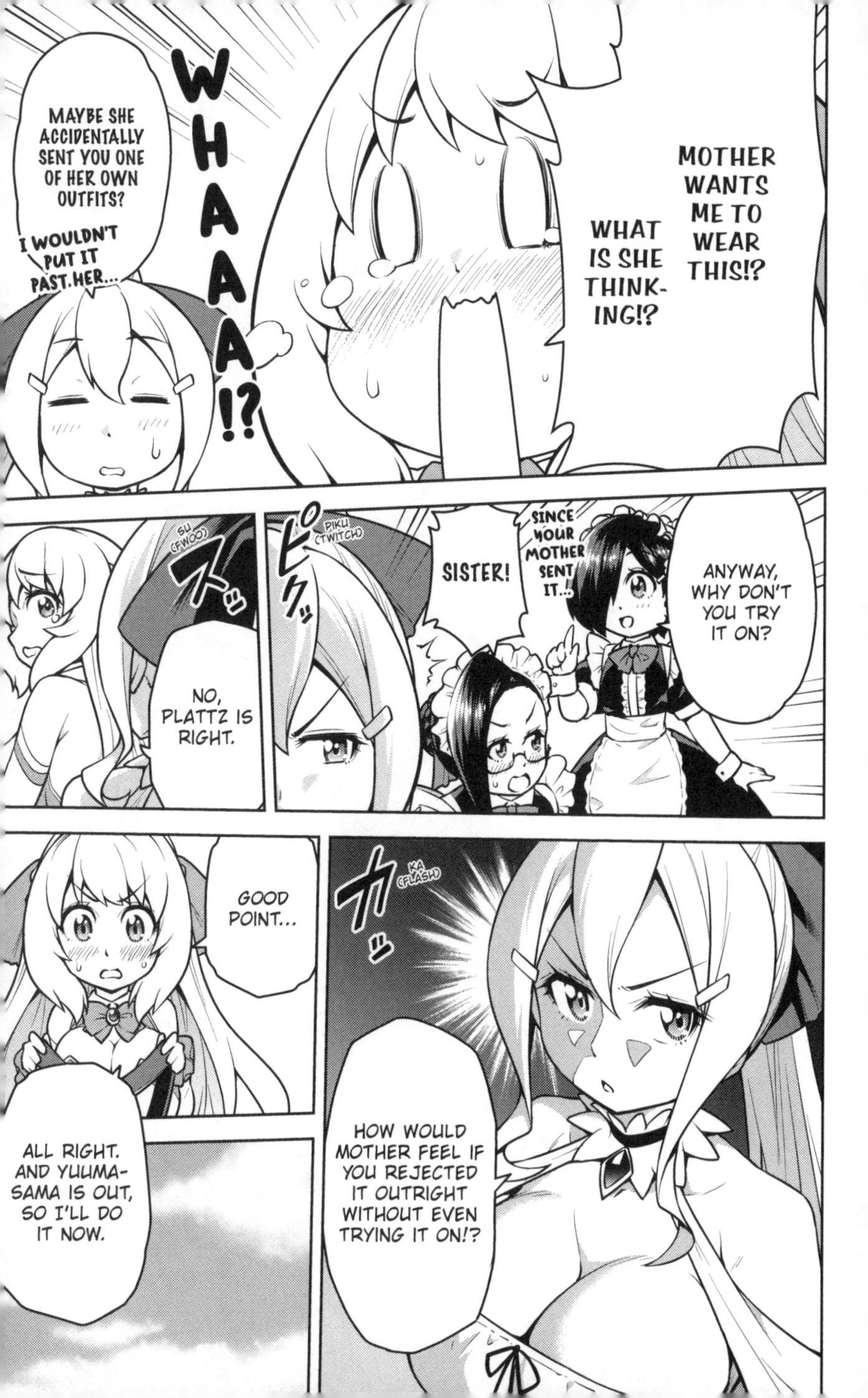
MOTHER WANTS ME TO WEAR THIS!?
WHAT IS SHE THINKING!?
WHAAAA!?
MAYBE SHE ACCIDENTALLY SENT YOU ONE OF HER OWN OUTFITS?
I WOULDN'T PUT IT PAST HER...
ANYWAY, WHY DON'T YOU TRY IT ON?
SINCE YOUR MOTHER SENT IT...
SISTER!
PIKU (TWITCH)
SU (FWOO)
NO, PLATTZ IS RIGHT.
KA (FLASH)
HOW WOULD MOTHER FEEL IF YOU REJECTED IT OUTRIGHT WITHOUT EVEN TRYING IT ON!?
GOOD POINT...
ALL RIGHT. AND YUUMA-SAMA IS OUT, SO I'LL DO IT NOW.

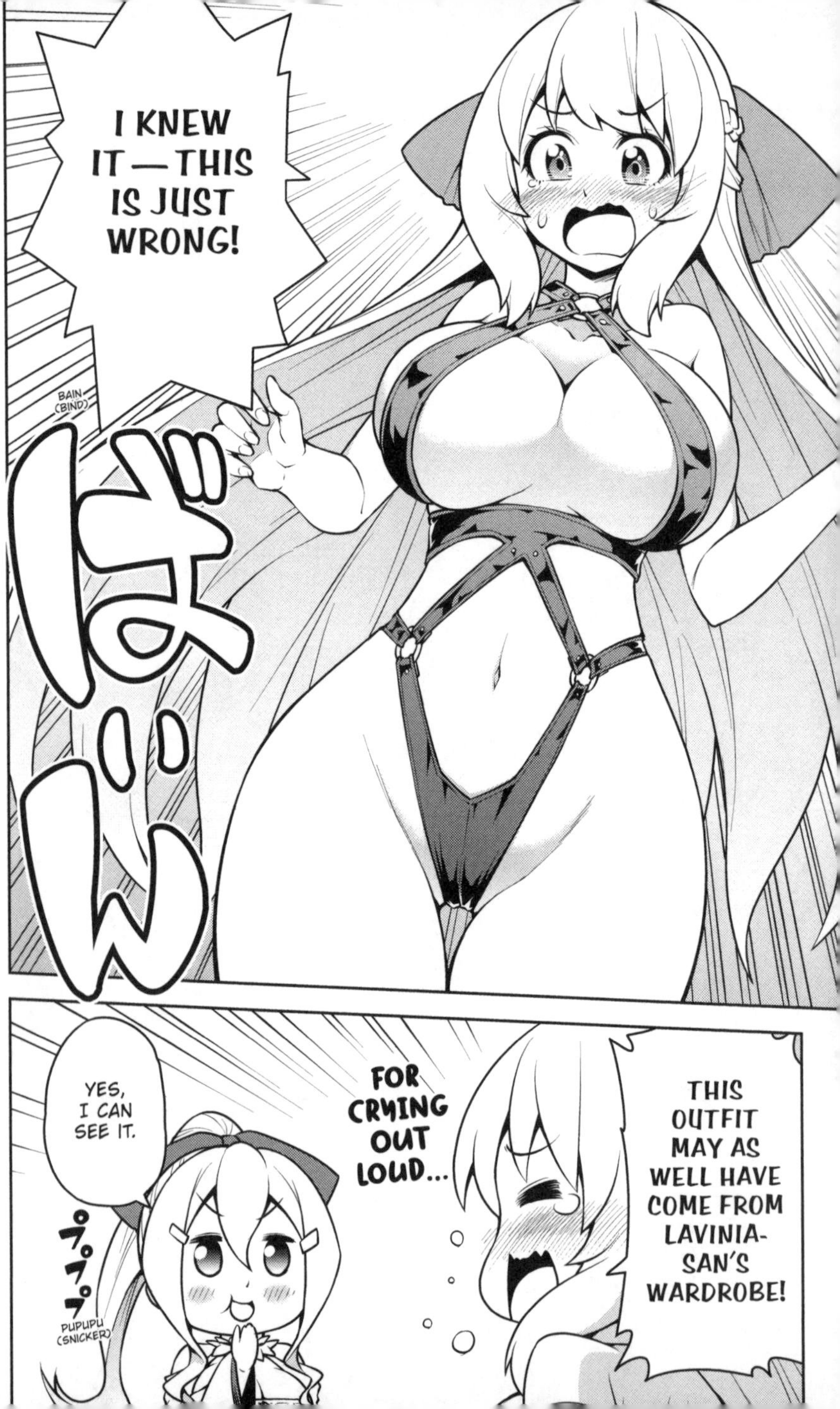
I KNEW IT—THIS IS JUST WRONG!
BAIN (BIND)
ばいん
THIS OUTFIT MAY AS WELL HAVE COME FROM LAVINIA-SAN'S WARDROBE!
FOR CRYING OUT LOUD...
YES, I CAN SEE IT.
ぷぷぷ
PUPUPU (SNICKER)

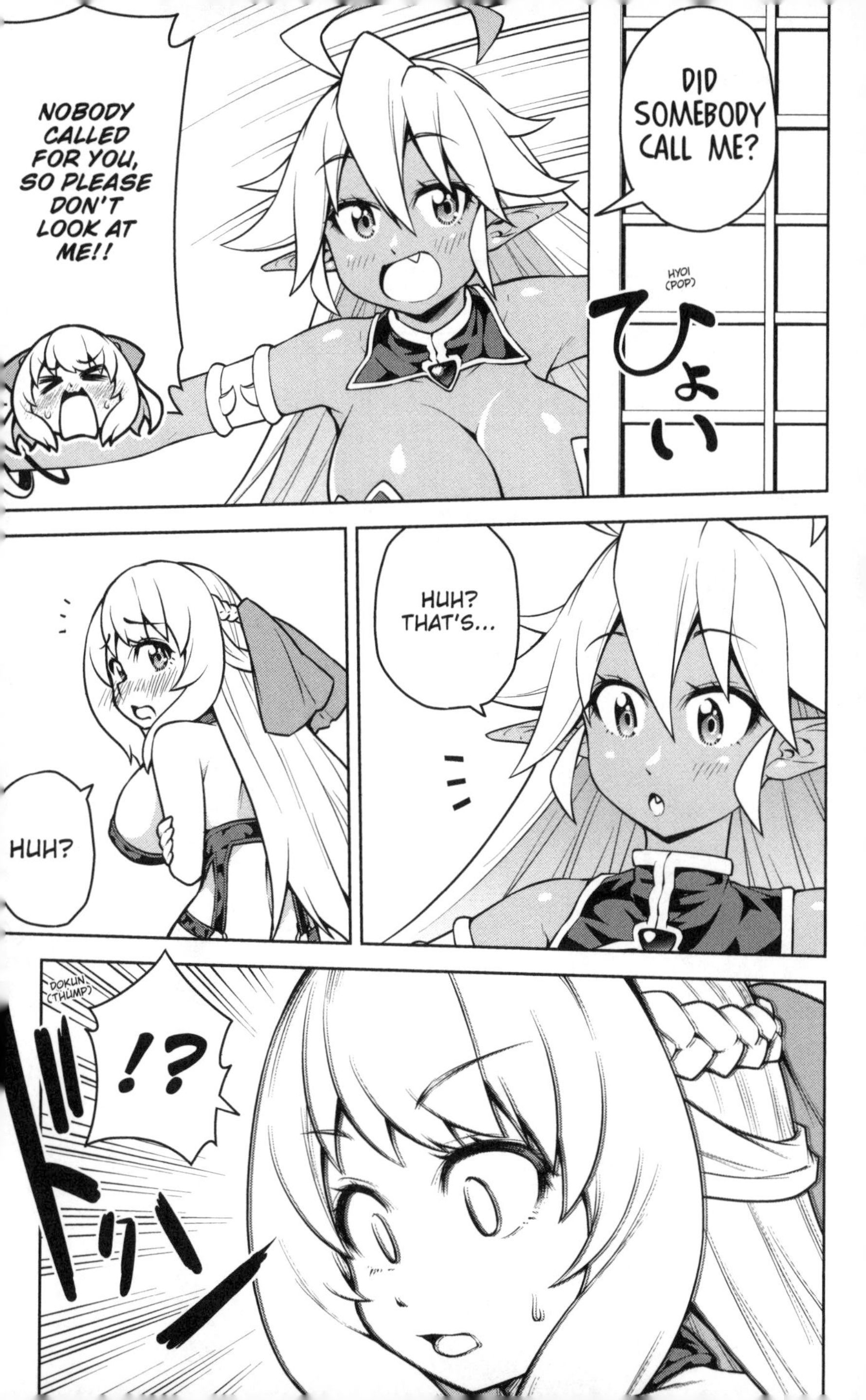
DID SOMEBODY CALL ME?
HYOI (POP)
ひょい
NOBODY CALLED FOR YOU, SO PLEASE DON'T LOOK AT ME!!
HUH? THAT'S...
HUH?
DOKUN (THUMP)
!?

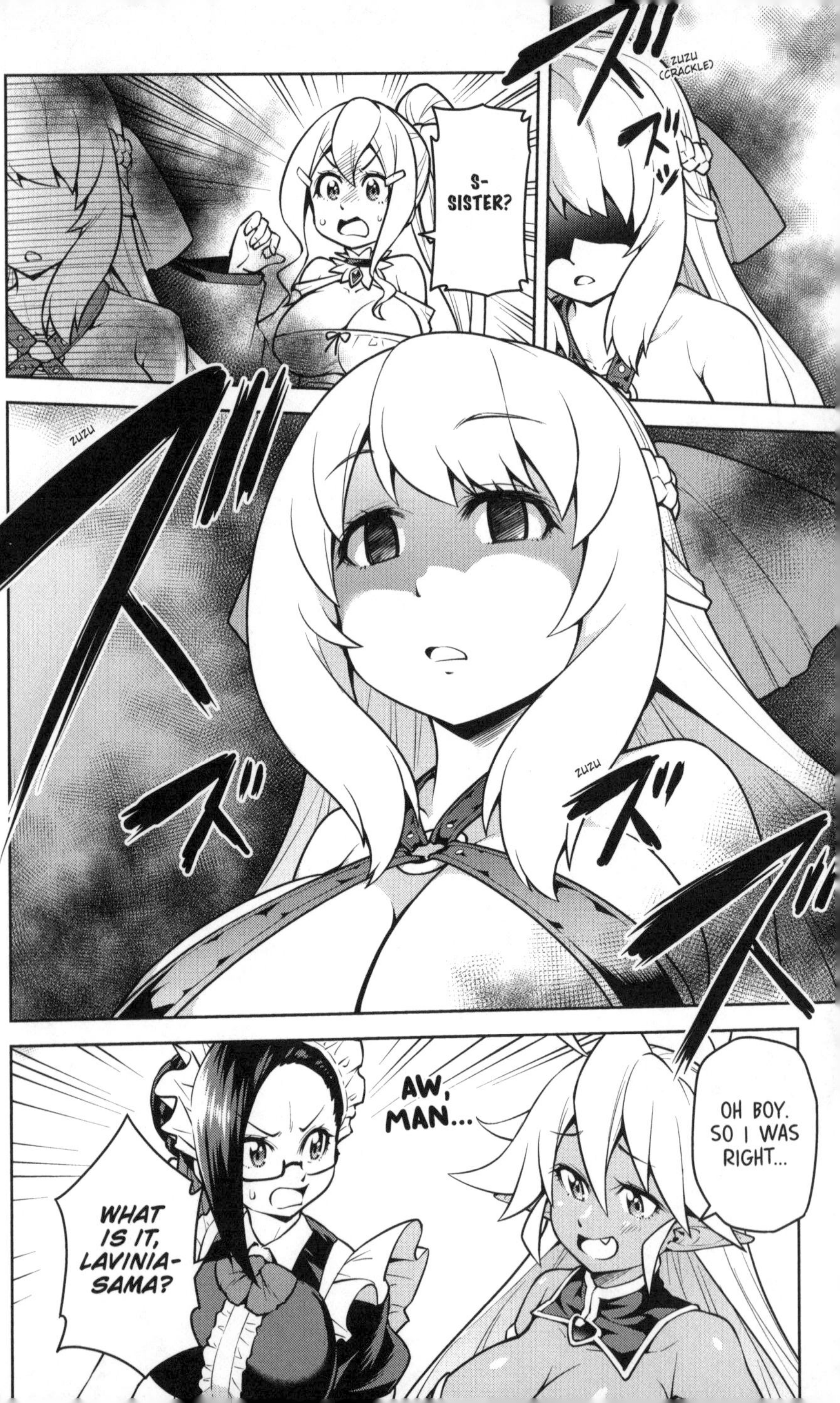

ZUZU (CRACKLE)
S-SISTER?
ZUZU
ZUZU
OH BOY. SO I WAS RIGHT...
AW, MAN...
WHAT IS IT, LAVINIA-SAMA?

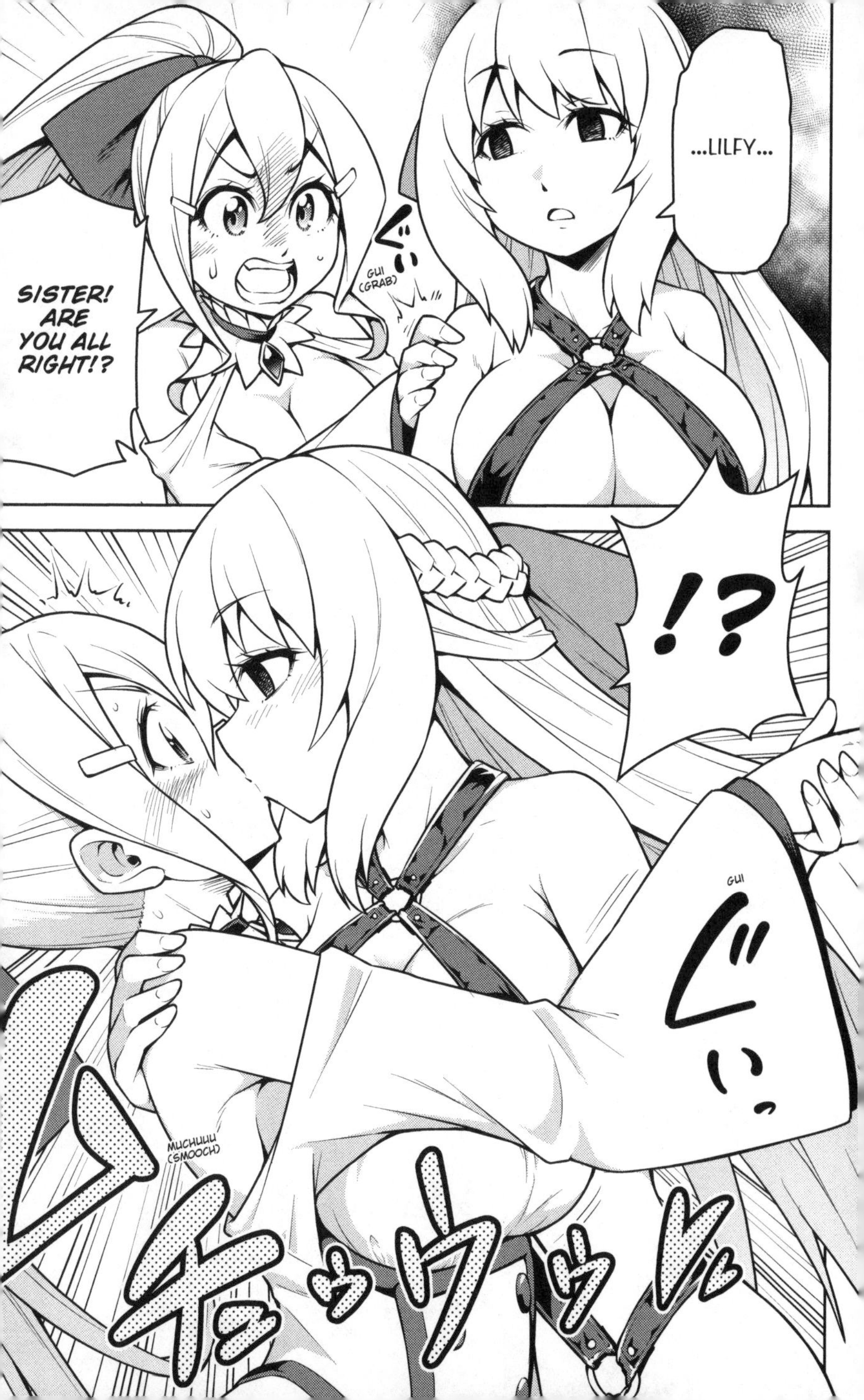
...LILFY...
GUI (GRAB)
SISTER! ARE YOU ALL RIGHT!?
!?
GUI
MUCHUUU (SMOOCH)

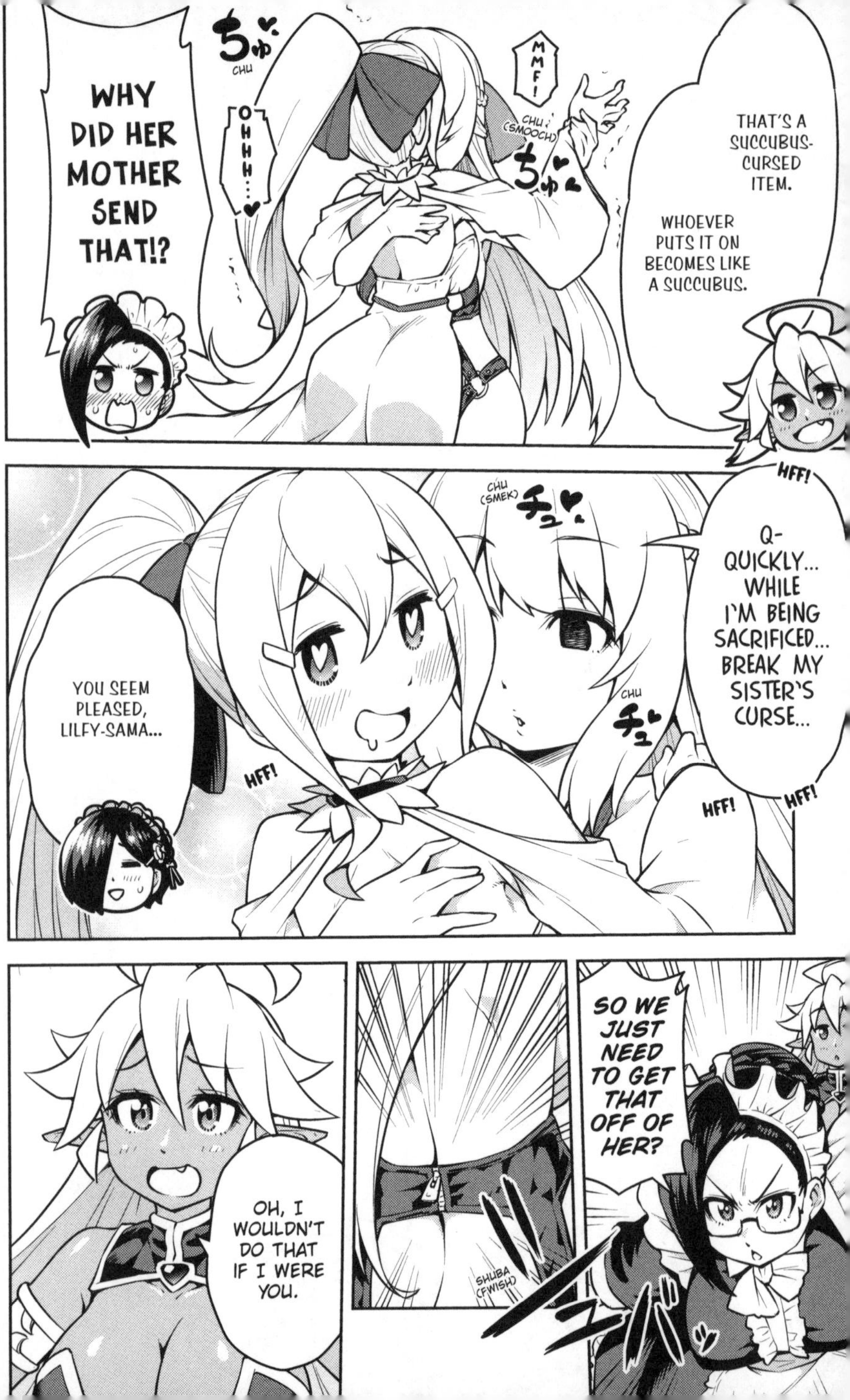
THAT'S A SUCCUBUS-CURSED ITEM.
WHOEVER PUTS IT ON BECOMES LIKE A SUCCUBUS.
MMF!
ちゅ CHU (SMOOCH)
ちゅ CHU
OHHH...
WHY DID HER MOTHER SEND THAT!?
HFF!
チュ CHU (SMEK)
Q-QUICKLY... WHILE I'M BEING SACRIFICED... BREAK MY SISTER'S CURSE...
チュ CHU
HFF!
HFF!
HFF!
YOU SEEM PLEASED, LILFY-SAMA...
SO WE JUST NEED TO GET THAT OFF OF HER?
SHUBA (FWISH)
OH, I WOULDN'T DO THAT IF I WERE YOU.

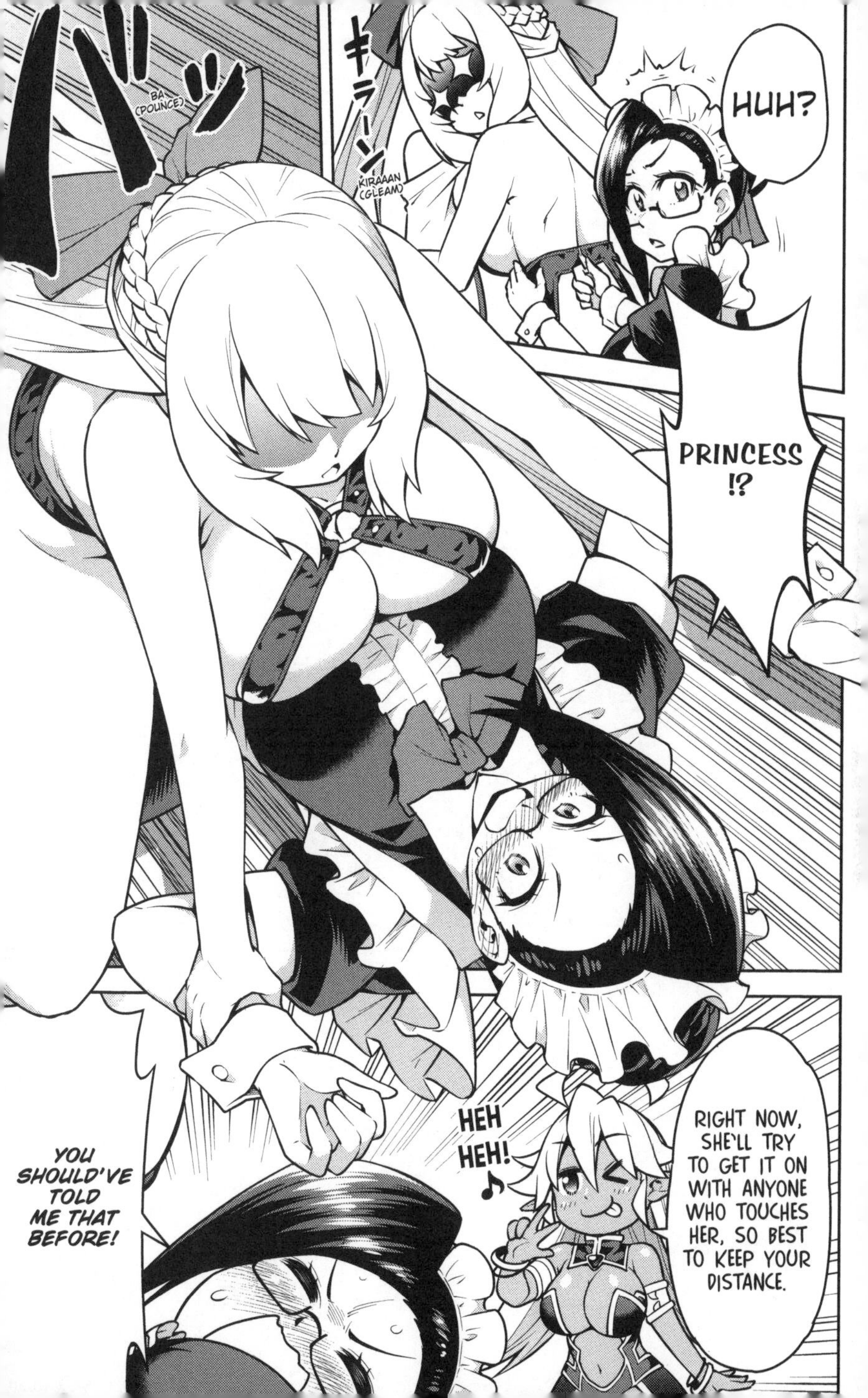
キラーン
KIRAAAN (GLEAM)
HUH?
バッ
BA (POUNCE)
PRINCESS !?
RIGHT NOW, SHE'LL TRY TO GET IT ON WITH ANYONE WHO TOUCHES HER, SO BEST TO KEEP YOUR DISTANCE.
HEH HEH! ♪
YOU SHOULD'VE TOLD ME THAT BEFORE!

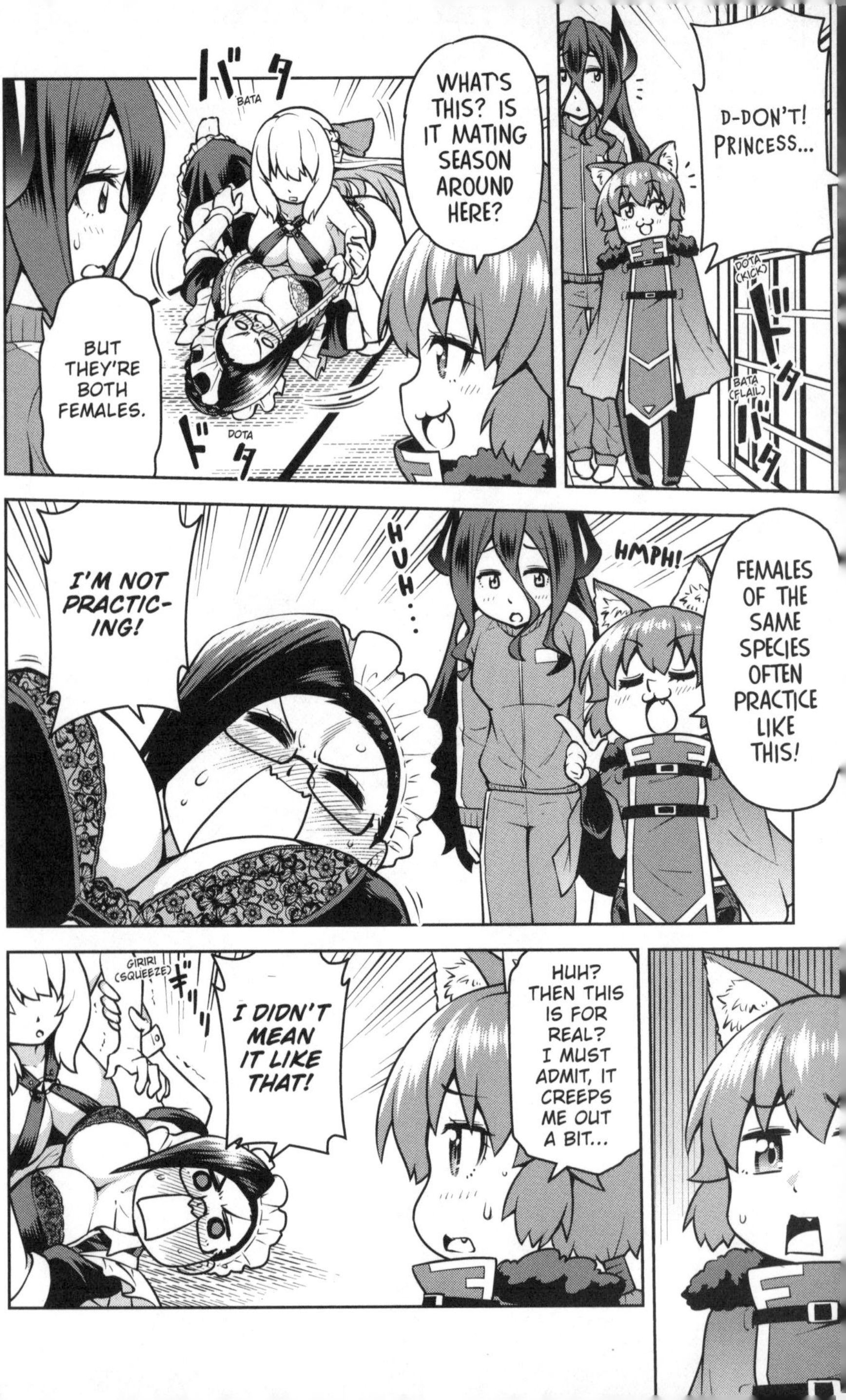
D-DON'T! PRINCESS...
DOTA (KICK)
BATA (FLAIL)
WHAT'S THIS? IS IT MATING SEASON AROUND HERE?
BATA
BUT THEY'RE BOTH FEMALES.
DOTA
FEMALES OF THE SAME SPECIES OFTEN PRACTICE LIKE THIS!
HMPH!
HUH...
I'M NOT PRACTICING!
HUH? THEN THIS IS FOR REAL? I MUST ADMIT, IT CREEPS ME OUT A BIT...
I DIDN'T MEAN IT LIKE THAT!
GIRIRI (SQUEEZE)

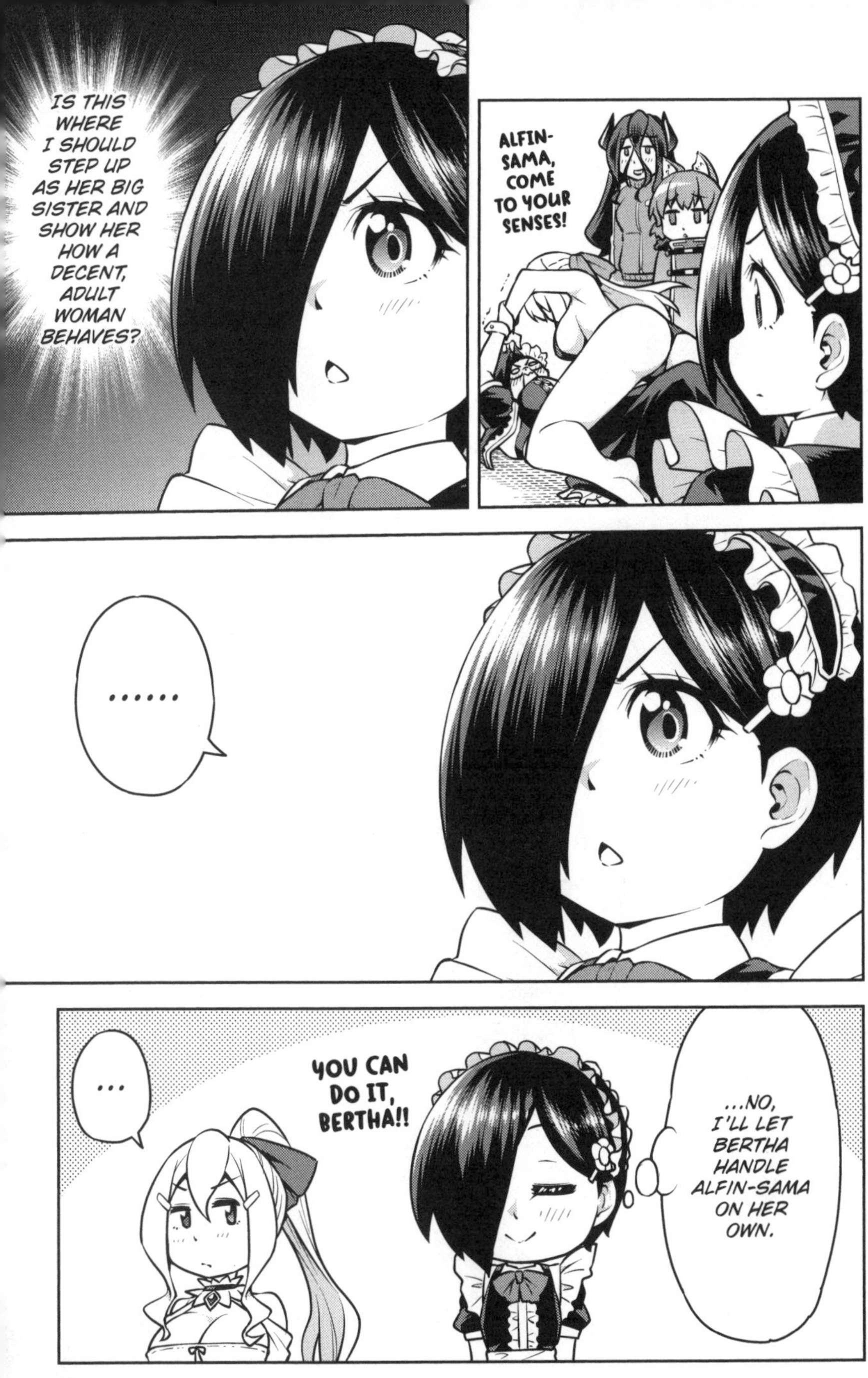
ALFIN-SAMA, COME TO YOUR SENSES!
IS THIS WHERE I SHOULD STEP UP AS HER BIG SISTER AND SHOW HER HOW A DECENT, ADULT WOMAN BEHAVES?
......
...NO, I'LL LET BERTHA HANDLE ALFIN-SAMA ON HER OWN.
YOU CAN DO IT, BERTHA!!
...

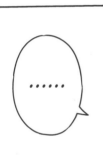

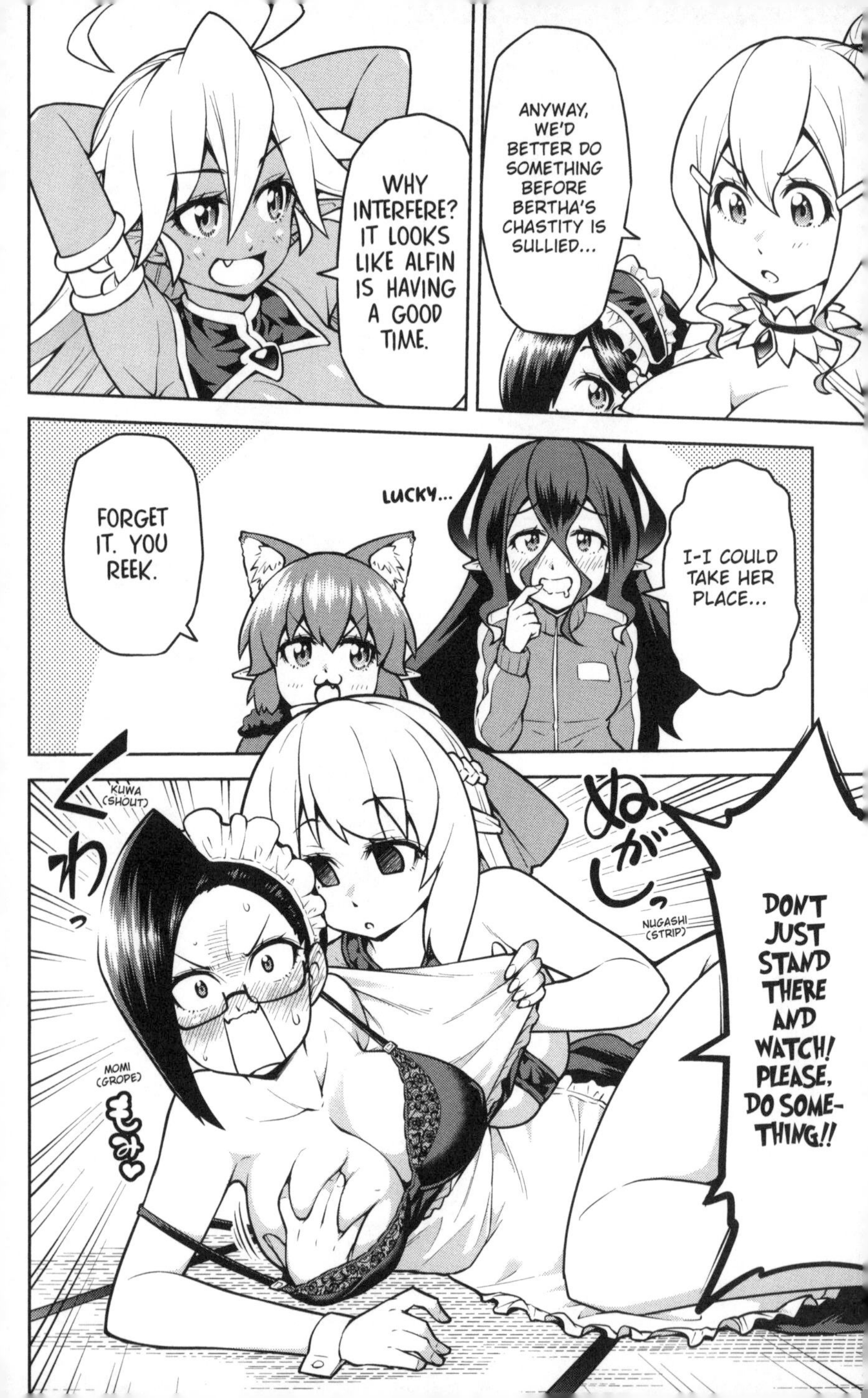
ANYWAY, WE'D BETTER DO SOMETHING BEFORE BERTHA'S CHASTITY IS SULLIED...
WHY INTERFERE? IT LOOKS LIKE ALFIN IS HAVING A GOOD TIME.
I-I COULD TAKE HER PLACE...
LUCKY...
FORGET IT. YOU REEK.
DON'T JUST STAND THERE AND WATCH! PLEASE, DO SOME-THING!!
ぬがしっ
NUGASHI (STRIP)
くわっ
KUWA (SHOUT)
もみ
MOMI (GROPE)

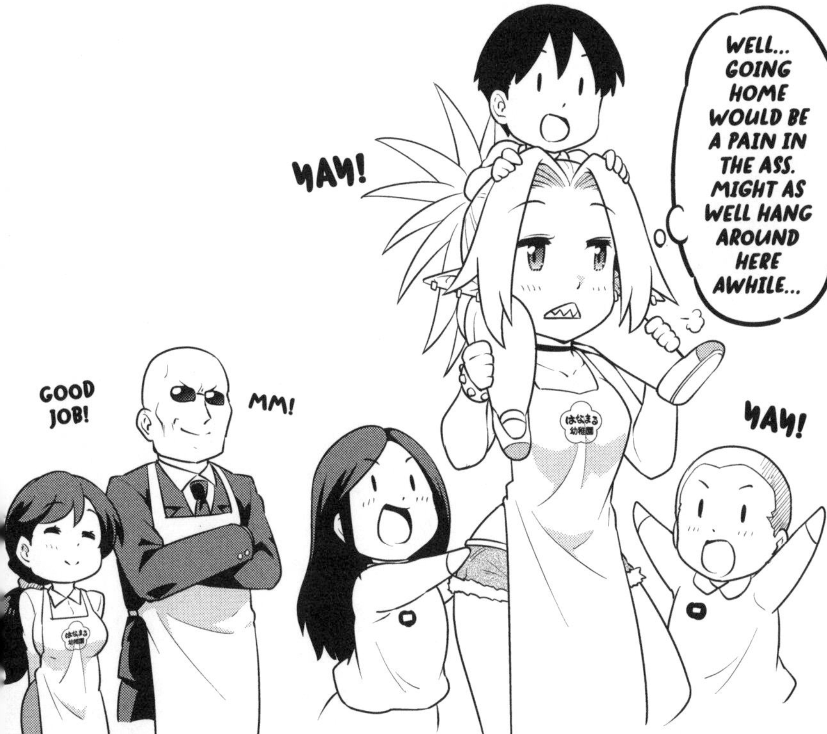
WELL... GOING HOME WOULD BE A PAIN IN THE ASS. MIGHT AS WELL HANG AROUND HERE AWHILE...
YAY!
YAY!
MM!
GOOD JOB!

I'm the HERO, but the DEMON LORD's Also Me

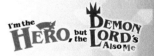

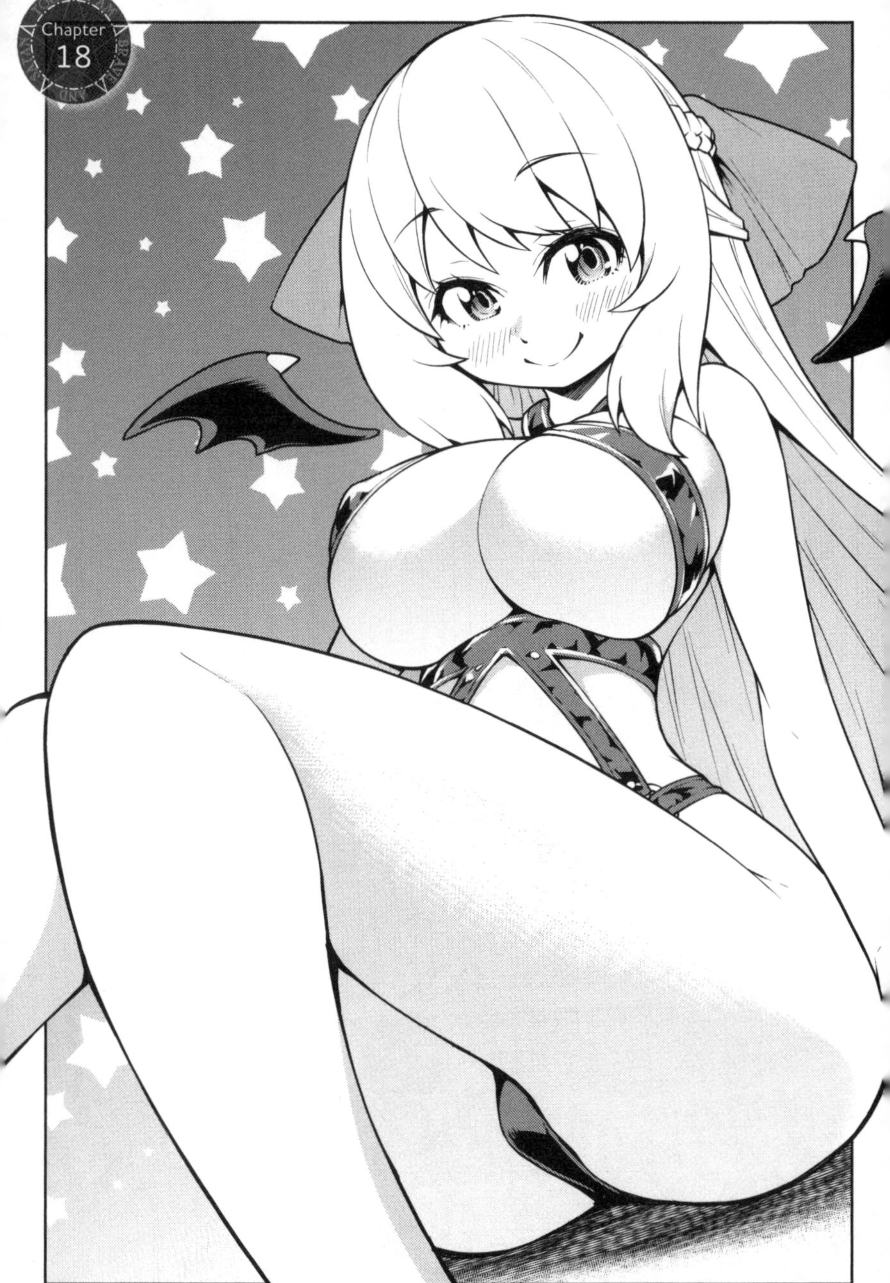
Chapter
18

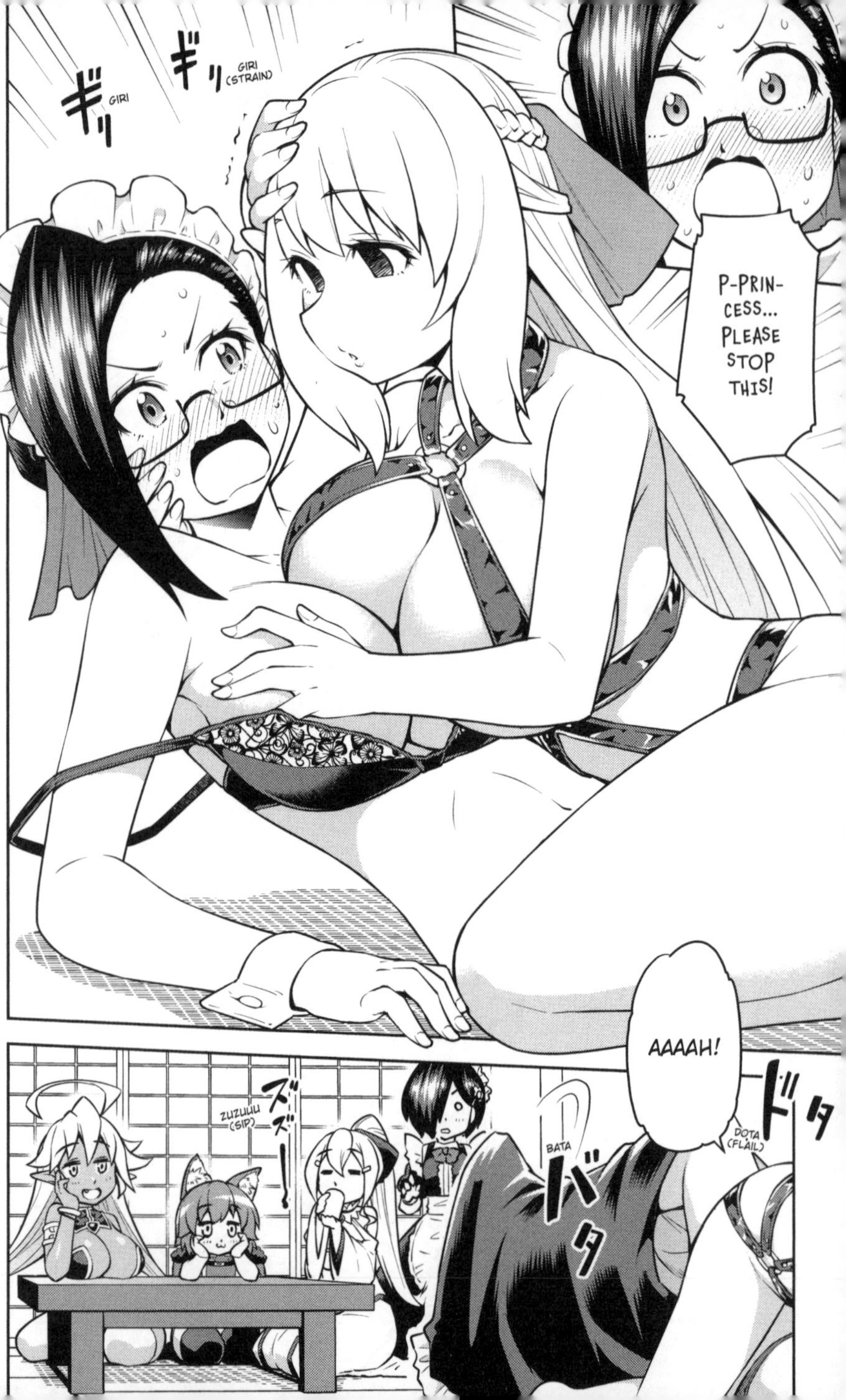
P-PRIN-CESS... PLEASE STOP THIS!
GIRI (STRAIN)
GIRI
AAAAH!
DOTA (FLAIL)
BATA
ZUZUUU (SIP)

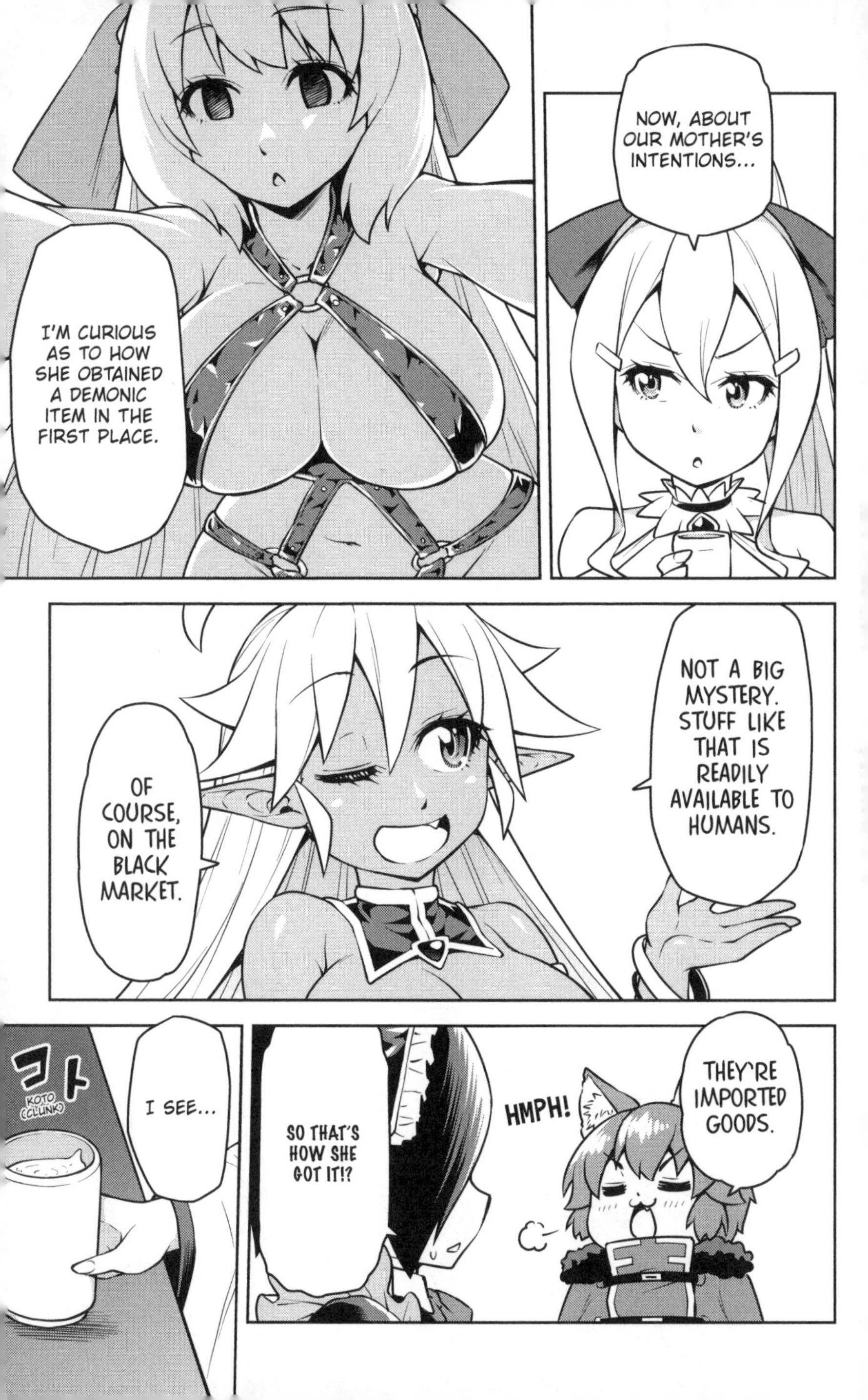
NOW, ABOUT OUR MOTHER'S INTENTIONS...
I'M CURIOUS AS TO HOW SHE OBTAINED A DEMONIC ITEM IN THE FIRST PLACE.
NOT A BIG MYSTERY. STUFF LIKE THAT IS READILY AVAILABLE TO HUMANS.
OF COURSE, ON THE BLACK MARKET.
THEY'RE IMPORTED GOODS.
HMPH!
SO THAT'S HOW SHE GOT IT!?
I SEE...
コト
KOTO (CLUNK)

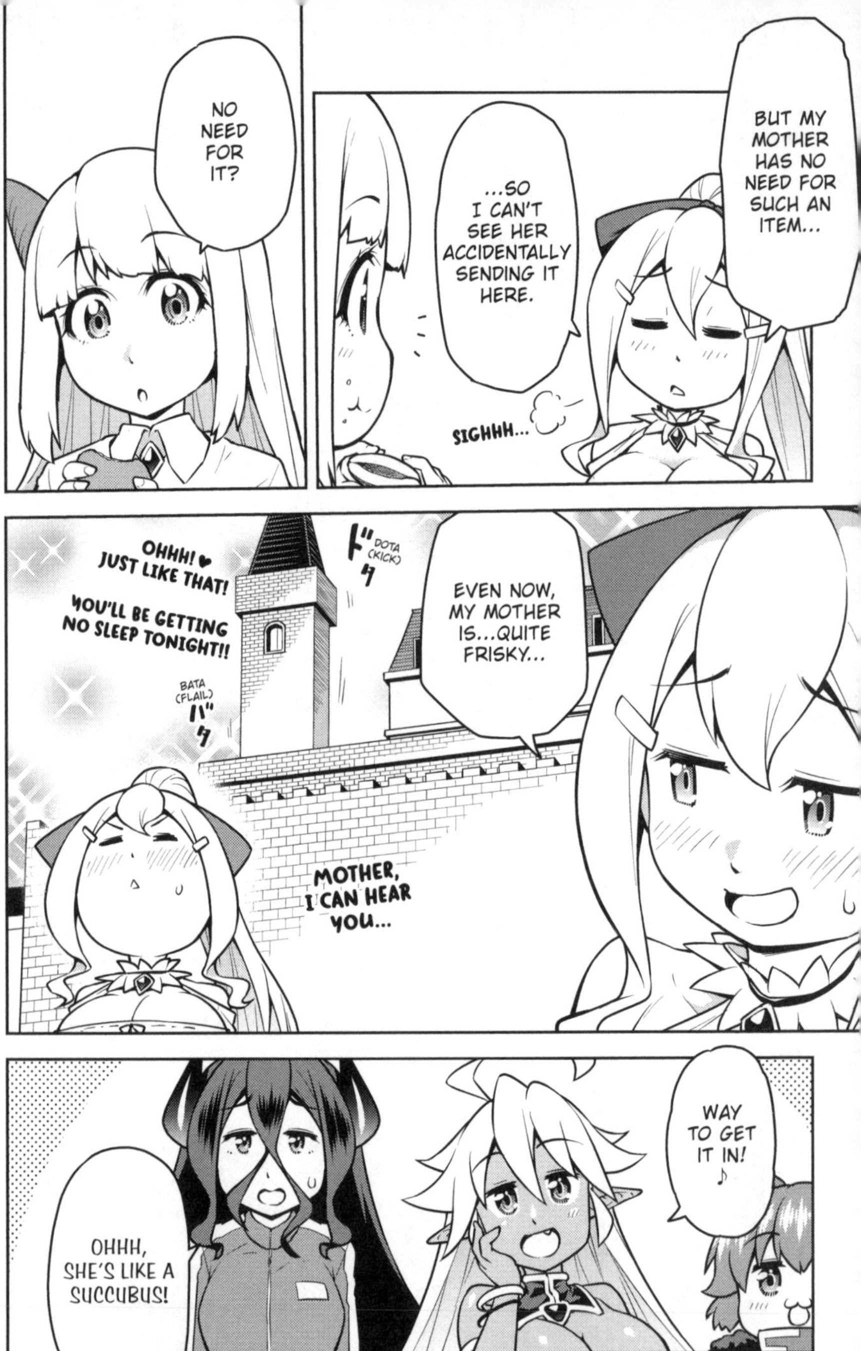
BUT MY MOTHER HAS NO NEED FOR SUCH AN ITEM...
...SO I CAN'T SEE HER ACCIDENTALLY SENDING IT HERE.
SIGHHH...
NO NEED FOR IT?
EVEN NOW, MY MOTHER IS...QUITE FRISKY...
DOTA (KICK)
OHHH! ♥ JUST LIKE THAT!
YOU'LL BE GETTING NO SLEEP TONIGHT!!
BATA (FLAIL)
MOTHER, I CAN HEAR YOU...
WAY TO GET IT IN! ♪
OHHH, SHE'S LIKE A SUCCUBUS!

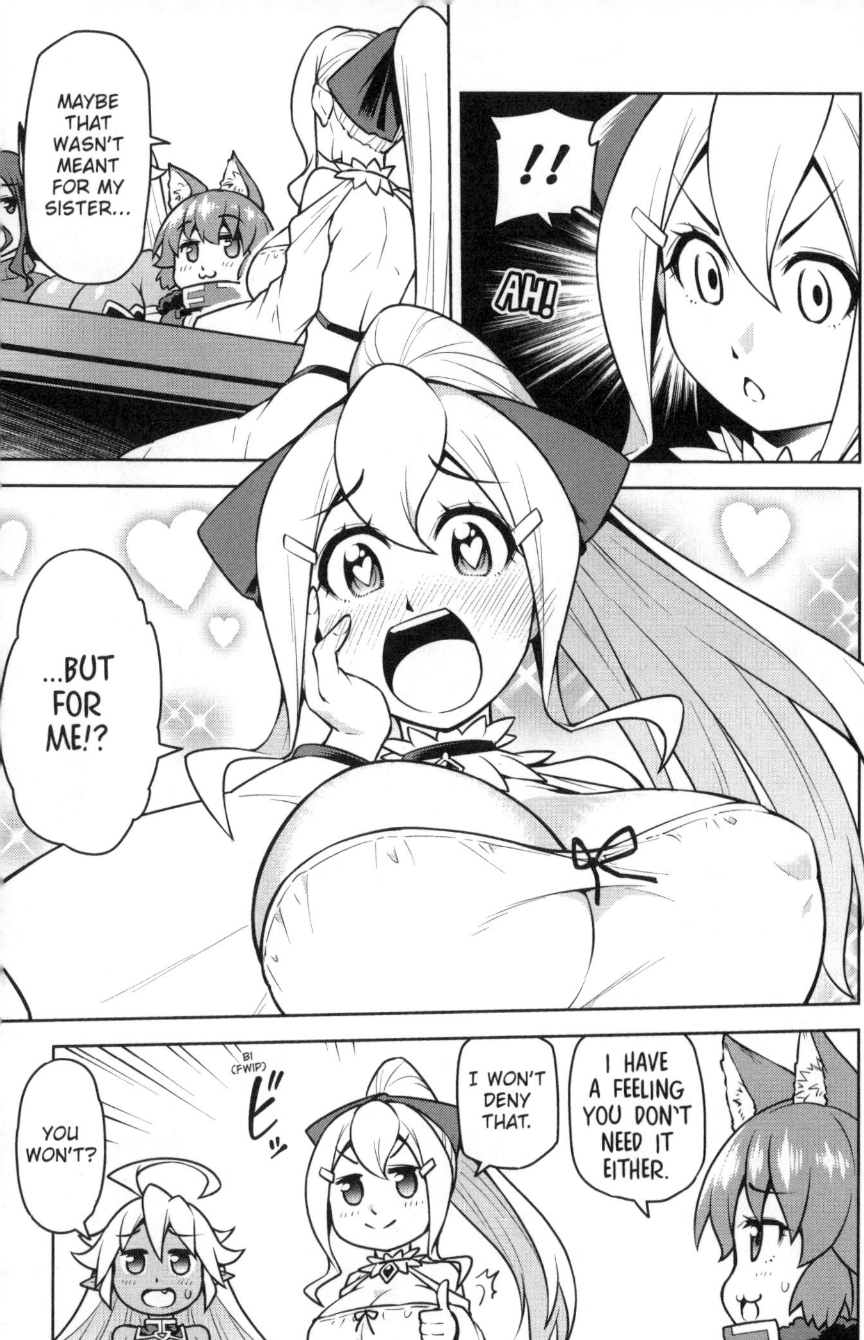
!!
AH!
MAYBE THAT WASN'T MEANT FOR MY SISTER...
...BUT FOR ME!?
I HAVE A FEELING YOU DON'T NEED IT EITHER.
I WON'T DENY THAT.
BI (FWIP)
YOU WON'T?

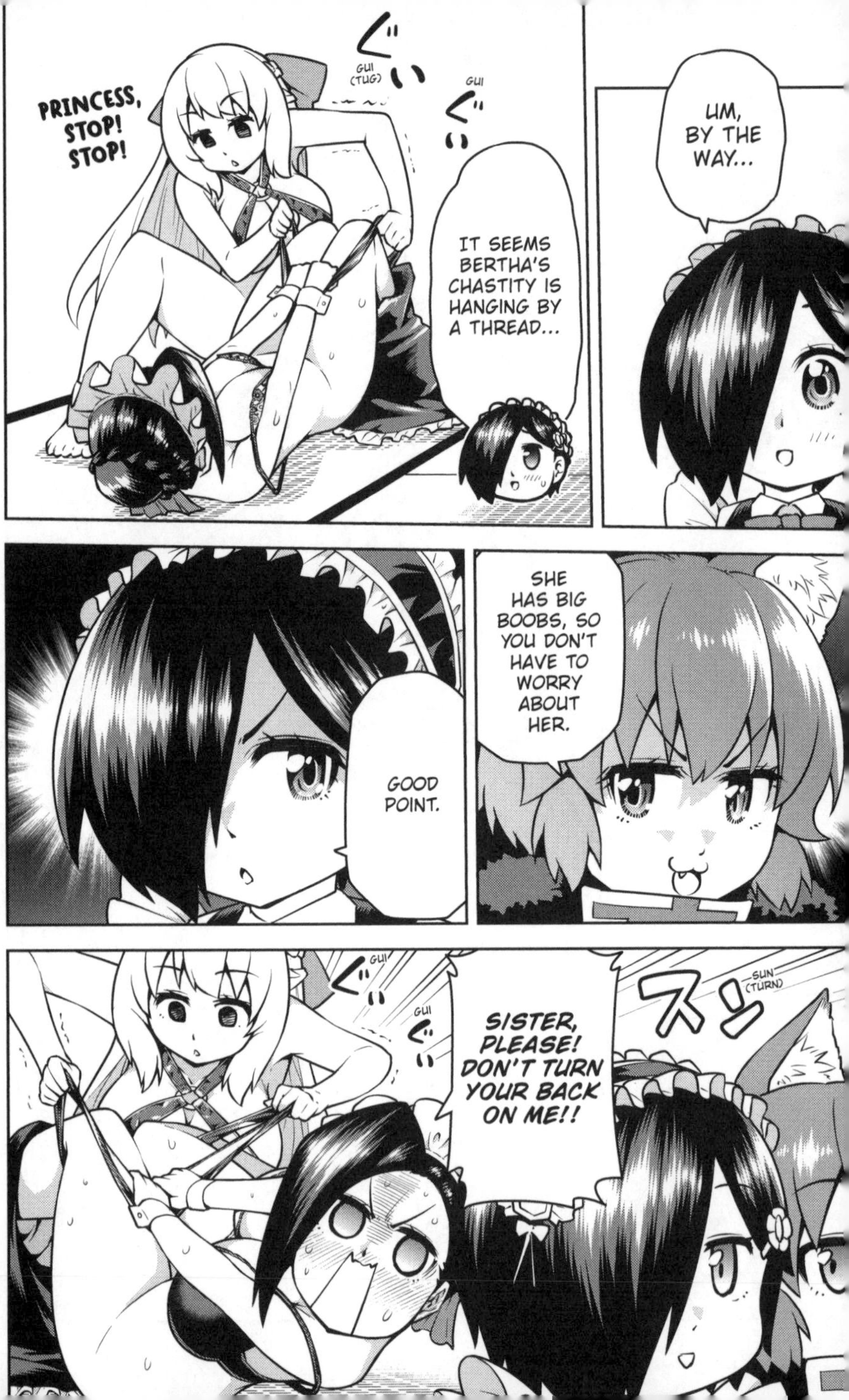
UM, BY THE WAY...
ぐい
GUI
ぐい
GUI (TUG)
IT SEEMS BERTHA'S CHASTITY IS HANGING BY A THREAD...
PRINCESS, STOP! STOP!
SHE HAS BIG BOOBS, SO YOU DON'T HAVE TO WORRY ABOUT HER.
GOOD POINT.
スン
SUN (TURN)
SISTER, PLEASE! DON'T TURN YOUR BACK ON ME!!
ぐい
GUI
ぐい
GUI

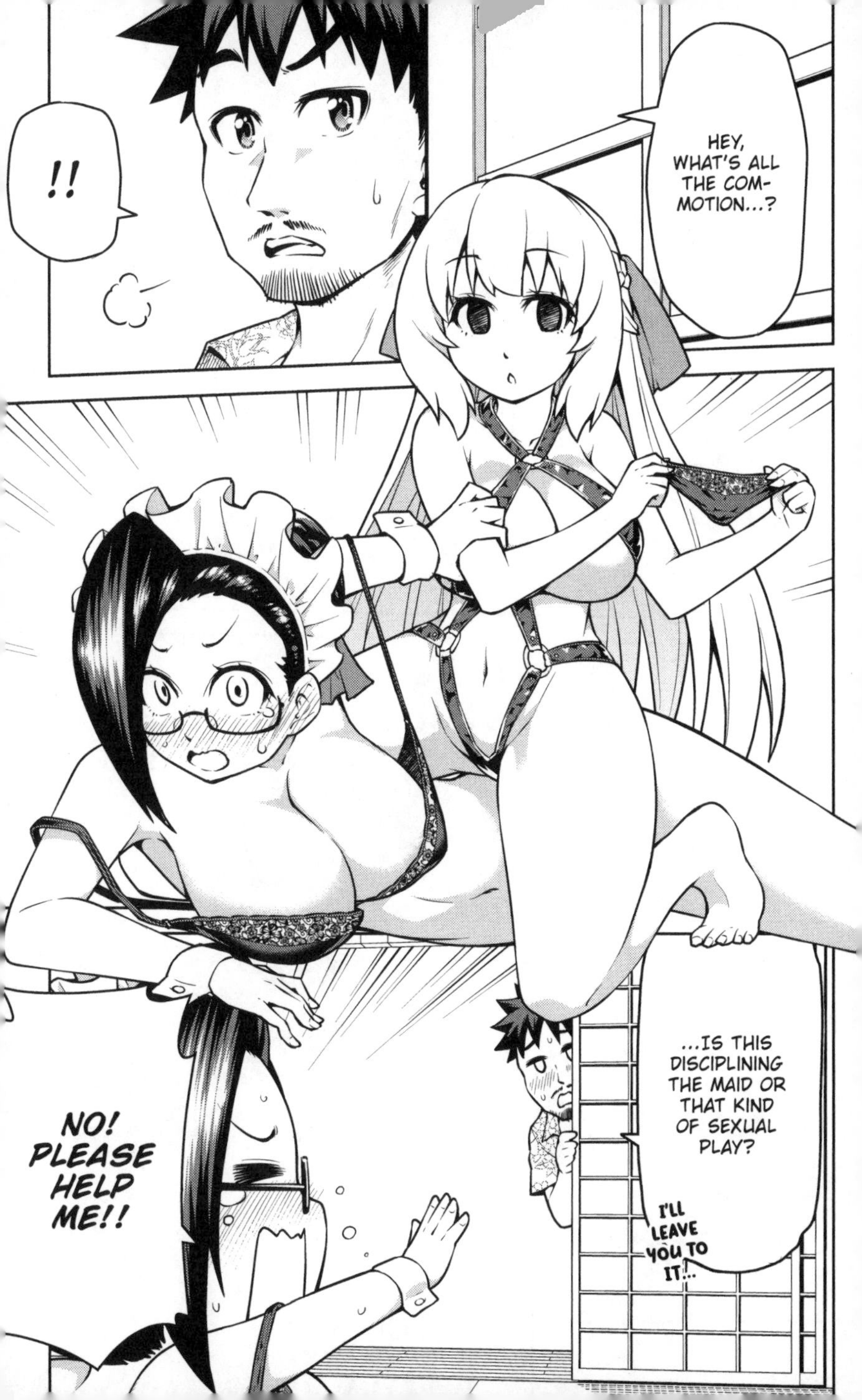
HEY, WHAT'S ALL THE COM-MOTION...?
!!
...IS THIS DISCIPLINING THE MAID OR THAT KIND OF SEXUAL PLAY?
I'LL LEAVE YOU TO IT...
NO! PLEASE HELP ME!!

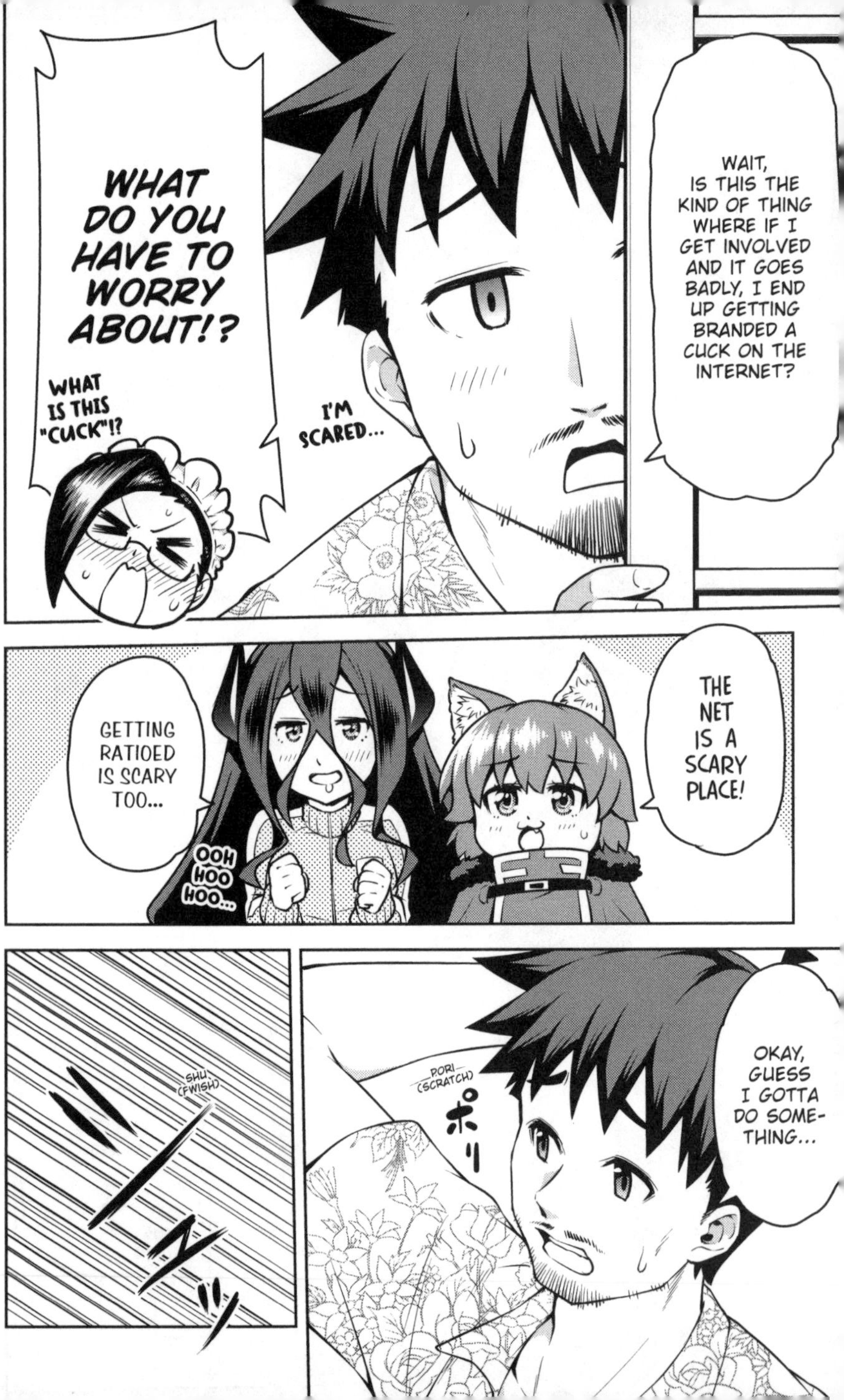
WAIT, IS THIS THE KIND OF THING WHERE IF I GET INVOLVED AND IT GOES BADLY, I END UP GETTING BRANDED A CUCK ON THE INTERNET?
I'M SCARED...
WHAT DO YOU HAVE TO WORRY ABOUT!?
WHAT IS THIS "CUCK"!?
THE NET IS A SCARY PLACE!
GETTING RATIOED IS SCARY TOO...
OOH HOO HOO...
OKAY, GUESS I GOTTA DO SOME-THING...
PORI (SCRATCH)
ポリ
SHU (FWISH)

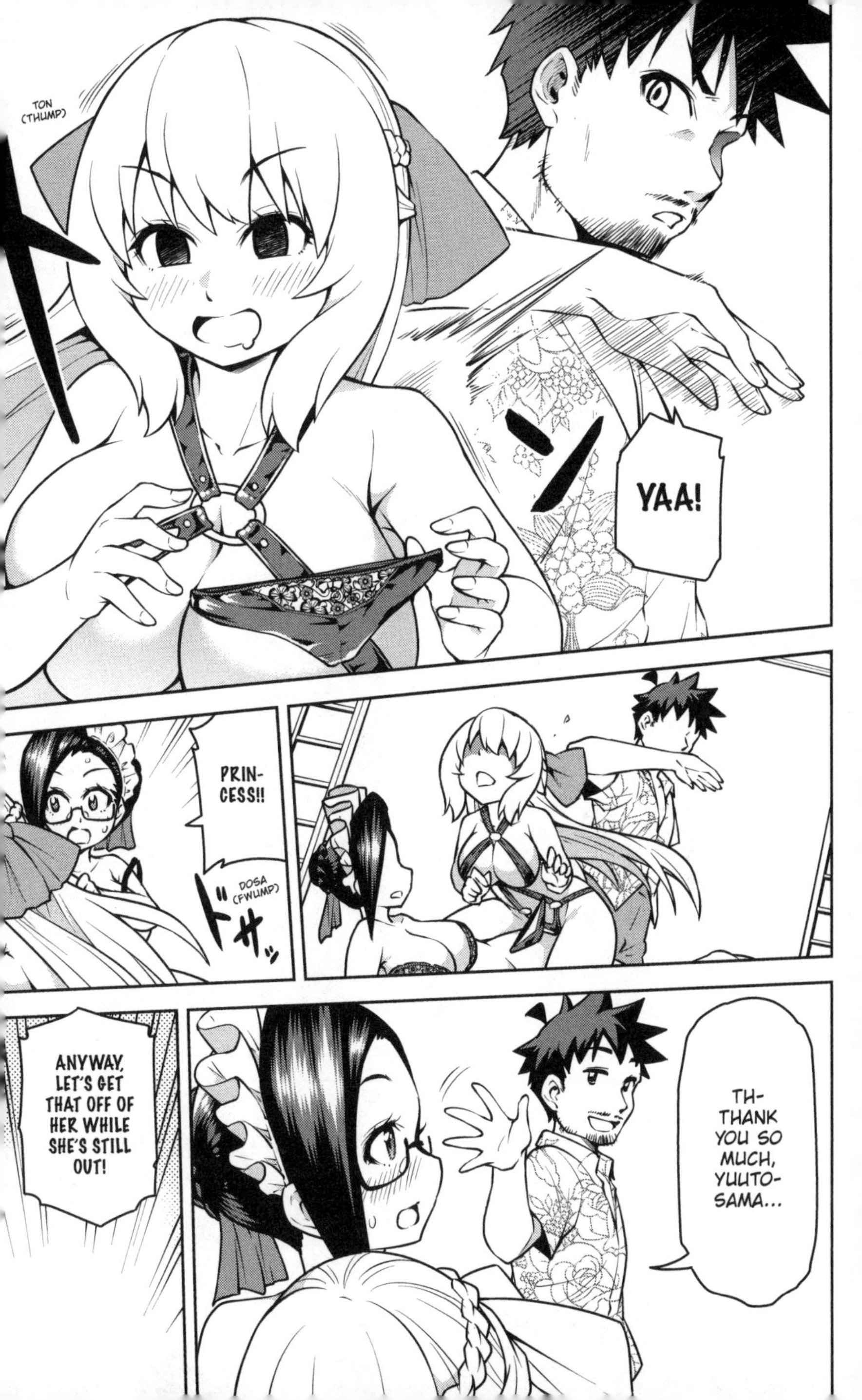
YAA!
TON (THUMP)
PRIN-CESS!!
DOSA (FWUMP)
TH-THANK YOU SO MUCH, YUUTO-SAMA...
ANYWAY, LET'S GET THAT OFF OF HER WHILE SHE'S STILL OUT!

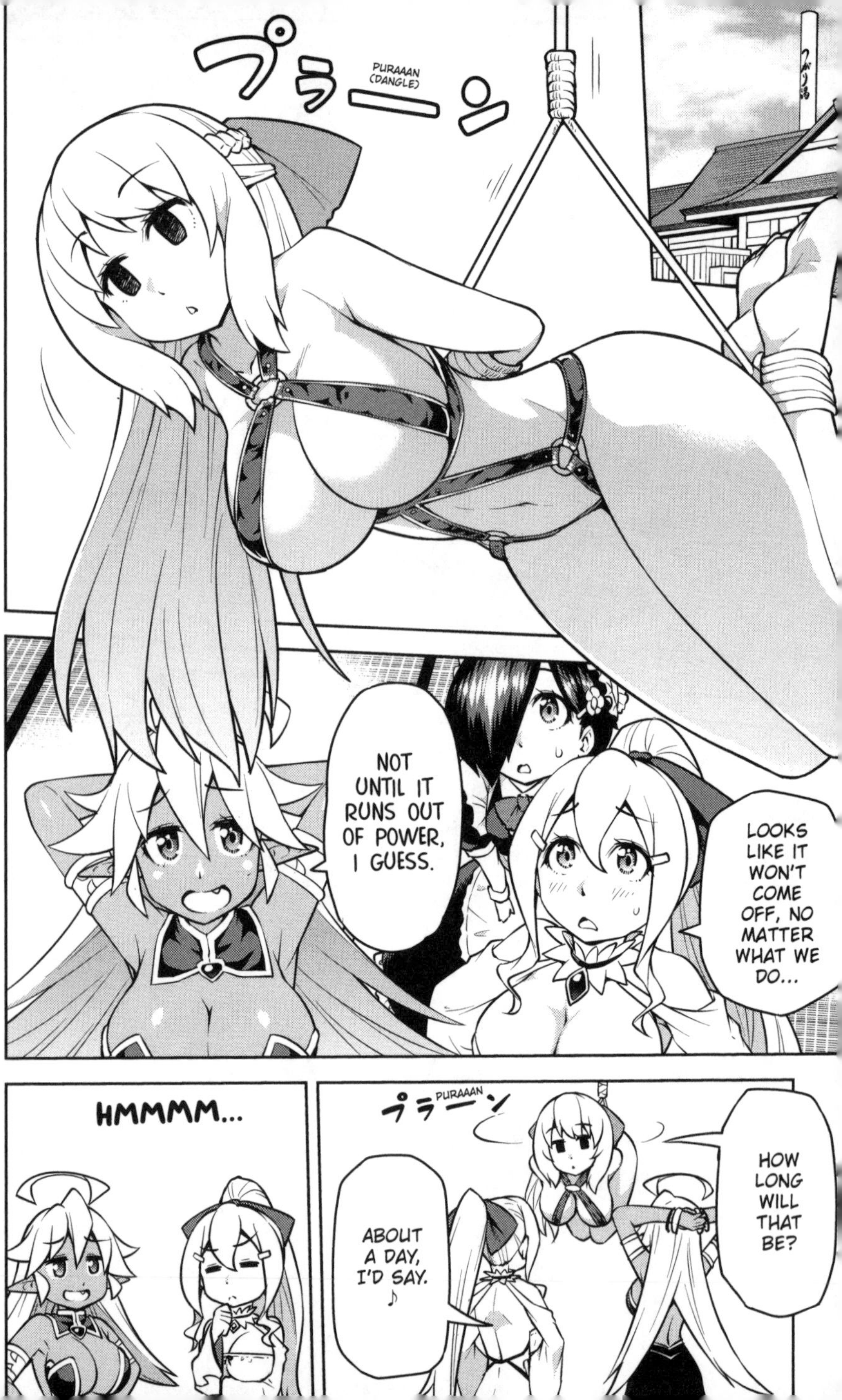

プラーン
PURAAAN (DANGLE)
LOOKS LIKE IT WON'T COME OFF, NO MATTER WHAT WE DO...
NOT UNTIL IT RUNS OUT OF POWER, I GUESS.
プラーン
PURAAAN
HOW LONG WILL THAT BE?
ABOUT A DAY, I'D SAY. ♪
HMMMM...

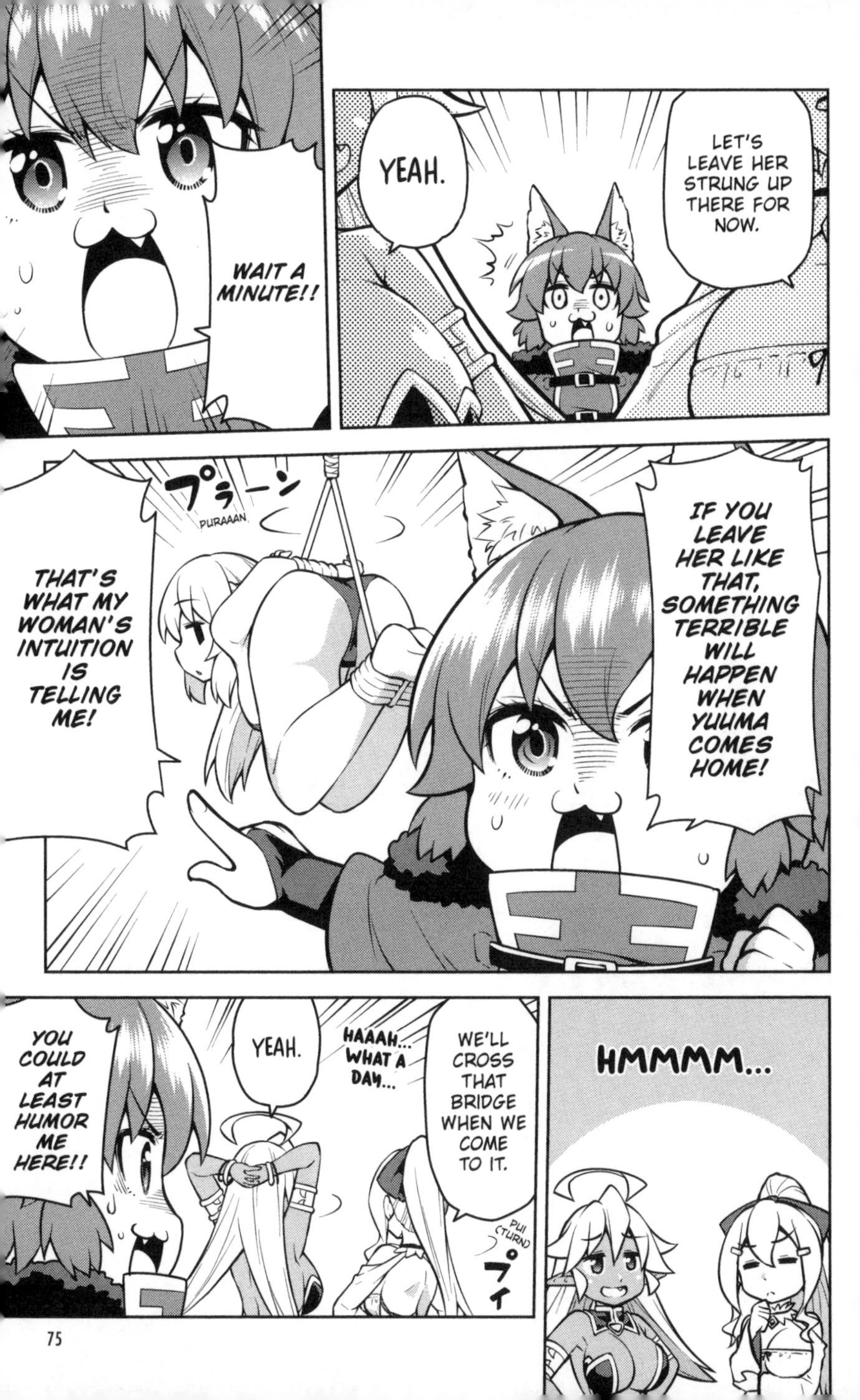
LET'S LEAVE HER STRUNG UP THERE FOR NOW.
YEAH.
WAIT A MINUTE!!
IF YOU LEAVE HER LIKE THAT, SOMETHING TERRIBLE WILL HAPPEN WHEN YUUMA COMES HOME!
プラーン
PURAAAN
THAT'S WHAT MY WOMAN'S INTUITION IS TELLING ME!
HMMMM...
WE'LL CROSS THAT BRIDGE WHEN WE COME TO IT.
HAAAH... WHAT A DAY...
YEAH.
YOU COULD AT LEAST HUMOR ME HERE!!
PUI (TURN)
プイ

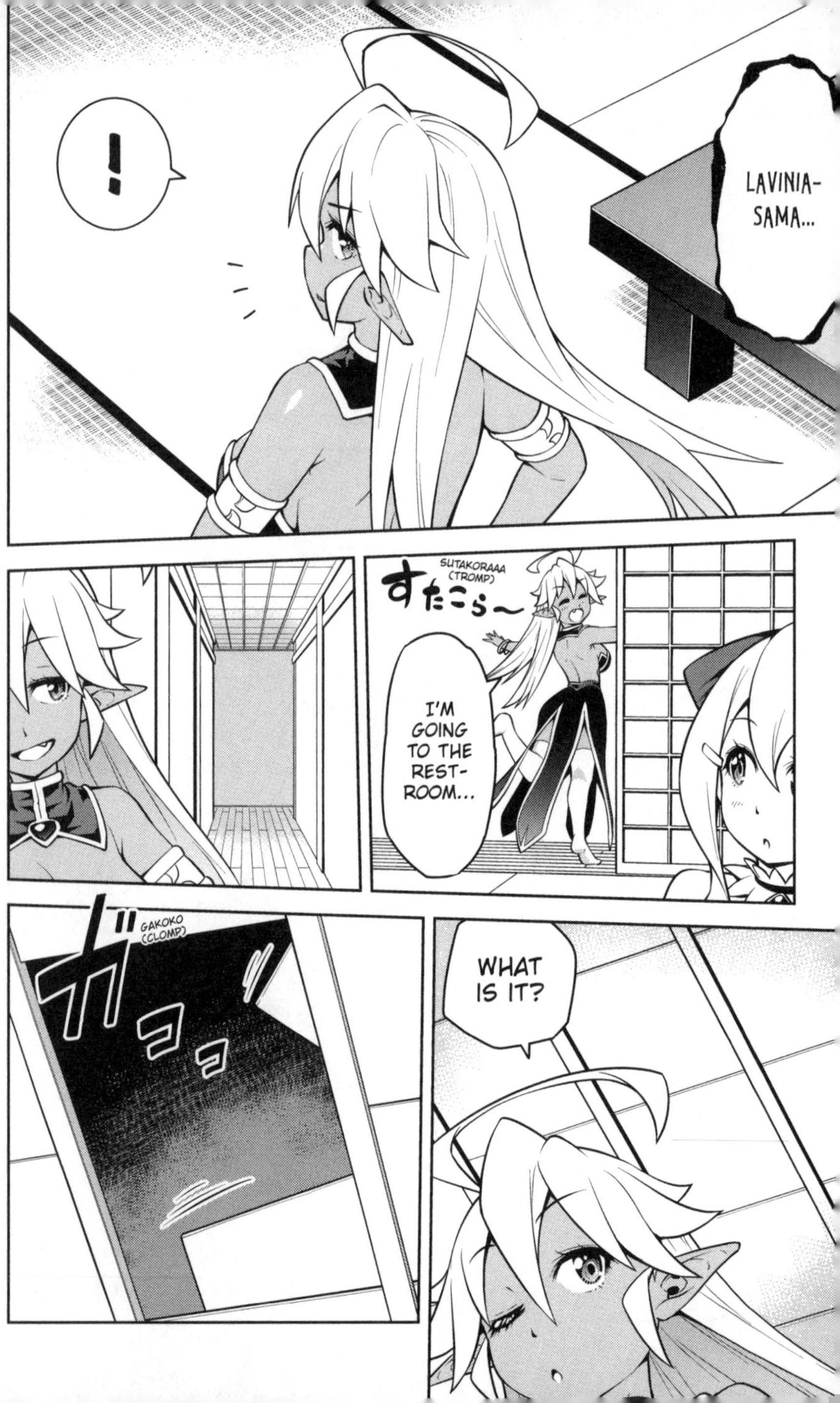

LAVINIA-SAMA...
!
すたこら～
SUTAKORAAA (TROMP)
I'M GOING TO THE REST-ROOM...
WHAT IS IT?
ガコココ
GAKOKO (CLOMP)

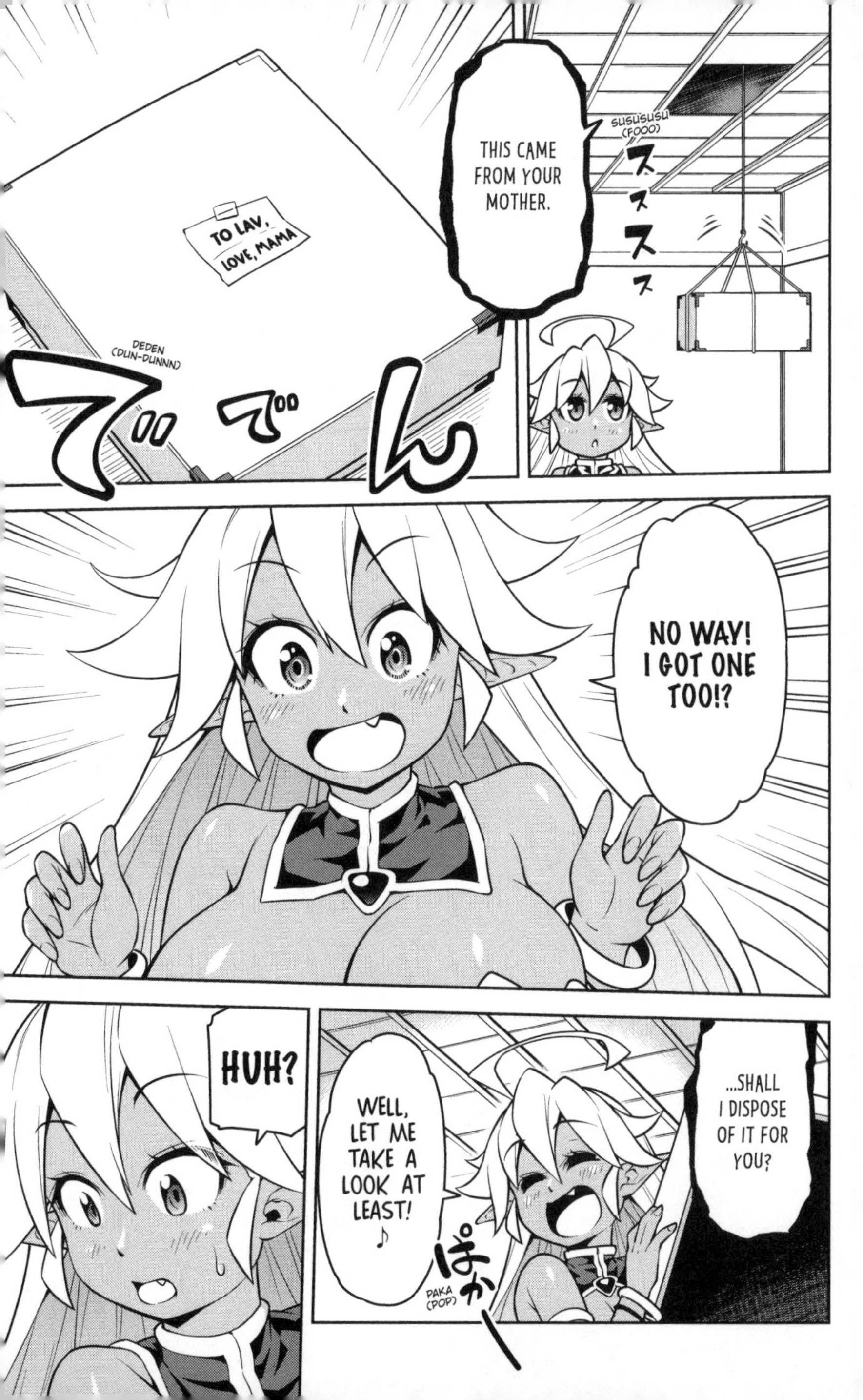
SUSUSUSU (FOOO)
THIS CAME FROM YOUR MOTHER.
TO LAV, LOVE, MAMA
DEDEN (DUN-DUNNN)
NO WAY! I GOT ONE TOO!?
...SHALL I DISPOSE OF IT FOR YOU?
WELL, LET ME TAKE A LOOK AT LEAST! ♪
PAKA (POP)
HUH?

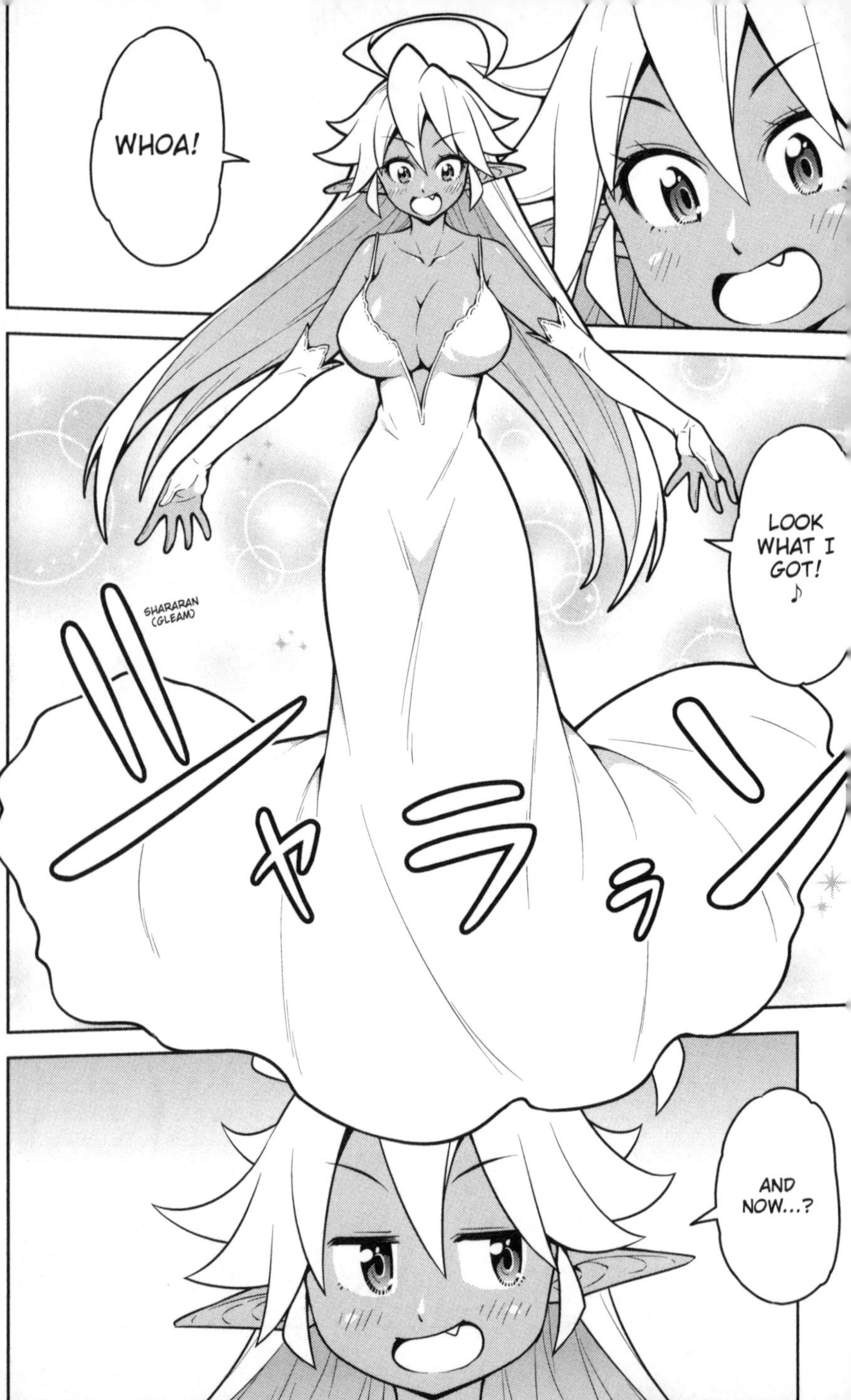
WHOA!
LOOK WHAT I GOT! ♪
SHARARAN (GLEAM)
AND NOW...?

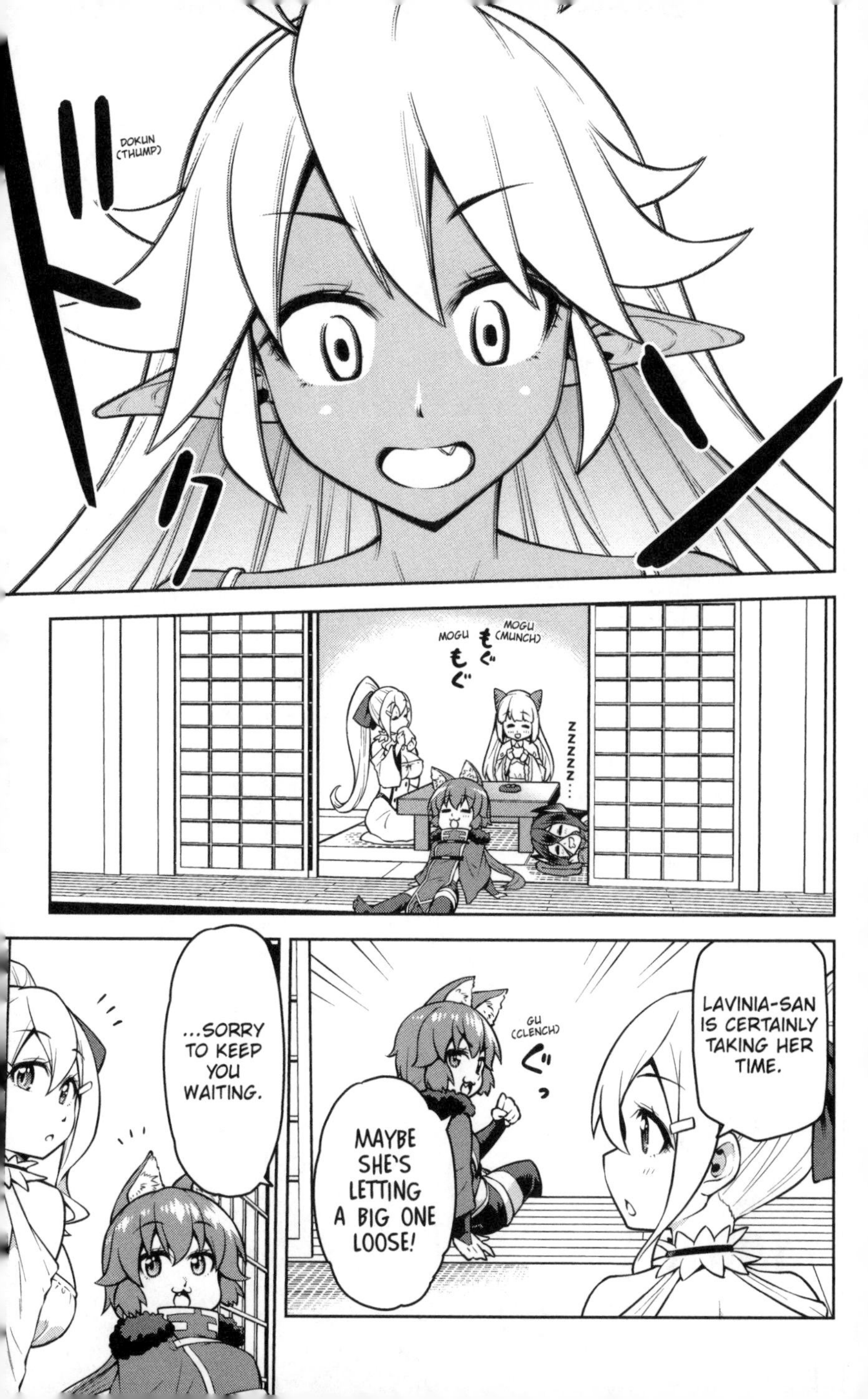
DOKUN (THUMP)
MOGU (MUNCH)
MOGU
ZZZZZ...
LAVINIA-SAN IS CERTAINLY TAKING HER TIME.
GU (CLENCH)
MAYBE SHE'S LETTING A BIG ONE LOOSE!
...SORRY TO KEEP YOU WAITING.

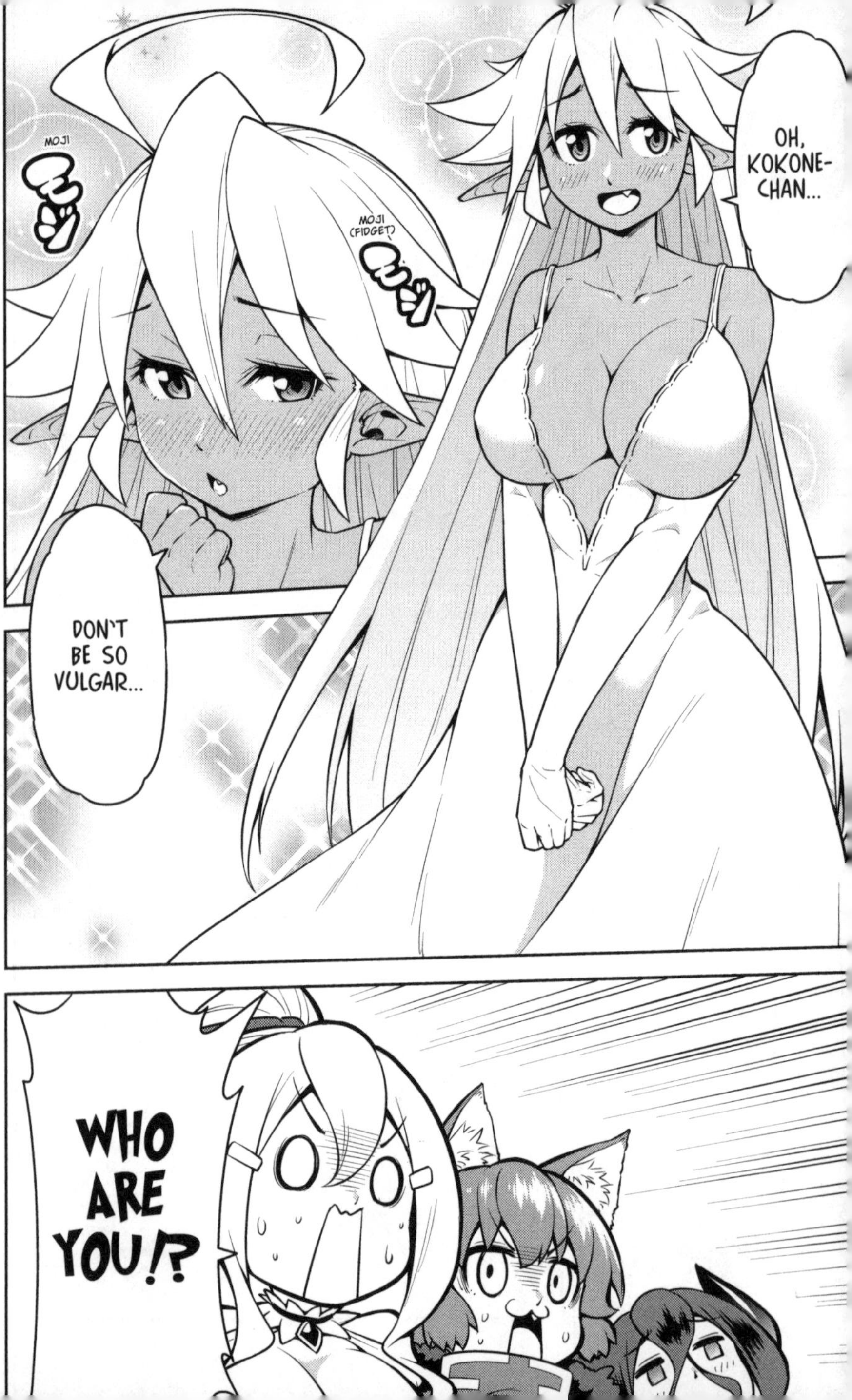
OH, KOKONE-CHAN...
MOJI
MOJI (FIDGET)
DON'T BE SO VULGAR...
WHO ARE YOU!?

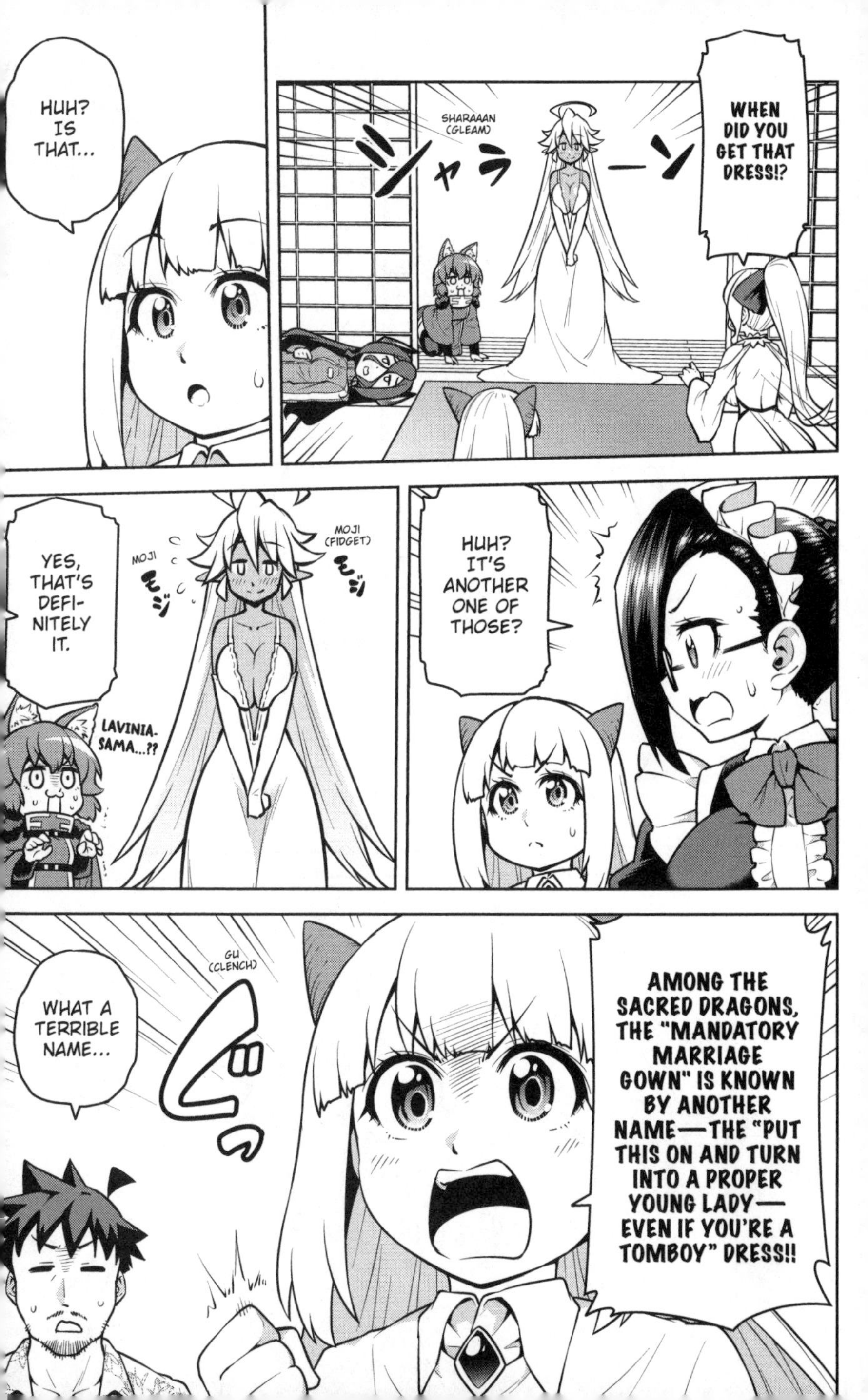
WHEN DID YOU GET THAT DRESS!?
SHARAAAN (GLEAM)
シャラーン
HUH? IS THAT...
HUH? IT'S ANOTHER ONE OF THOSE?
MOJI (FIDGET)
モジ
MOJI
モジ
YES, THAT'S DEFI-NITELY IT.
LAVINIA-SAMA...??
AMONG THE SACRED DRAGONS, THE "MANDATORY MARRIAGE GOWN" IS KNOWN BY ANOTHER NAME—THE "PUT THIS ON AND TURN INTO A PROPER YOUNG LADY—EVEN IF YOU'RE A TOMBOY" DRESS!!
GU (CLENCH)
ぐっ
WHAT A TERRIBLE NAME...

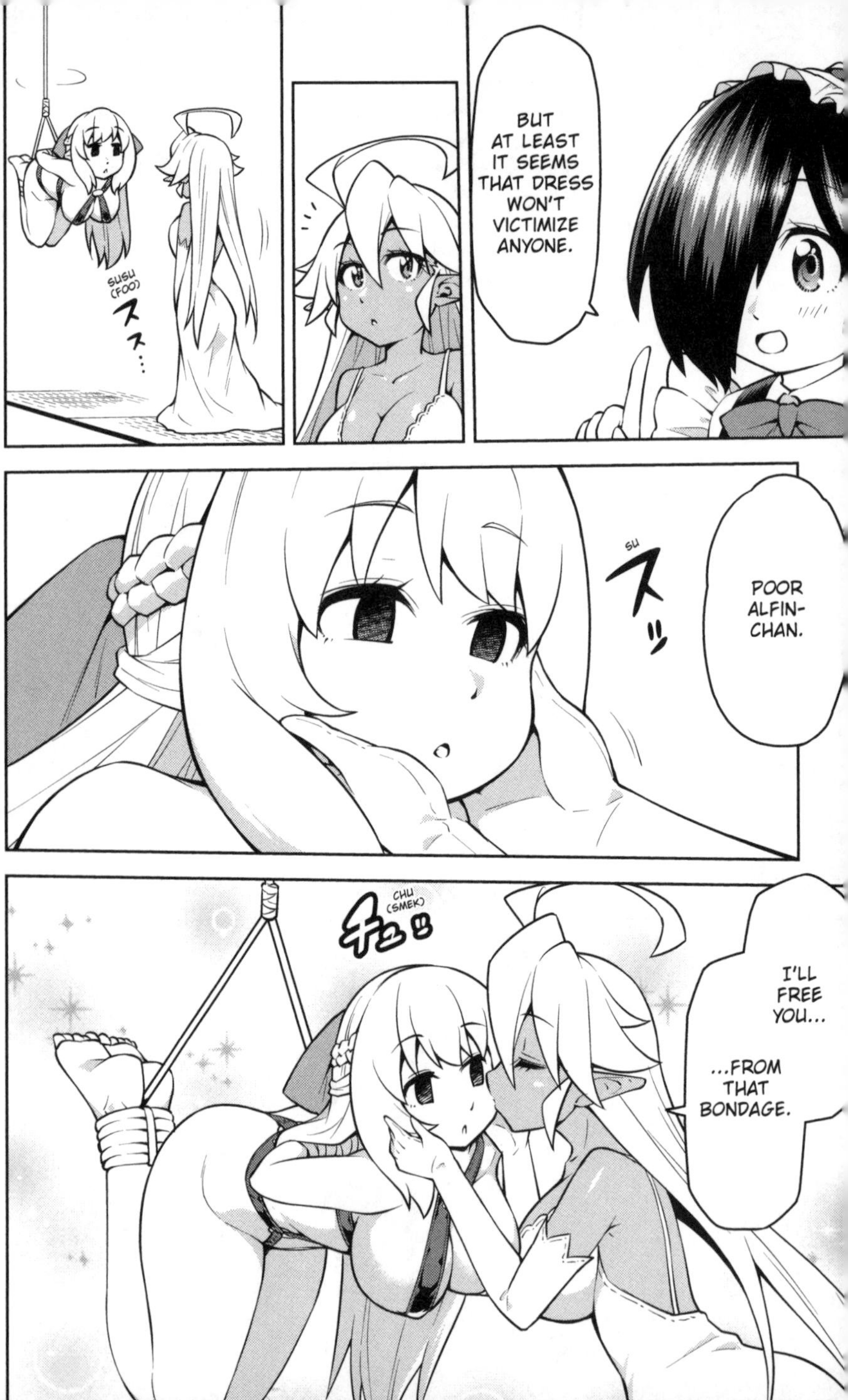
BUT AT LEAST IT SEEMS THAT DRESS WON'T VICTIMIZE ANYONE.
SUSU (FOO)
スス…
POOR ALFIN-CHAN.
SU
スッ
I'LL FREE YOU...
...FROM THAT BONDAGE.
CHU (SMEK)
チュ!!

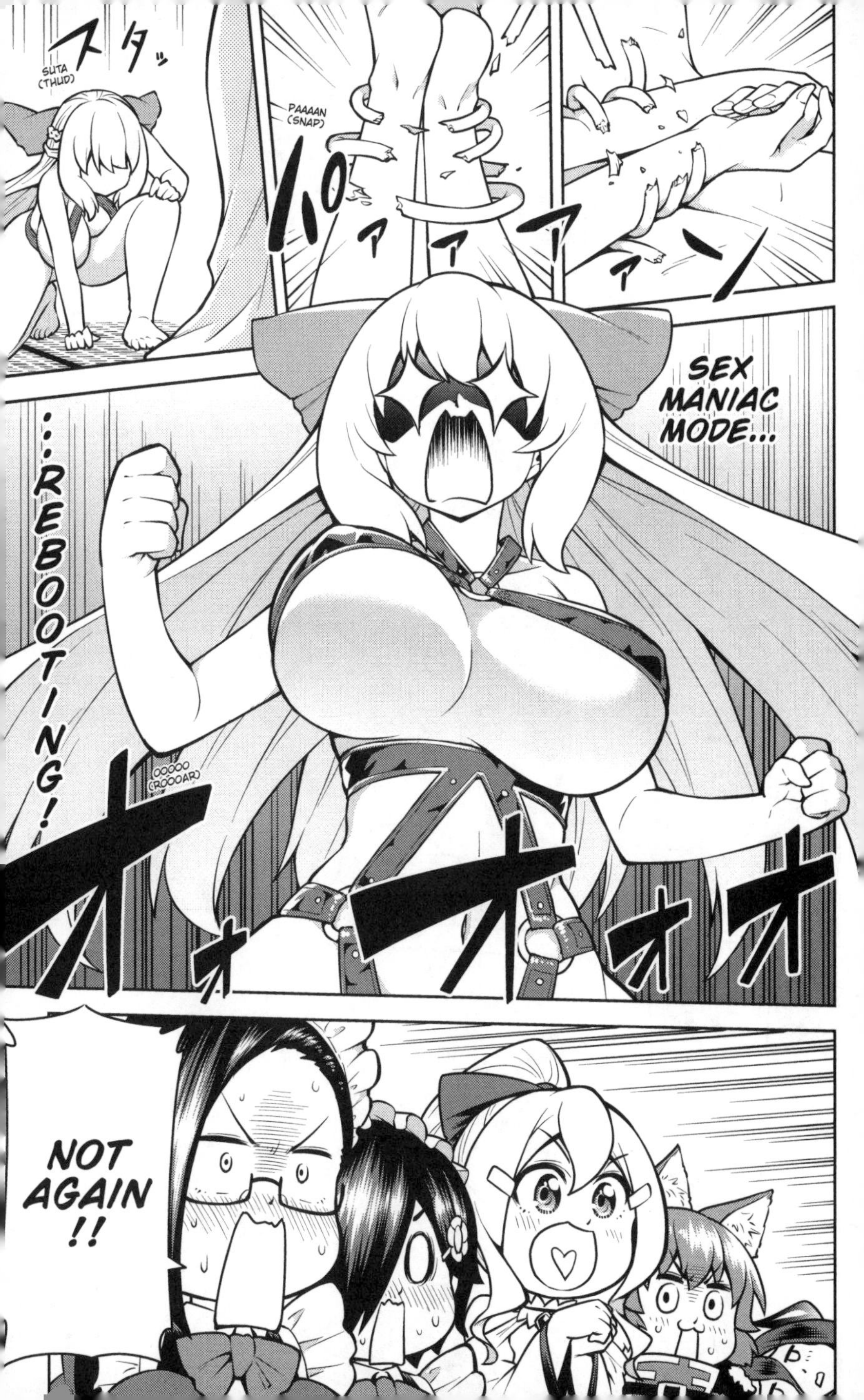

PAAAAN (SNAP)
パァァァァン
SUTA (THUD)
スタッ
SEX MANIAC MODE...
...REBOOTING!!
OOOOO (ROOOAR)
オォォオォオ
NOT AGAIN!!

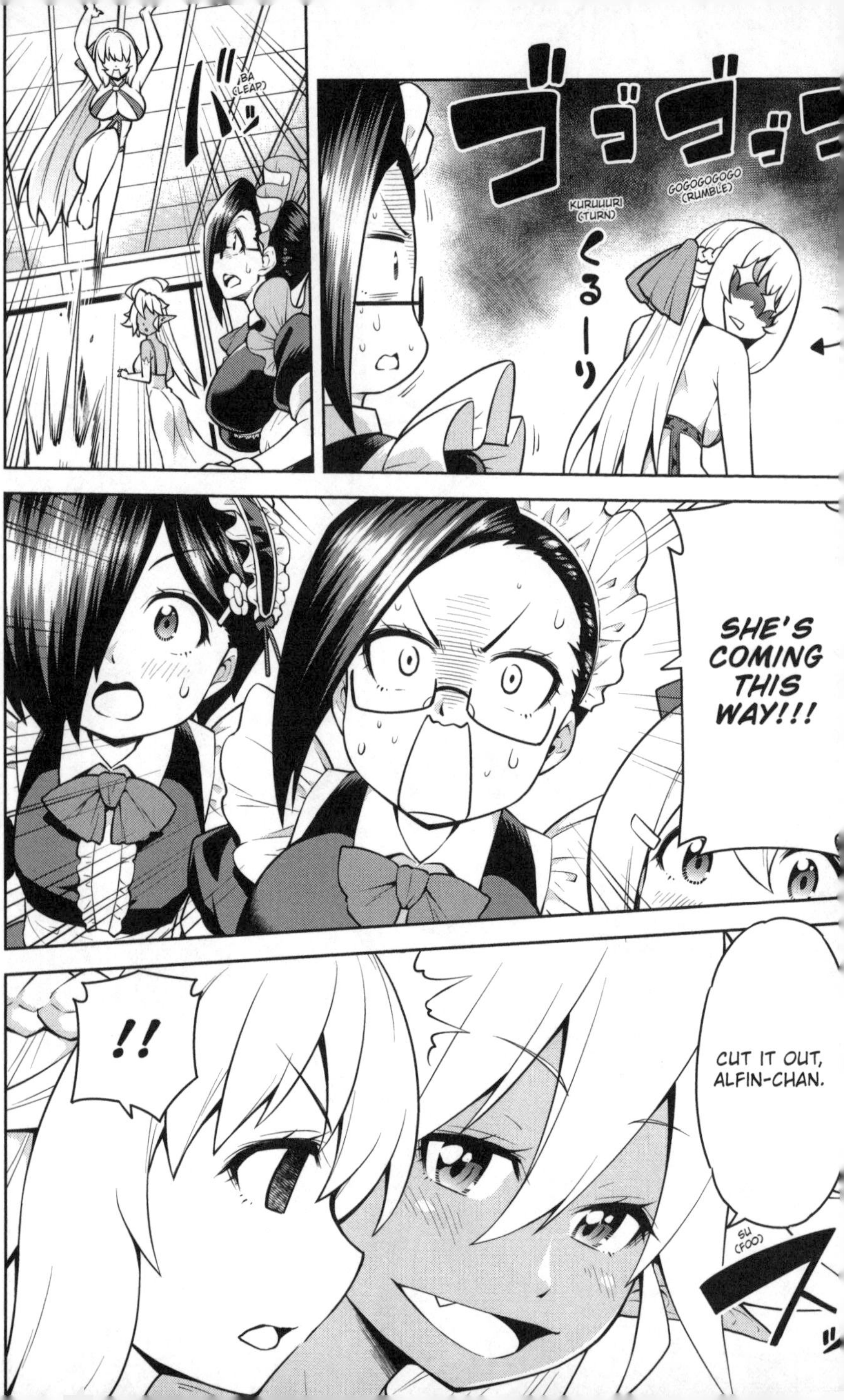
GOGOGOGOGO (RUMBLE)
KURUUURI (TURN)
くるーり
BA (LEAP)
バッ
SHE'S COMING THIS WAY!!!
CUT IT OUT, ALFIN-CHAN.
!!
SU (FOO)

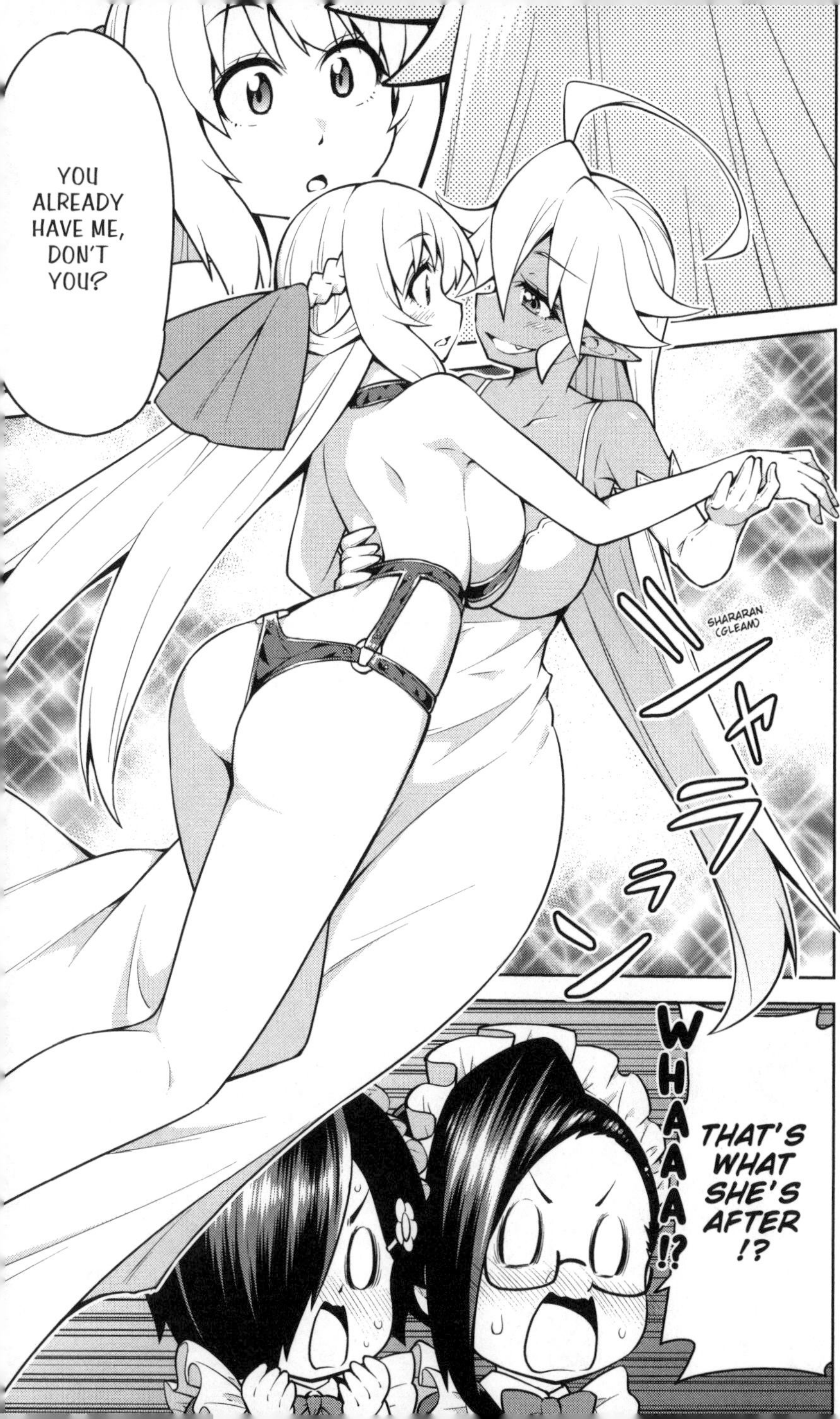
YOU ALREADY HAVE ME, DON'T YOU?
SHARARAN (GLEAM)
THAT'S WHAT SHE'S AFTER!?
WHAAAA!?

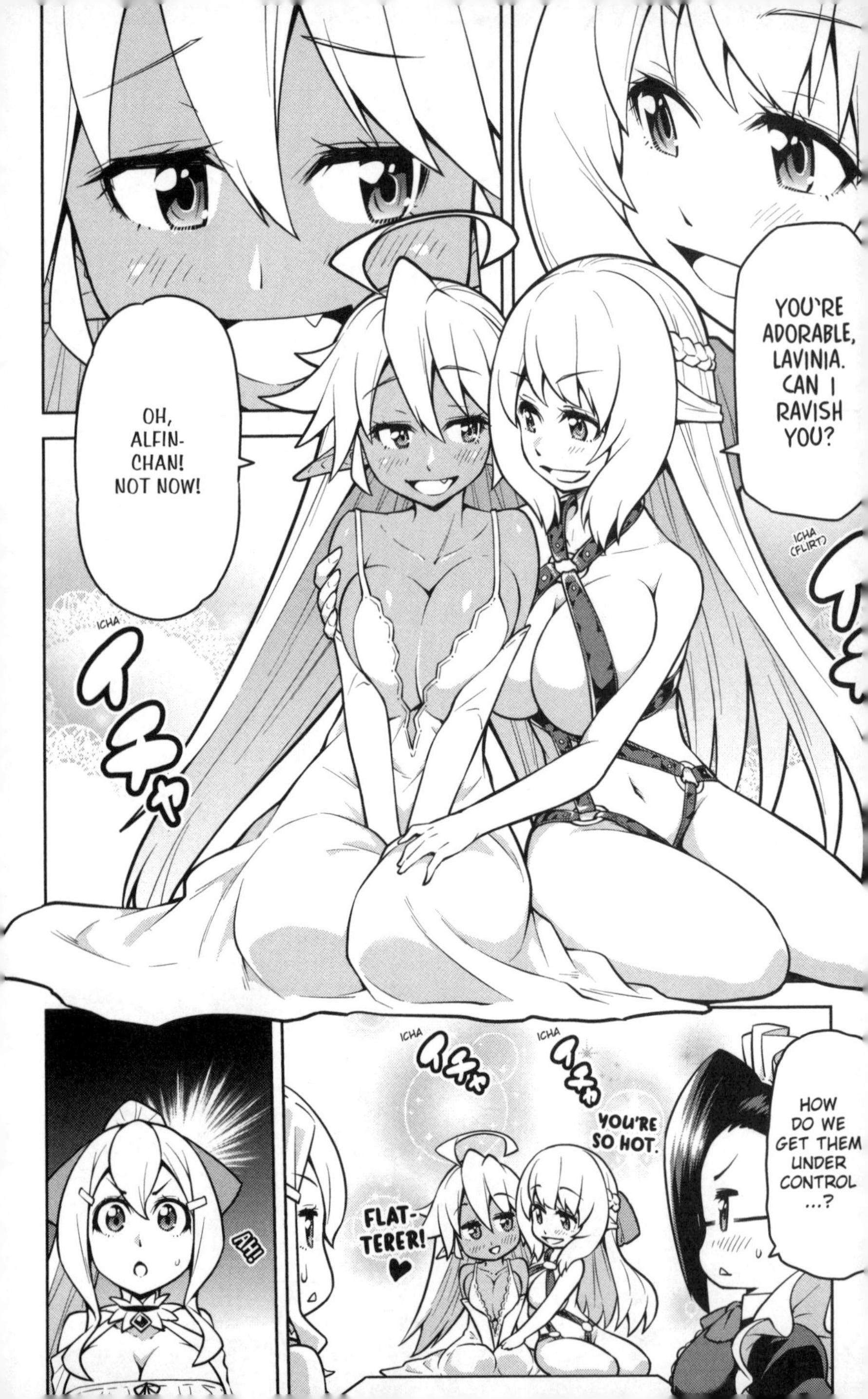
YOU'RE ADORABLE, LAVINIA. CAN I RAVISH YOU?
ICHA (FLIRT)
OH, ALFIN-CHAN! NOT NOW!
ICHA
HOW DO WE GET THEM UNDER CONTROL ...?
ICHA
ICHA
YOU'RE SO HOT.
FLAT-TERER!
AH!

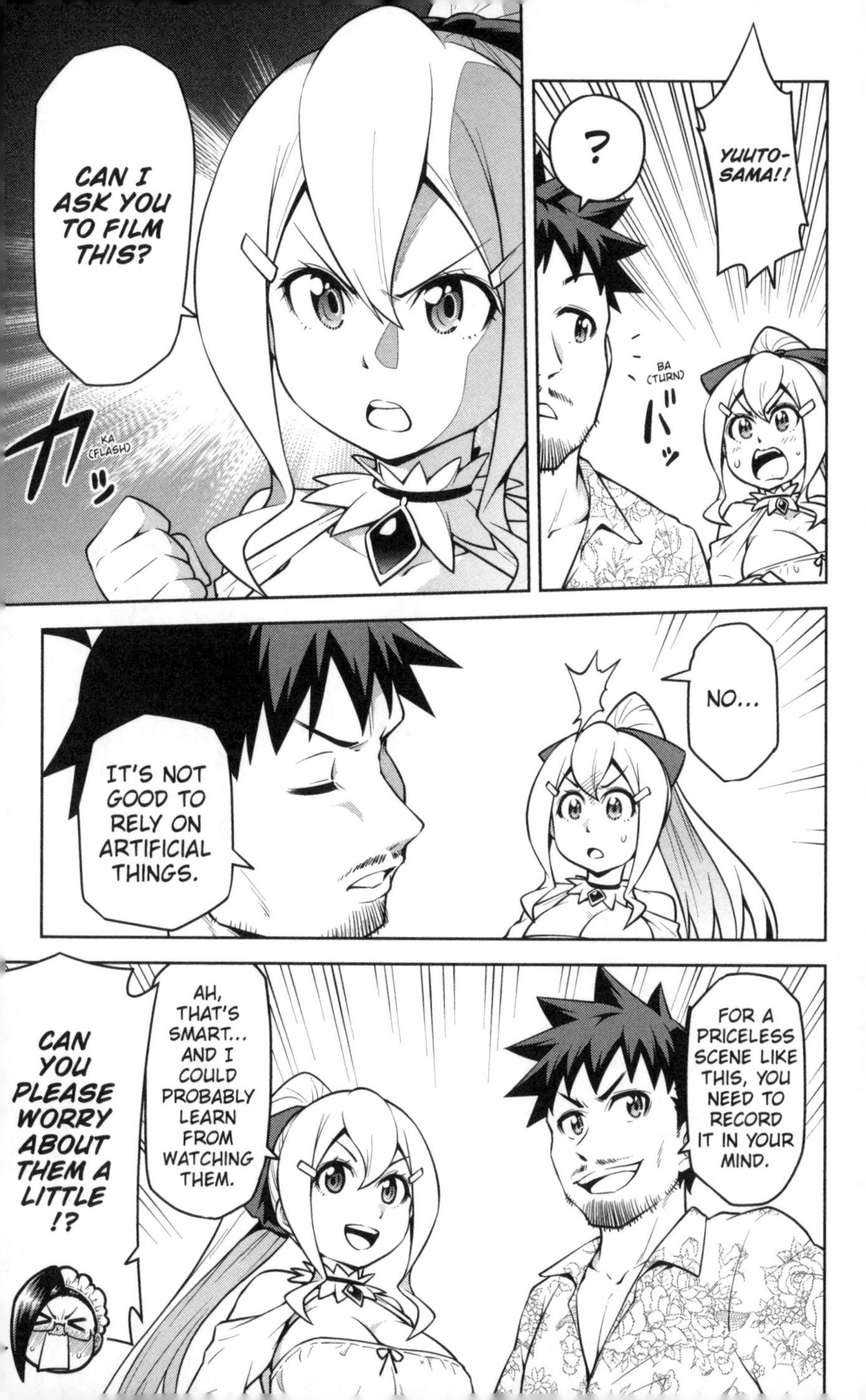
YUUTO-SAMA!!
?
BA (TURN)
CAN I ASK YOU TO FILM THIS?
KA (FLASH)
NO...
IT'S NOT GOOD TO RELY ON ARTIFICIAL THINGS.
FOR A PRICELESS SCENE LIKE THIS, YOU NEED TO RECORD IT IN YOUR MIND.
AH, THAT'S SMART... AND I COULD PROBABLY LEARN FROM WATCHING THEM.
CAN YOU PLEASE WORRY ABOUT THEM A LITTLE!?

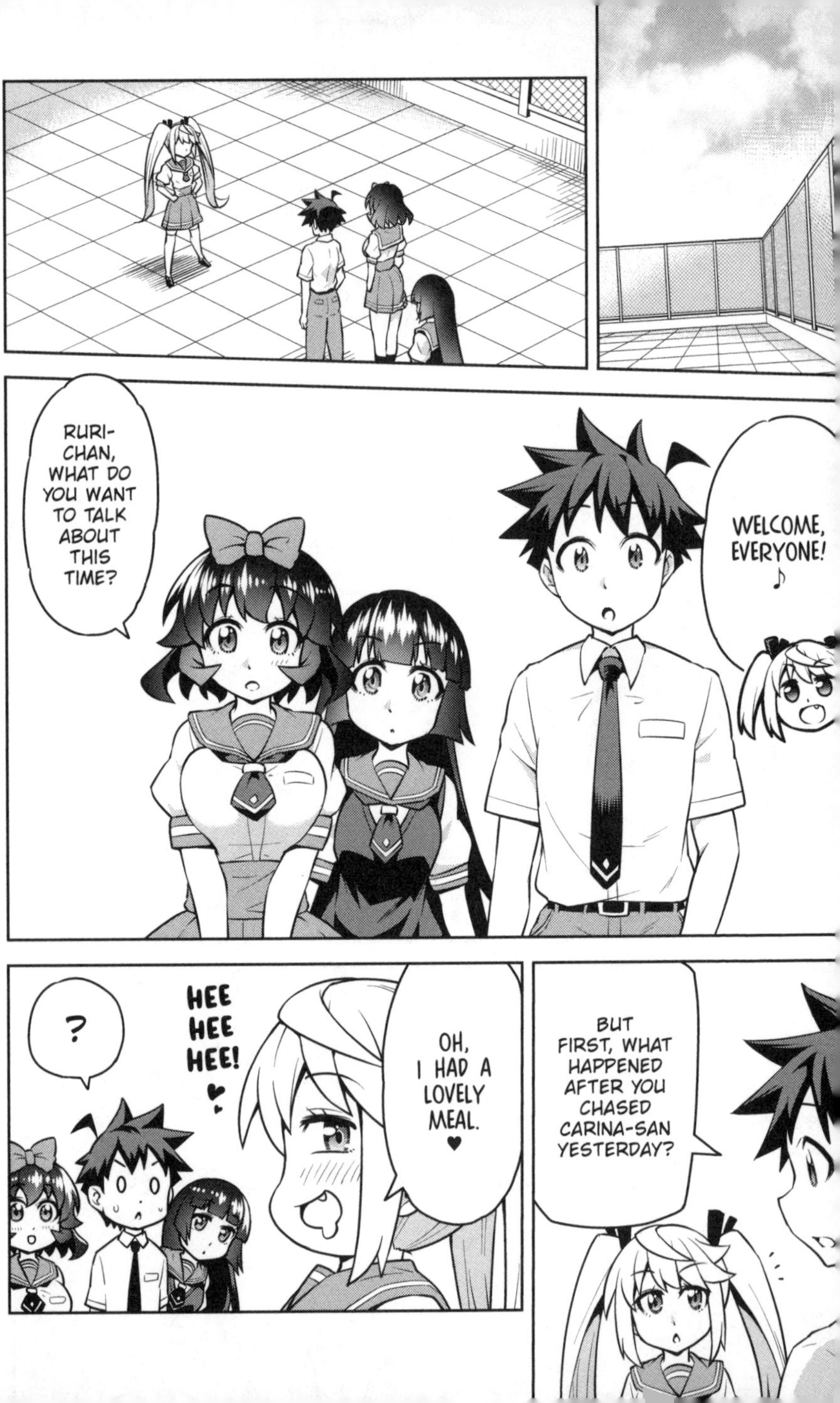
WELCOME, EVERYONE! ♪
RURI-CHAN, WHAT DO YOU WANT TO TALK ABOUT THIS TIME?
BUT FIRST, WHAT HAPPENED AFTER YOU CHASED CARINA-SAN YESTERDAY?
OH, I HAD A LOVELY MEAL. ♥
HEE HEE HEE! ♥
?

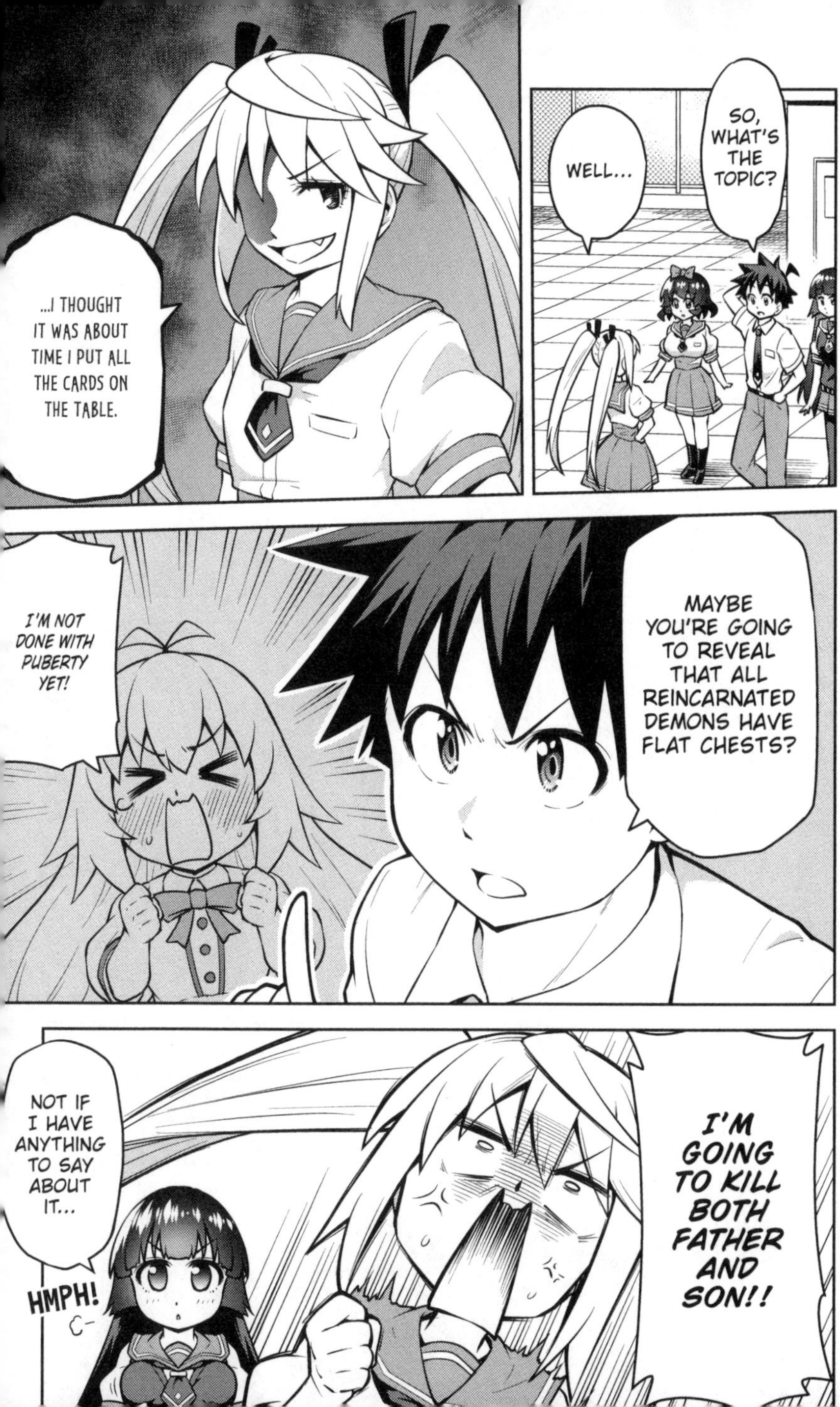
SO, WHAT'S THE TOPIC?
WELL...
...I THOUGHT IT WAS ABOUT TIME I PUT ALL THE CARDS ON THE TABLE.
MAYBE YOU'RE GOING TO REVEAL THAT ALL REINCARNATED DEMONS HAVE FLAT CHESTS?
I'M NOT DONE WITH PUBERTY YET!
I'M GOING TO KILL BOTH FATHER AND SON!!
NOT IF I HAVE ANYTHING TO SAY ABOUT IT...
HMPH!

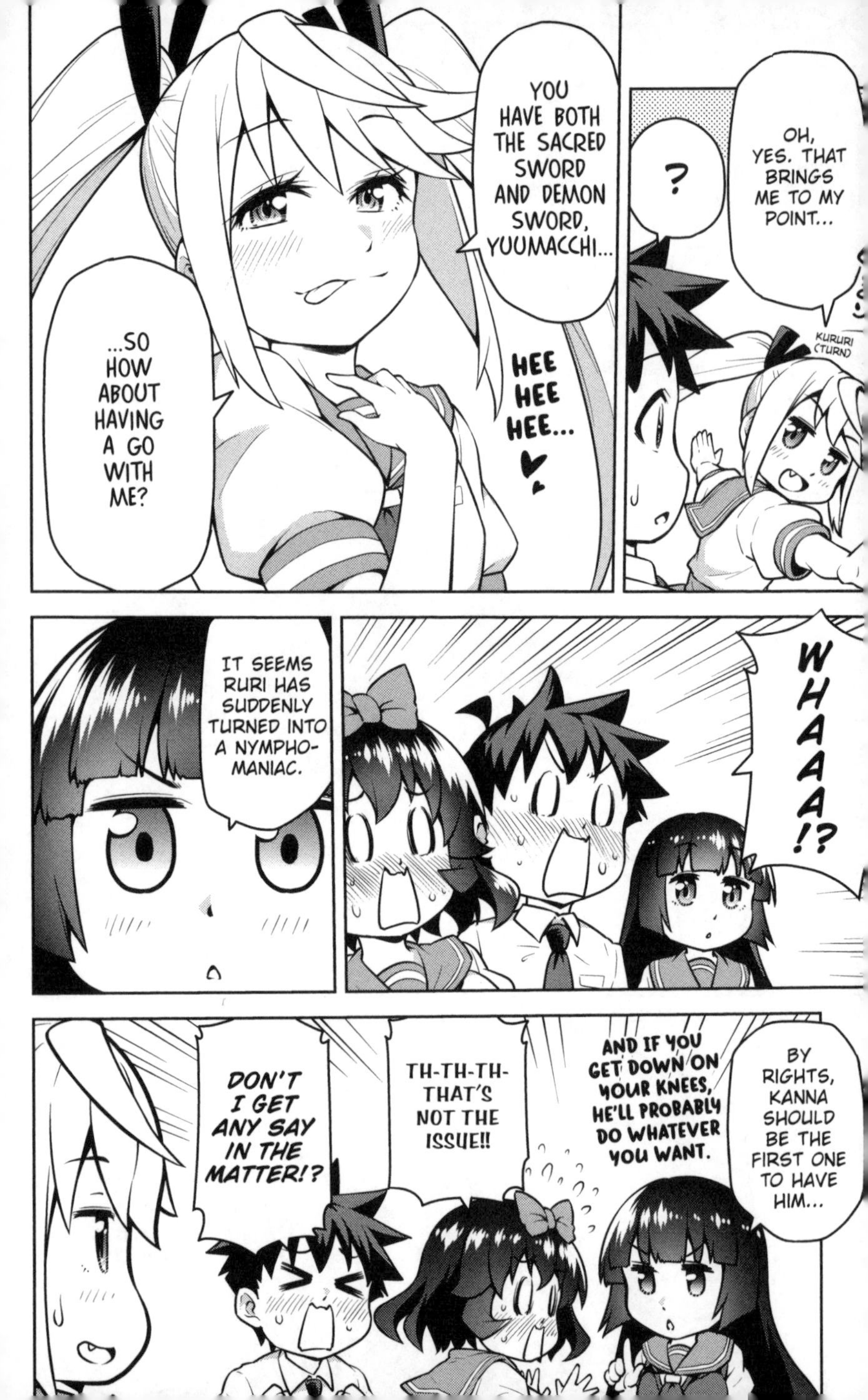
OH, YES. THAT BRINGS ME TO MY POINT...
?
KURURI (TURN)
YOU HAVE BOTH THE SACRED SWORD AND DEMON SWORD, YUUMACCHI...
HEE HEE HEE...
...SO HOW ABOUT HAVING A GO WITH ME?
WHAAAA!?
IT SEEMS RURI HAS SUDDENLY TURNED INTO A NYMPHO-MANIAC.
BY RIGHTS, KANNA SHOULD BE THE FIRST ONE TO HAVE HIM...
AND IF YOU GET DOWN ON YOUR KNEES, HE'LL PROBABLY DO WHATEVER YOU WANT.
TH-TH-TH-THAT'S NOT THE ISSUE!!
DON'T I GET ANY SAY IN THE MATTER!?

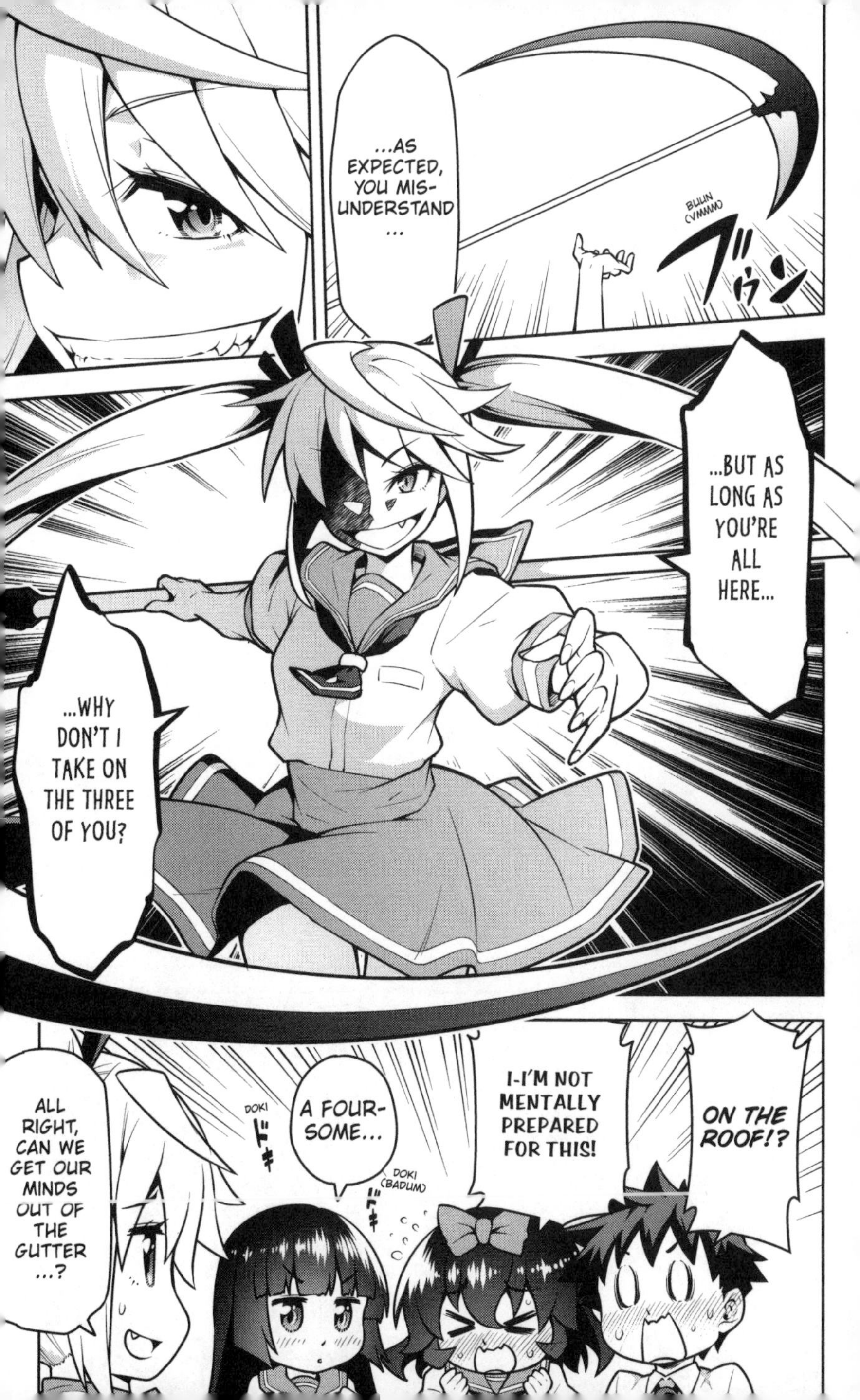
...AS EXPECTED, YOU MIS-UNDERSTAND...
BULUN (VMMM)
ブゥン
...BUT AS LONG AS YOU'RE ALL HERE...
...WHY DON'T I TAKE ON THE THREE OF YOU?
ON THE ROOF!?
I-I'M NOT MENTALLY PREPARED FOR THIS!
DOKI (BADUM)
ドキ
A FOUR-SOME...
DOKI
ドキ
ALL RIGHT, CAN WE GET OUR MINDS OUT OF THE GUTTER...?

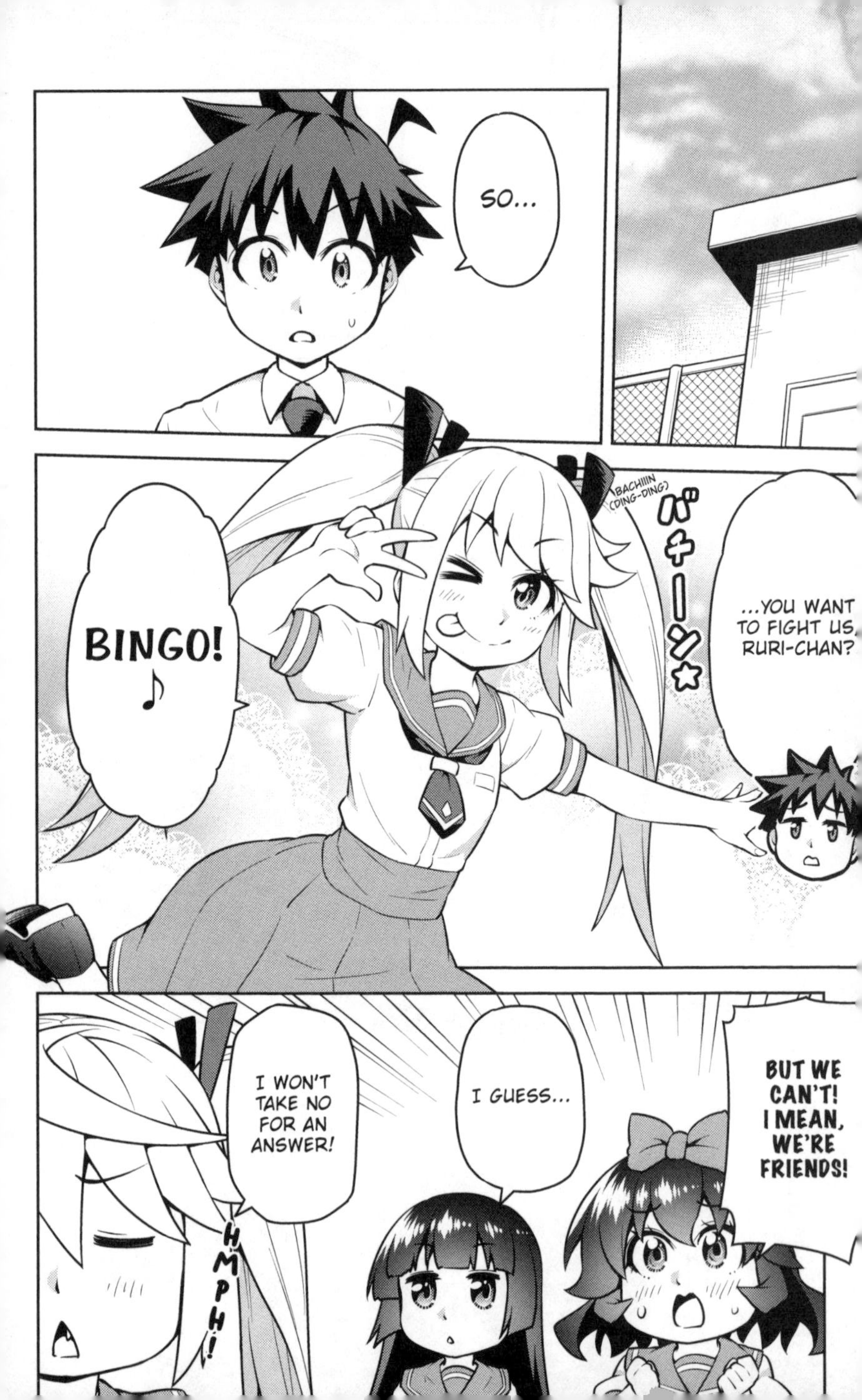
SO...
...YOU WANT TO FIGHT US, RURI-CHAN?
BACHIIN (DING-DING)
バチーン☆
BINGO! ♪
BUT WE CAN'T! I MEAN, WE'RE FRIENDS!
I GUESS...
I WON'T TAKE NO FOR AN ANSWER!
HMPH!

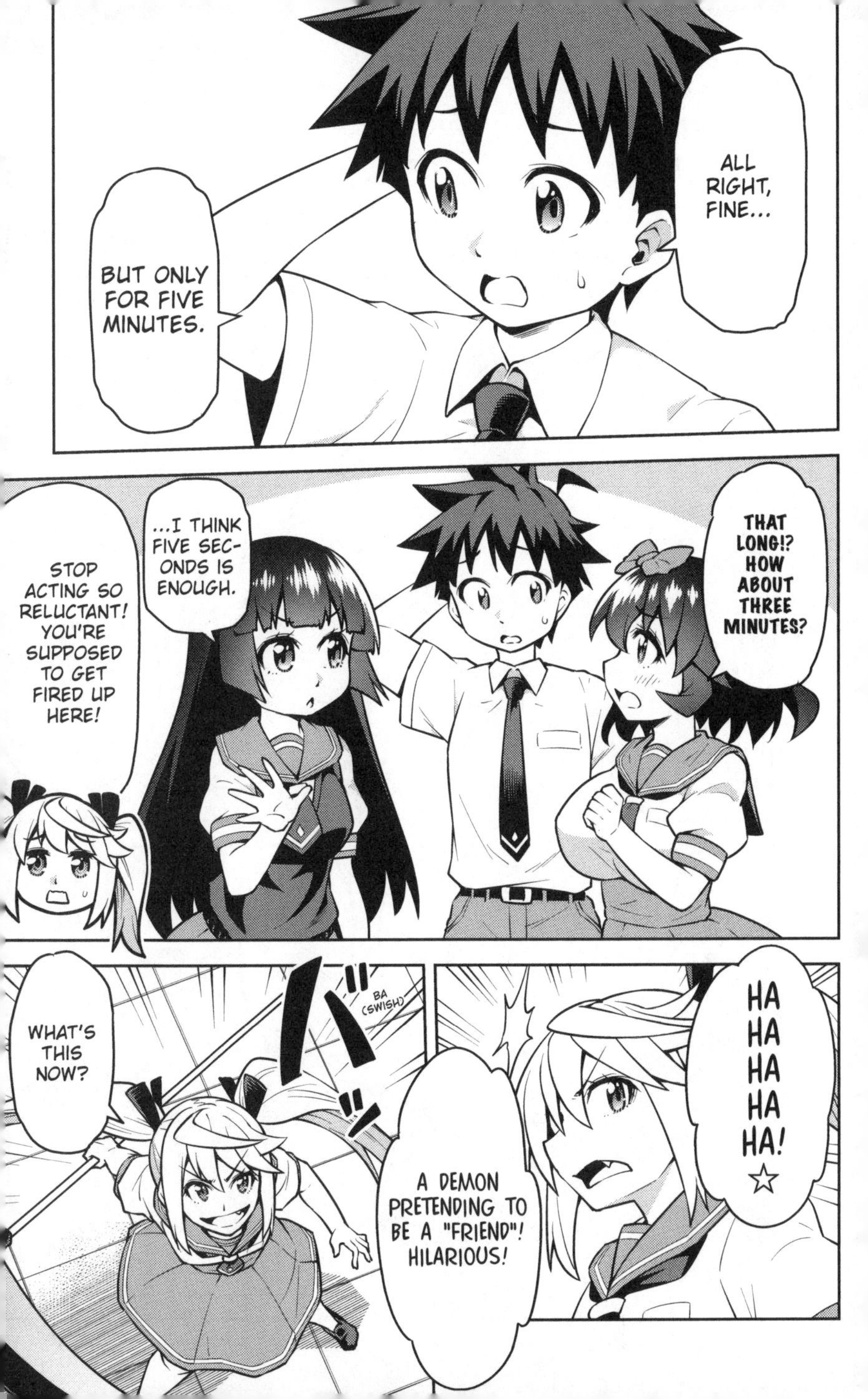
ALL RIGHT, FINE...
BUT ONLY FOR FIVE MINUTES.
THAT LONG!? HOW ABOUT THREE MINUTES?
...I THINK FIVE SEC-ONDS IS ENOUGH.
STOP ACTING SO RELUCTANT! YOU'RE SUPPOSED TO GET FIRED UP HERE!
HA HA HA HA HA! ☆
A DEMON PRETENDING TO BE A "FRIEND"! HILARIOUS!
BA (SWISH)
WHAT'S THIS NOW?

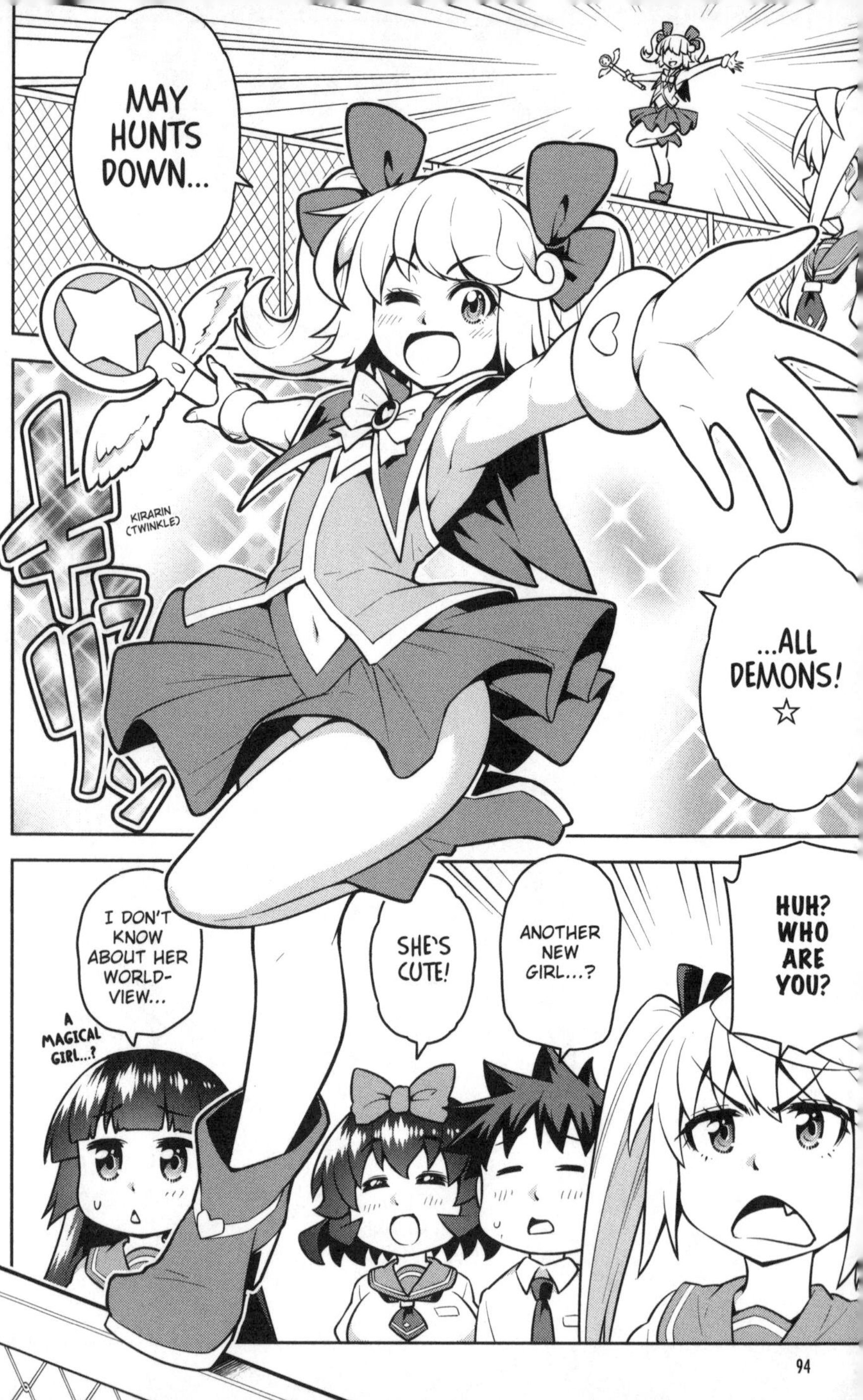
MAY HUNTS DOWN...
...ALL DEMONS! ☆
KIRARIN (TWINKLE)
HUH? WHO ARE YOU?
ANOTHER NEW GIRL...?
SHE'S CUTE!
I DON'T KNOW ABOUT HER WORLD-VIEW...
A MAGICAL GIRL...?

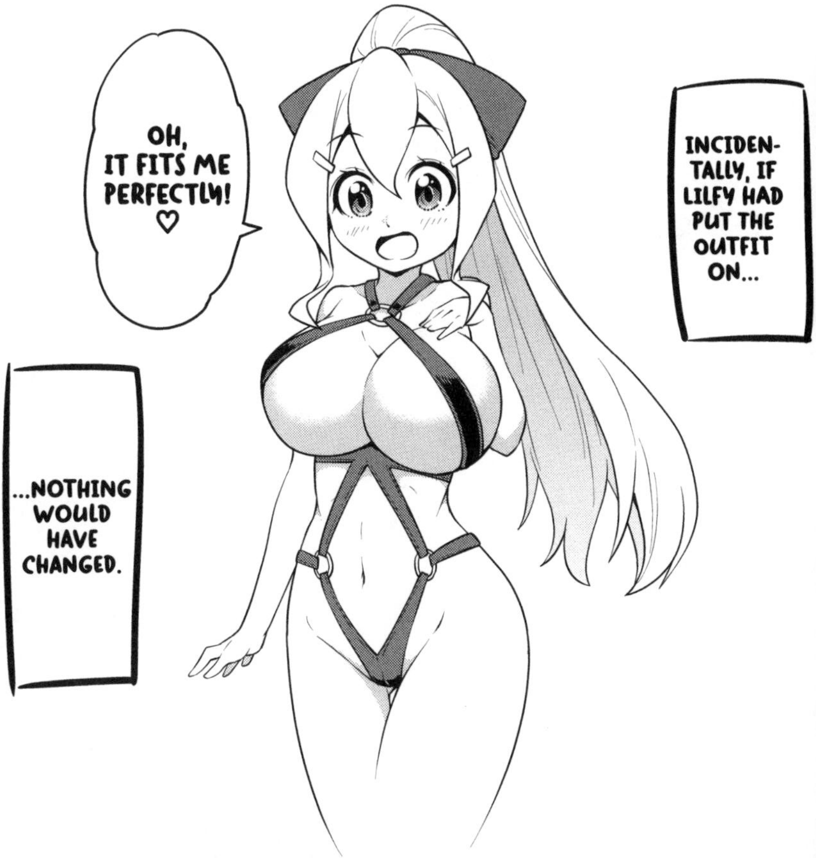
OH, IT FITS ME PERFECTLY! ♡
INCIDENTALLY, IF LILFY HAD PUT THE OUTFIT ON...
...NOTHING WOULD HAVE CHANGED.

I'm the HERO, but the DEMON LORD's Also Me

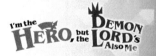

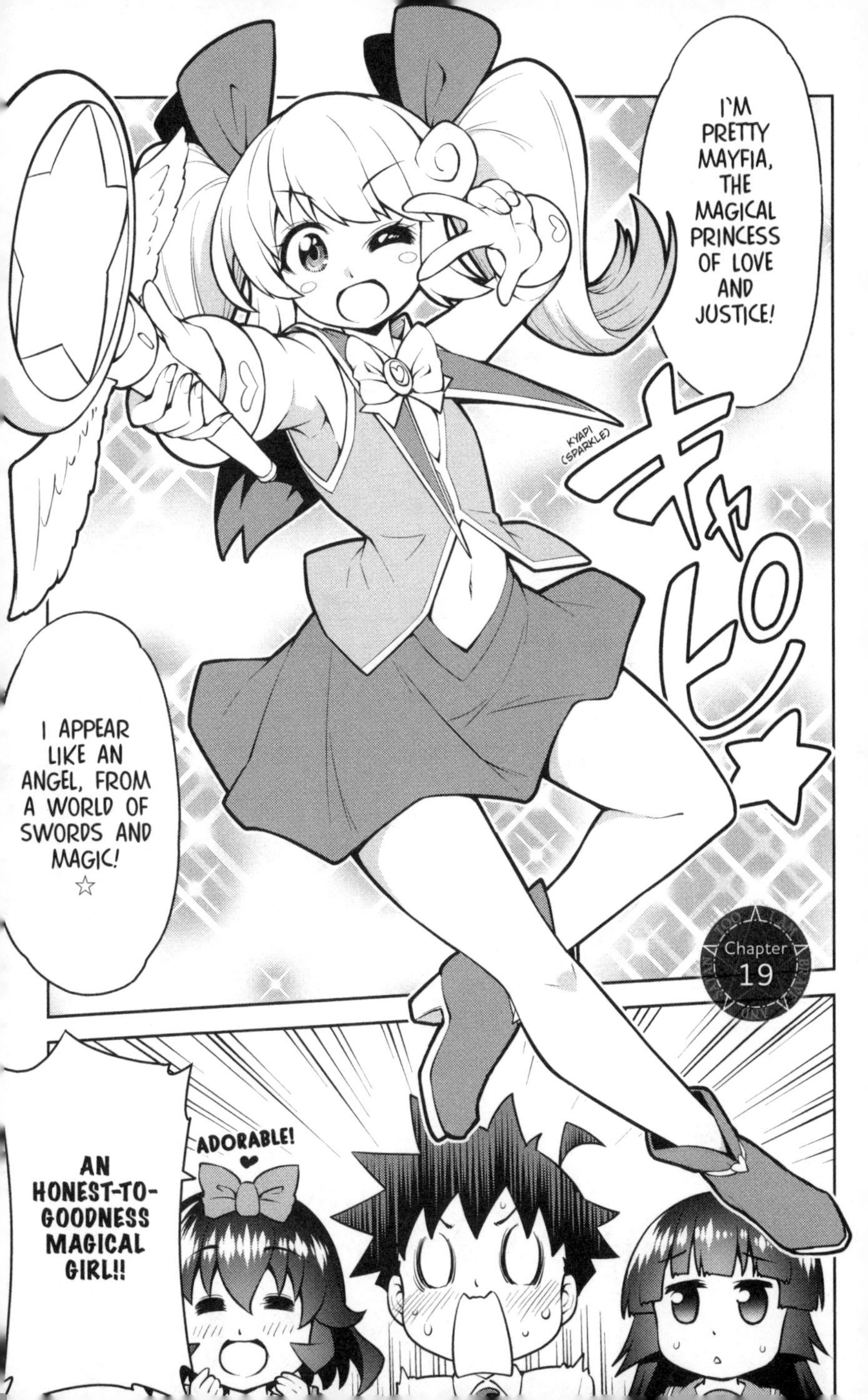
I'M PRETTY MAYFIA, THE MAGICAL PRINCESS OF LOVE AND JUSTICE!
KYAPI (SPARKLE)
I APPEAR LIKE AN ANGEL, FROM A WORLD OF SWORDS AND MAGIC! ☆
Chapter 19
ADORABLE! ♥
AN HONEST-TO-GOODNESS MAGICAL GIRL!!

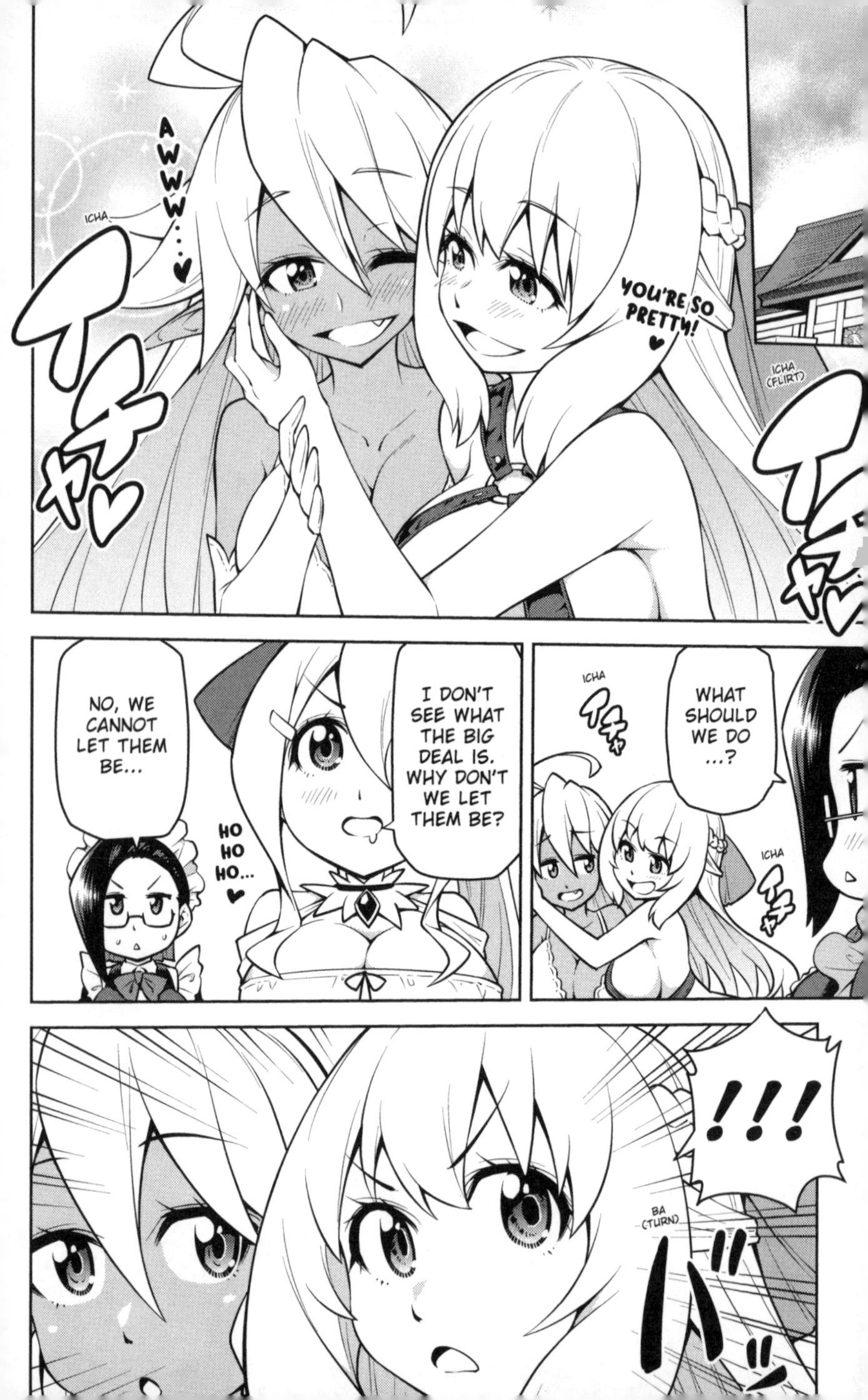

YOU'RE SO PRETTY! ♥
ICHA (FLIRT)
AWWW...♥
ICHA
WHAT SHOULD WE DO ...?
ICHA
ICHA
I DON'T SEE WHAT THE BIG DEAL IS. WHY DON'T WE LET THEM BE?
HO HO HO...♥
NO, WE CANNOT LET THEM BE...
!!!
BA (TURN)

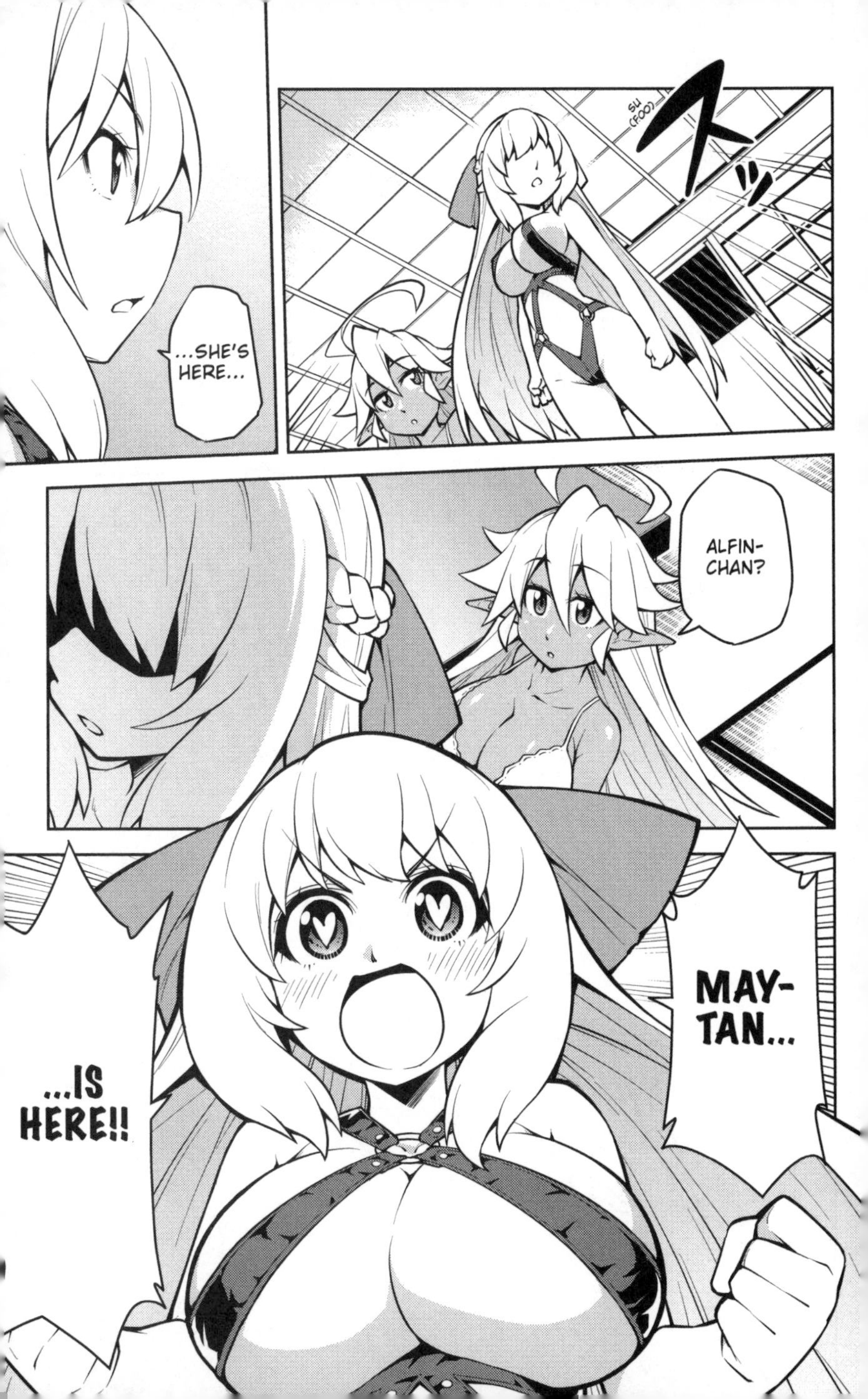
SU (FOO)
...SHE'S HERE...
ALFIN-CHAN?
MAY-TAN...
...IS HERE!!

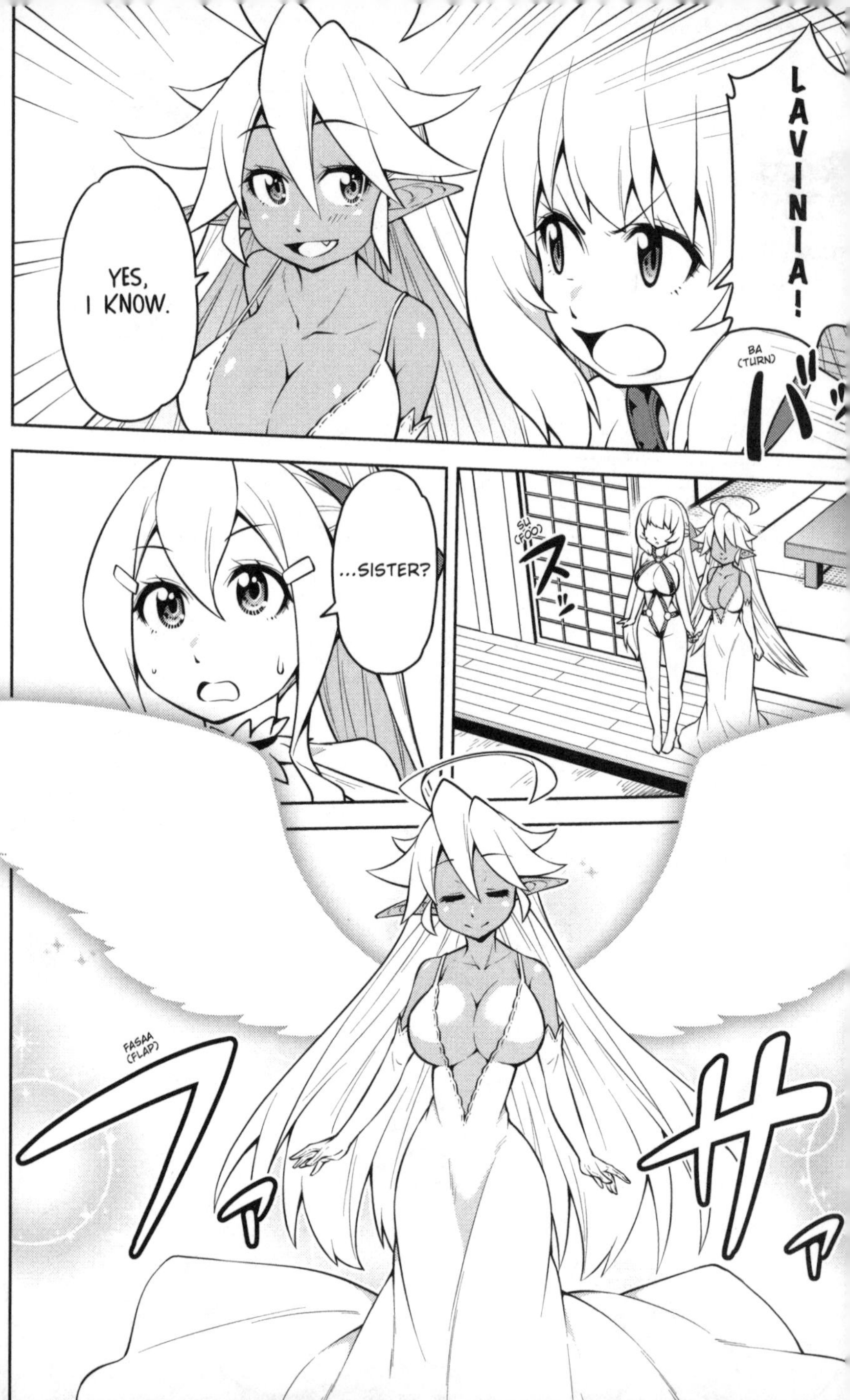
LAVINIA!
BA (TURN)
YES, I KNOW.
SU (FOO)
...SISTER?
FASAA (FLAP)

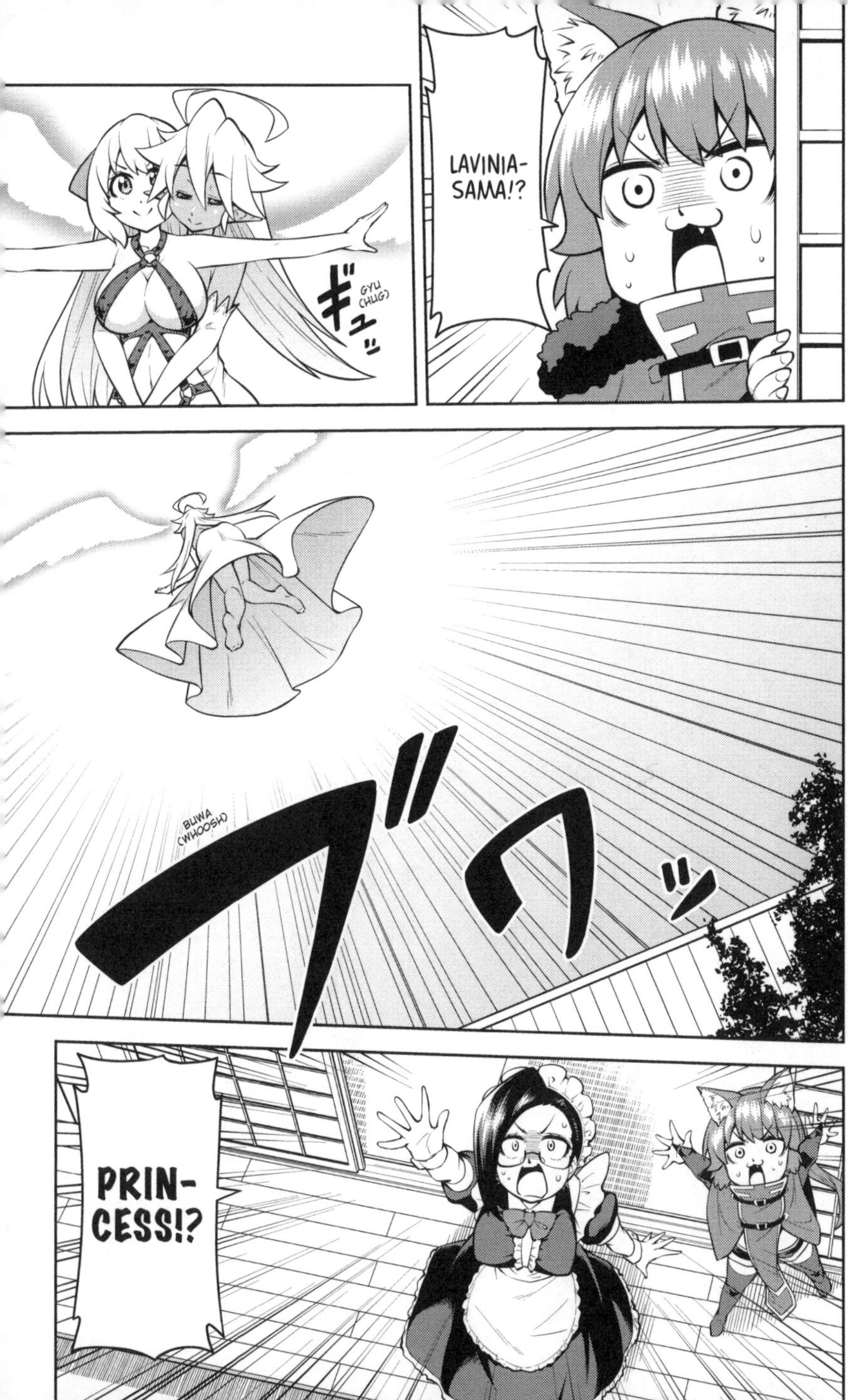
LAVINIA-SAMA!?
ギュッ
GYU (HUG)
ブワッ
BUWA (WHOOSH)
PRIN-CESS!?

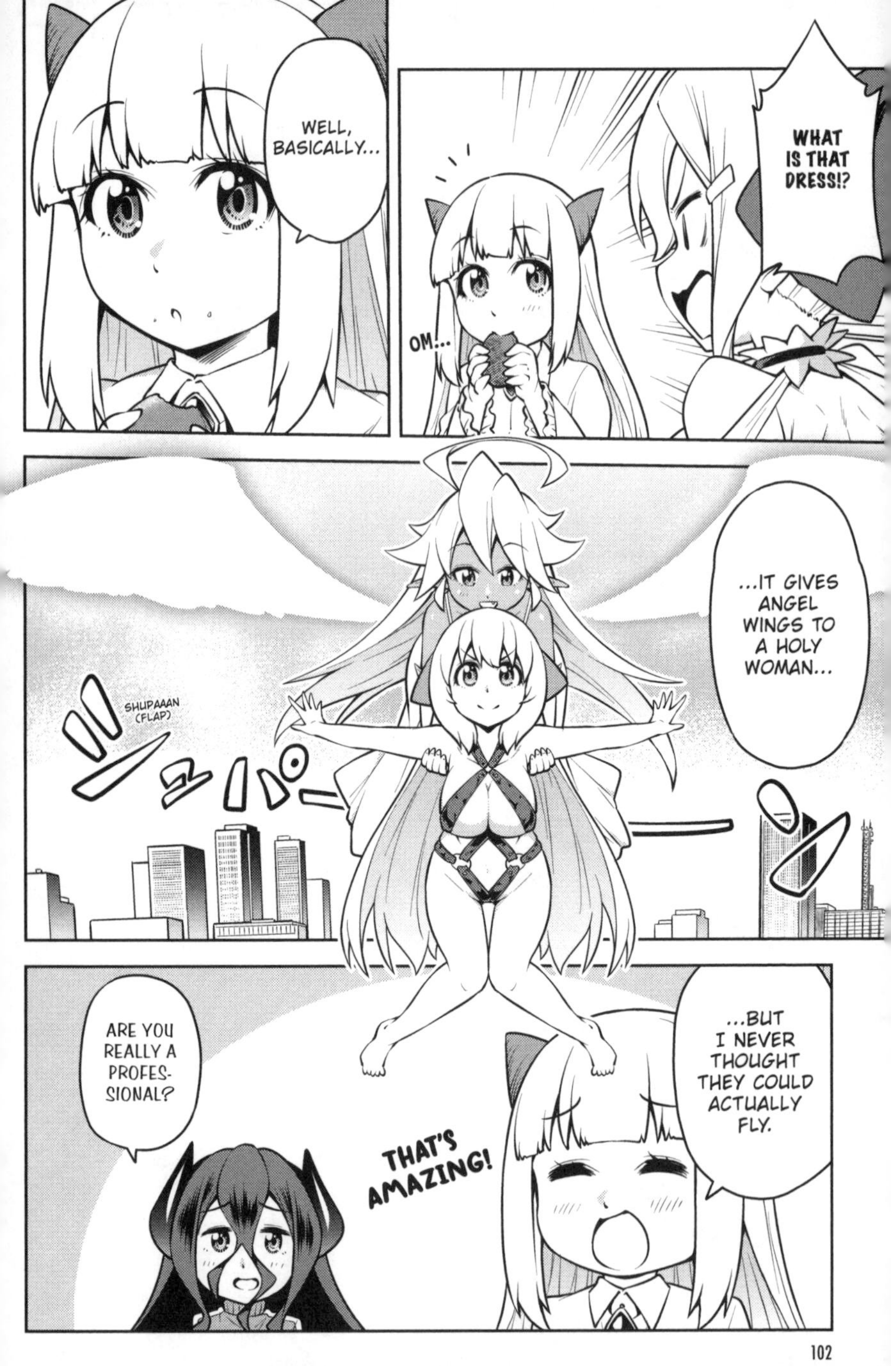

WHAT IS THAT DRESS!?
OM...
WELL, BASICALLY...
...IT GIVES ANGEL WINGS TO A HOLY WOMAN...
シュパーン
SHUPAAAN (FLAP)
...BUT I NEVER THOUGHT THEY COULD ACTUALLY FLY.
THAT'S AMAZING!
ARE YOU REALLY A PROFES-SIONAL?

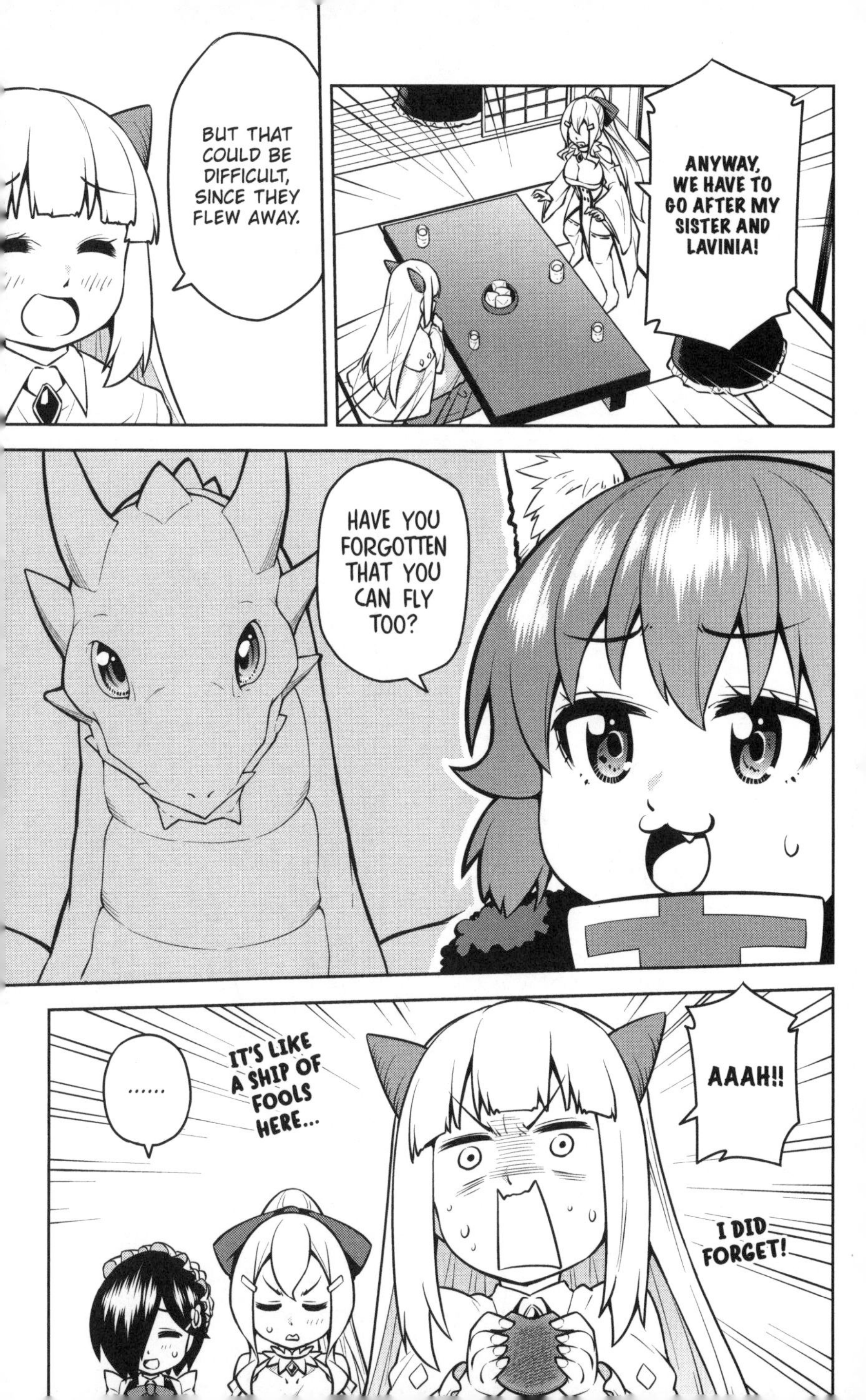
ANYWAY, WE HAVE TO GO AFTER MY SISTER AND LAVINIA!
BUT THAT COULD BE DIFFICULT, SINCE THEY FLEW AWAY.
HAVE YOU FORGOTTEN THAT YOU CAN FLY TOO?
AAAH!!
I DID FORGET!
IT'S LIKE A SHIP OF FOOLS HERE...
......

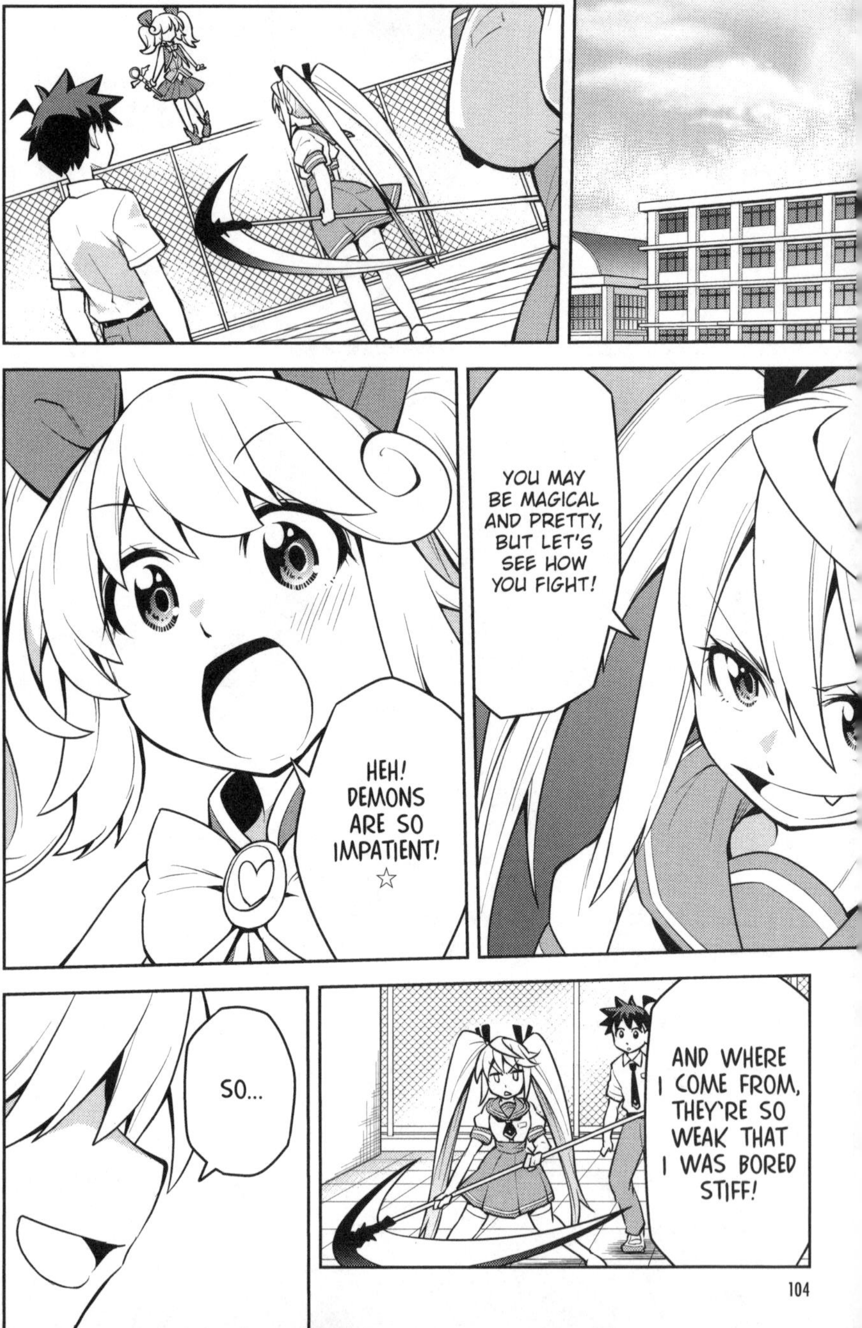
YOU MAY BE MAGICAL AND PRETTY, BUT LET'S SEE HOW YOU FIGHT!
HEH! DEMONS ARE SO IMPATIENT! ☆
AND WHERE I COME FROM, THEY'RE SO WEAK THAT I WAS BORED STIFF!
SO...

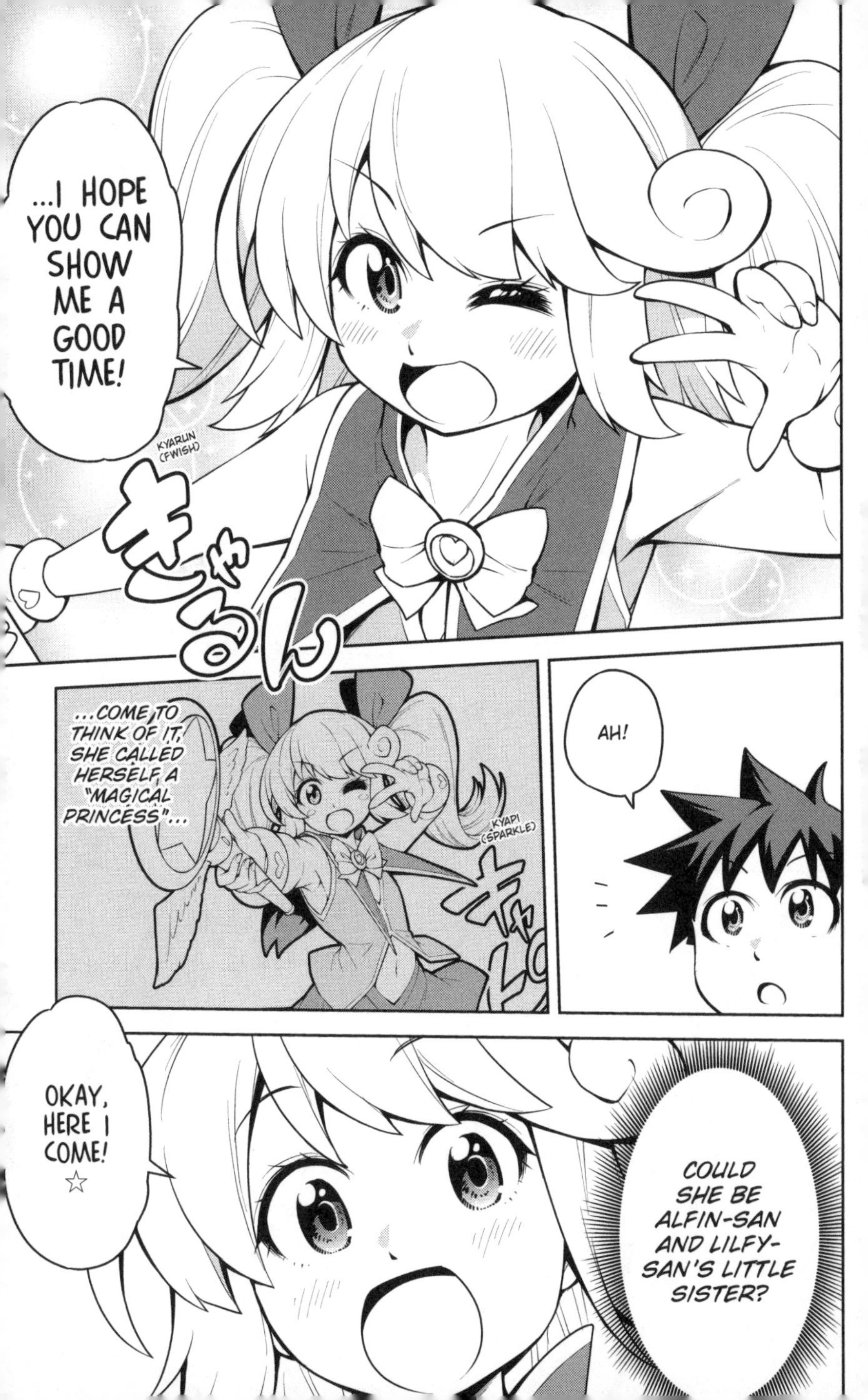
...I HOPE YOU CAN SHOW ME A GOOD TIME!
KYARUN (FWISH)
きゃるん
AH!
...COME TO THINK OF IT, SHE CALLED HERSELF A "MAGICAL PRINCESS"...
KYAPI (SPARKLE)
COULD SHE BE ALFIN-SAN AND LILFY-SAN'S LITTLE SISTER?
OKAY, HERE I COME! ☆

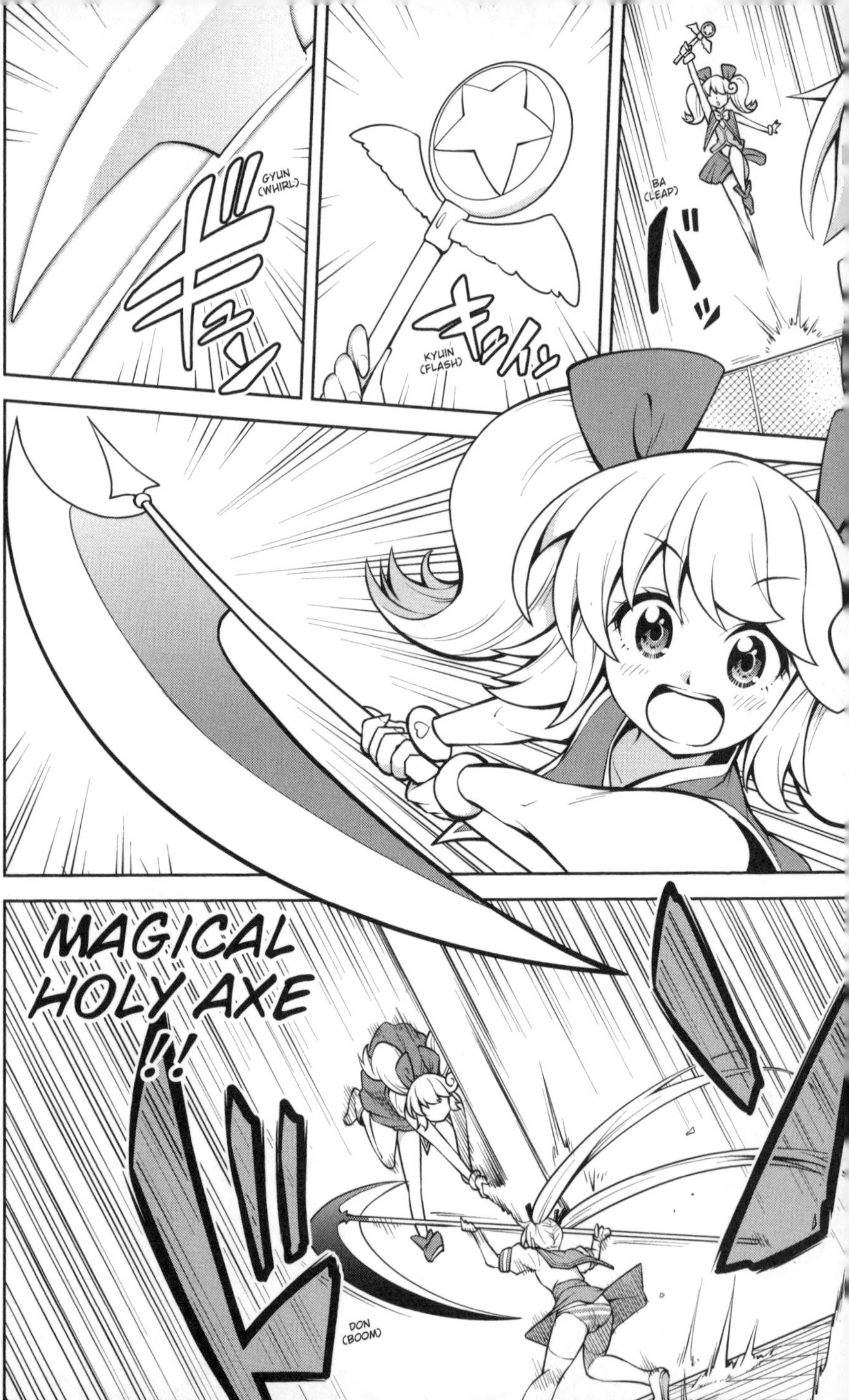
BA
(LEAP)
KYUIN
(FLASH)
GYUN
(WHIRL)
MAGICAL HOLY AXE!!
DON
(BOOM)

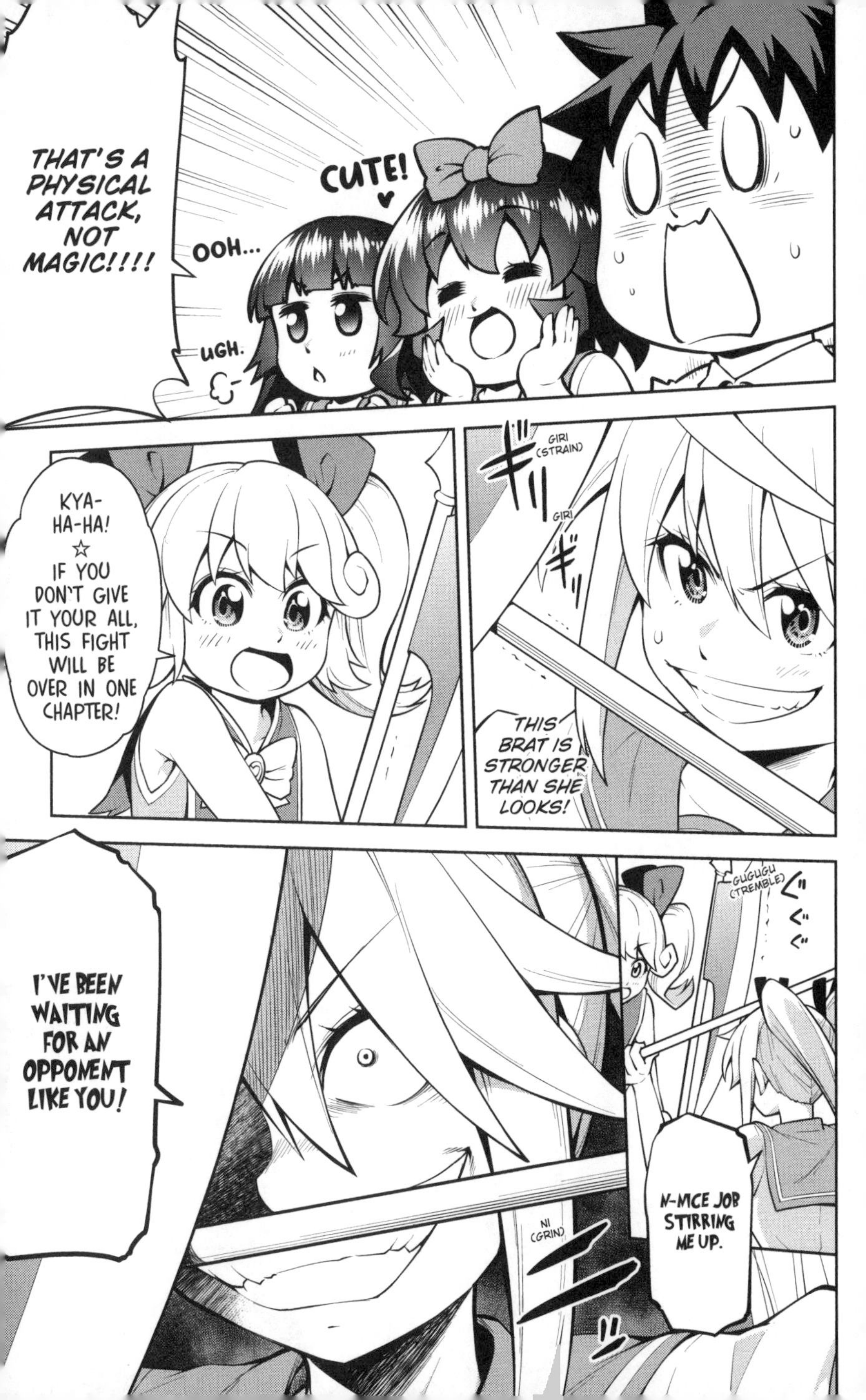
CUTE! ♥
OOH...
THAT'S A PHYSICAL ATTACK, NOT MAGIC!!!!
UGH.
GIRI (STRAIN)
GIRI
THIS BRAT IS STRONGER THAN SHE LOOKS!
KYA-HA-HA! ☆ IF YOU DON'T GIVE IT YOUR ALL, THIS FIGHT WILL BE OVER IN ONE CHAPTER!
GUGUGU (TREMBLE)
N-NICE JOB STIRRING ME UP.
NI (GRIN)
I'VE BEEN WAITING FOR AN OPPONENT LIKE YOU!

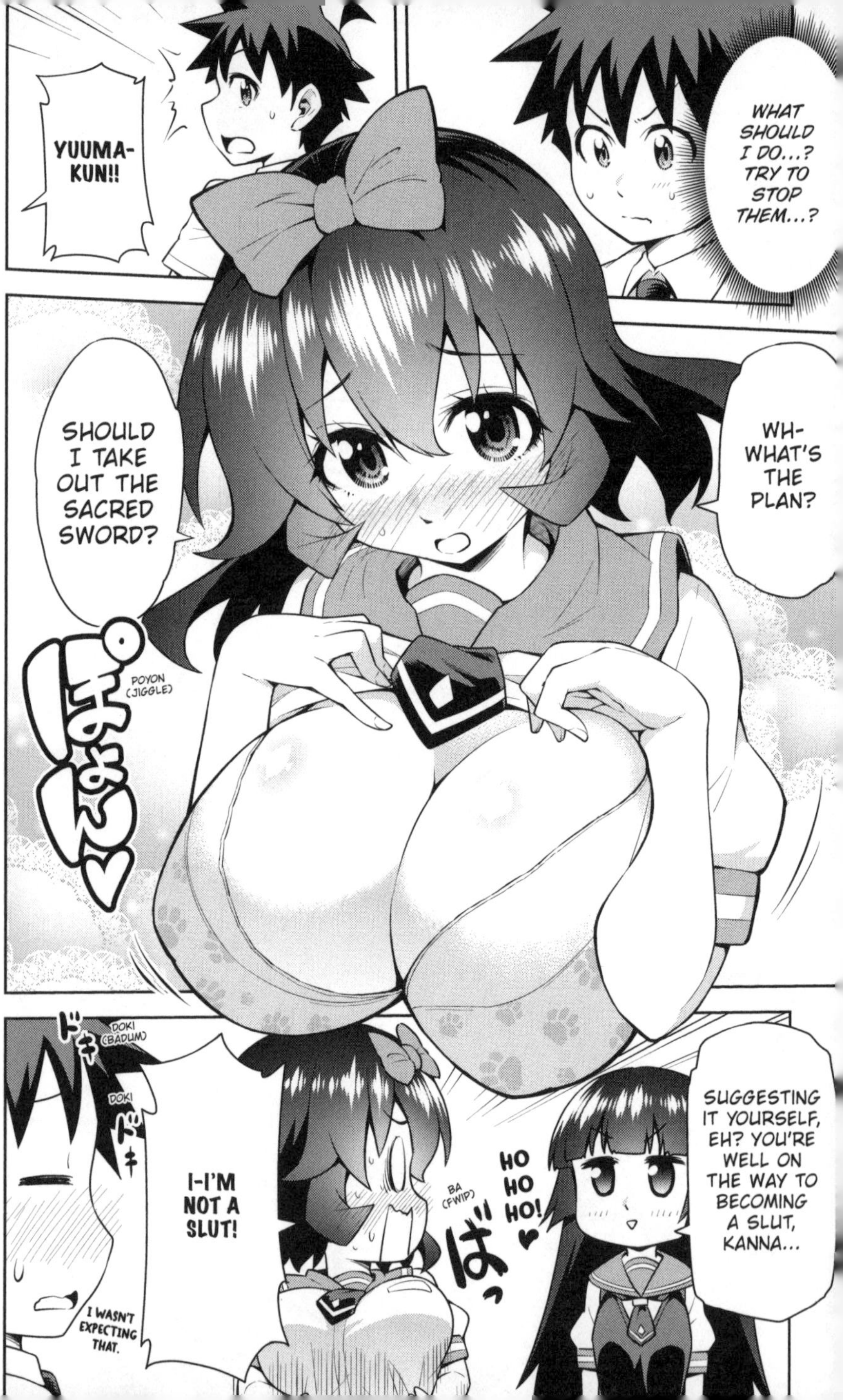
WHAT SHOULD I DO...? TRY TO STOP THEM...?
YUUMA-KUN!!
WH-WHAT'S THE PLAN?
SHOULD I TAKE OUT THE SACRED SWORD?
ぽよん
POYON (JIGGLE)
SUGGESTING IT YOURSELF, EH? YOU'RE WELL ON THE WAY TO BECOMING A SLUT, KANNA...
HO HO HO!
ばっ
BA (FWIP)
I-I'M NOT A SLUT!
ドキ
DOKI (BADUM)
ドキ
DOKI
I WASN'T EXPECTING THAT.

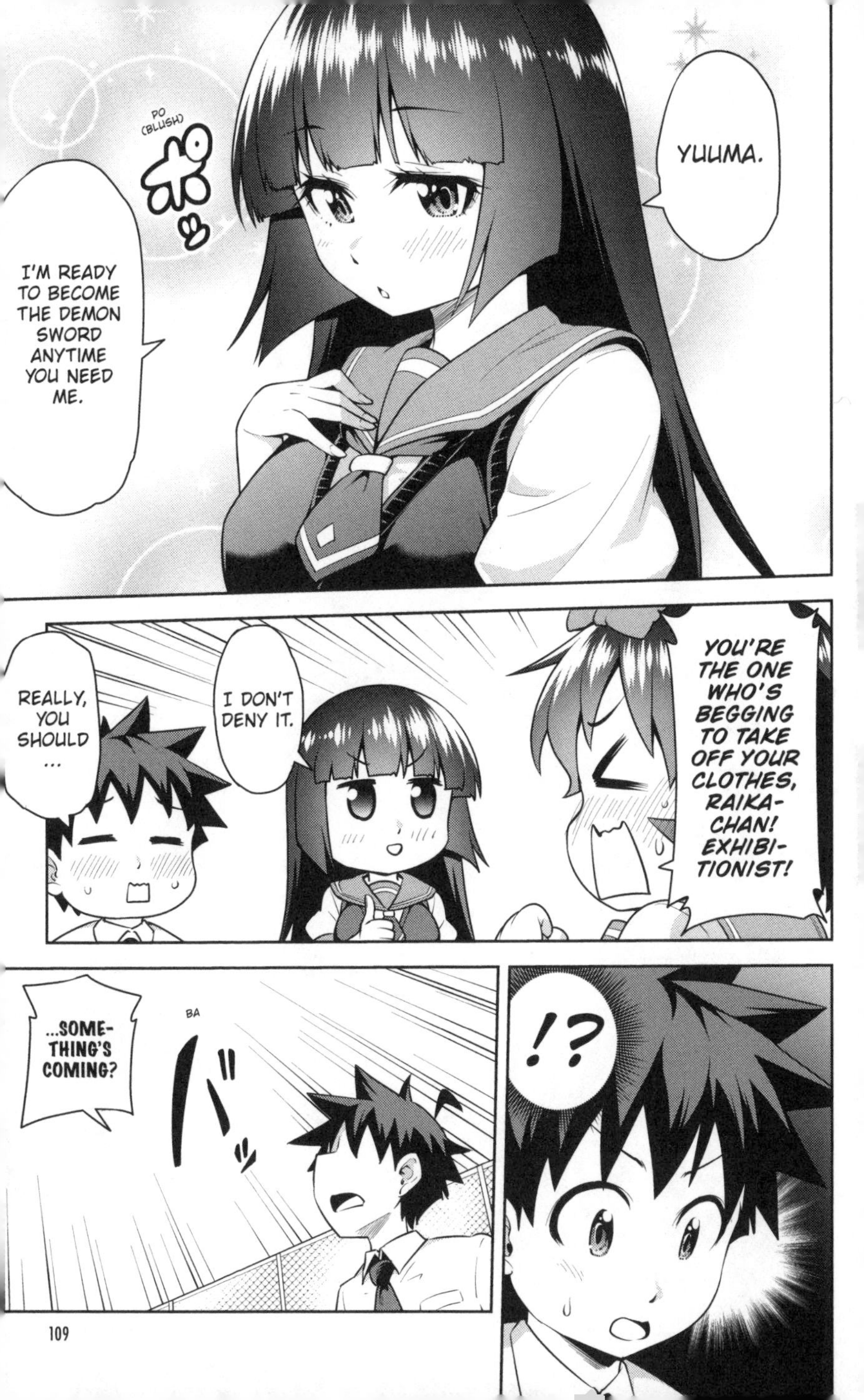
YUUMA.
PO (BLUSH)
I'M READY TO BECOME THE DEMON SWORD ANYTIME YOU NEED ME.
YOU'RE THE ONE WHO'S BEGGING TO TAKE OFF YOUR CLOTHES, RAIKA-CHAN! EXHIBITIONIST!
I DON'T DENY IT.
REALLY, YOU SHOULD ...
!?
BA
...SOMETHING'S COMING?

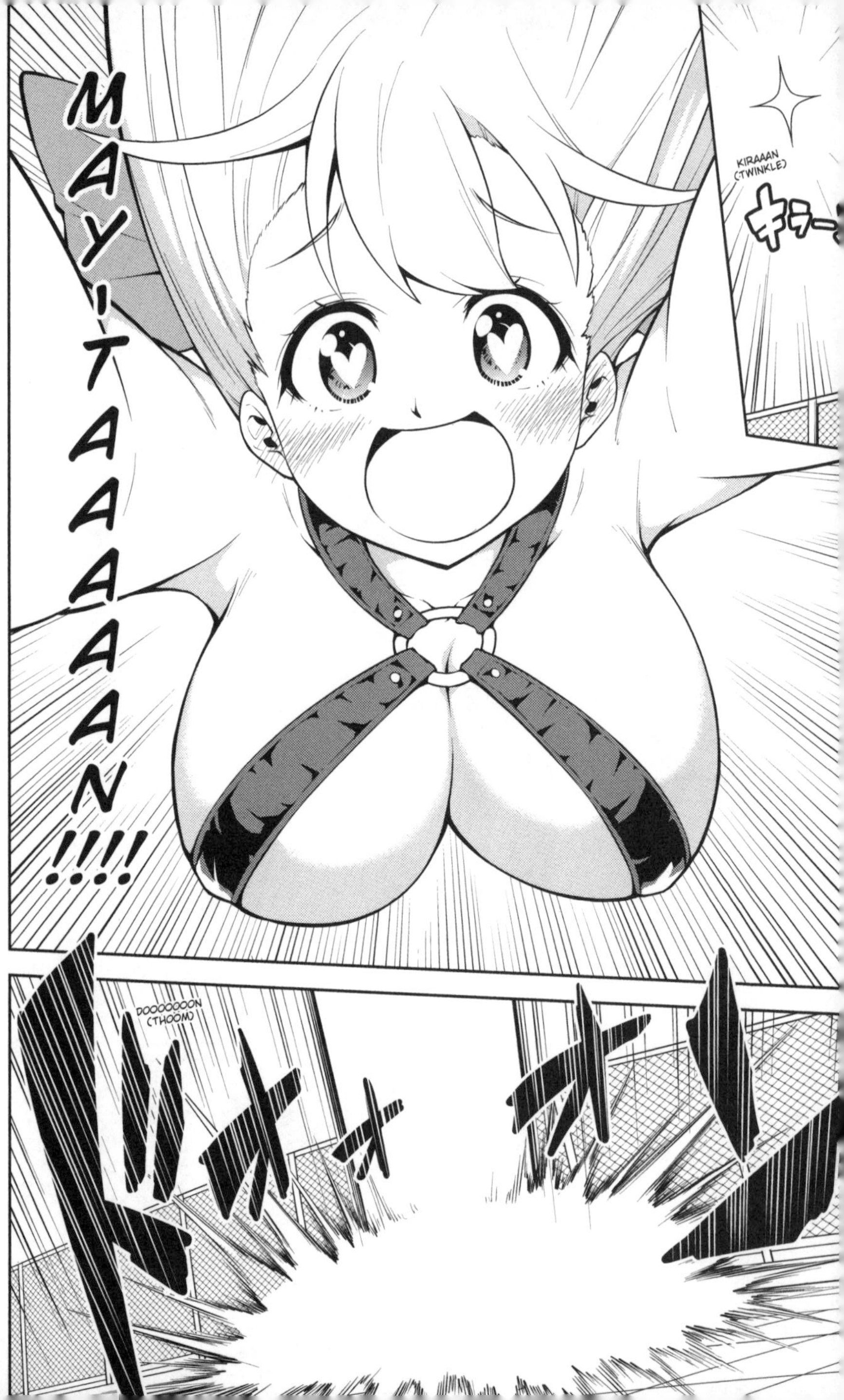
KIRAAAN (TWINKLE)
MAY-TAAAAAN!!!!
DOOOOOOON (THOOM)

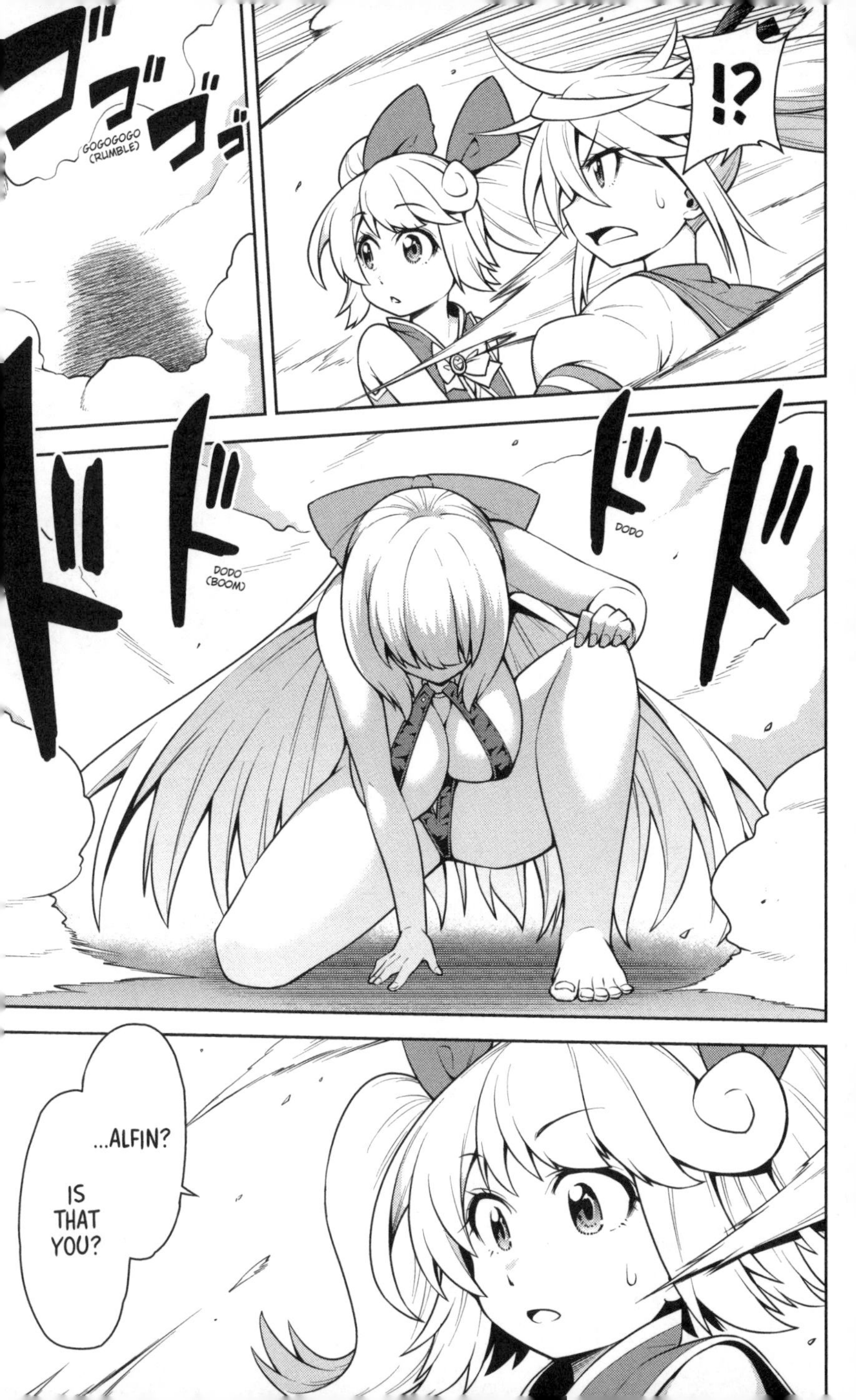
!?
GOGOGOGO (RUMBLE)
DODO
DODO (BOOM)
...ALFIN?
IS THAT YOU?

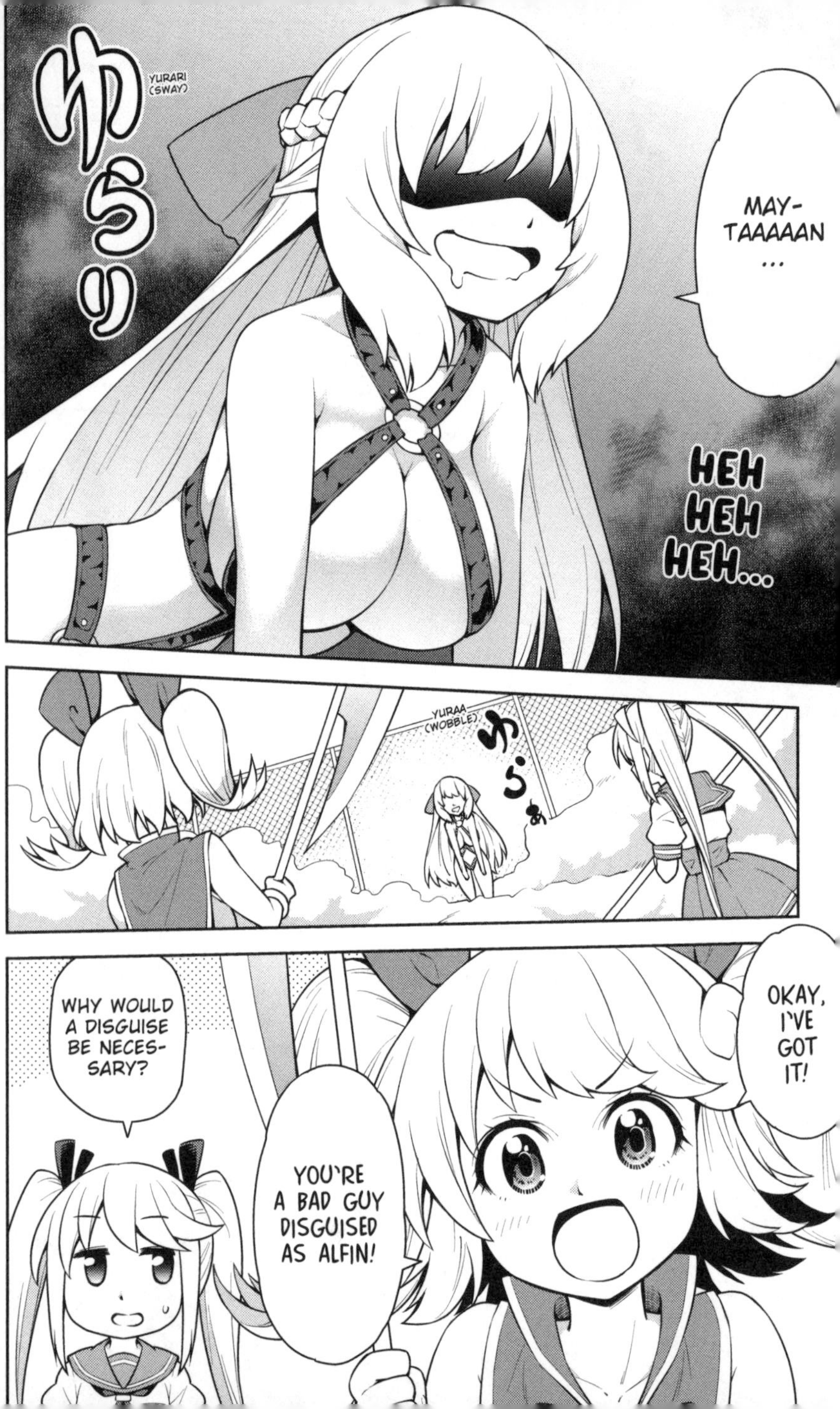
MAY-TAAAAAN...
HEH HEH HEH...
ゆらり
YURARI (SWAY)
ゆらぁ
YURAA (WOBBLE)
OKAY, I'VE GOT IT!
YOU'RE A BAD GUY DISGUISED AS ALFIN!
WHY WOULD A DISGUISE BE NECES-SARY?

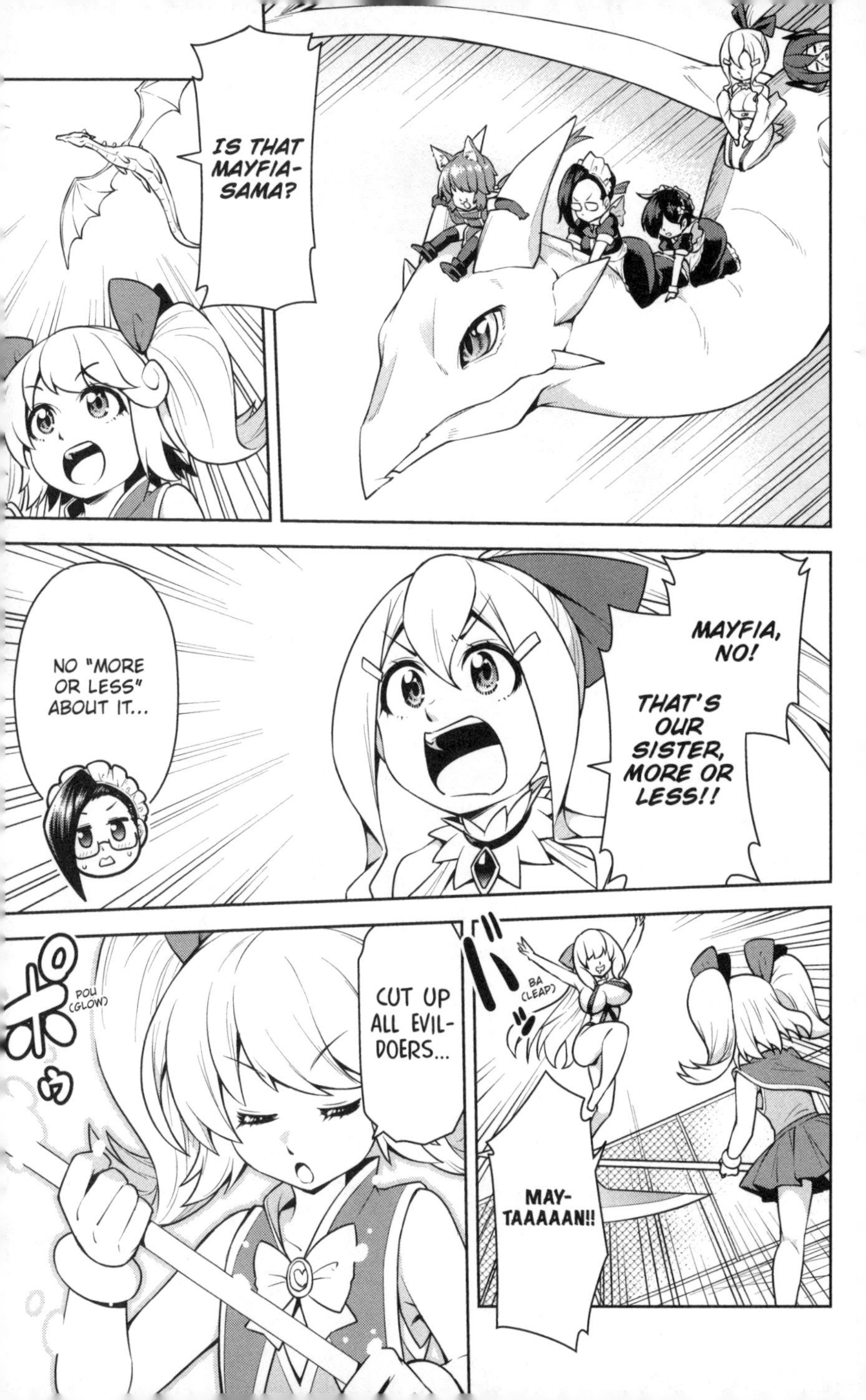
IS THAT MAYFIA-SAMA?
MAYFIA, NO!
THAT'S OUR SISTER, MORE OR LESS!!
NO "MORE OR LESS" ABOUT IT...
BA (LEAP)
MAY-TAAAAAN!!
CUT UP ALL EVIL-DOERS...
POU (GLOW)

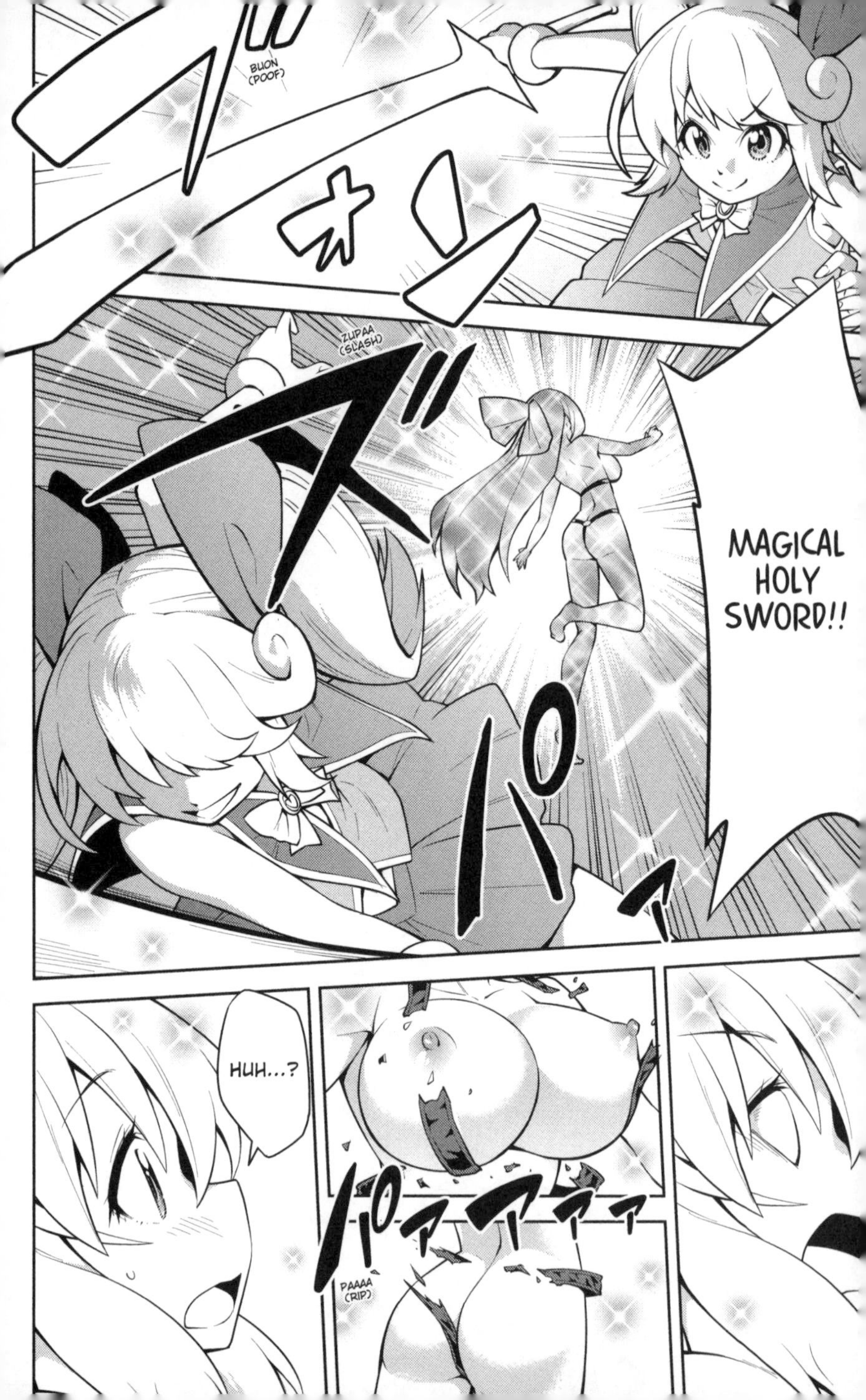
BUON (POOF)
ZUPAA (SLASH)
MAGICAL HOLY SWORD!!
PAAAA (RIP)
HUH...?

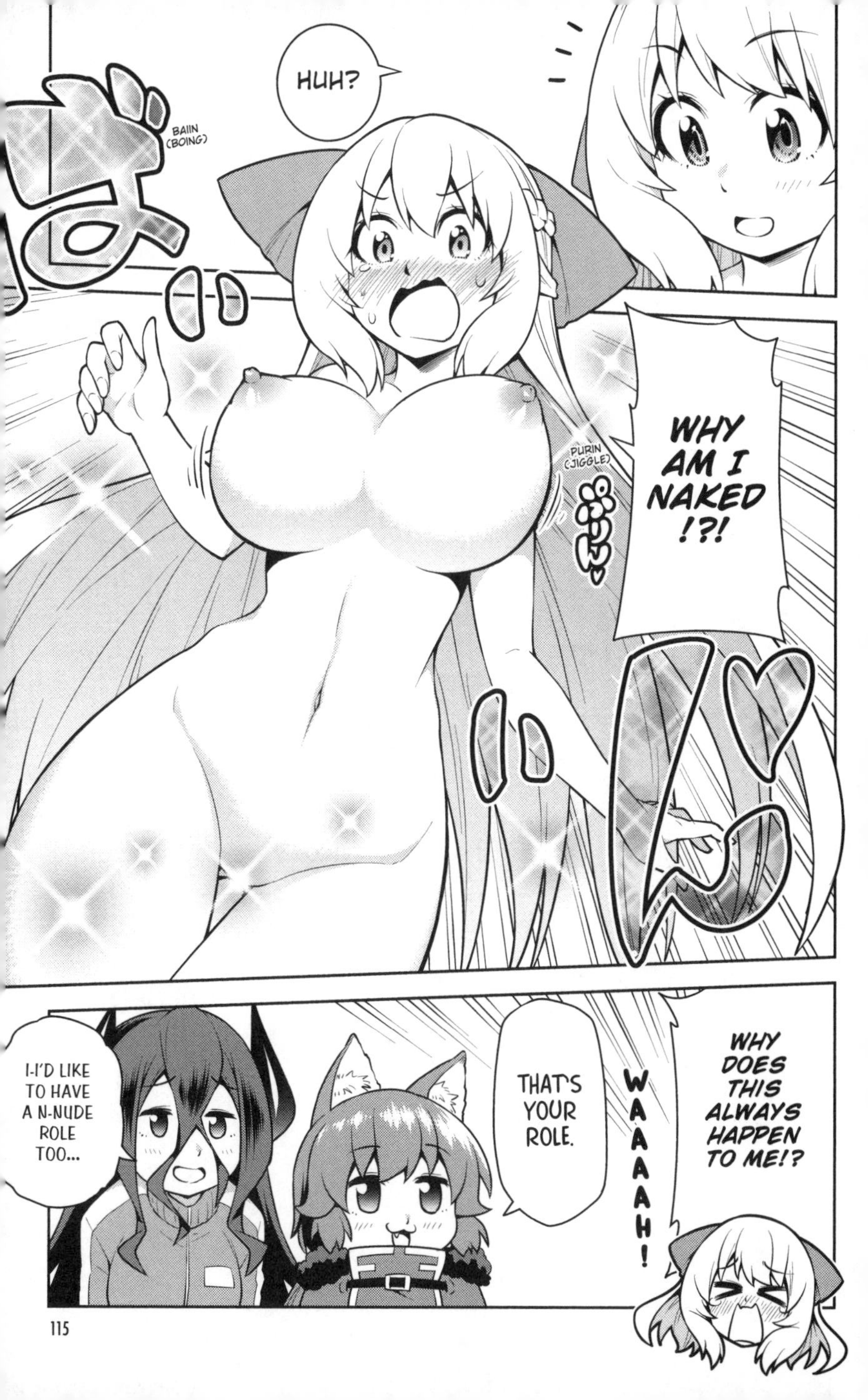
HUH?
BAIIN (BOING)
WHY AM I NAKED !?!
PURIN (JIGGLE)
WHY DOES THIS ALWAYS HAPPEN TO ME!?
WAAAAAH!
THAT'S YOUR ROLE.
I-I'D LIKE TO HAVE A N-NUDE ROLE TOO...

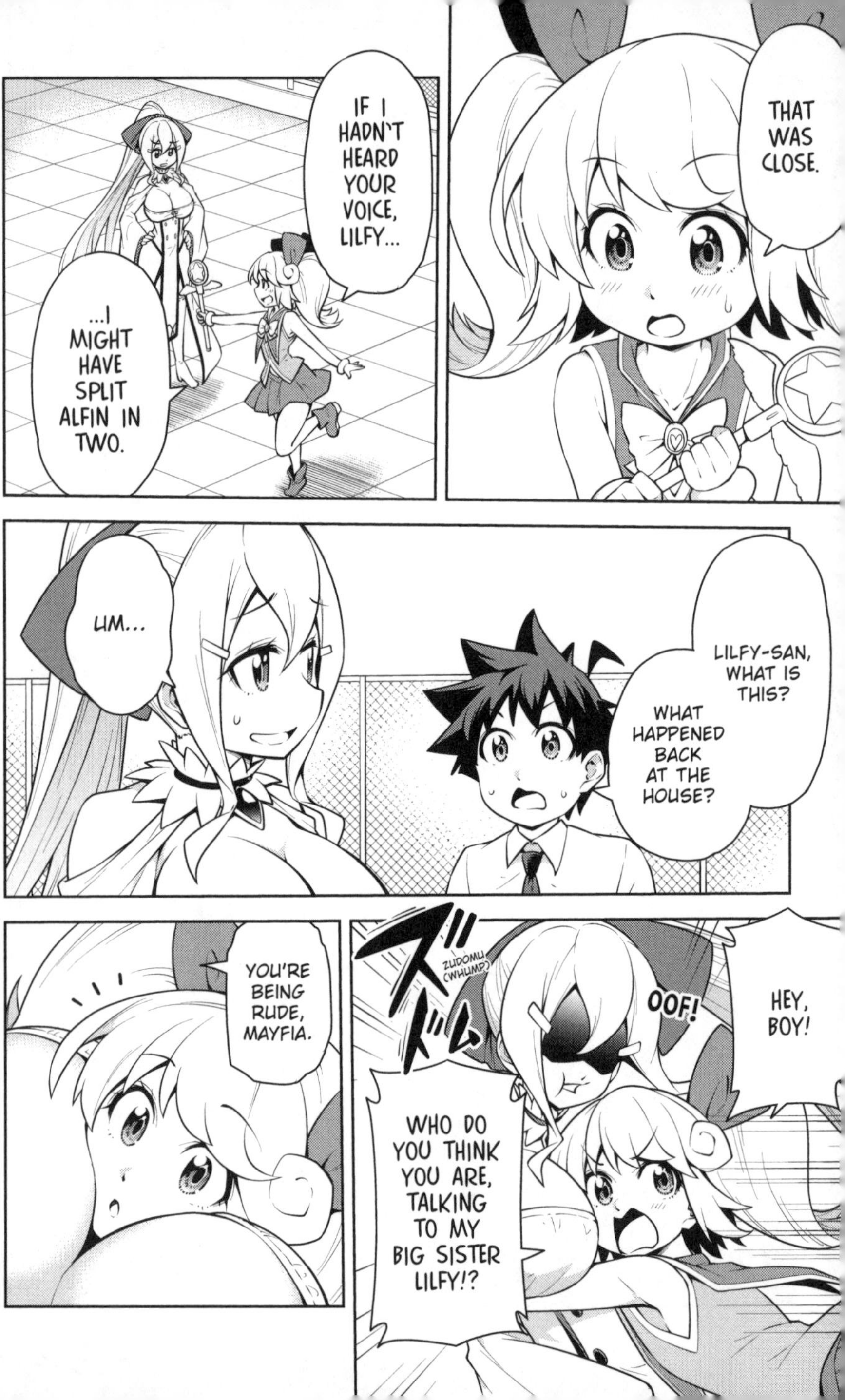
THAT WAS CLOSE.
IF I HADN'T HEARD YOUR VOICE, LILFY...
...I MIGHT HAVE SPLIT ALFIN IN TWO.
LILFY-SAN, WHAT IS THIS?
WHAT HAPPENED BACK AT THE HOUSE?
UM...
HEY, BOY!
OOF!
ZUDOMU (WHUMP)
WHO DO YOU THINK YOU ARE, TALKING TO MY BIG SISTER LILFY!?
YOU'RE BEING RUDE, MAYFIA.

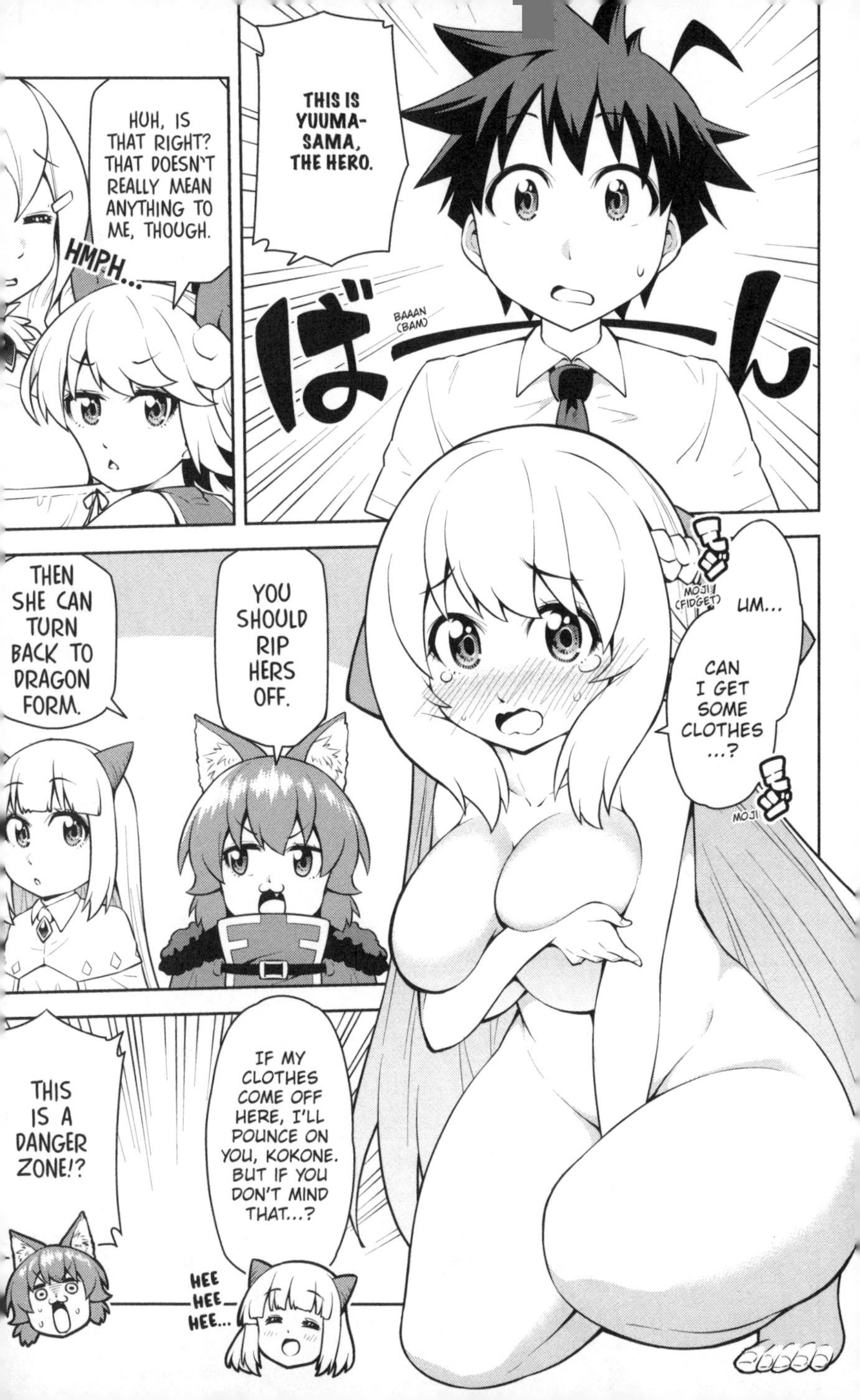
THIS IS YUUMA-SAMA, THE HERO.
ばーん
BAAAN (BAM)
HUH, IS THAT RIGHT? THAT DOESN'T REALLY MEAN ANYTHING TO ME, THOUGH.
HMPH...
MOJI (FIDGET)
UM...
CAN I GET SOME CLOTHES ...?
MOJI
YOU SHOULD RIP HERS OFF.
THEN SHE CAN TURN BACK TO DRAGON FORM.
IF MY CLOTHES COME OFF HERE, I'LL POUNCE ON YOU, KOKONE. BUT IF YOU DON'T MIND THAT...?
HEE HEE HEE...
THIS IS A DANGER ZONE!?

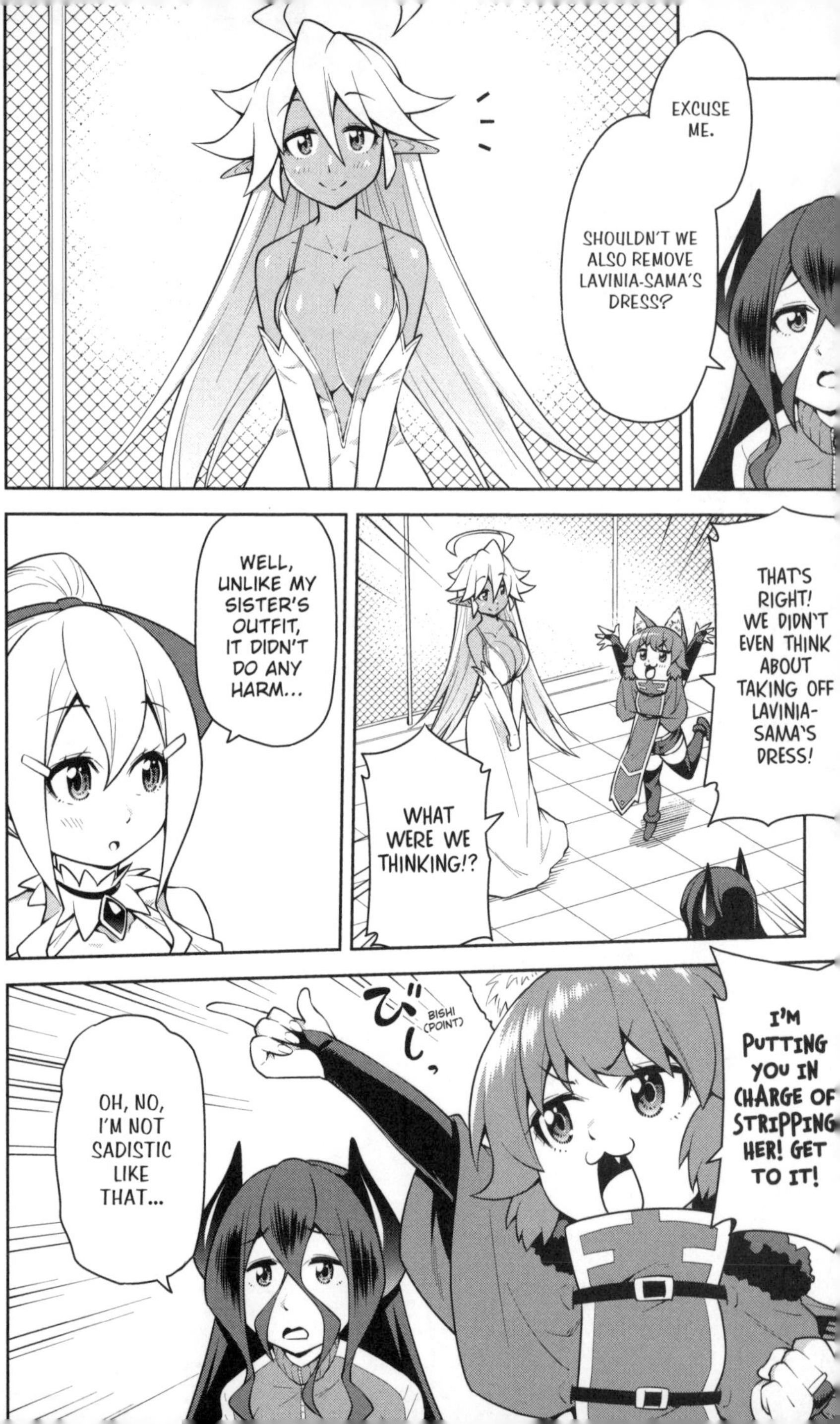
EXCUSE ME.
SHOULDN'T WE ALSO REMOVE LAVINIA-SAMA'S DRESS?
THAT'S RIGHT! WE DIDN'T EVEN THINK ABOUT TAKING OFF LAVINIA-SAMA'S DRESS!
WHAT WERE WE THINKING!?
WELL, UNLIKE MY SISTER'S OUTFIT, IT DIDN'T DO ANY HARM...
I'M PUTTING YOU IN CHARGE OF STRIPPING HER! GET TO IT!
びしっ
BISHI (POINT)
OH, NO, I'M NOT SADISTIC LIKE THAT...

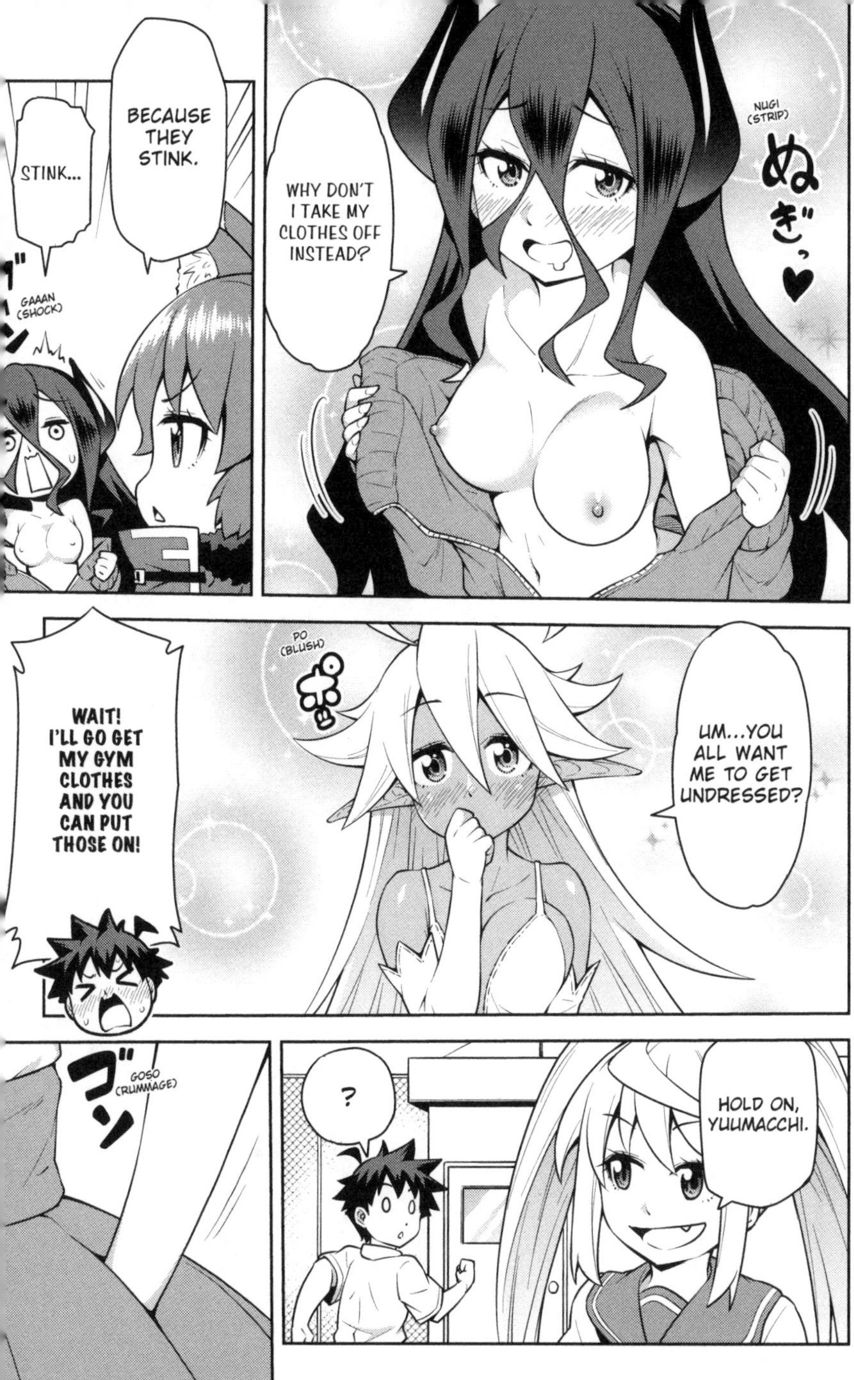
NUGI (STRIP)
ぬぎっ♥
WHY DON'T I TAKE MY CLOTHES OFF INSTEAD?
BECAUSE THEY STINK.
STINK...
GAAAN (SHOCK)
PO (BLUSH)
UM...YOU ALL WANT ME TO GET UNDRESSED?
WAIT! I'LL GO GET MY GYM CLOTHES AND YOU CAN PUT THOSE ON!
HOLD ON, YUUMACCHI.
?
GOSO (RUMMAGE)

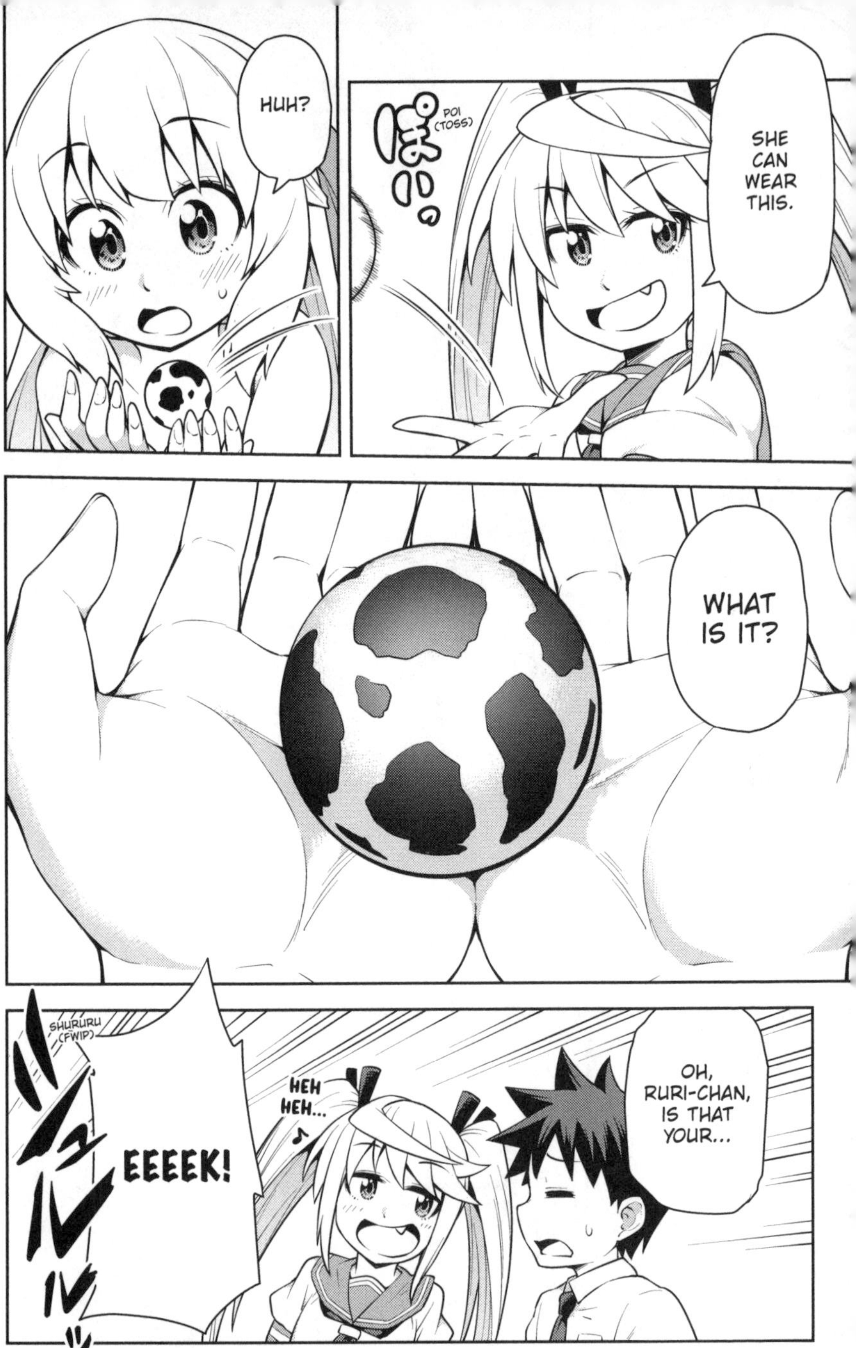
SHE CAN WEAR THIS.
POI (TOSS)
HUH?
WHAT IS IT?
OH, RURI-CHAN, IS THAT YOUR...
HEH HEH...
SHURURU (FWIP)
EEEEK!

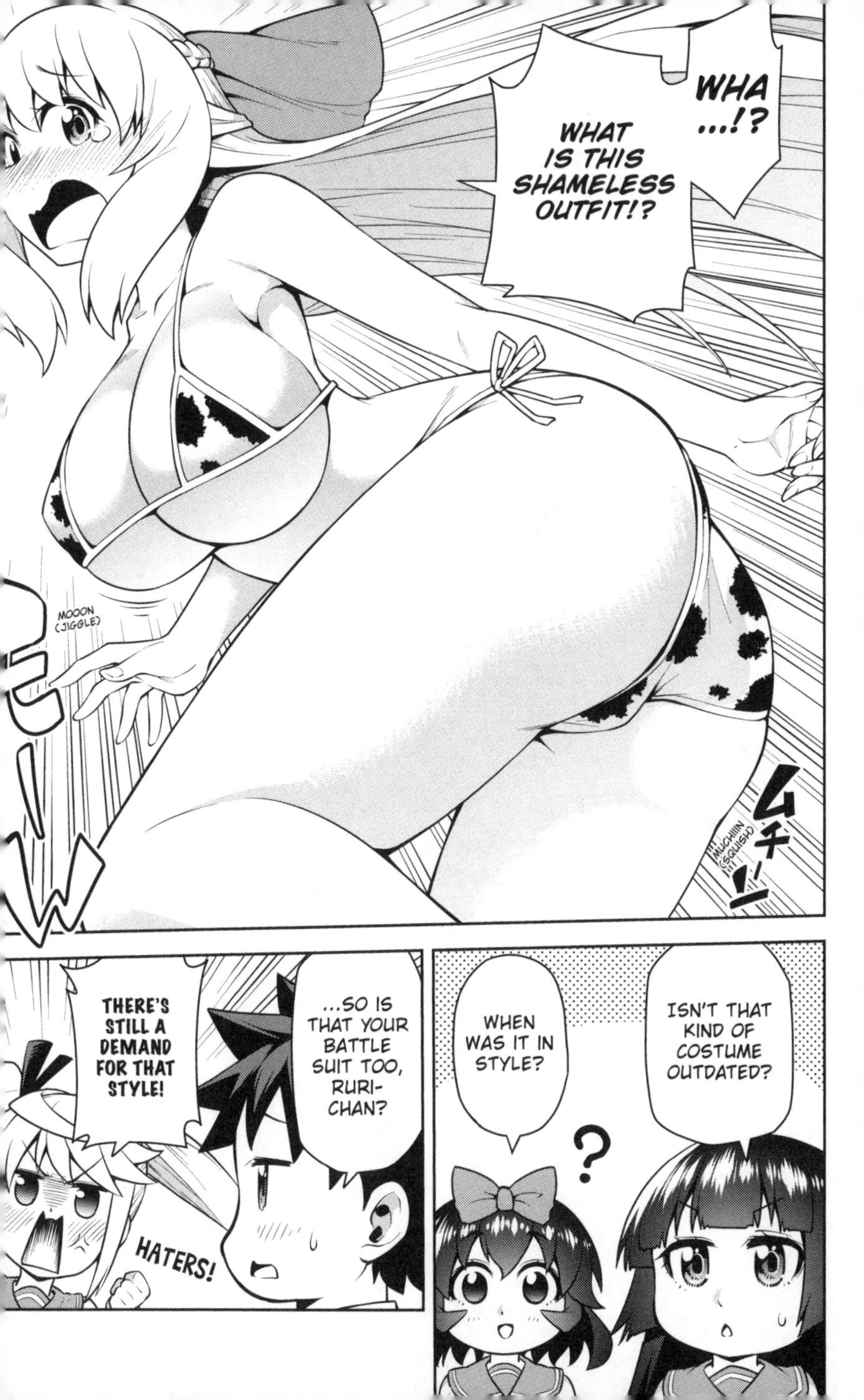
WHA ...!?
WHAT IS THIS SHAMELESS OUTFIT!?
MOOON (JIGGLE)
MUCHIIIN (SQUISH)
ISN'T THAT KIND OF COSTUME OUTDATED?
WHEN WAS IT IN STYLE?
...SO IS THAT YOUR BATTLE SUIT TOO, RURI-CHAN?
THERE'S STILL A DEMAND FOR THAT STYLE!
HATERS!

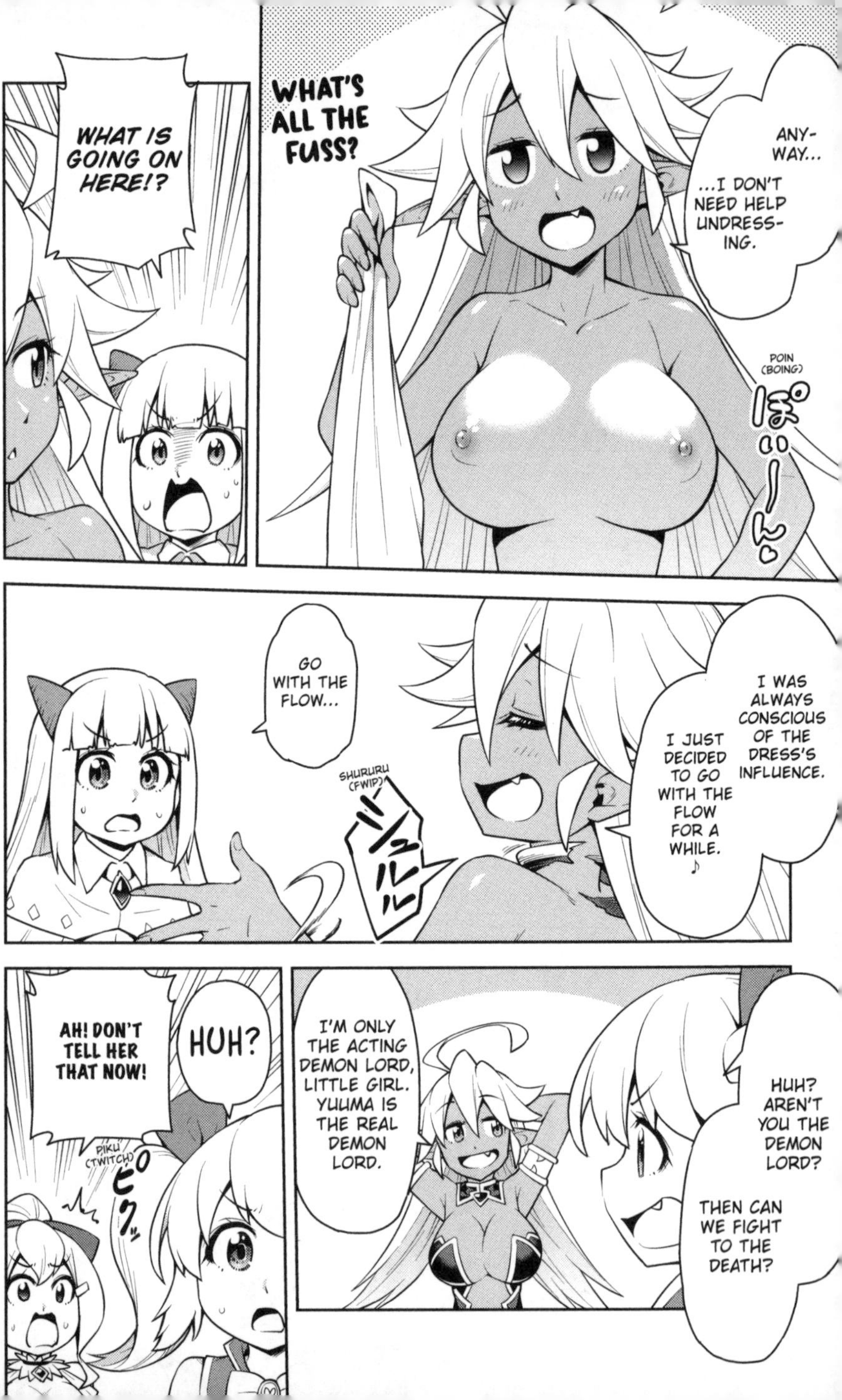
ANY-WAY... ...I DON'T NEED HELP UNDRESS-ING.
WHAT'S ALL THE FUSS?
POIN (BOING)
ぽいーん♡
WHAT IS GOING ON HERE!?
I WAS ALWAYS CONSCIOUS OF THE DRESS'S INFLUENCE.
I JUST DECIDED TO GO WITH THE FLOW FOR A WHILE. ♪
SHURURU (FWIP)
シュルル
GO WITH THE FLOW...
HUH? AREN'T YOU THE DEMON LORD?
THEN CAN WE FIGHT TO THE DEATH?
I'M ONLY THE ACTING DEMON LORD, LITTLE GIRL. YUUMA IS THE REAL DEMON LORD.
HUH?
AH! DON'T TELL HER THAT NOW!
PIKU (TWITCH)
ピクッ

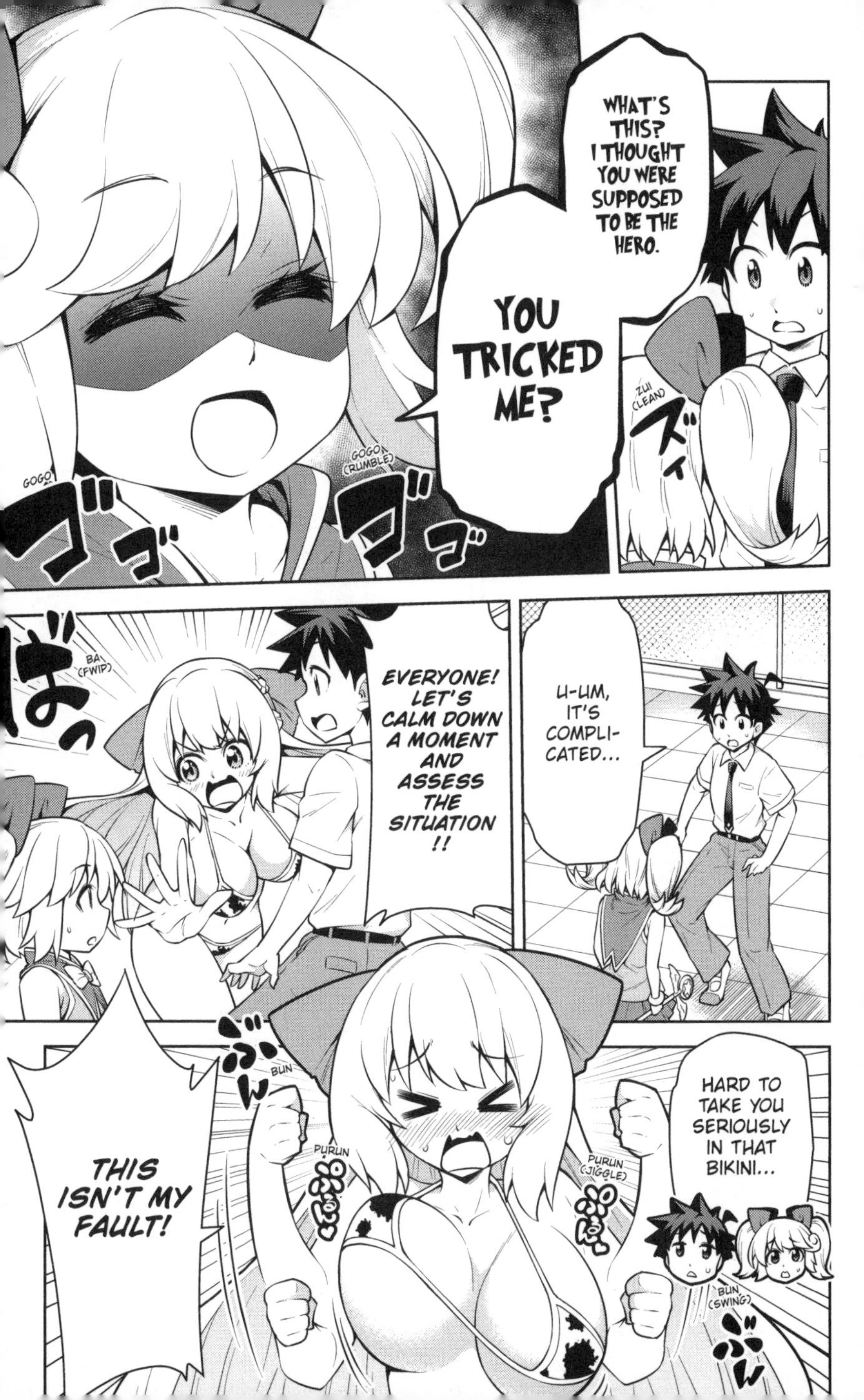
WHAT'S THIS? I THOUGHT YOU WERE SUPPOSED TO BE THE HERO.
ZUI (LEAN)
YOU TRICKED ME?
GOGO (RUMBLE)
GOGO
U-UM, IT'S COMPLI-CATED...
EVERYONE! LET'S CALM DOWN A MOMENT AND ASSESS THE SITUATION !!
BA (FWIP)
HARD TO TAKE YOU SERIOUSLY IN THAT BIKINI...
BUN (SWING)
PURUN (JIGGLE)
PURUN
BUN
THIS ISN'T MY FAULT!

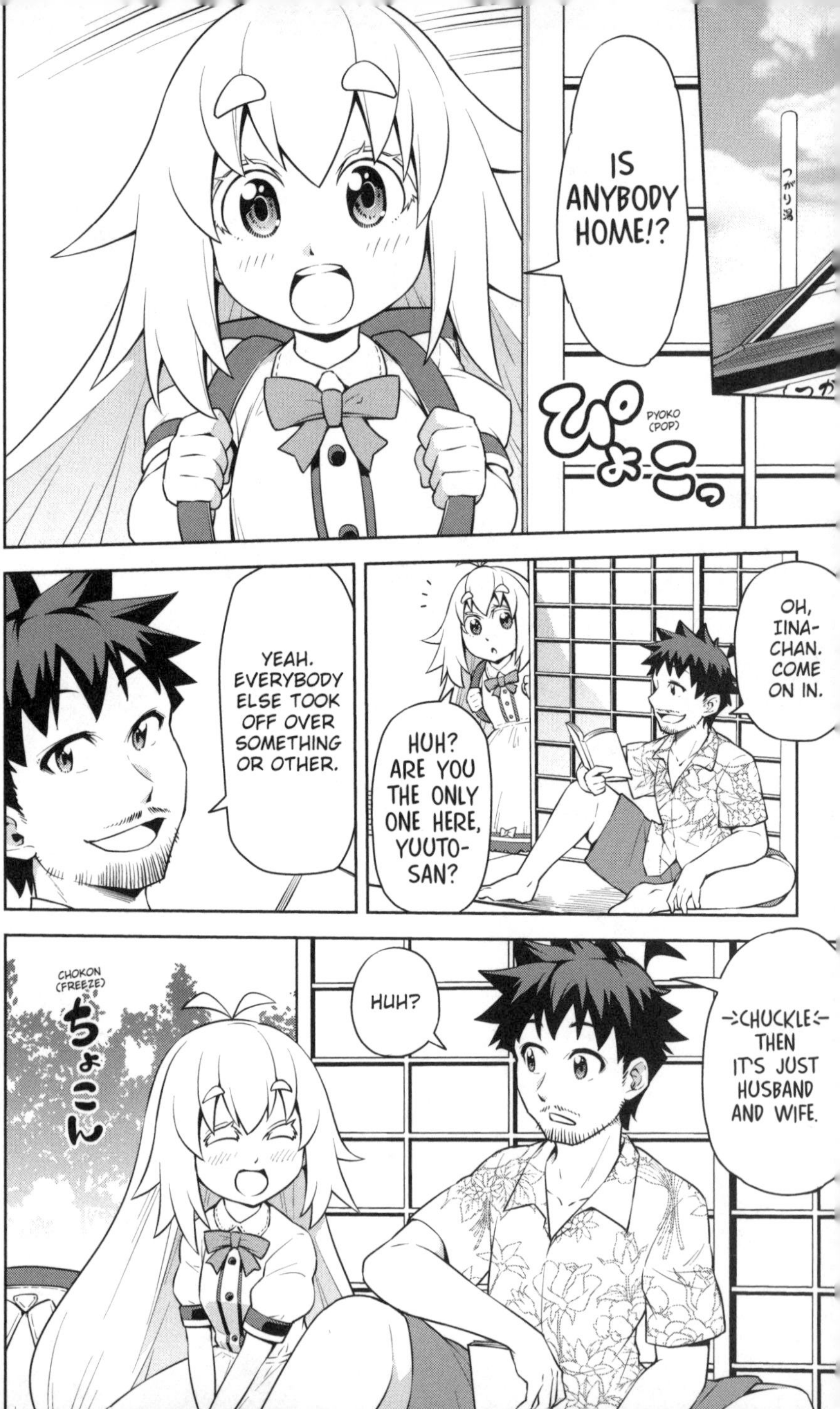
つかり湯
IS ANYBODY HOME!?
ぴょこっ
PYOKO (POP)
OH, INA-CHAN. COME ON IN.
HUH? ARE YOU THE ONLY ONE HERE, YUUTO-SAN?
YEAH. EVERYBODY ELSE TOOK OFF OVER SOMETHING OR OTHER.
-CHUCKLE- THEN IT'S JUST HUSBAND AND WIFE.
HUH?
ちょこん
CHOKON (FREEZE)

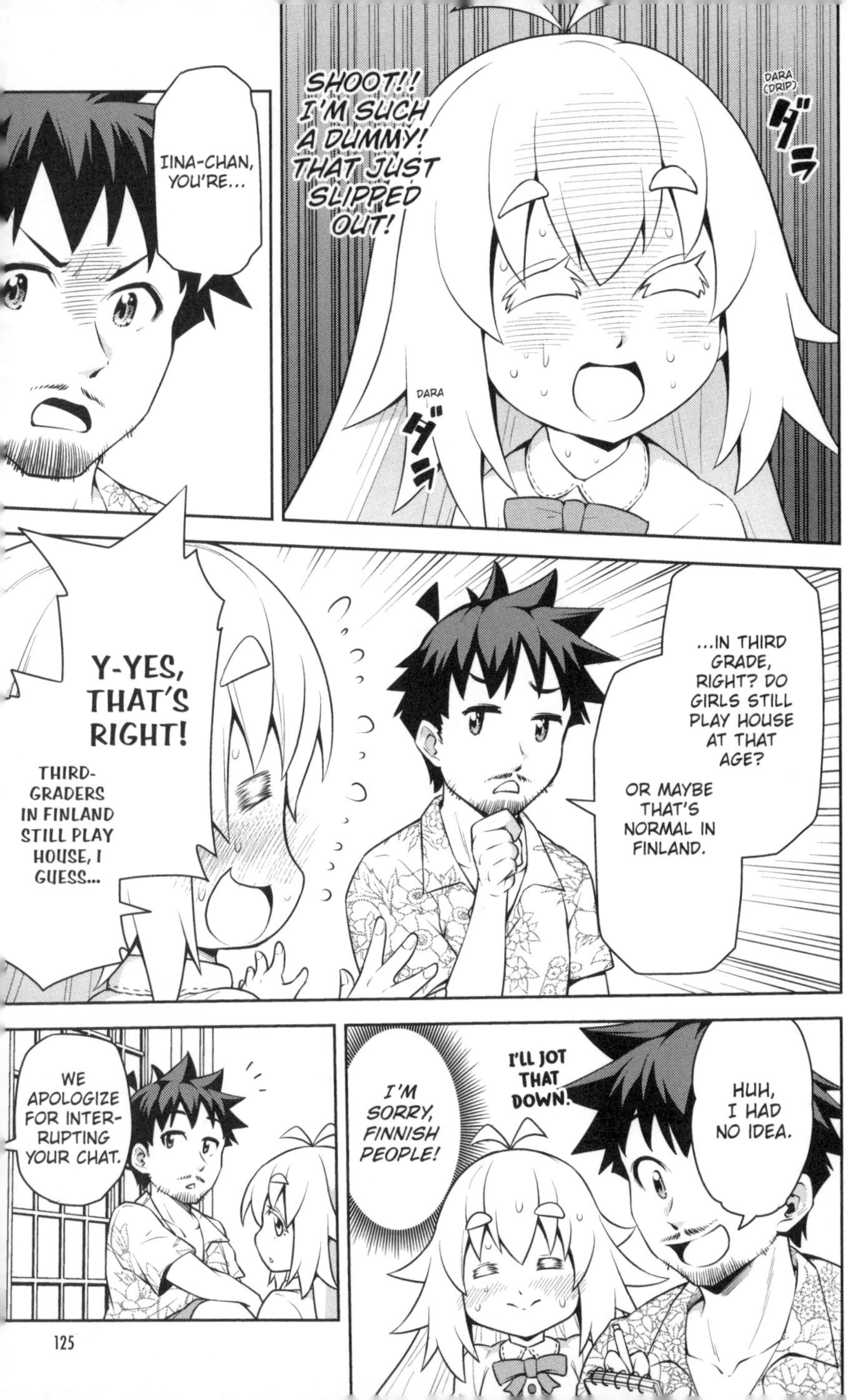
SHOOT!! I'M SUCH A DUMMY! THAT JUST SLIPPED OUT!
DARA (DRIP)
ダラ
DARA
ダラ
IINA-CHAN, YOU'RE...
...IN THIRD GRADE, RIGHT? DO GIRLS STILL PLAY HOUSE AT THAT AGE?
OR MAYBE THAT'S NORMAL IN FINLAND.
Y-YES, THAT'S RIGHT!
THIRD-GRADERS IN FINLAND STILL PLAY HOUSE, I GUESS...
HUH, I HAD NO IDEA.
I'LL JOT THAT DOWN.
I'M SORRY, FINNISH PEOPLE!
WE APOLOGIZE FOR INTER-RUPTING YOUR CHAT.

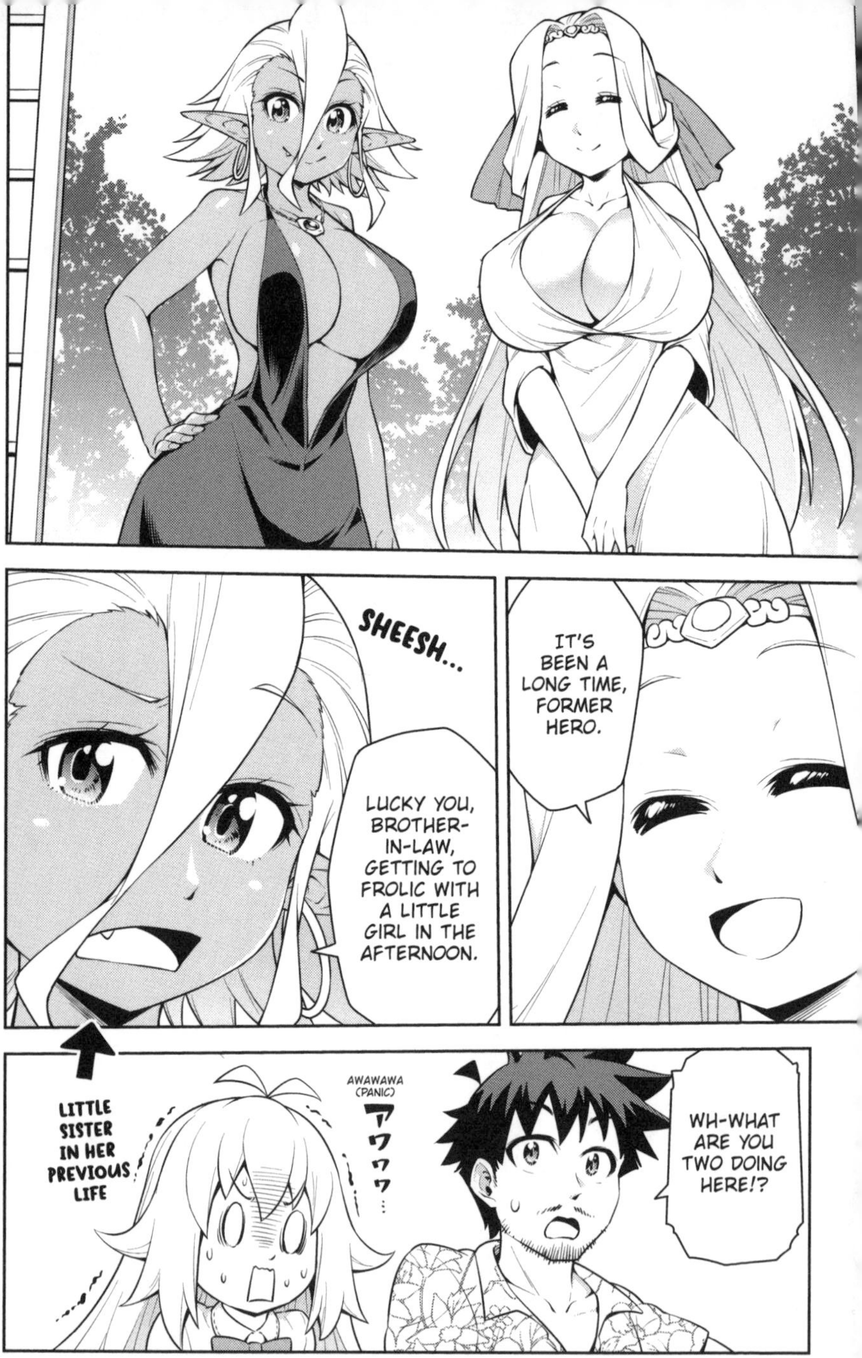
IT'S BEEN A LONG TIME, FORMER HERO.
SHEESH...
LUCKY YOU, BROTHER-IN-LAW, GETTING TO FROLIC WITH A LITTLE GIRL IN THE AFTERNOON.
WH-WHAT ARE YOU TWO DOING HERE!?
AWAWAWA (PANIC)
アワワワ…
LITTLE SISTER IN HER PREVIOUS LIFE

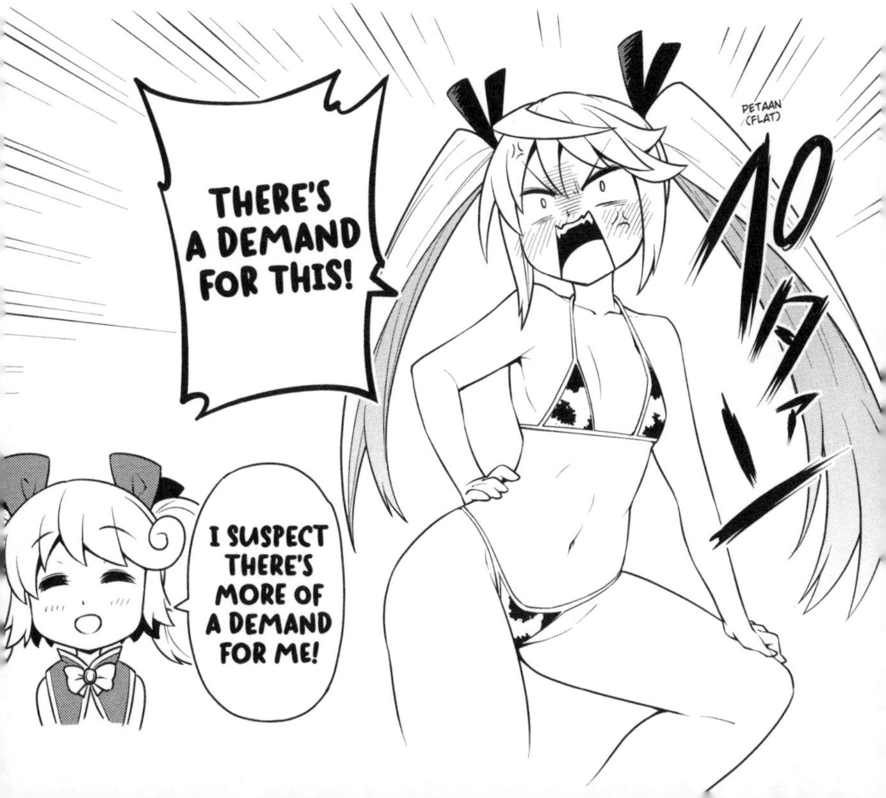
PETAAN (FLAT)
THERE'S A DEMAND FOR THIS!
I SUSPECT THERE'S MORE OF A DEMAND FOR ME!

I'm the HERO, but the DEMON LORD's Also Me

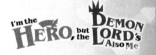

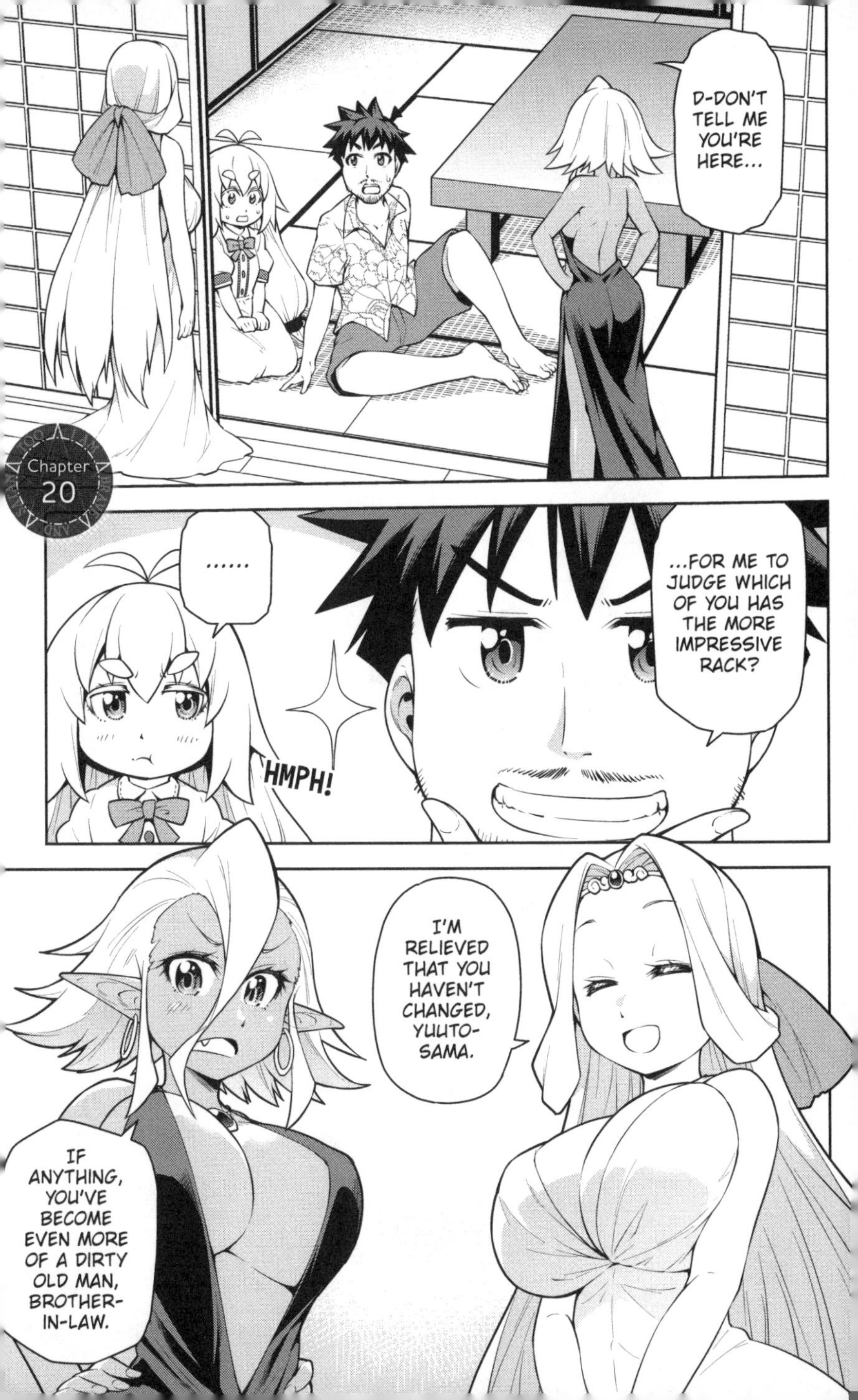
D-DON'T TELL ME YOU'RE HERE...
Chapter 20
...FOR ME TO JUDGE WHICH OF YOU HAS THE MORE IMPRESSIVE RACK?
......
HMPH!
I'M RELIEVED THAT YOU HAVEN'T CHANGED, YUUTO-SAMA.
IF ANYTHING, YOU'VE BECOME EVEN MORE OF A DIRTY OLD MAN, BROTHER-IN-LAW.

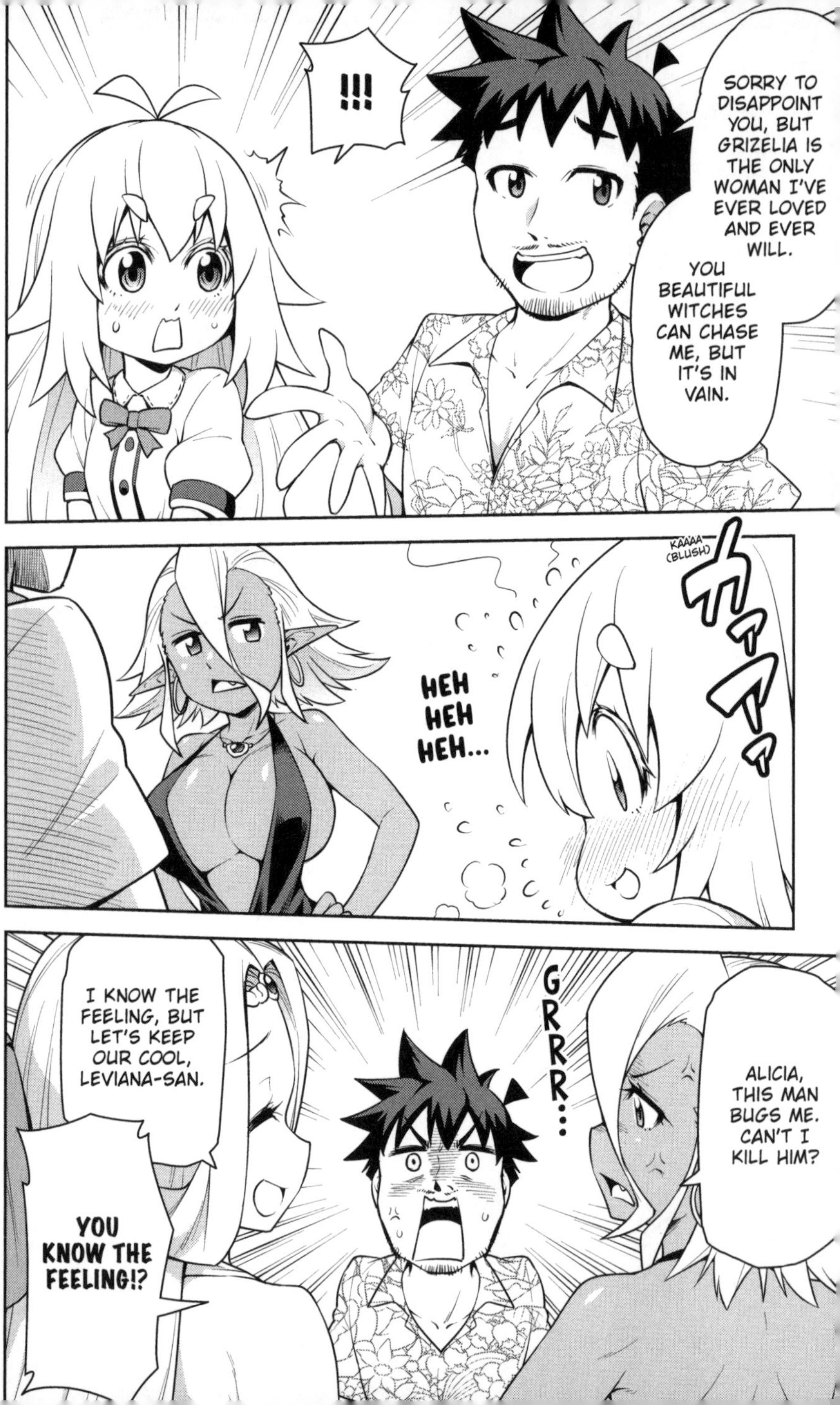
SORRY TO DISAPPOINT YOU, BUT GRIZELIA IS THE ONLY WOMAN I'VE EVER LOVED AND EVER WILL.
YOU BEAUTIFUL WITCHES CAN CHASE ME, BUT IT'S IN VAIN.
!!!
KAAAA (BLUSH)
HEH HEH HEH...
ALICIA, THIS MAN BUGS ME. CAN'T I KILL HIM?
GRRR...
I KNOW THE FEELING, BUT LET'S KEEP OUR COOL, LEVIANA-SAN.
YOU KNOW THE FEELING!?

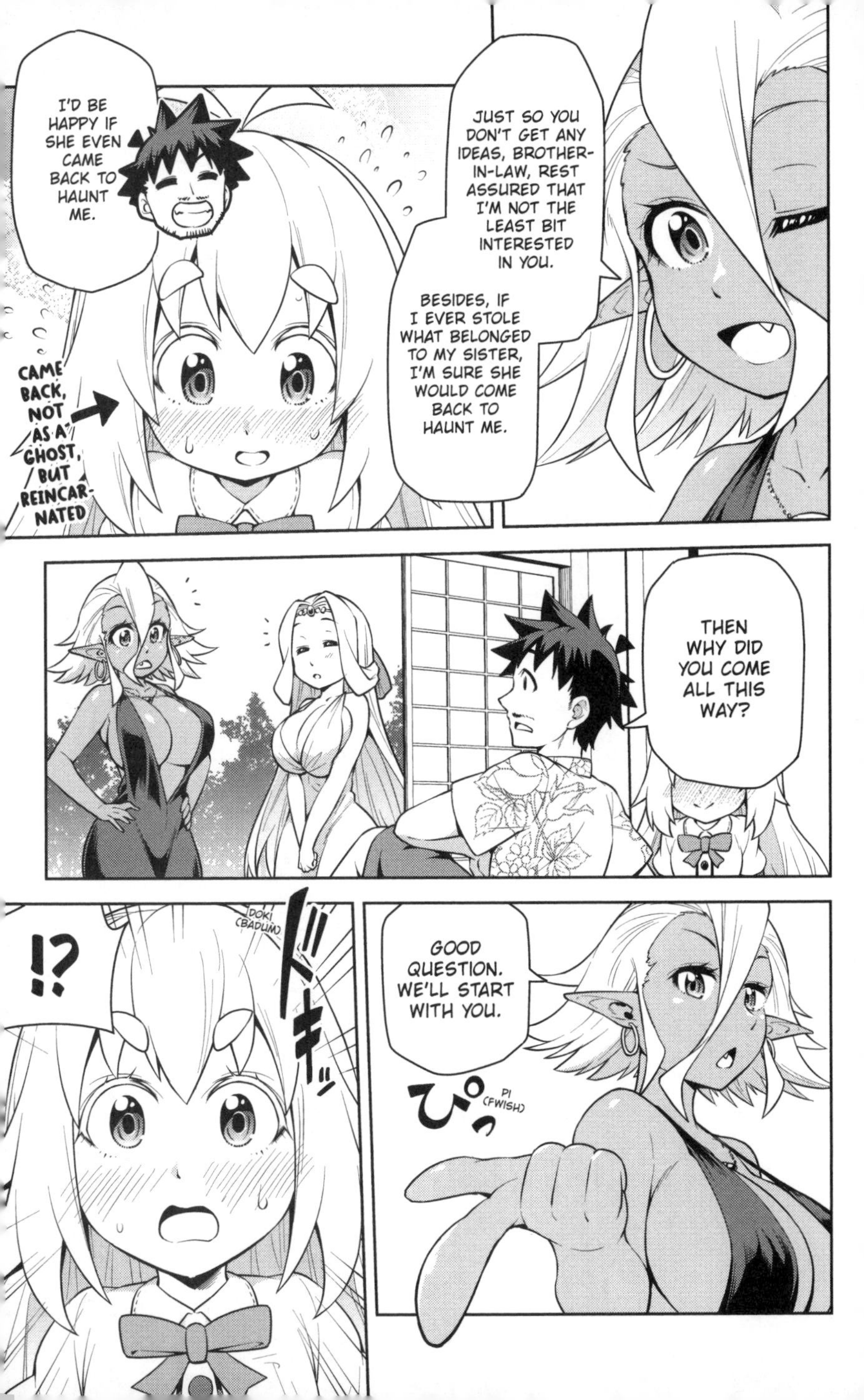
JUST SO YOU DON'T GET ANY IDEAS, BROTHER-IN-LAW, REST ASSURED THAT I'M NOT THE LEAST BIT INTERESTED IN YOU.
BESIDES, IF I EVER STOLE WHAT BELONGED TO MY SISTER, I'M SURE SHE WOULD COME BACK TO HAUNT ME.
I'D BE HAPPY IF SHE EVEN CAME BACK TO HAUNT ME.
CAME BACK, NOT AS A GHOST, BUT REINCARNATED
THEN WHY DID YOU COME ALL THIS WAY?
GOOD QUESTION. WE'LL START WITH YOU.
ぴっ
PI (FWISH)
ドキッ
DOKI (BADUM)
!?

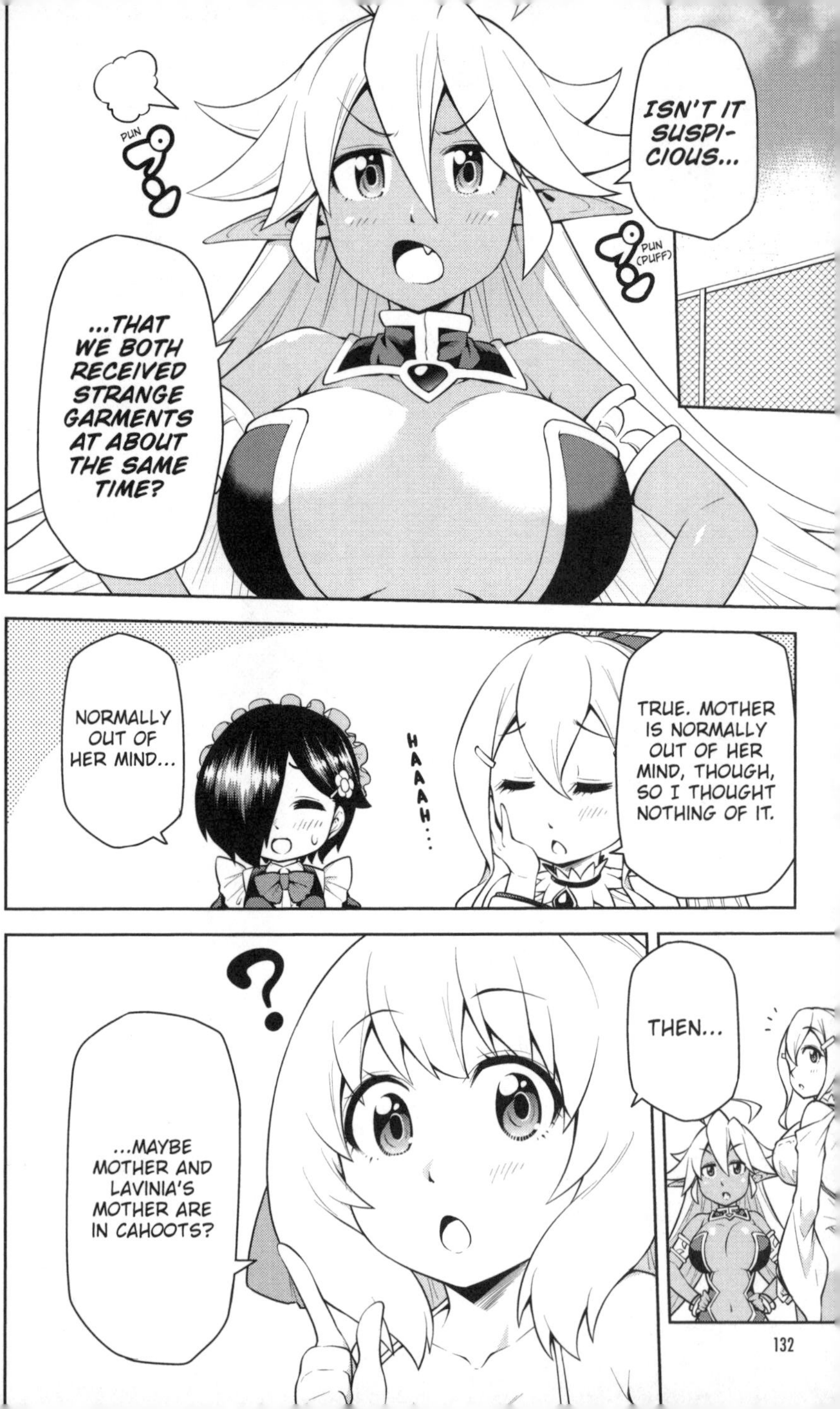
ISN'T IT SUSPICIOUS...
PUN (PUFF)
PUN
...THAT WE BOTH RECEIVED STRANGE GARMENTS AT ABOUT THE SAME TIME?
TRUE. MOTHER IS NORMALLY OUT OF HER MIND, THOUGH, SO I THOUGHT NOTHING OF IT.
HAAAH...
NORMALLY OUT OF HER MIND...
THEN...
...MAYBE MOTHER AND LAVINIA'S MOTHER ARE IN CAHOOTS?

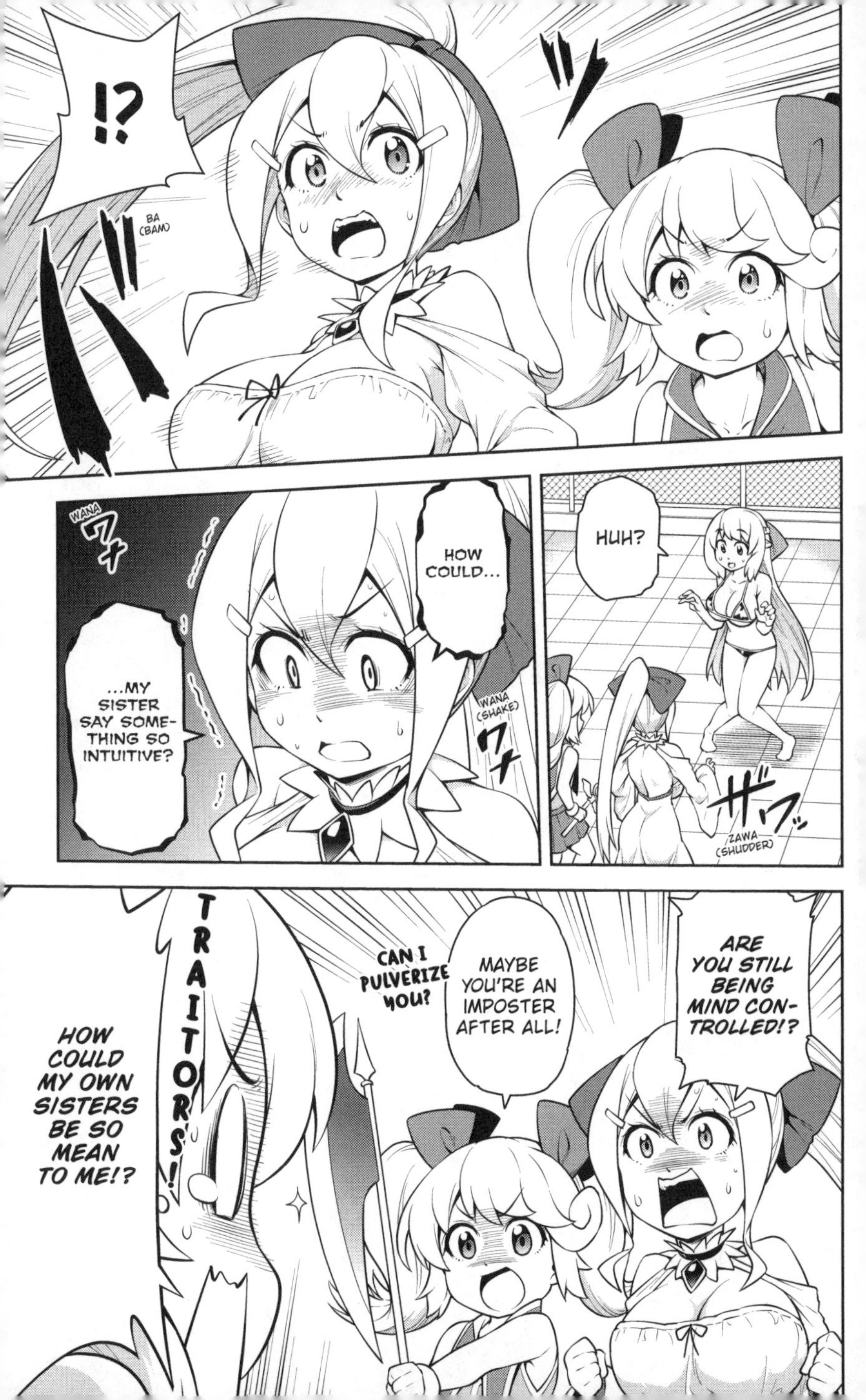
!?
BA (BAM)
HUH?
ZAWA (SHUDDER)
HOW COULD...
...MY SISTER SAY SOME-THING SO INTUITIVE?
WANA (SHAKE)
WANA
ARE YOU STILL BEING MIND CON-TROLLED!?
MAYBE YOU'RE AN IMPOSTER AFTER ALL!
CAN I PULVERIZE YOU?
TRAITORS!
HOW COULD MY OWN SISTERS BE SO MEAN TO ME!?

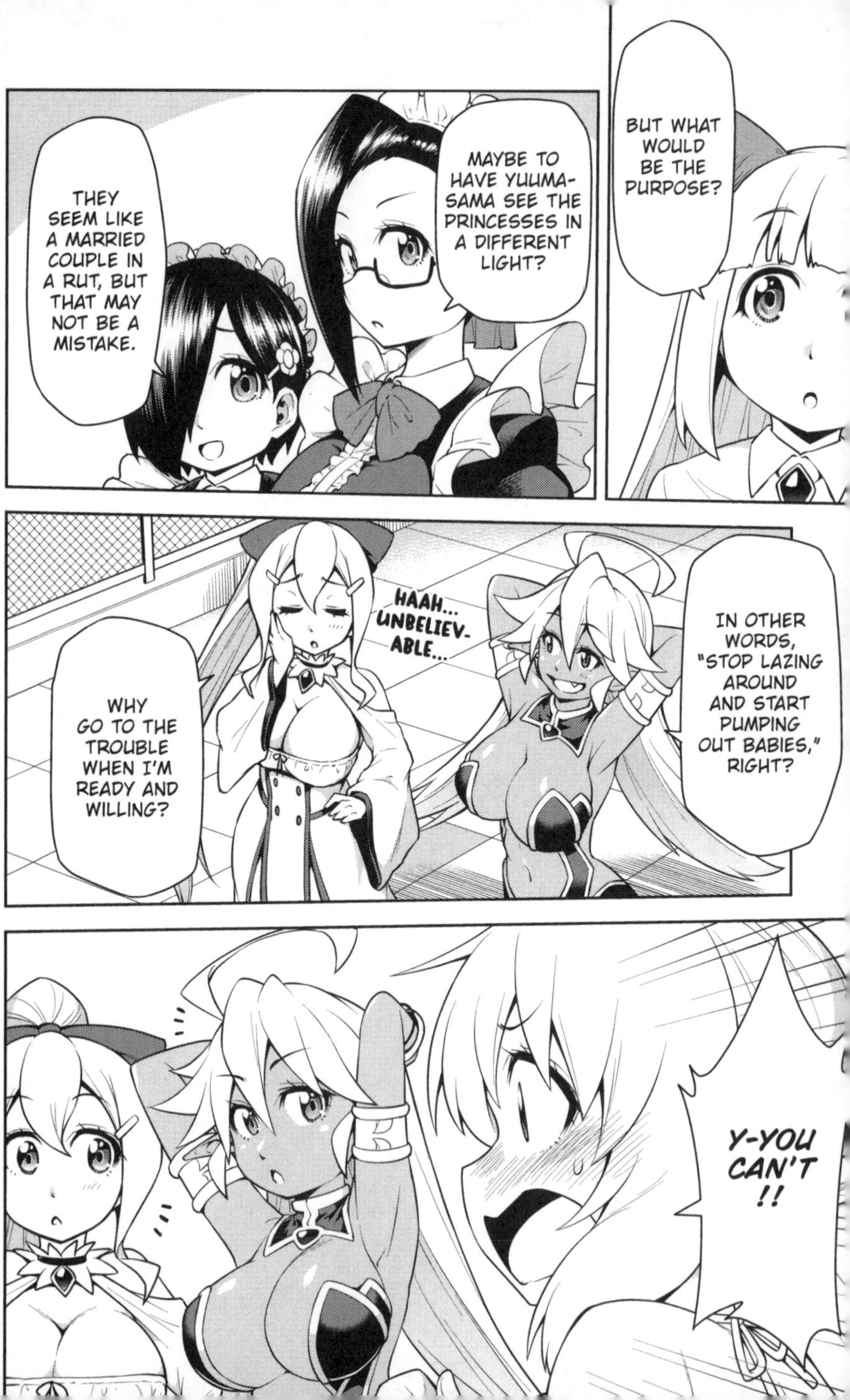
BUT WHAT WOULD BE THE PURPOSE?
MAYBE TO HAVE YUUMA-SAMA SEE THE PRINCESSES IN A DIFFERENT LIGHT?
THEY SEEM LIKE A MARRIED COUPLE IN A RUT, BUT THAT MAY NOT BE A MISTAKE.
IN OTHER WORDS, "STOP LAZING AROUND AND START PUMPING OUT BABIES," RIGHT?
HAAH... UNBELIEV-ABLE...
WHY GO TO THE TROUBLE WHEN I'M READY AND WILLING?
Y-YOU CAN'T!!

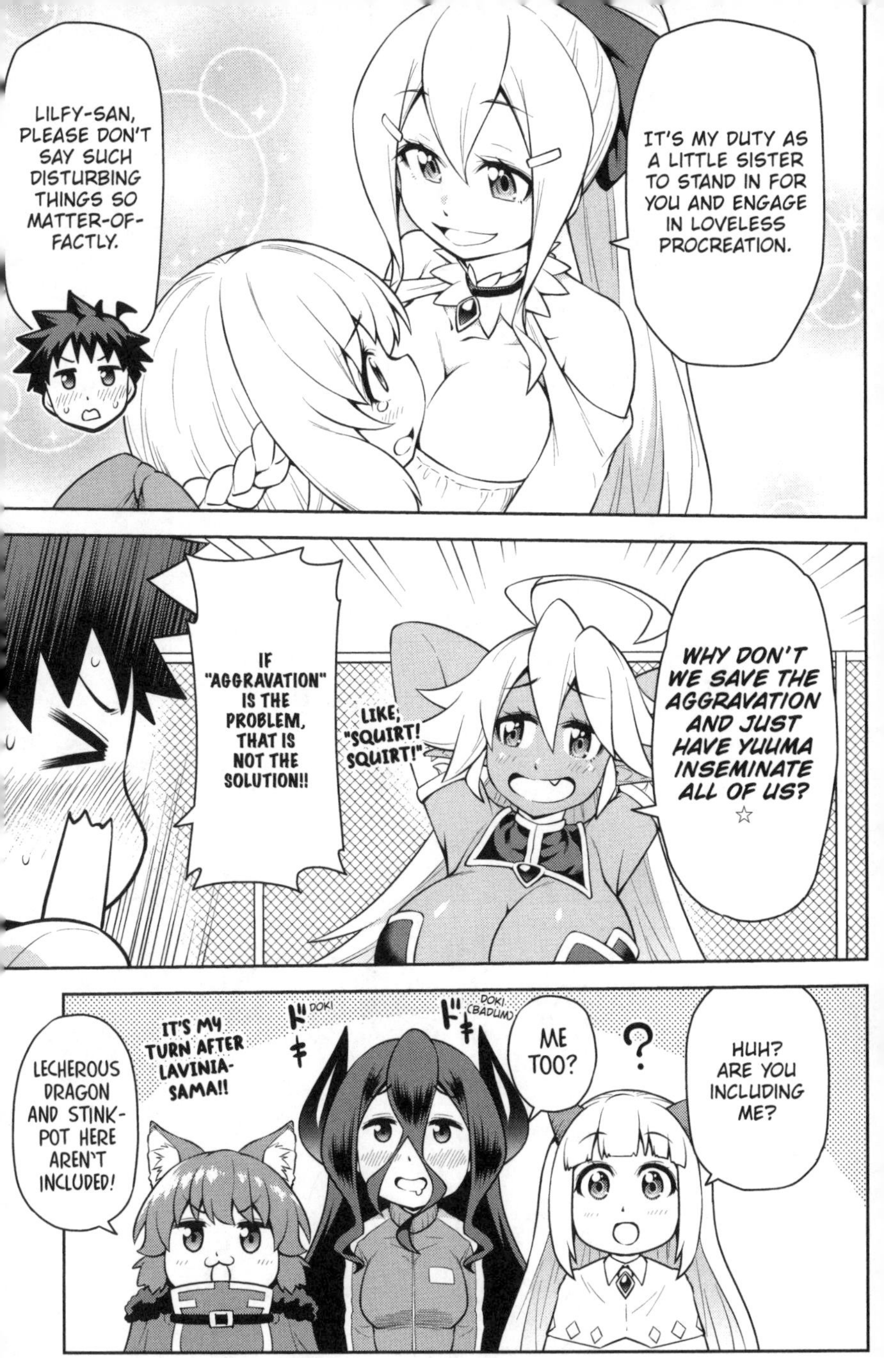
IT'S MY DUTY AS A LITTLE SISTER TO STAND IN FOR YOU AND ENGAGE IN LOVELESS PROCREATION.
LILFY-SAN, PLEASE DON'T SAY SUCH DISTURBING THINGS SO MATTER-OF-FACTLY.
WHY DON'T WE SAVE THE AGGRAVATION AND JUST HAVE YUUMA INSEMINATE ALL OF US? ☆
LIKE; "SQUIRT! SQUIRT!"
IF "AGGRAVATION" IS THE PROBLEM, THAT IS NOT THE SOLUTION!!
HUH? ARE YOU INCLUDING ME?
?
ME TOO?
ドキ
DOKI (BADUM)
ドキ
DOKI
IT'S MY TURN AFTER LAVINIA-SAMA!!
LECHEROUS DRAGON AND STINK-POT HERE AREN'T INCLUDED!

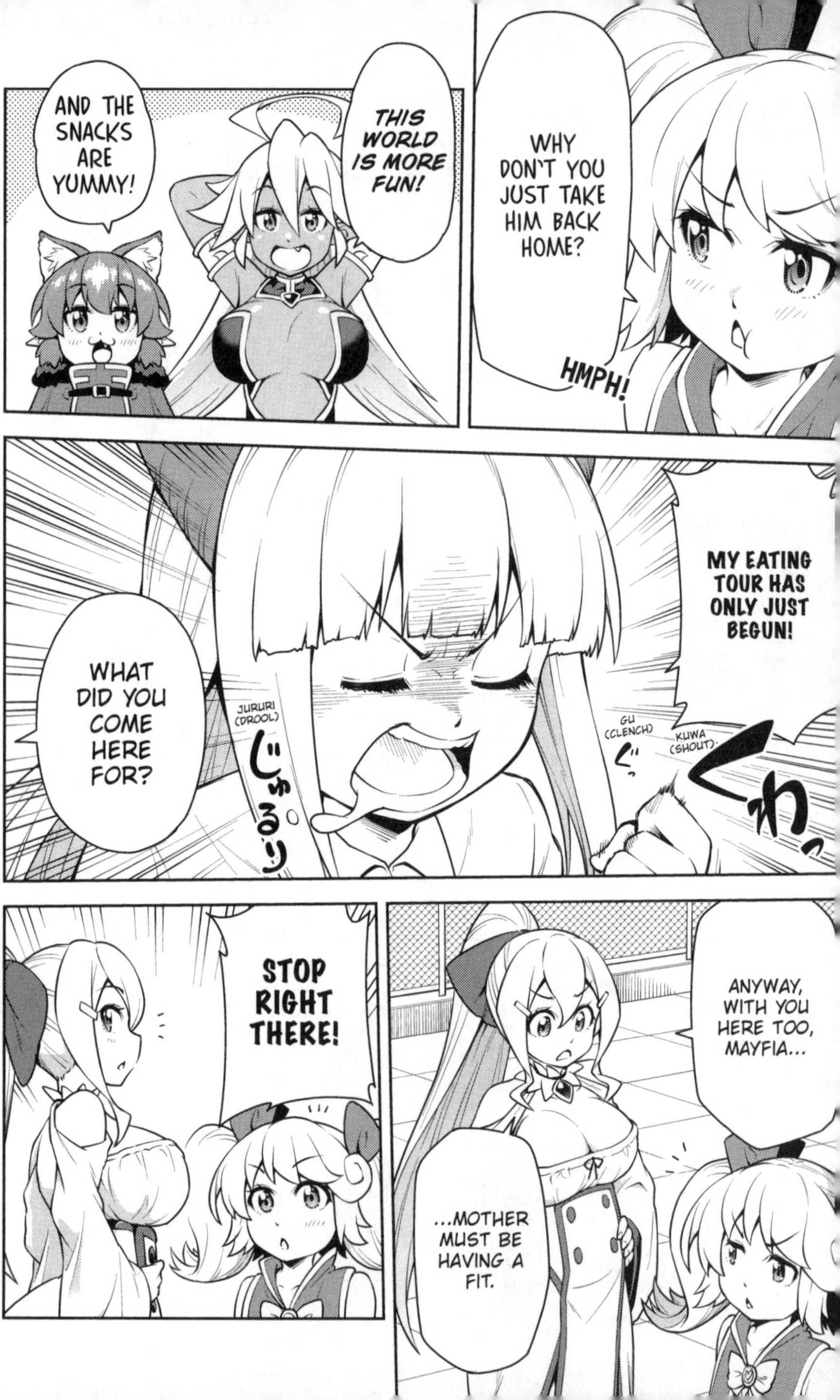
WHY DON'T YOU JUST TAKE HIM BACK HOME?
HMPH!
THIS WORLD IS MORE FUN!
AND THE SNACKS ARE YUMMY!
MY EATING TOUR HAS ONLY JUST BEGUN!
KUWA (SHOUT)
くわっ
GU (CLENCH)
ぐっ
JURURI (DROOL)
じゅるり
WHAT DID YOU COME HERE FOR?
ANYWAY, WITH YOU HERE TOO, MAYFIA...
...MOTHER MUST BE HAVING A FIT.
STOP RIGHT THERE!

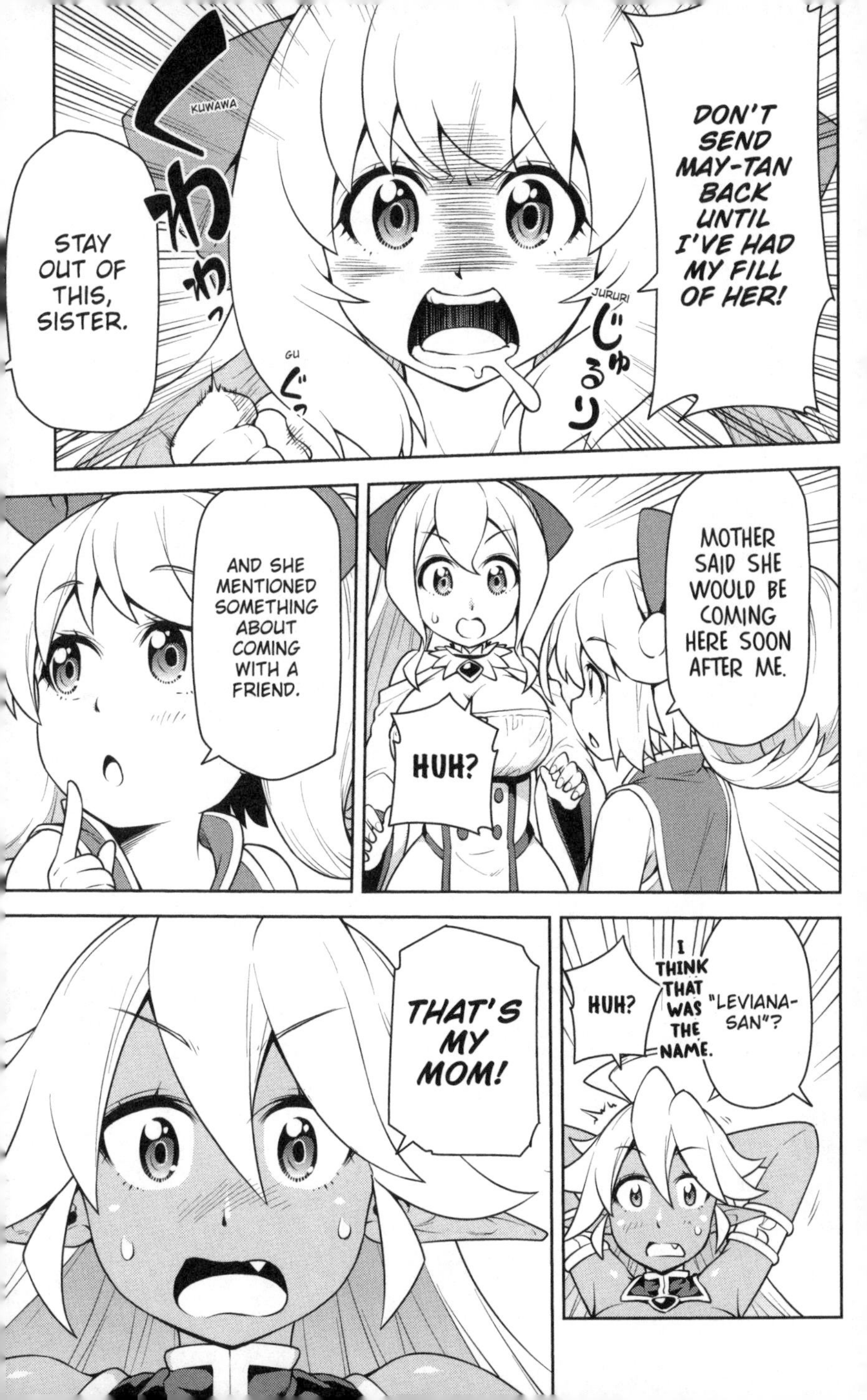
DON'T SEND MAY-TAN BACK UNTIL I'VE HAD MY FILL OF HER!
JURURI
じゅるり
GU
ぐっ
KUWAWA
くわわっ
STAY OUT OF THIS, SISTER.
MOTHER SAID SHE WOULD BE COMING HERE SOON AFTER ME.
HUH?
AND SHE MENTIONED SOMETHING ABOUT COMING WITH A FRIEND.
"LEVIANA-SAN"?
I THINK THAT WAS THE NAME.
HUH?
THAT'S MY MOM!

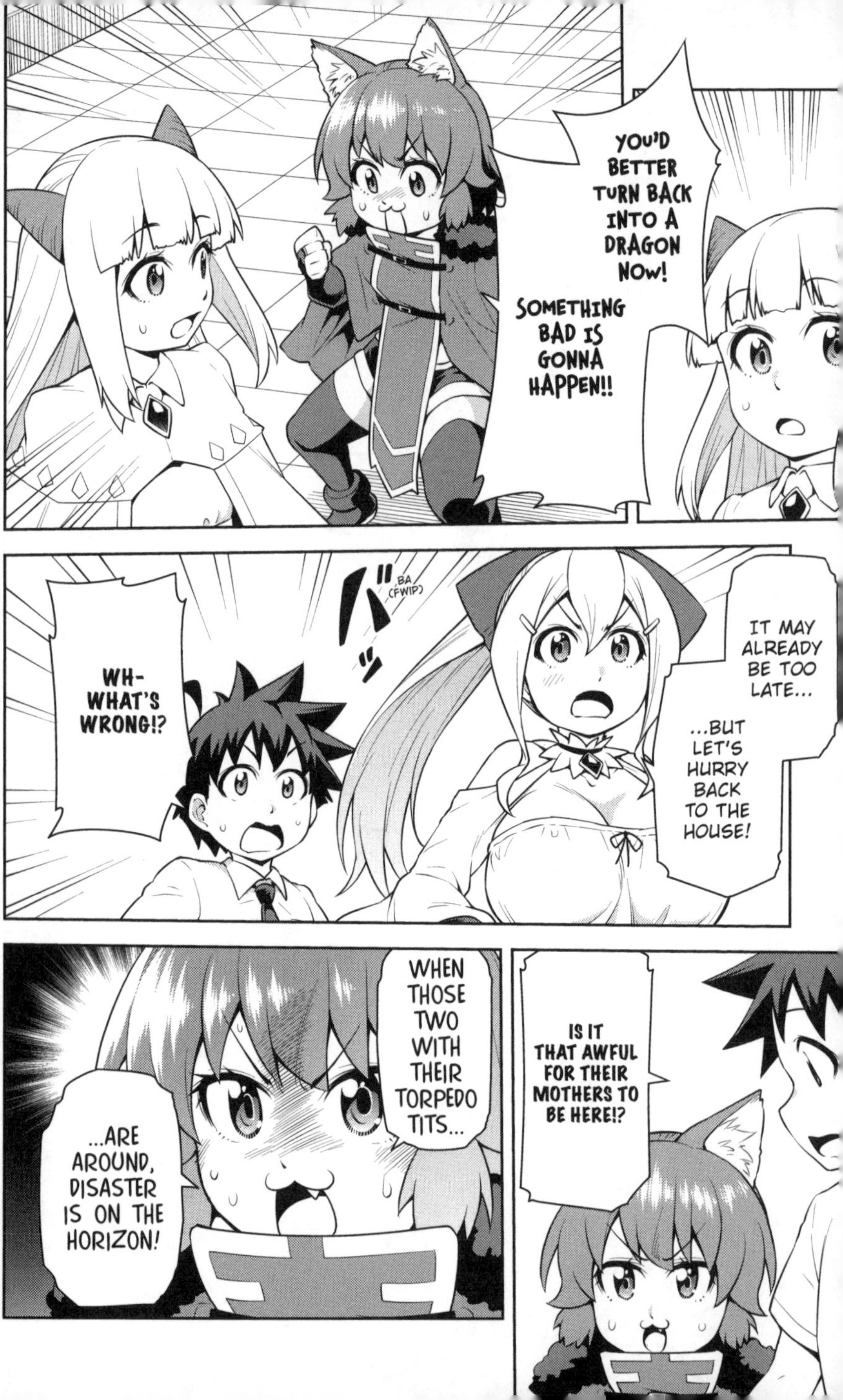
YOU'D BETTER TURN BACK INTO A DRAGON NOW!
SOMETHING BAD IS GONNA HAPPEN!!
IT MAY ALREADY BE TOO LATE...
...BUT LET'S HURRY BACK TO THE HOUSE!
BA (FWIP)
WH-WHAT'S WRONG!?
IS IT THAT AWFUL FOR THEIR MOTHERS TO BE HERE!?
WHEN THOSE TWO WITH THEIR TORPEDO TITS...
...ARE AROUND, DISASTER IS ON THE HORIZON!

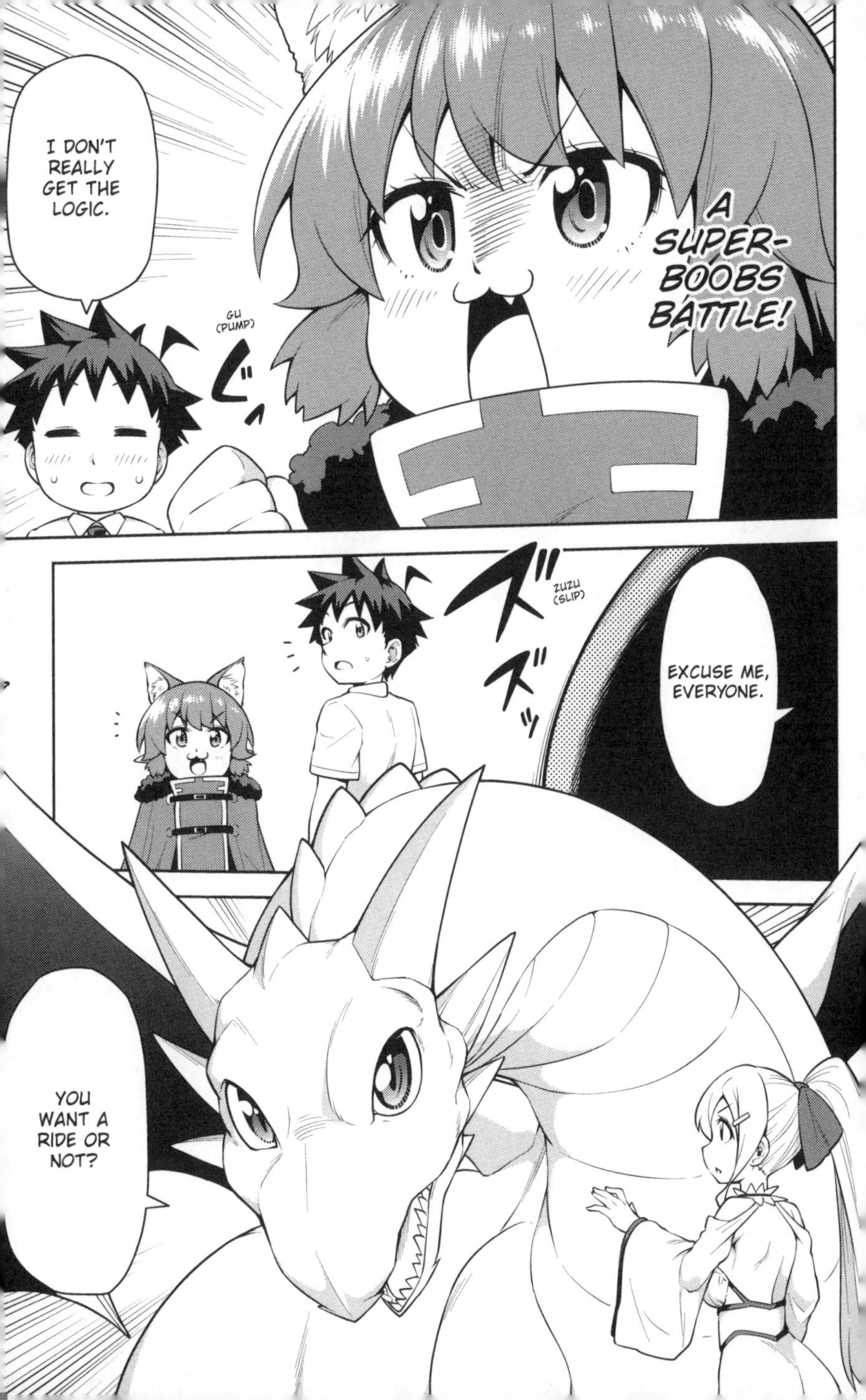
A SUPER-BOOBS BATTLE!
ぐっ
GU (PUMP)
I DON'T REALLY GET THE LOGIC.
EXCUSE ME, EVERYONE.
ズズッ
ZUZU (SLIP)
YOU WANT A RIDE OR NOT?

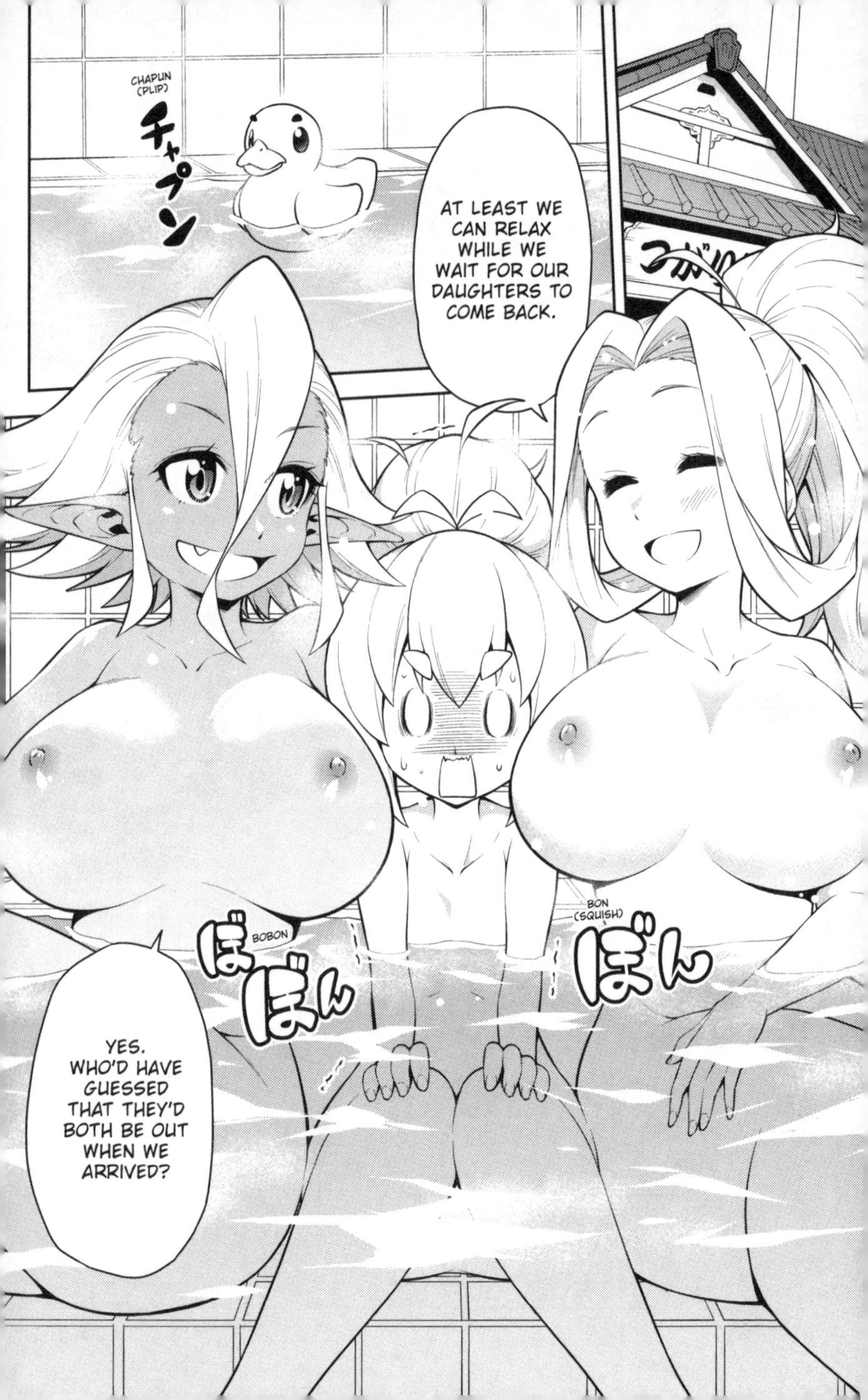
AT LEAST WE CAN RELAX WHILE WE WAIT FOR OUR DAUGHTERS TO COME BACK.
CHAPUN (PLIP)
チャプン
BON (SQUISH)
ぼん
BOBON
ぼぼん
YES. WHO'D HAVE GUESSED THAT THEY'D BOTH BE OUT WHEN WE ARRIVED?

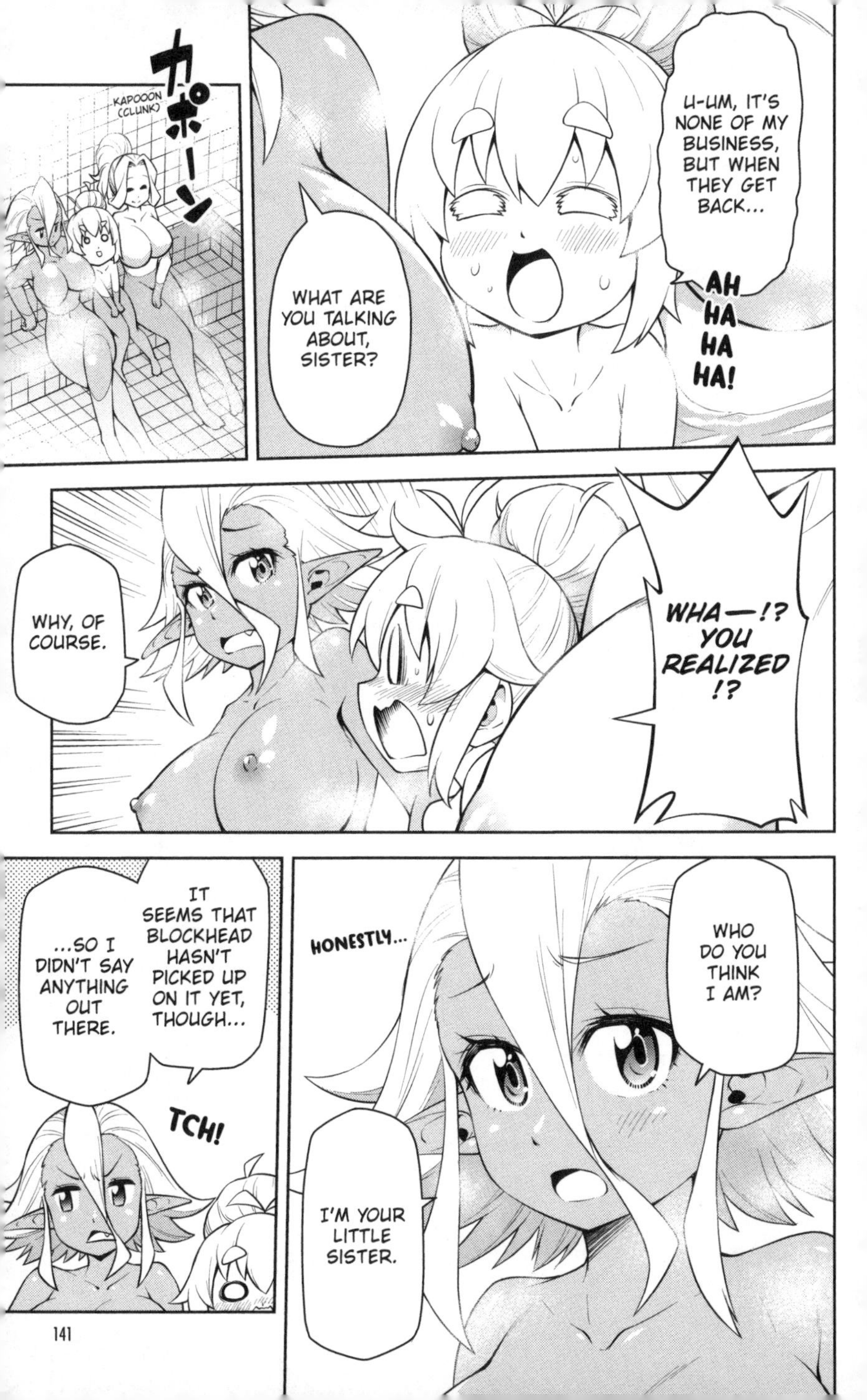
U-UM, IT'S NONE OF MY BUSINESS, BUT WHEN THEY GET BACK...
AH HA HA HA!
WHAT ARE YOU TALKING ABOUT, SISTER?
カポーン
KAPOOON (CLUNK)
WHA—!? YOU REALIZED !?
WHY, OF COURSE.
WHO DO YOU THINK I AM?
HONESTLY...
I'M YOUR LITTLE SISTER.
IT SEEMS THAT BLOCKHEAD HASN'T PICKED UP ON IT YET, THOUGH...
...SO I DIDN'T SAY ANYTHING OUT THERE.
TCH!

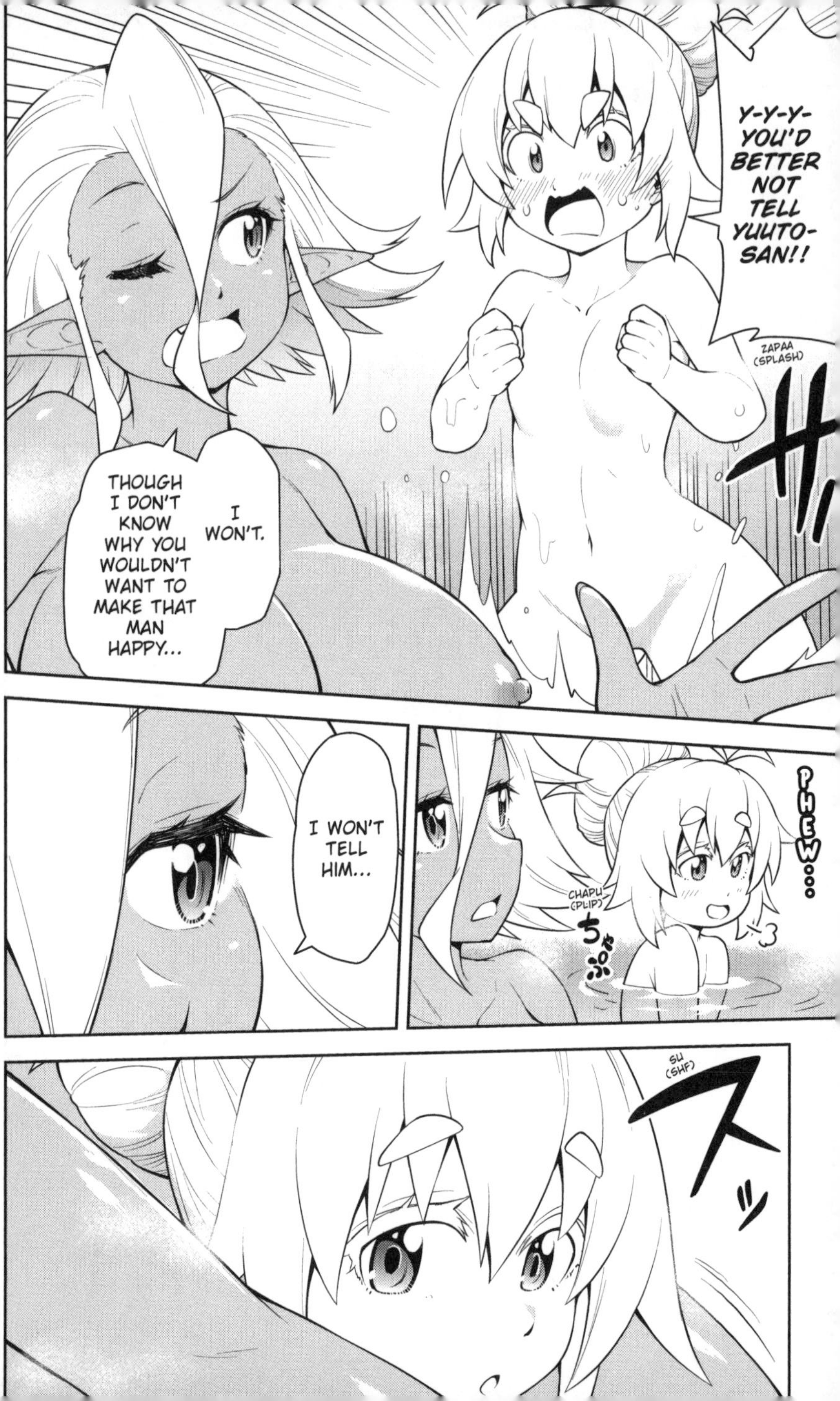

Y-Y-Y-YOU'D BETTER NOT TELL YUUTO-SAN!!
ZAPAA (SPLASH)
I WON'T.
THOUGH I DON'T KNOW WHY YOU WOULDN'T WANT TO MAKE THAT MAN HAPPY...
PHEW...
CHAPU (PLIP)
ちゃぷ
I WON'T TELL HIM...
SU (SHF)
スッ

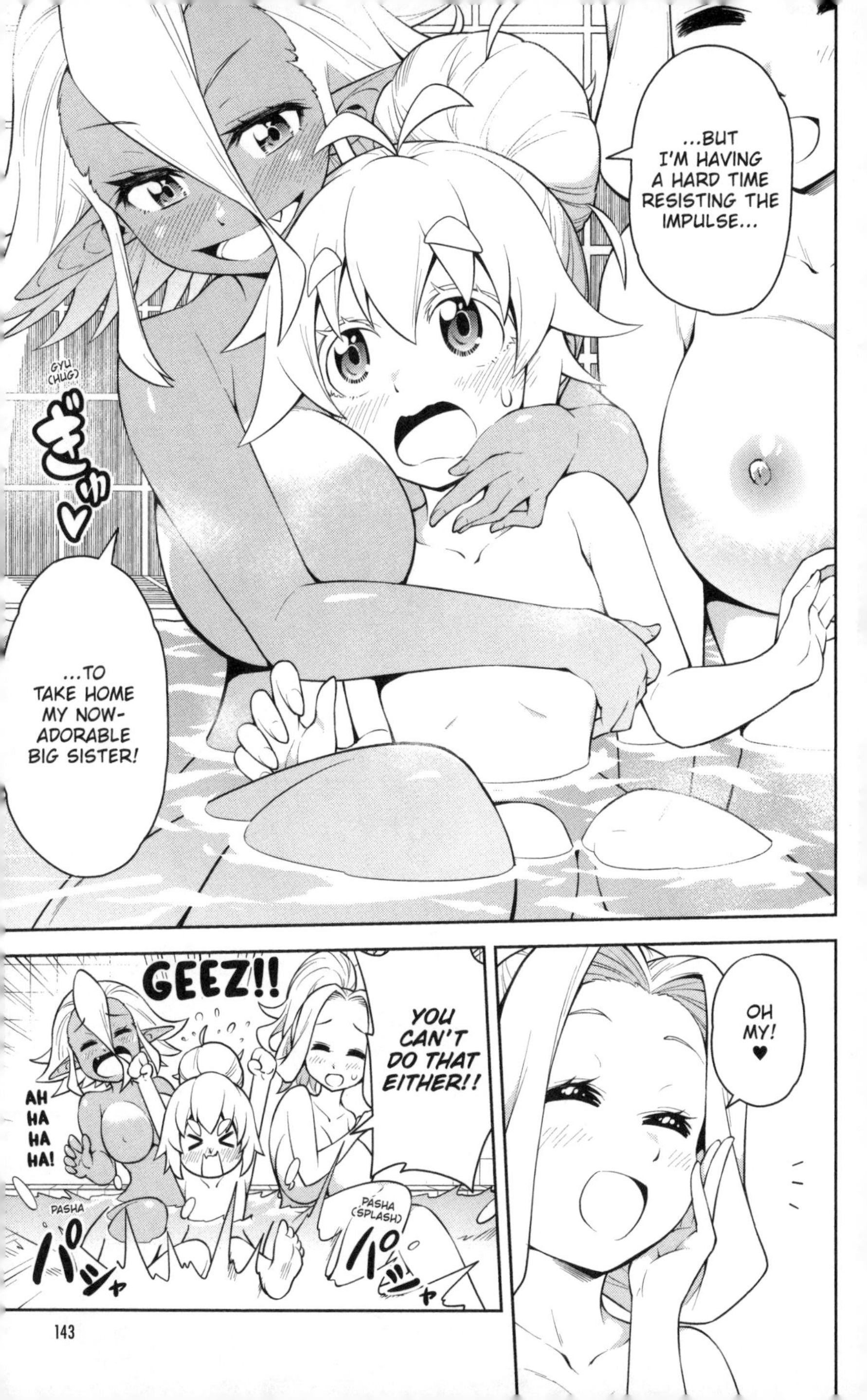
...BUT I'M HAVING A HARD TIME RESISTING THE IMPULSE...
GYU (HUG)
...TO TAKE HOME MY NOW-ADORABLE BIG SISTER!
OH MY! ♥
YOU CAN'T DO THAT EITHER!!
GEEZ!!
AH HA HA HA HA!
PASHA (SPLASH)
PASHA

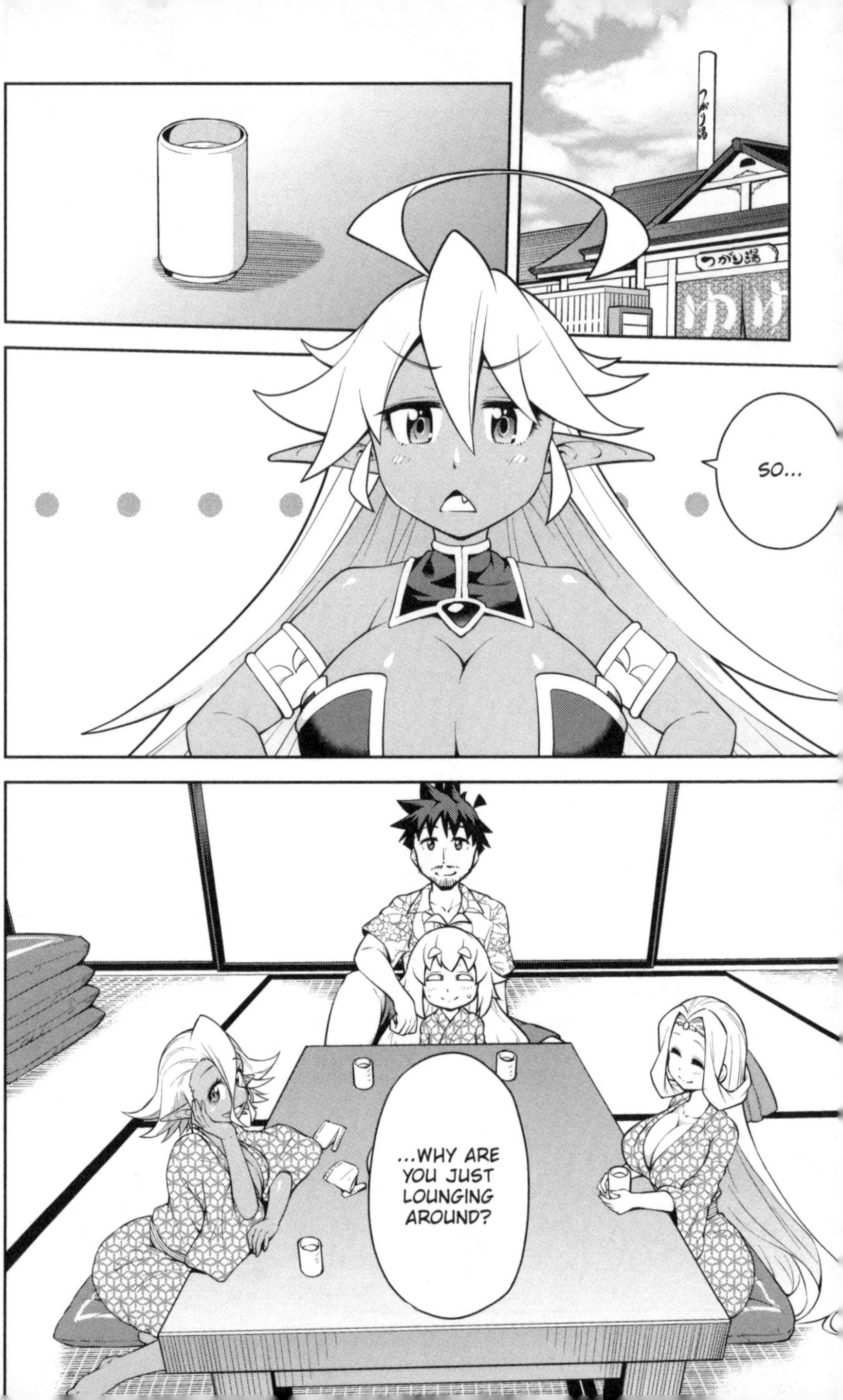
つがり湯
SO...
...WHY ARE YOU JUST LOUNGING AROUND?

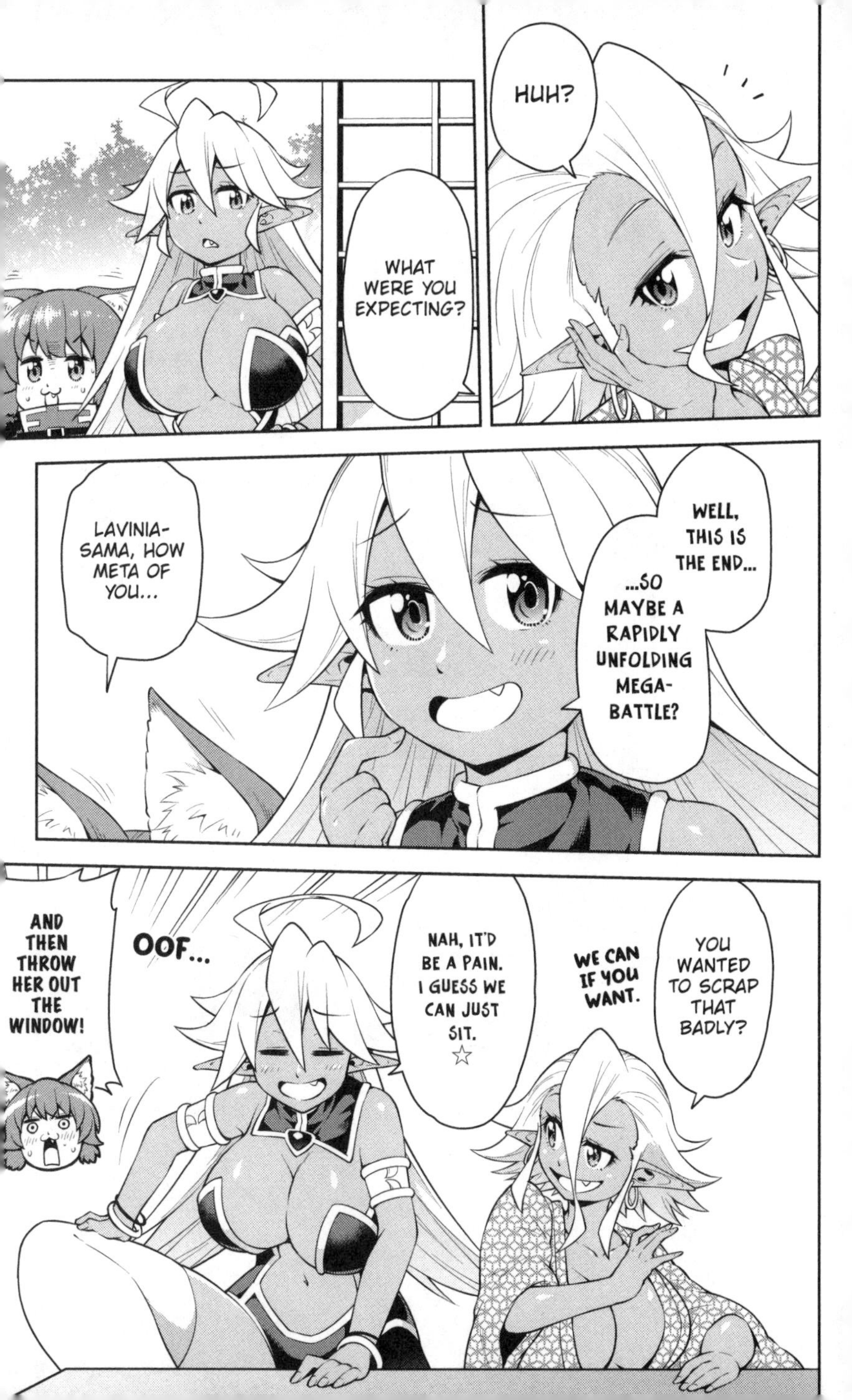
HUH?
WHAT WERE YOU EXPECTING?
WELL, THIS IS THE END...
...SO MAYBE A RAPIDLY UNFOLDING MEGA-BATTLE?
LAVINIA-SAMA, HOW META OF YOU...
YOU WANTED TO SCRAP THAT BADLY?
WE CAN IF YOU WANT.
NAH, IT'D BE A PAIN. I GUESS WE CAN JUST SIT. ☆
OOF...
AND THEN THROW HER OUT THE WINDOW!

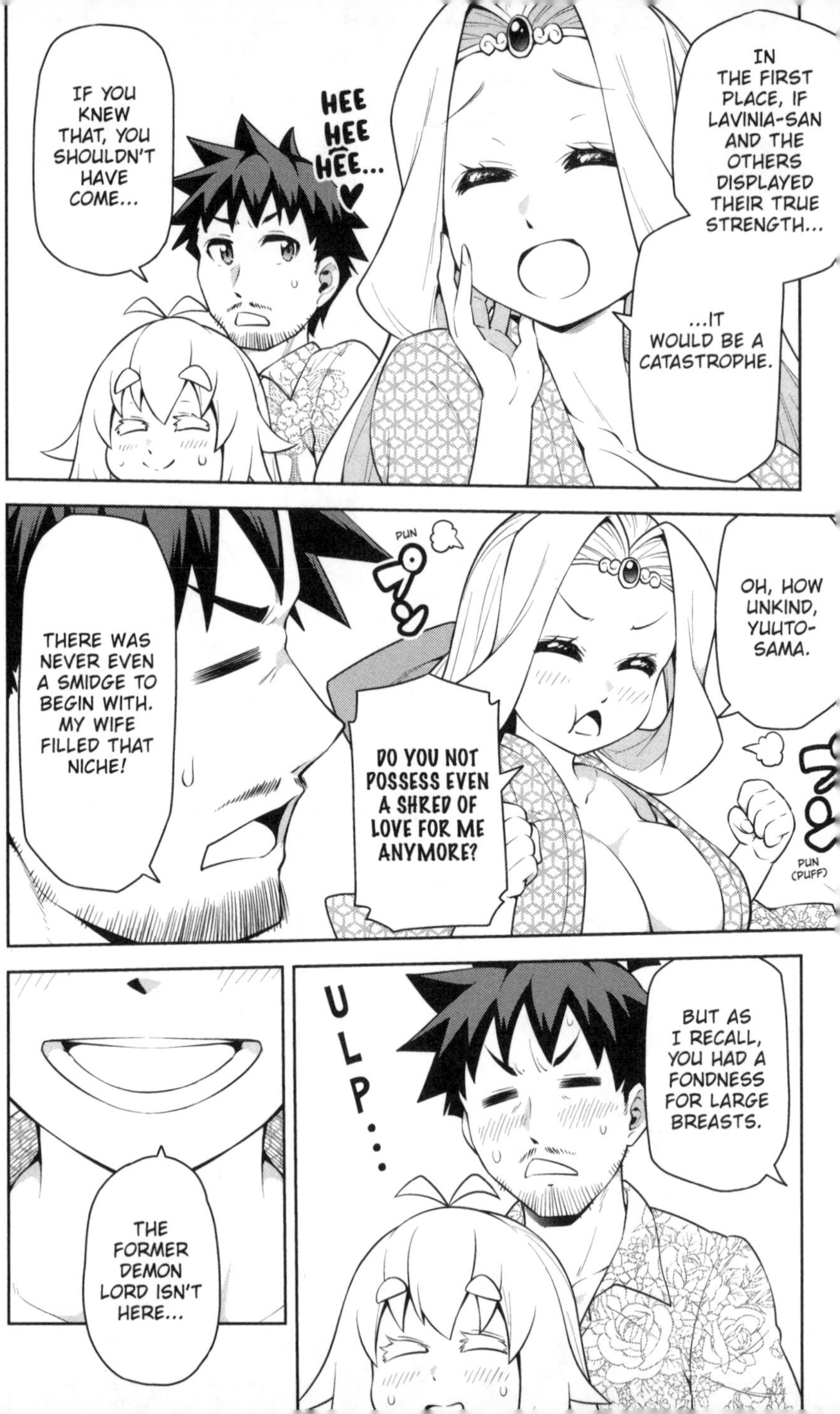
IN THE FIRST PLACE, IF LAVINIA-SAN AND THE OTHERS DISPLAYED THEIR TRUE STRENGTH...
...IT WOULD BE A CATASTROPHE.
HEE HEE HEE...
IF YOU KNEW THAT, YOU SHOULDN'T HAVE COME...
OH, HOW UNKIND, YUUTO-SAMA.
PUN (PUFF)
DO YOU NOT POSSESS EVEN A SHRED OF LOVE FOR ME ANYMORE?
PUN
THERE WAS NEVER EVEN A SMIDGE TO BEGIN WITH. MY WIFE FILLED THAT NICHE!
BUT AS I RECALL, YOU HAD A FONDNESS FOR LARGE BREASTS.
ULP...
THE FORMER DEMON LORD ISN'T HERE...

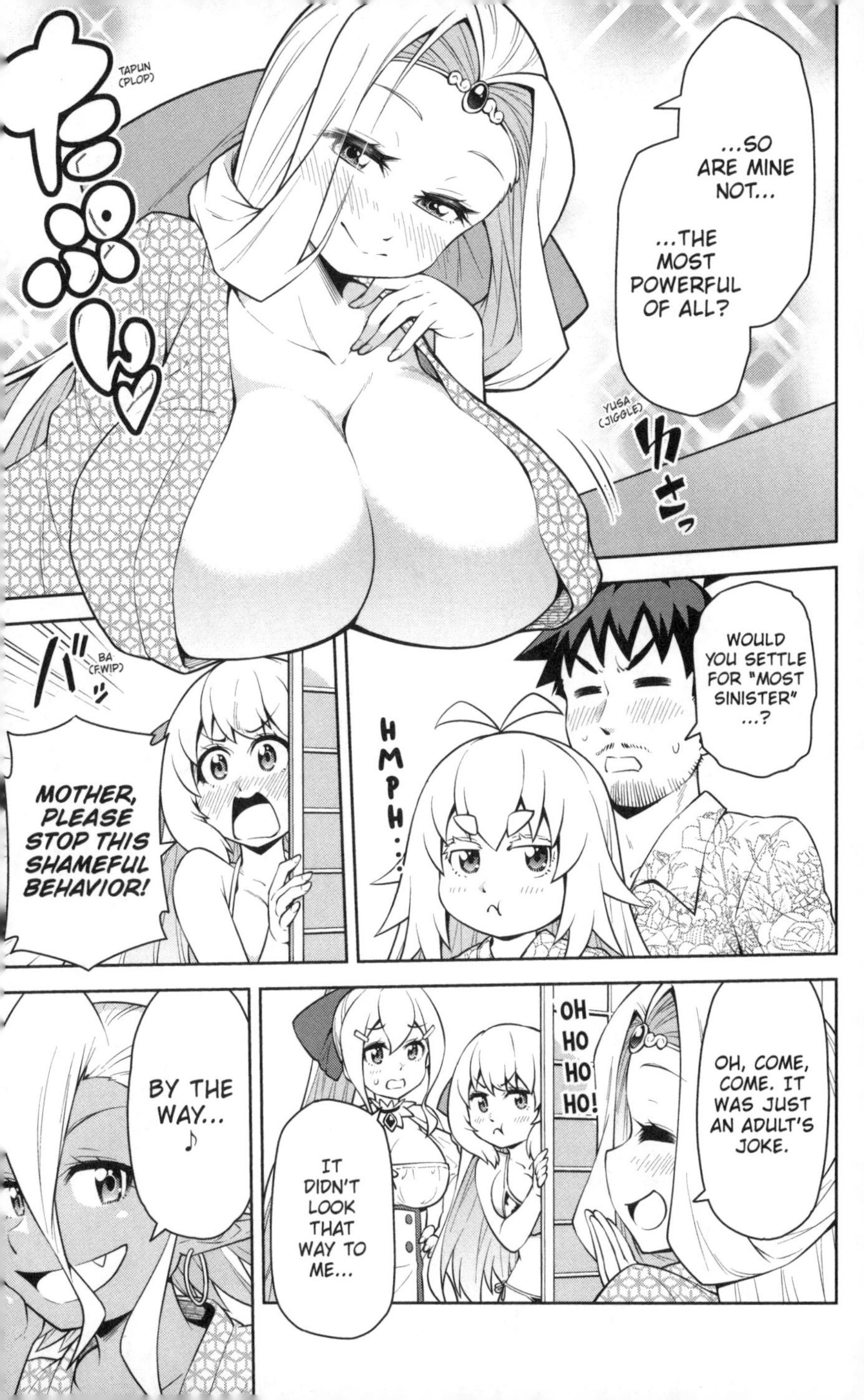
TAPUN (PLOP)
...SO ARE MINE NOT...
...THE MOST POWERFUL OF ALL?
YUSA (JIGGLE)
WOULD YOU SETTLE FOR "MOST SINISTER" ...?
HMPH...
BA (FWIP)
MOTHER, PLEASE STOP THIS SHAMEFUL BEHAVIOR!
OH, COME, COME. IT WAS JUST AN ADULT'S JOKE.
OH HO HO HO!
IT DIDN'T LOOK THAT WAY TO ME...
BY THE WAY... ♪

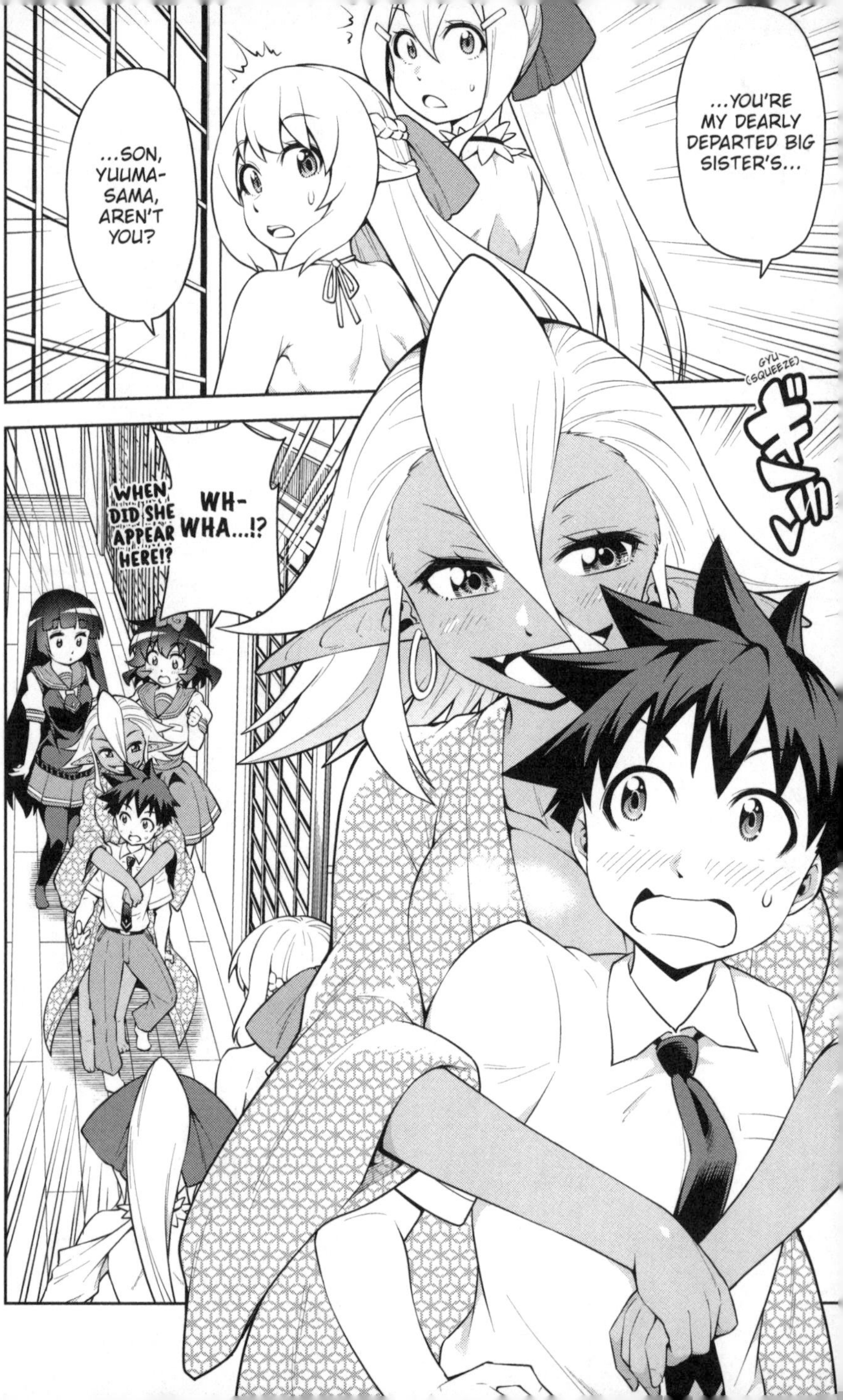
...YOU'RE MY DEARLY DEPARTED BIG SISTER'S...
...SON, YUUMA-SAMA, AREN'T YOU?
GYU (SQUEEZE)
WH- WHA...!?
WHEN DID SHE APPEAR HERE!?

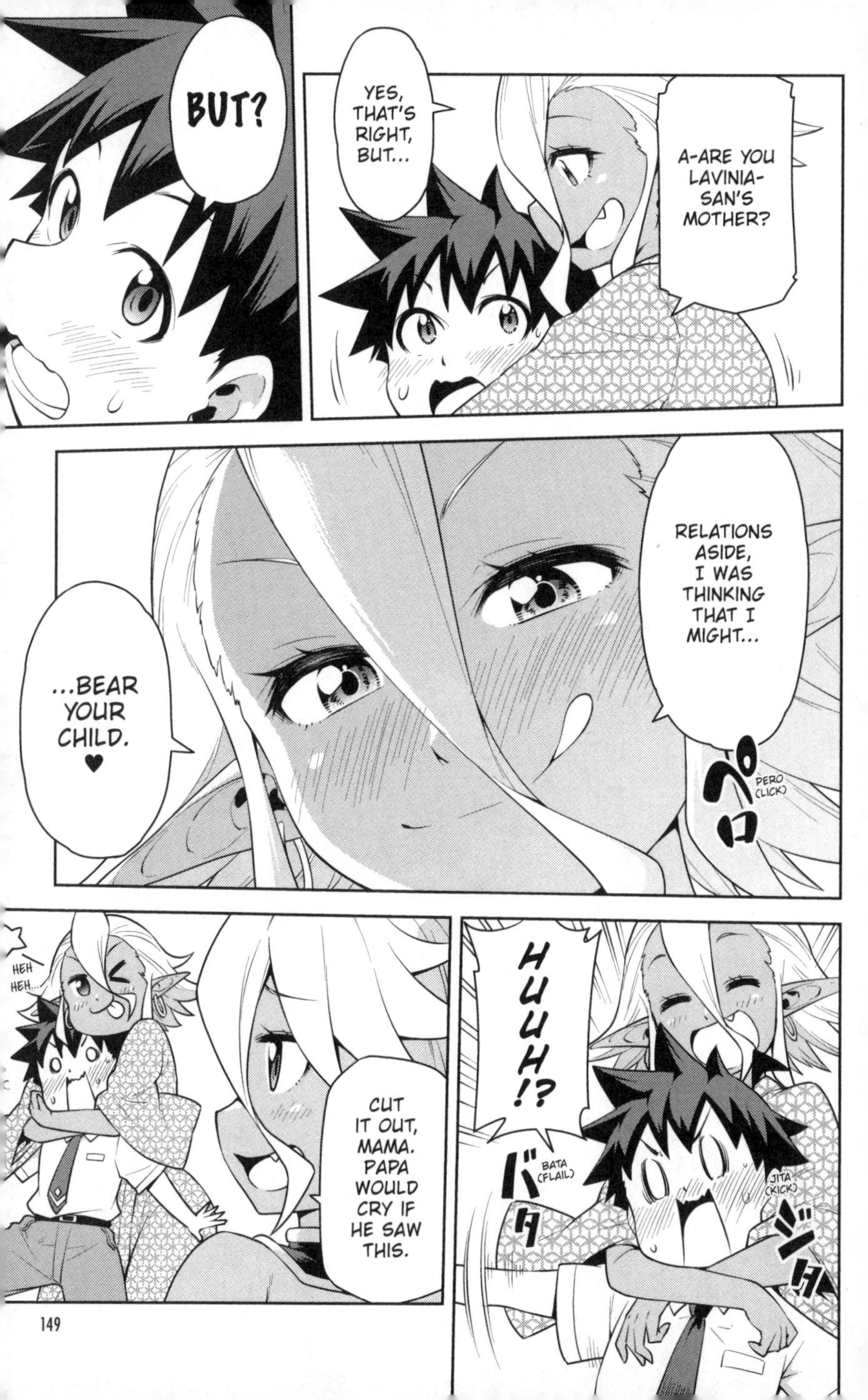
A-ARE YOU LAVINIA-SAN'S MOTHER?
YES, THAT'S RIGHT, BUT...
BUT?
RELATIONS ASIDE, I WAS THINKING THAT I MIGHT...
PERO (LICK)
...BEAR YOUR CHILD. ♥
HUUUH!?
JITA (KICK)
BATA (FLAIL)
CUT IT OUT, MAMA. PAPA WOULD CRY IF HE SAW THIS.
HEH HEH...

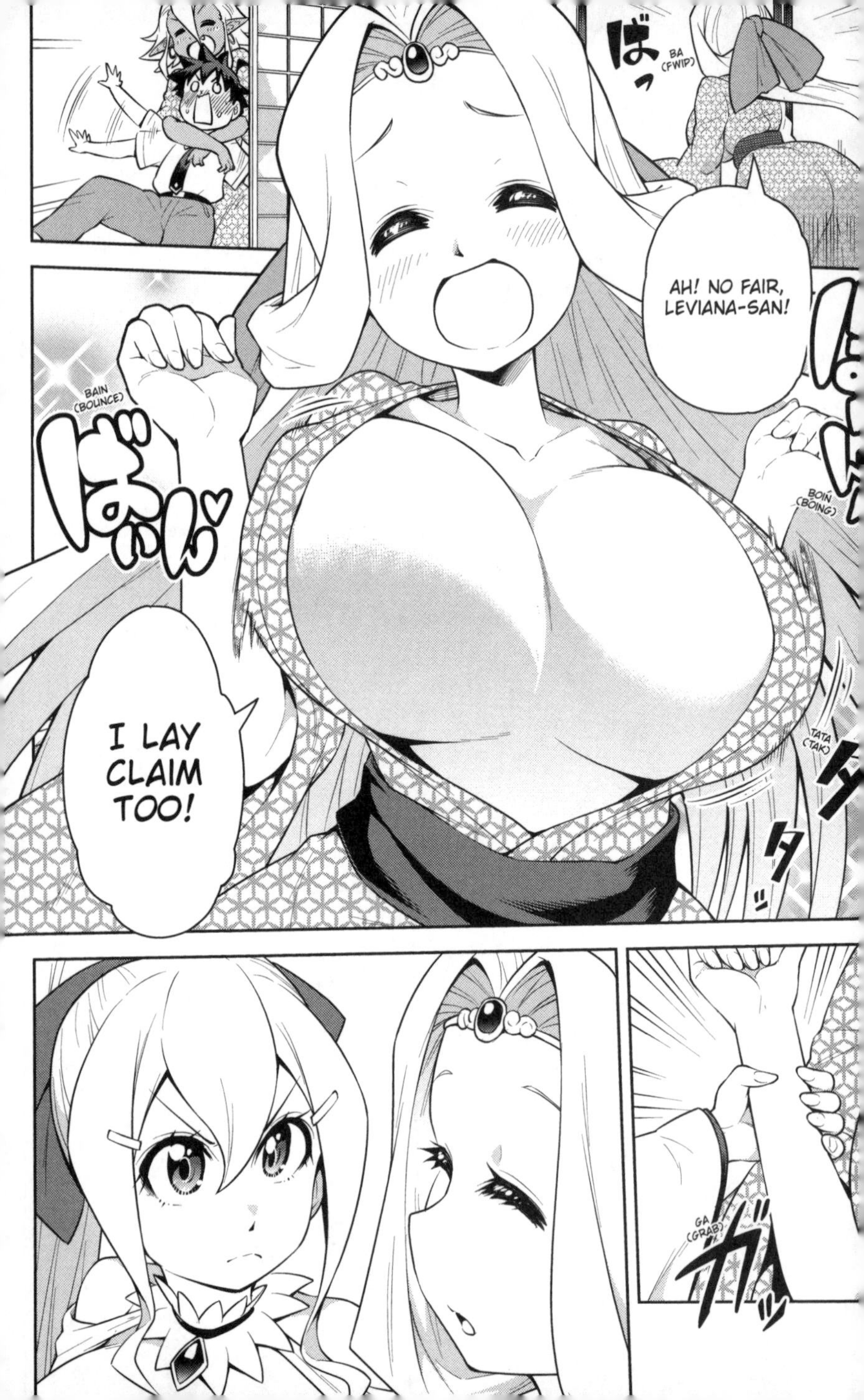

ばっ
BA (FWIP)
AH! NO FAIR, LEVIANA-SAN!
BOIN (BOING)
TATA (TAK)
タタッ
BAIN (BOUNCE)
I LAY CLAIM TOO!
GA (GRAB)
ガッ

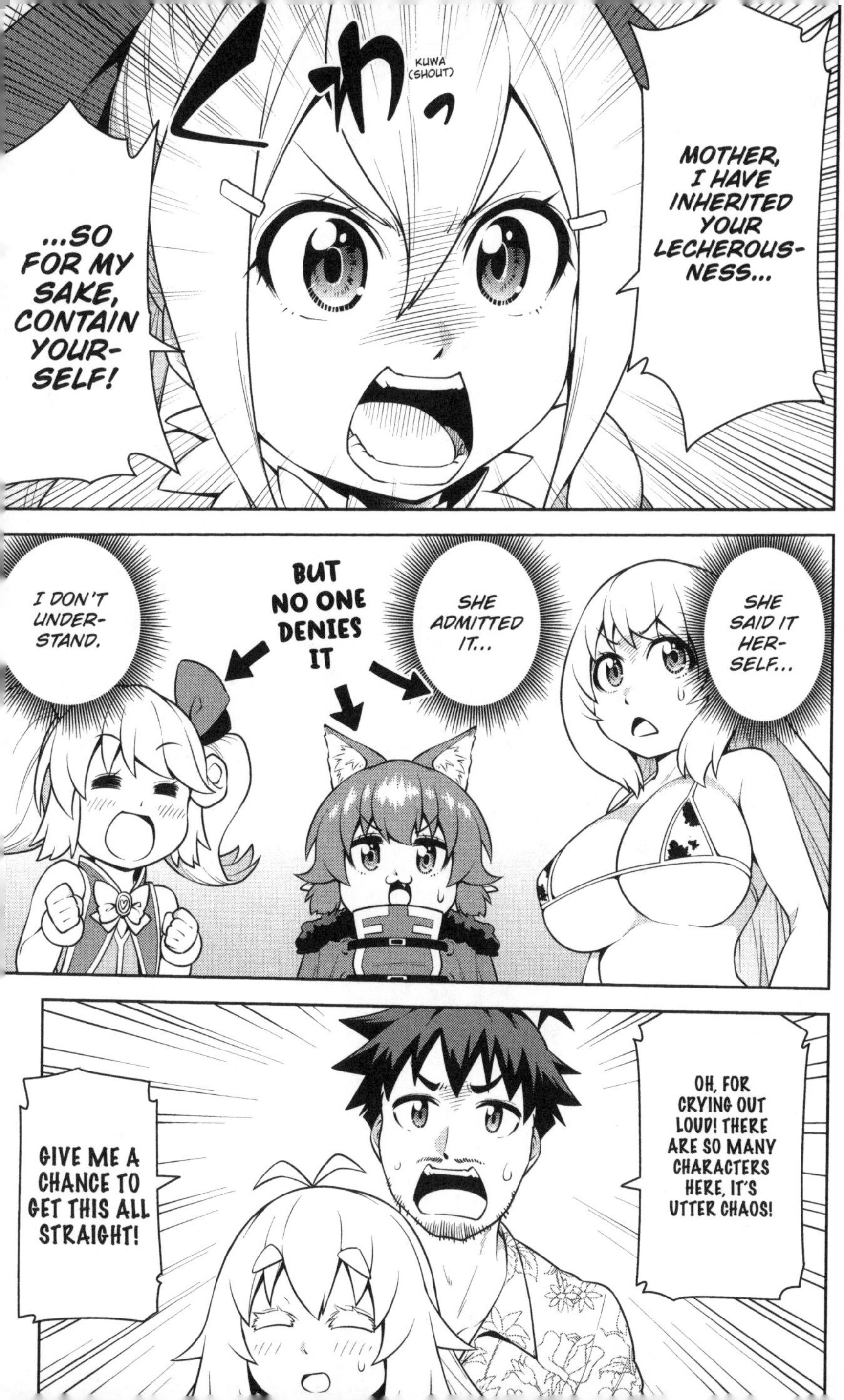
KUWA (SHOUT)
MOTHER, I HAVE INHERITED YOUR LECHEROUSNESS...
...SO FOR MY SAKE, CONTAIN YOURSELF!
SHE SAID IT HERSELF...
SHE ADMITTED IT...
BUT NO ONE DENIES IT
I DON'T UNDERSTAND.
OH, FOR CRYING OUT LOUD! THERE ARE SO MANY CHARACTERS HERE, IT'S UTTER CHAOS!
GIVE ME A CHANCE TO GET THIS ALL STRAIGHT!

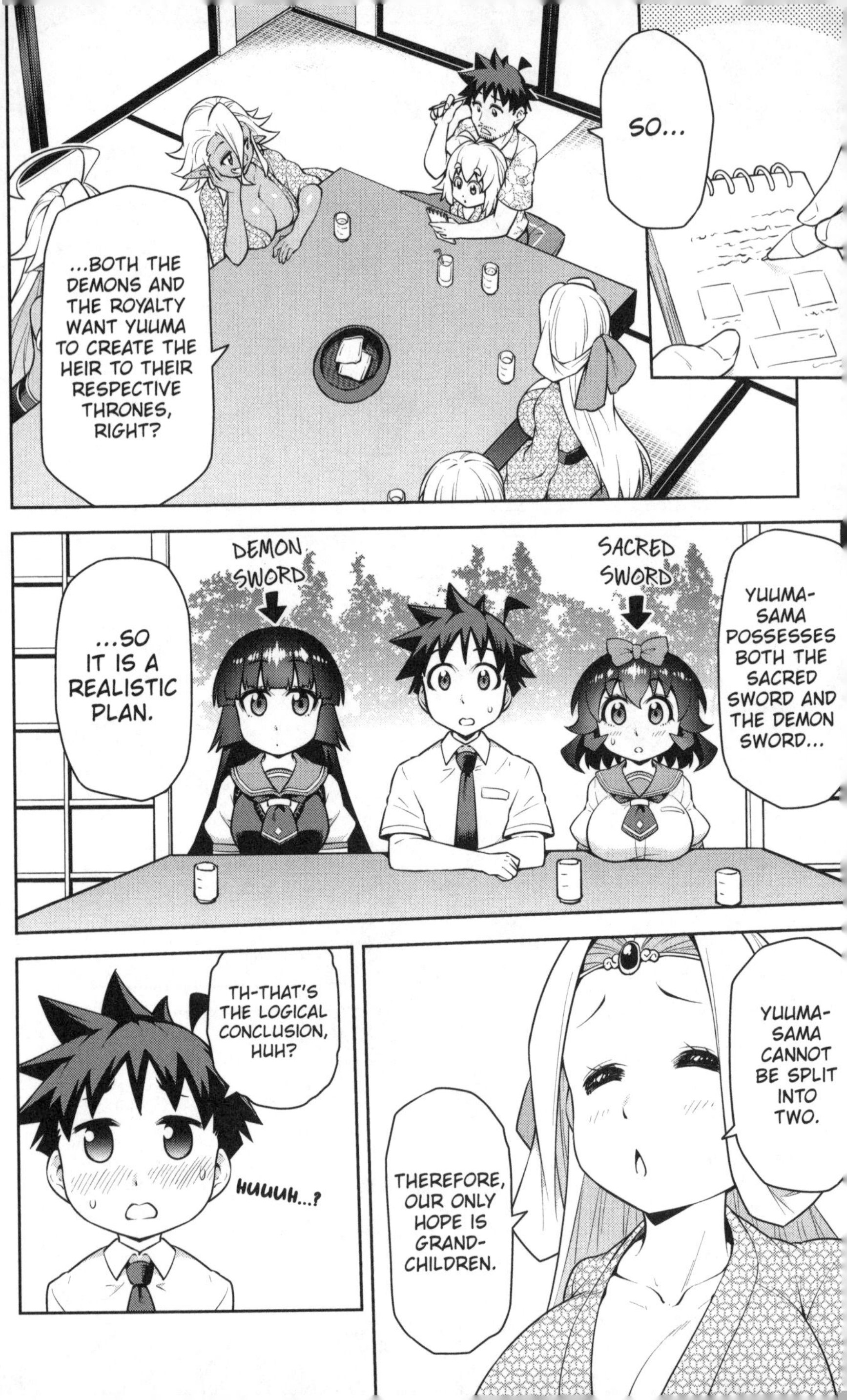
SO...
...BOTH THE DEMONS AND THE ROYALTY WANT YUUMA TO CREATE THE HEIR TO THEIR RESPECTIVE THRONES, RIGHT?
YUUMA-SAMA POSSESSES BOTH THE SACRED SWORD AND THE DEMON SWORD...
SACRED SWORD
DEMON SWORD
...SO IT IS A REALISTIC PLAN.
YUUMA-SAMA CANNOT BE SPLIT INTO TWO.
THEREFORE, OUR ONLY HOPE IS GRAND-CHILDREN.
TH-THAT'S THE LOGICAL CONCLUSION, HUH?
HUUUH...?

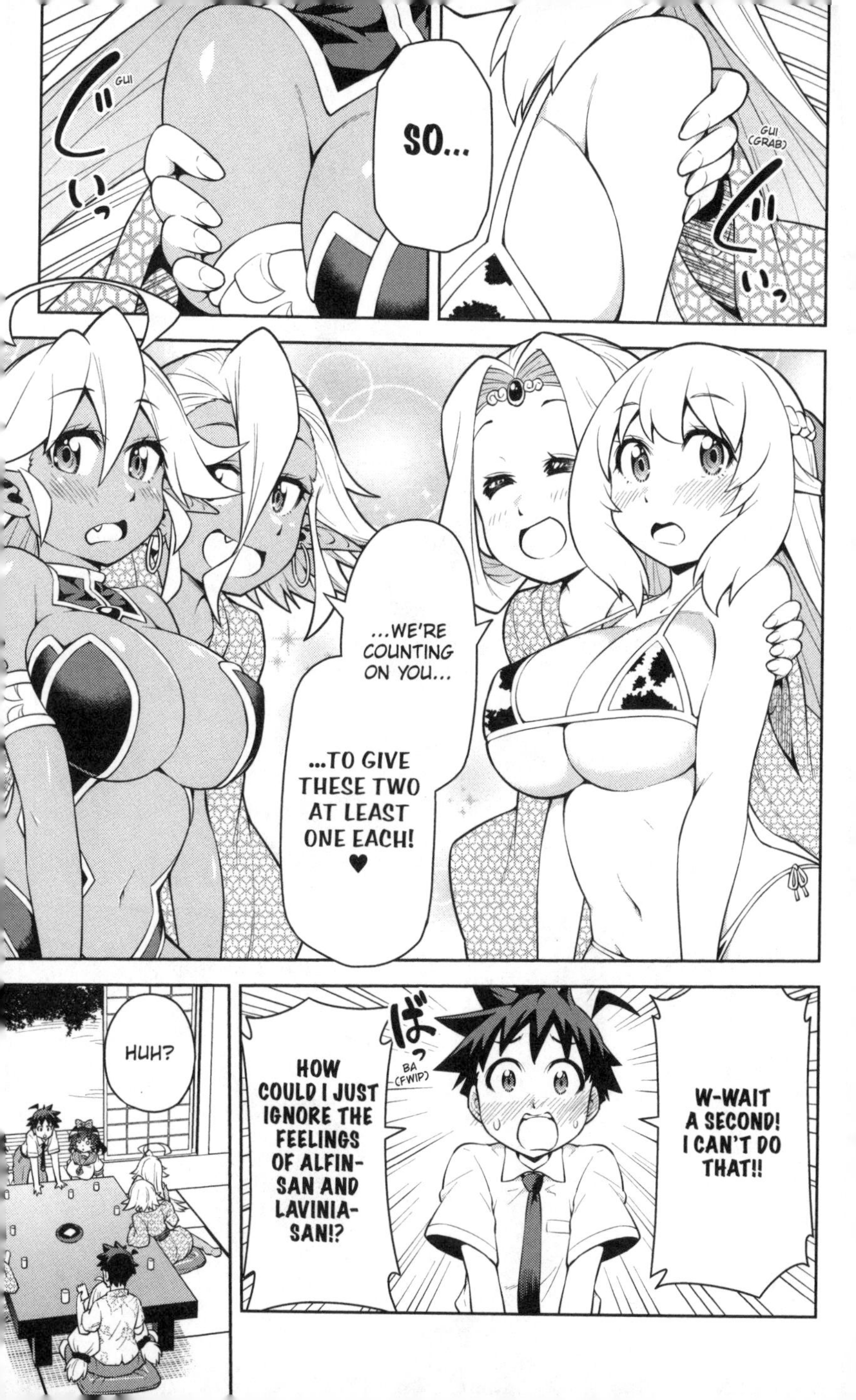
GUI (GRAB)
SO...
GUI
...WE'RE COUNTING ON YOU...
...TO GIVE THESE TWO AT LEAST ONE EACH! ♥
W-WAIT A SECOND! I CAN'T DO THAT!!
BA (FWIP)
HOW COULD I JUST IGNORE THE FEELINGS OF ALFIN-SAN AND LAVINIA-SAN!?
HUH?

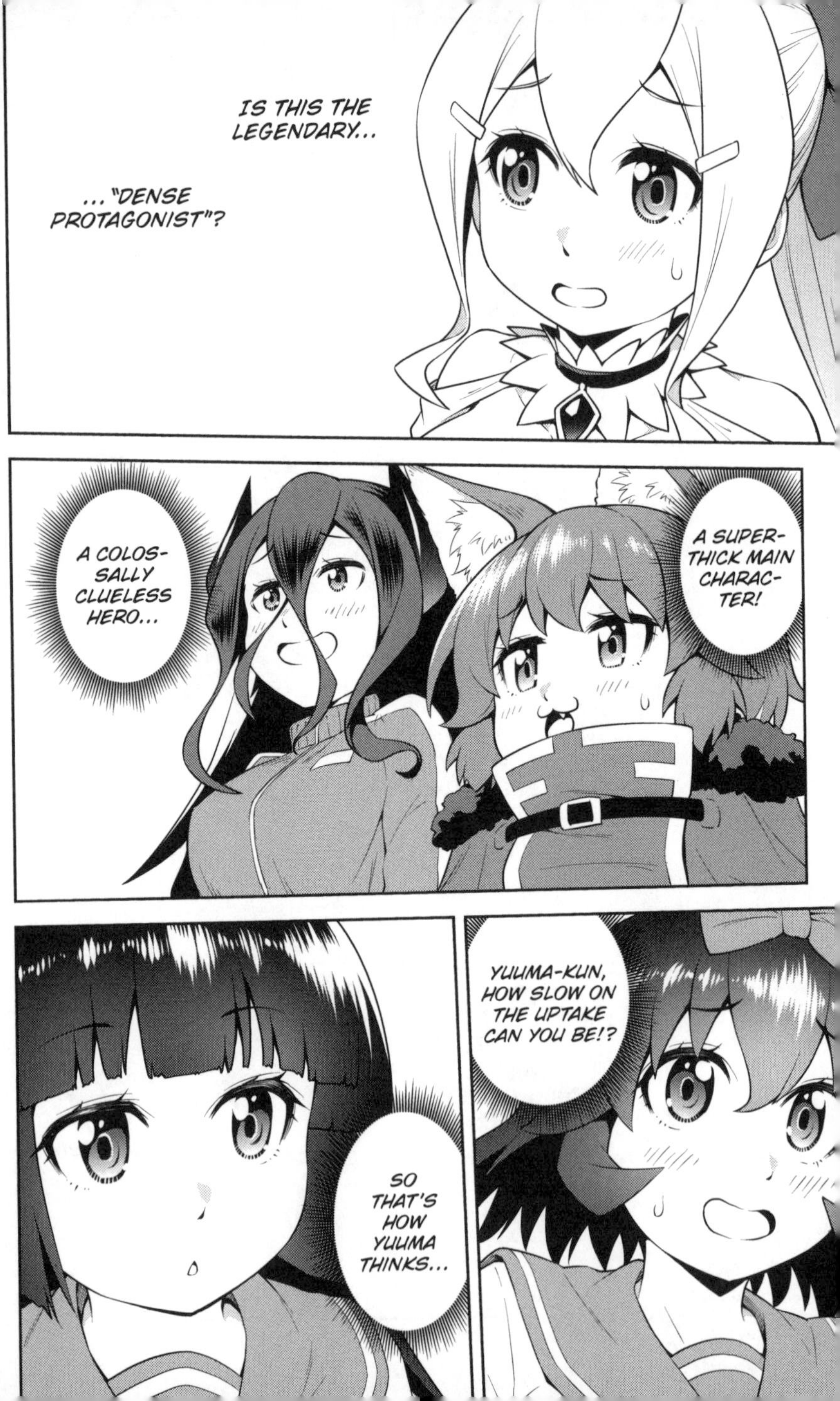
IS THIS THE LEGENDARY...
..."DENSE PROTAGONIST"?
A SUPER-THICK MAIN CHARAC-TER!
A COLOS-SALLY CLUELESS HERO...
YUUMA-KUN, HOW SLOW ON THE UPTAKE CAN YOU BE!?
SO THAT'S HOW YUUMA THINKS...

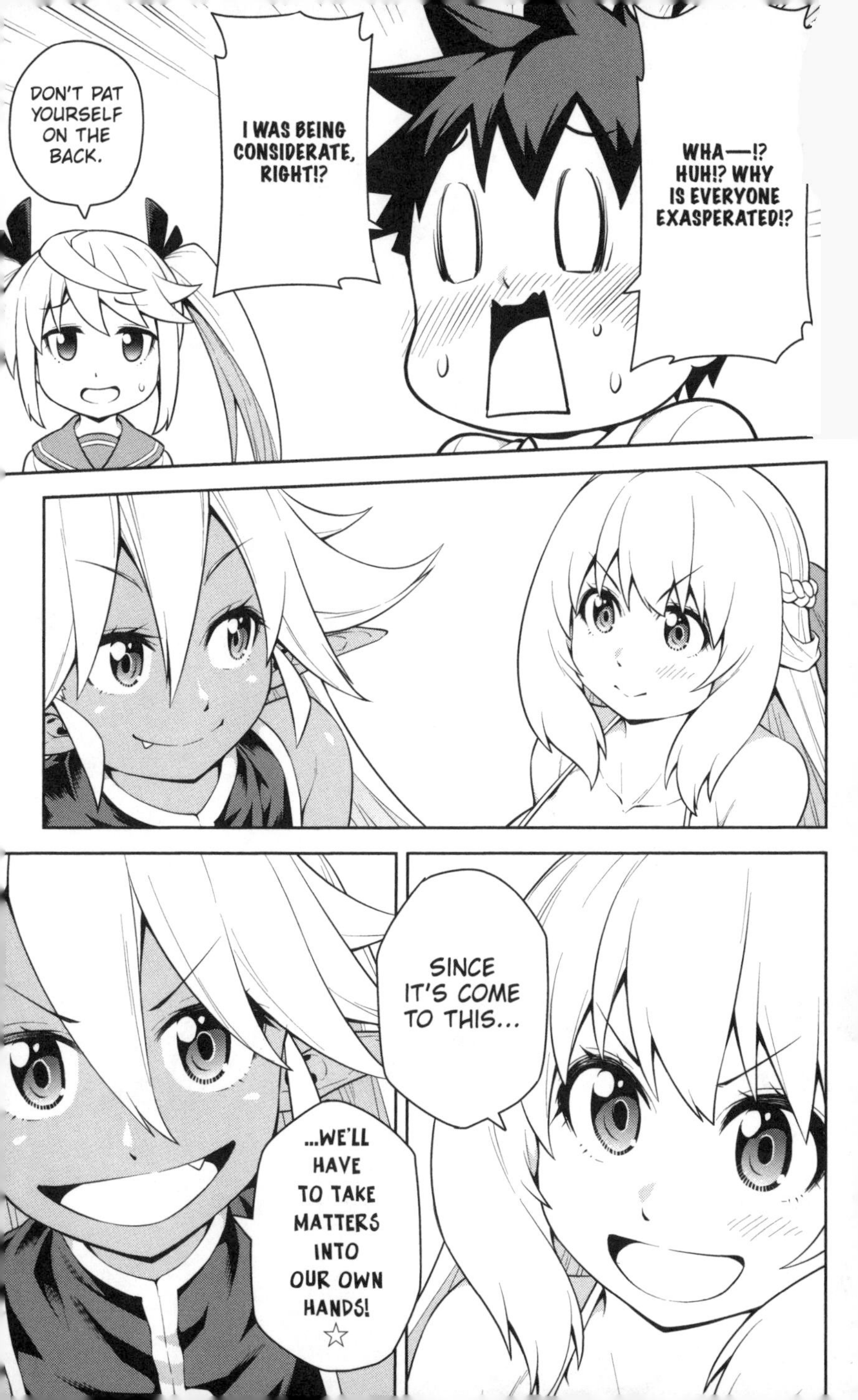
WHA—!? HUH!? WHY IS EVERYONE EXASPERATED!?
I WAS BEING CONSIDERATE, RIGHT!?
DON'T PAT YOURSELF ON THE BACK.
SINCE IT'S COME TO THIS...
...WE'LL HAVE TO TAKE MATTERS INTO OUR OWN HANDS! ☆

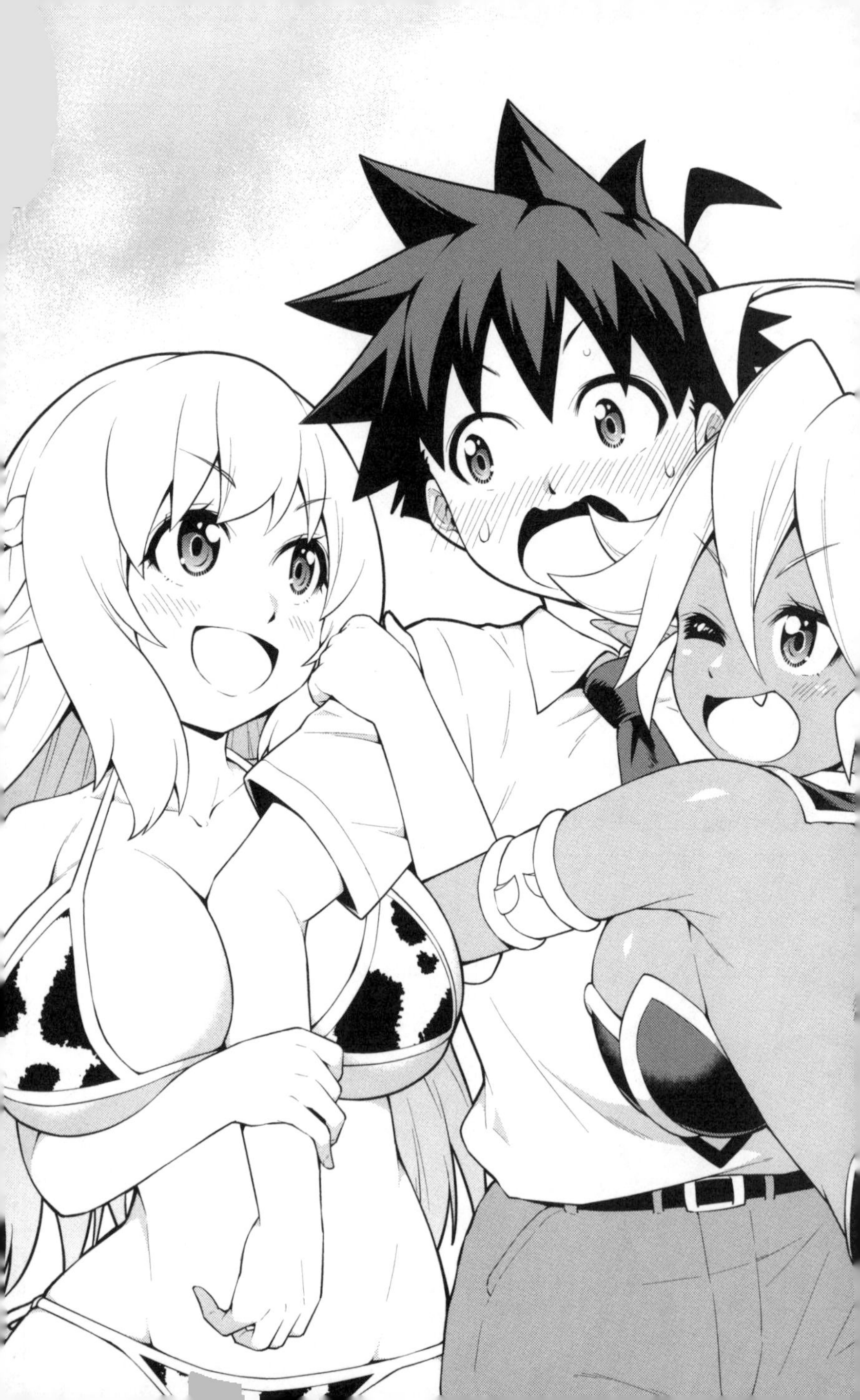

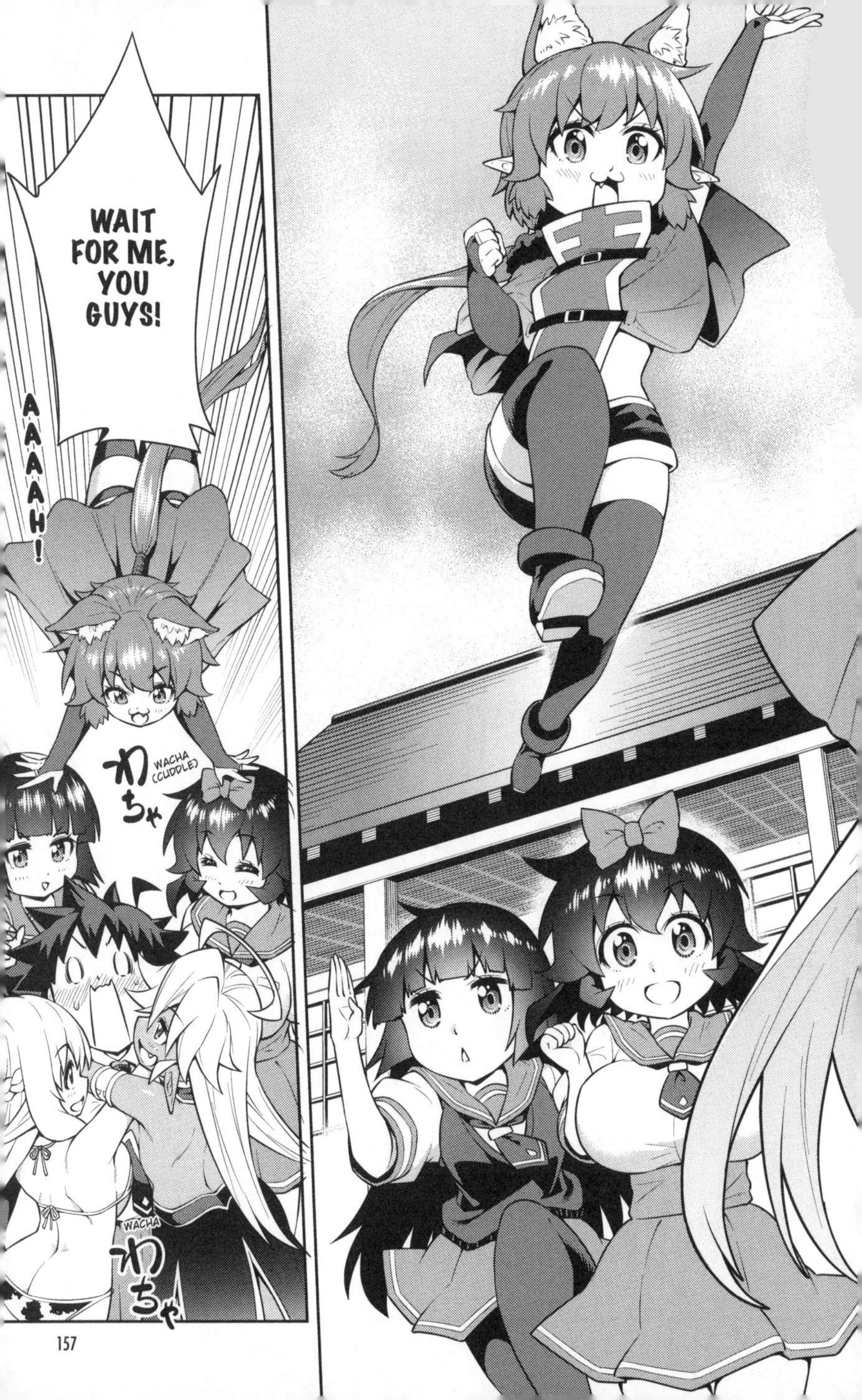
WAIT FOR ME, YOU GUYS!
AAAAAH!
わちゃ
WACHA (CUDDLE)
わちゃ
WACHA

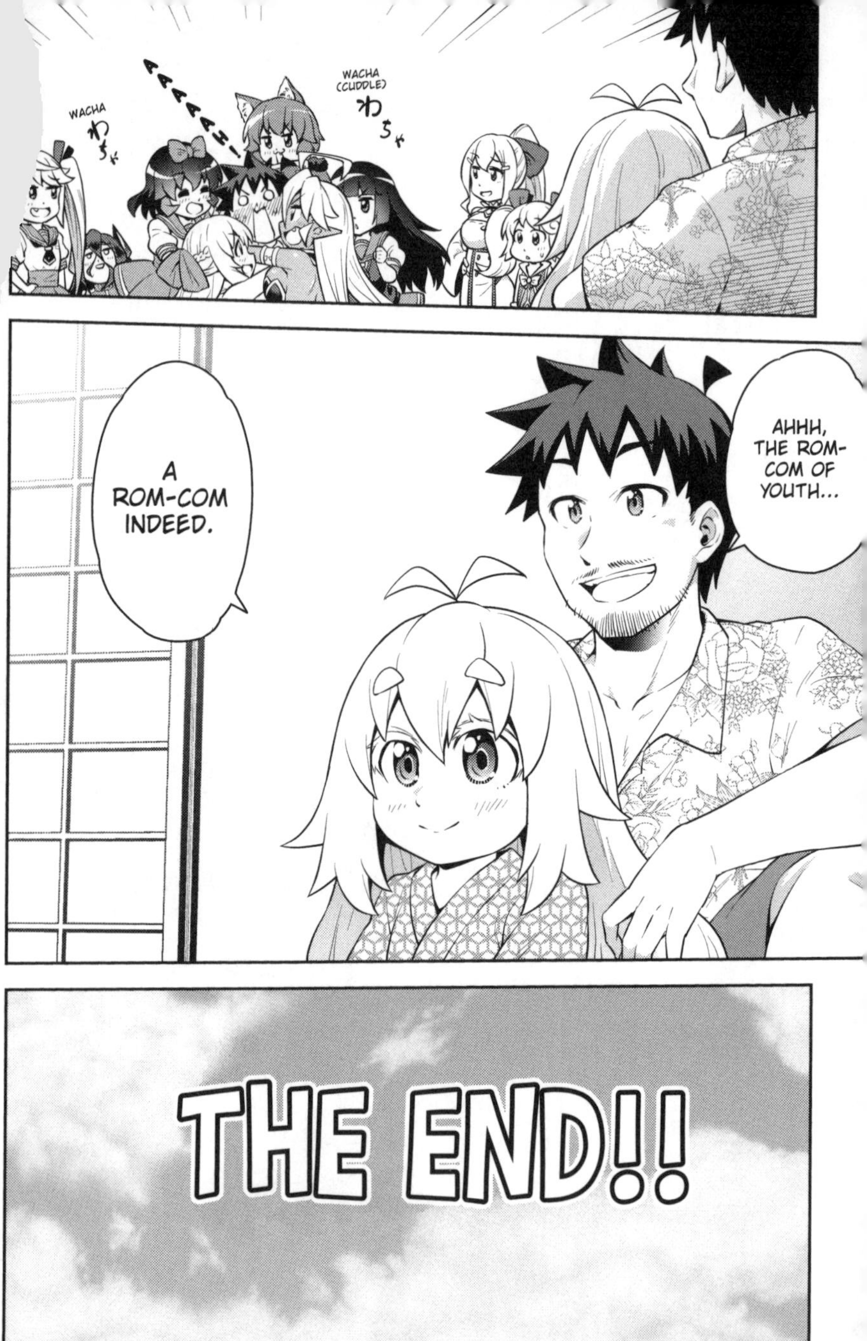
WACHA (CUDDLE) わちゃ
AAAAAAA!!
WACHA わちゃ
AHHH, THE ROM-COM OF YOUTH...
A ROM-COM INDEED.
THE END!!

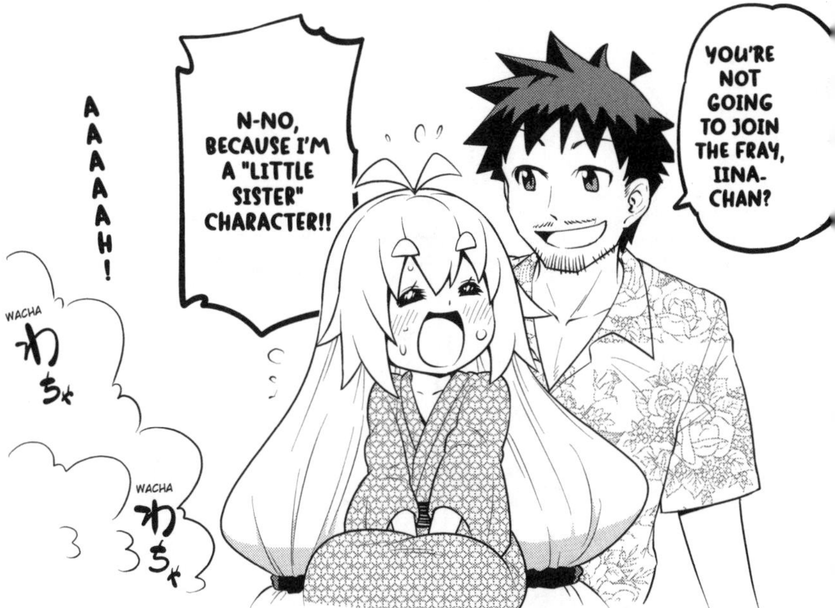
YOU'RE NOT GOING TO JOIN THE FRAY, IINA-CHAN?
N-NO, BECAUSE I'M A "LITTLE SISTER" CHARACTER!!
AAAAAH!
WACHA
わちゃ
WACHA
わちゃ

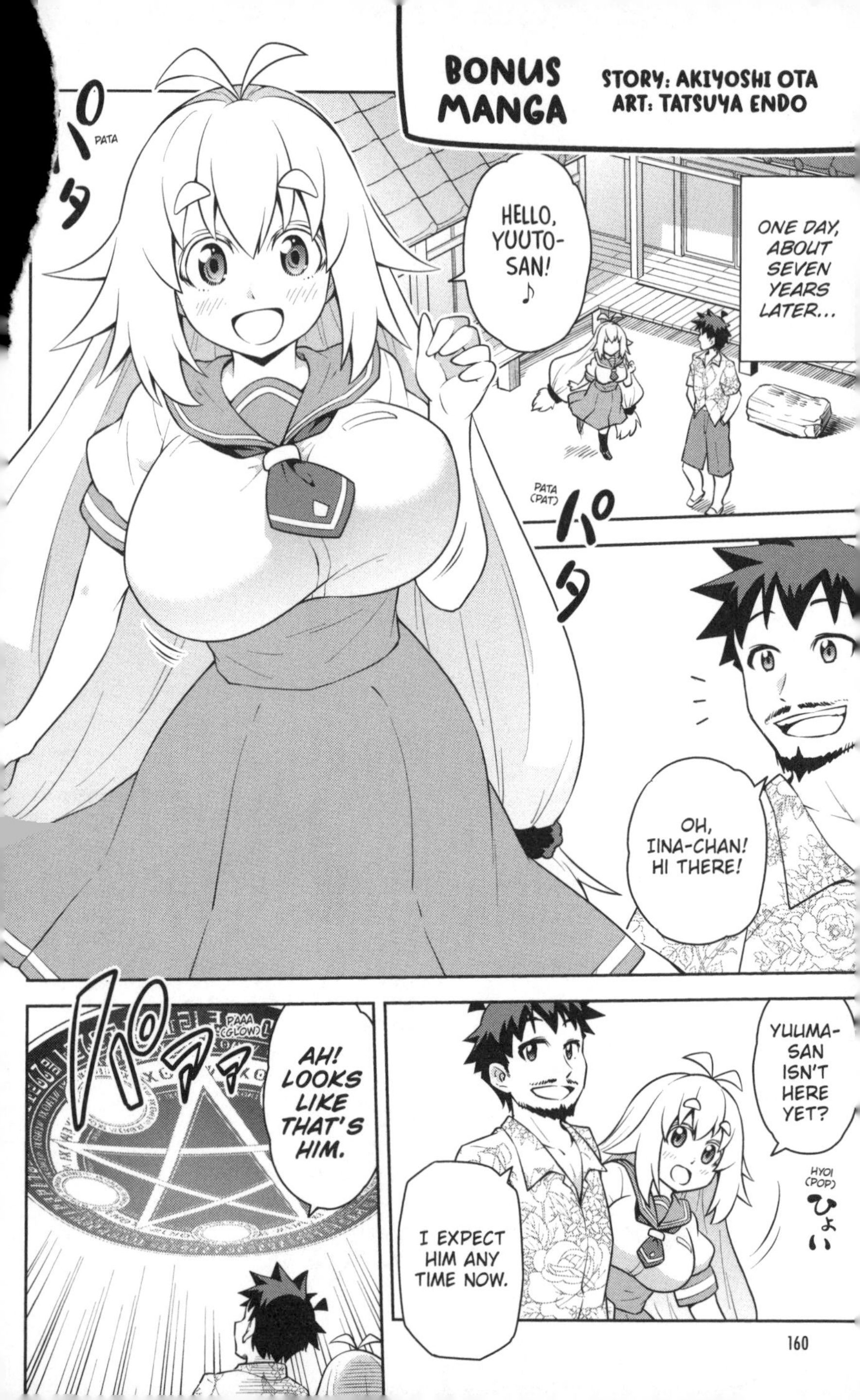
BONUS MANGA
STORY: AKIYOSHI OTA
ART: TATSUYA ENDO
ONE DAY, ABOUT SEVEN YEARS LATER...
HELLO, YUUTO-SAN! ♪
PATA (PAT)
パタ
PATA
パタ
OH, IINA-CHAN! HI THERE!
YUUMA-SAN ISN'T HERE YET?
HYOI (POP)
ひょい
I EXPECT HIM ANY TIME NOW.
PAAA (GLOW)
パァァ
AH! LOOKS LIKE THAT'S HIM.

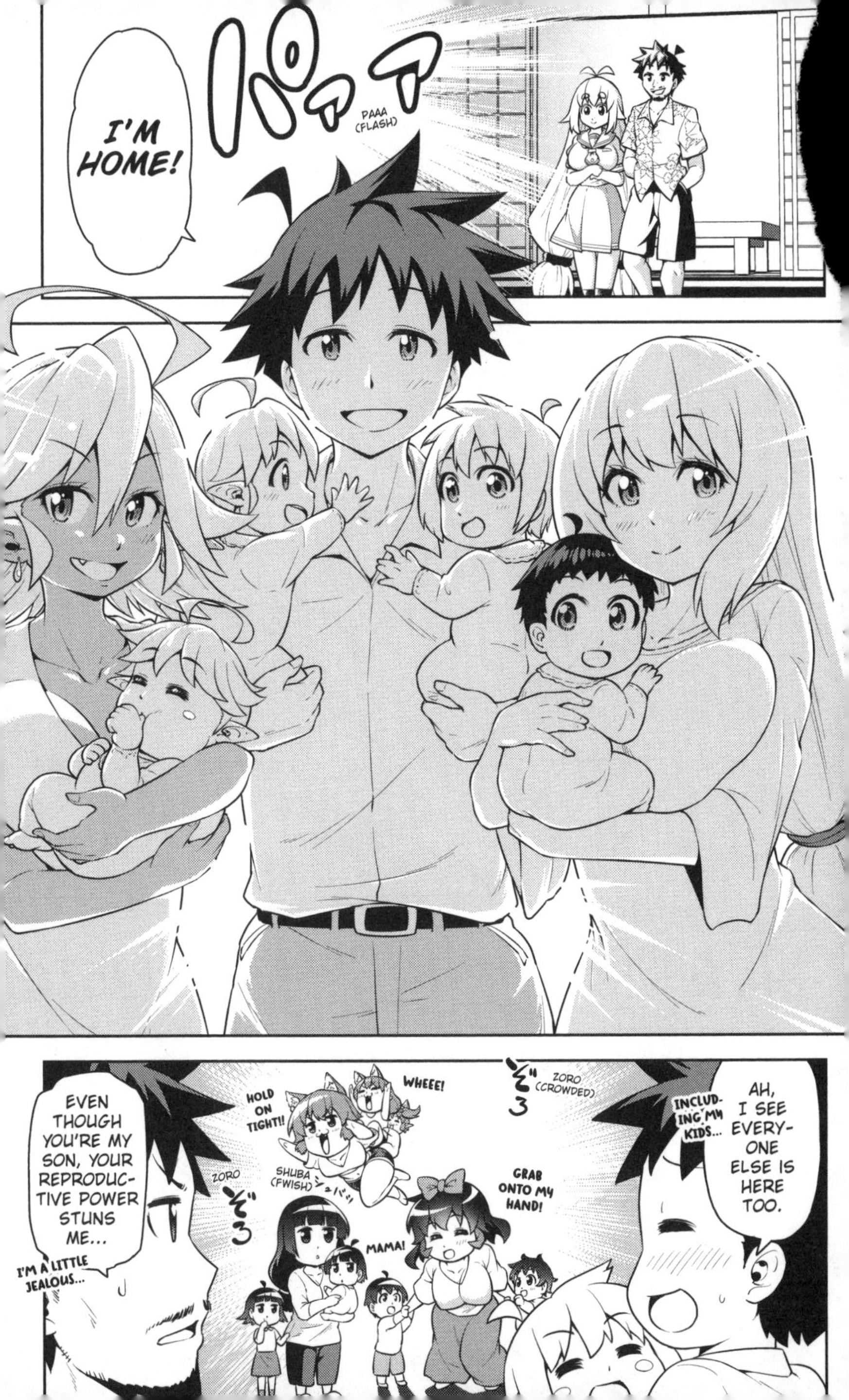
パァァ
PAAA (FLASH)
I'M HOME!
AH, I SEE EVERYONE ELSE IS HERE TOO.
INCLUDING MY KIDS...
ぞろ
ZORO (CROWDED)
WHEEE!
HOLD ON TIGHT!!
GRAB ONTO MY HAND!
SHUBA (FWISH)
シュバッ
ZORO
ぞろ
MAMA!
EVEN THOUGH YOU'RE MY SON, YOUR REPRODUCTIVE POWER STUNS ME...
I'M A LITTLE JEALOUS...

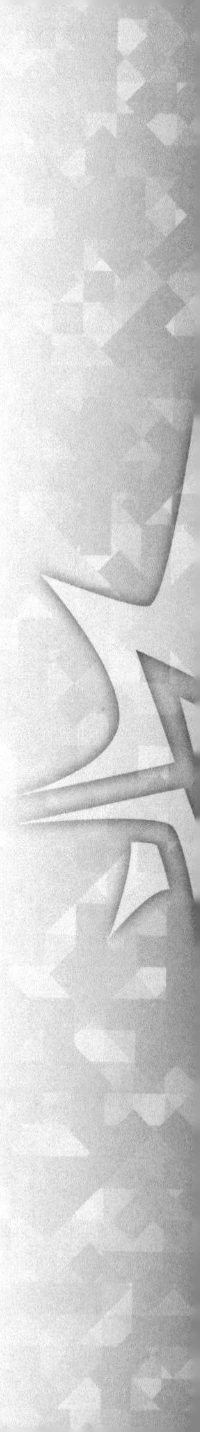